THE UNITED NATIONS
& REGIONAL SECURITY

A project of the International Peace Academy

THE UNITED NATIONS & REGIONAL SECURITY

Europe and Beyond

EDITED BY
Michael Pugh
Waheguru Pal Singh Sidhu

LYNNE
RIENNER
PUBLISHERS

BOULDER
LONDON

Published in the United States of America in 2003 by
Lynne Rienner Publishers, Inc.
1800 30th Street, Boulder, Colorado 80301
www.rienner.com

and in the United Kingdom by
Lynne Rienner Publishers, Inc.
3 Henrietta Street, Covenant Garden, London WC2E 8LU

Library of Congress Cataloging-in-Publication Data
The United Nations and regional security : Europe and beyond / Michael Pugh and
    Waheguru Pal Singh Sidhu, editors.
        p.   cm.
    Includes bibliographical references and index.
    ISBN 1-58826-207-3 (alk. paper) — ISBN 1-58826-232-4 (pbk. : alk. paper)
    1. United Nations. 2. Security, International. 3. Regionalism (International organization)
I. Pugh, Michael C. (Michael Charles), 1944–. II. Sidhu, Waheguru Pal Singh.

NZ4984.5.U538   2004
341.5'23—dc21

                                                                                    2003047049

British Cataloguing in Publication Data
A Cataloguing in Publication record for this book
is available from the British Library.

Printed and bound in the United States of America

The paper used in this publication meets the requirements
of the American National Standard for Permanence of
Paper for Printed Library Materials Z39.48-1992.

5   4   3   2   1

For
Kamlesh and Mridula

Contents

Foreword

David M. Malone
President, International Peace Academy

The United Nations and the North Atlantic Treaty Organization (NATO) are the two major security institutions created following the end of World War II, but they have widely different approaches to the maintenance of international peace and security. For five decades, under the prevailing Cold War politico-ideological divide, most of their member states saw little cause for or value in cooperation between the global collective security arrangement of the UN and the regional collective defense mechanism of NATO. However, developments in post–Cold War Europe, particularly in the Balkans, saw not only these two institutions but other European security organizations thrust together in Bosnia during the implementation of the 1995 Dayton Peace Agreement and in Kosovo during and after the intervention of 1999. In these circumstances, the UN and the European security organizations cooperated well in the field, but developed too little understanding at the headquarters level of the mutual benefit to be derived from reaching a better understanding on issues relevant to their future collaboration.

In 1998, well before the climax of the Kosovo crisis, the International Peace Academy (IPA) started examining the UN-NATO relationship more closely. IPA board members Hans Jacob Biørn Lian and Nicolaas Biegman, serving as permanent representatives to the North Atlantic Council for Norway and the Netherlands, respectively, after previous assignments at the UN, had been struck by the many gaps of knowledge and understanding between the two organizations. They proposed that the IPA tackle this challenge.

Subsequently, with the strong personal support of Secretary-General Kofi Annan at the UN, Secretary-General Lord George Robertson at NATO, and Secretary-General Ján Kubiš at the Organization for Security and Cooperation in Europe (OSCE), as well as key officials in other regional security organizations, the IPA embarked on an ambitious research project addressing (1) the role of the UN and European security organizations in responding to conflict in Europe and beyond, and (2) the implications of this relationship for other regional organizations in the field of peace operations.

This volume is the final product of this multiyear project, which has explored a constructive and sustained relationship between the UN and European security organizations in conflict management and examined the implications of these interactions for other regional actors in Asia, Africa, and Latin America in their ties to the UN.

We are, as ever, very grateful for the generous funding provided by the governments of Canada, Denmark, France, Germany, Luxembourg, the Netherlands, Norway, Switzerland, and the United Kingdom, which made this project and this volume possible.

The International Peace Academy is greatly indebted to the editors and authors of this volume, valued colleagues all.

The leadership of Jacob Biørn Lian and Nicolaas Biegman in suggesting this project is typical of the activist, highly supportive role of the IPA's board of directors. We are very grateful to them and to their board colleagues for their participation in this and other IPA projects.

Introduction:
The United Nations and
Regional Actors

Michael Pugh and Waheguru Pal Singh Sidhu

Since the end of the Cold War, intervention in intrastate conflicts has risen dramatically, with a corresponding increase in peace operations intended to manage these conflicts. Simultaneously, the 1990 intervention in Liberia by the Economic Community of West African States (ECOWAS) Ceasefire Monitoring Group (ECOMOG) marked the beginning of a trend toward "regionalization," whereby regional actors became increasingly engaged in peace operations, either alongside the United Nations or occasionally autonomously. In Latin America the trend evident in the preference of states has been to counterbalance the dominant U.S. influence by creating ad hoc groupings. Within Europe, developments in the 1990s, such as the dissolution of the Warsaw Pact, the subsequent transformation of Eastern Europe, as well as the rise of involvement in intrastate conflicts, created a dynamic requiring significant conceptual and practical adjustment on the part of the UN, the European Union (EU), the North Atlantic Treaty Organization (NATO), the Organization for Security and Cooperation in Europe (OSCE), the Western European Union (WEU), and other regional actors. Effective coordination became urgent as the UN and various European actors were thrust together in Bosnia and Herzegovina prior to and during the implementation of the 1995 Dayton Peace Agreement, and also during and after the 1999 intervention in Kosovo. These organizations and actors have often cooperated well in the field; nonetheless, a sense prevails that continued efforts to reach a better understanding at headquarters on a broad range of issues relevant to the organizations' future collaboration in Europe and beyond would prove to be mutually beneficial. Thus, as the above instances illustrate, regionalization of peace operations was not explicitly decreed or even necessarily desired; rather it has come about in an improvised way and in response to specific regional situations.

1

Indeed, even the term "regional," denoting spatial contiguity and geographical boundaries, reflects the ad hoc approach and is something of a misnomer in this context. Initially, the UN General Assembly distinguished between organizations formally recognized—such as the Organization of African Unity (OAU), the Organization of American States (OAS), and the OSCE—and military alliances such as NATO (and formerly the WEU). For their part, NATO and the WEU deliberately avoided reference to Chapter VIII of the UN Charter, which sanctions regional security mechanisms. Instead, they emphasized their autonomy in providing collective self-defense for their members under Article 51. But there has been a shift. Since the mid-1990s the UN Secretariat has taken a fairly relaxed, functional view of what constitutes a regional organization. The formula of "member states acting through regional agencies or arrangements" has been used, and in the annex of Security Council Resolution 1244 on Kosovo, NATO was explicitly named as a regional arrangement.[1] As Boutros Boutros-Ghali noted: "The Charter deliberately provides no precise definition of regional arrangements and agencies, thus allowing useful flexibility for undertakings by a group of States to deal with a matter appropriate for regional action which also could contribute to the maintenance of international peace and security."[2]

The fifteen organizations presently represented at high-level meetings with the UN include the Caribbean Community (CARICOM), the Commonwealth of Independent States (CIS), the British Commonwealth Secretariat, the Council of Europe, ECOWAS, the European Commission, the EU, the League of Arab States (LAS), NATO, the African Union (formerly the OAU), the OAS, the Organisation Internationale de la Francophonie, the Organization of the Islamic Conference (OIC), the OSCE, and the WEU. They are divergent in spatial designation as well as in structure, competence, and role. Thus the OSCE is not confined to Europe but includes Canada and the United States. The British Commonwealth and the Organisation Internationale de la Francophonie have memberships in many regions, reflecting links from a colonial past. On the other hand, subregional organizations (such as the Black Sea Economic Cooperation Organization) are not always represented.

The above list of organizations in a relationship with the UN, and the regular meetings at various levels between UN and regional representatives, suggest the emergence of institutionalized partnerships, if not in all cases, as a concept for sharing responsibility. This was always implicit in the logic of the UN Charter. Although universal interests, as determined by the Security Council and notably its five permanent members, take precedence over regional and individual interests, a division of labor was foreseen between regional and international organizations. Small crises that could be settled by peaceful means under Chapter VI of the UN Charter should be within the competence of regional arrangements, whereas major crises have to be settled at the world level, including potential resort to Chapter VII enforcement measures. This division of labor is implicit in the first paragraph of Article 52: "Nothing in the present Charter precludes the existence of regional arrangements or agencies for dealing with such matters relating to the maintenance of international peace and security as are appropriate for regional action."

Paragraph 2 underlines this by providing that "local disputes" should be first peacefully settled "through such regional arrangements or by such regional agencies before referring them to the Security Council." The Security Council would then have to authorize any enforcement action undertaken by regional arrangements, in effect meaning that the regional bodies are agents of the Security Council's decisions.

Regularizing the relationship was considered to be one of the major lessons of post–Cold War peace operations by the expert panel chaired by Lakhdar Brahimi. The Brahimi Report of 2000 recommended strengthening cooperation between the UN and regional organizations and establishing new regional partnerships on specific issues.[3]

This book takes a lead from the Brahimi Report in its exploration of a constructive and sustained relationship—a series of partnerships—between the UN and regional actors. There is a particular emphasis on the European experience of past and present collaborative efforts in peace operations, especially in southeast Europe. As there has been an intensity of interaction in this arena, unparalleled elsewhere, it is a logical line of inquiry to ask whether the UN-European experience has lessons for other parts of the world. The contributors to this volume seek to develop specific suggestions for future interaction between the UN and regional actors, particularly in the sphere of security sector reforms. Finally, this book explores the implications of the European experience for other regional actors in Asia, Africa, and Latin America in their ties to the UN, while noting the unique configuration of these partnerships.

The increasing and varied partnerships between the UN and regional actors notwithstanding, there remain fundamental questions about the concept of regionalization and its significance in maintaining peace and security. In Part 1, contributors address these fundamental and critical issues. In Chapter 1, Louise Fawcett examines the evolving architecture of regionalization and argues that there is a causal and interdependent relationship between robust globalism and robust regionalism because as regionalism and regionalization increase under a flexible security order, the pressures of international society will bring them closer into line with global processes in such a way that the two are mutually reinforcing. In Chapter 2, Michael Pugh's alternative and sometimes overlooked macro view, based on the politics of world order, offers an analytical framework to evaluate the potential and limitations of regionalization. He cautions that regionalization carries the risk of ghettoizing "undisciplined" parts of the world. In Chapter 3, in contrast, Ian Martin offers a practitioner's viewpoint of the regionalization of peace operations and concludes that even if this phenomenon is inevitable, regionalization will only produce desirable outcomes if satisfactory answers are found to the kinds of practical issues that became evident in divergent peace operations.

Part 2 focuses on the UN, the EU, NATO, the OSCE, and other regional actors in Europe. Its three chapters seek to clarify the evolving relationship between the UN and regional organizations in Europe on the political, doctrinal, and operational levels with the objective of examining how this cooperation can be improved to make peace operations more effective in the future. The role of the Russian Federation, a key actor in the region, is also examined to identify how best to enlist Moscow's support in peace operations. In Chapter 4, on the logic of primacy, Dick Leurdijk provides the historical perspective that defined the relationship between NATO and the UN and concludes that NATO probably is not interested in a further formalization of its relationships with the UN beyond the existing institutional framework and beyond the ad hoc operational peacebuilding frameworks in the field in Bosnia and Kosovo. However, in the wake of the U.S.-led interventions in Afghanistan and Iraq, an increasingly sidelined NATO might well be compelled to explore the prospect of expanding its partnership with the UN or other regional actors so as to justify its relevance as evidenced in its role in the security force in Kabul. In Chapter 5, in their examination of the role of the OSCE and the EU in regional cooperation with the UN, Nina Græger and Alexandra Novosseloff note that both entities are taking on new civilian and military activities that extend their original tasks and mandates, especially with regard to peace operations. This is partly an attempt to "assert" their profile on the international scene and to influence world politics through developments that have made the civilian and military management of complex crises the biggest challenge for cooperation between the UN on the one hand and the EU and the OSCE on the other. Subsequent events in Afghanistan and Iraq, however, have revealed the limits of European assertiveness on the global stage. The post-Iraq developments are also likely to confine the operational areas of European security organizations primarily to Europe and parts of Africa, areas where some of these countries had colonies and where the United States might be willing to subcontract some operations to European actors or areas that are not of vital strategic significance to Washington. In Chapter 6, Emily Metzgar and Andrei Zagorski provide Russia's perspective on the cooperation between the UN and European regional security organizations and suggest that there are reasons for cautious optimism in building cooperative relations between Russia and a variety of Western institutions, though derailment was threatened as a consequence of the U.S.-UK invasion of Iraq. This optimism, they argue, is based on Russia's participation in NATO-led, UN-sanctioned peacekeeping operations like the Stabilization Force (SFOR) and Kosovo Force (KFOR), which bodes well for the future.

The four chapters in Part 3 study how the UN's partnership with regional actors in Europe can be enhanced to promote postconflict peacebuilding, particularly in the sphere of security sector reform in the Balkans. Special emphasis is placed on the normative and practical aspects of coordinating institutional responses to security challenges in peacebuilding; the role of the military force in managing security sector challenges during and after the conflict; mechanisms to strengthen indigenous civil police capacity and the rule of law; and appropriate approaches to reviving the judicial and penal system. In Chapter 7, on coordinating action on security challenges in peacebuilding, John Cockell argues that the civil-military interface should move from cooperative relations to coordinated unity of effort. Such coordination, when pursued at the strategic, operational, and tactical levels, is best suited to manage the security sector challenges of demilitarization, demobilization, and police reforms. In Chapter 8, in his examination of the role of the military forces in managing public security challenges, Peter Viggo Jakobsen argues that while there is a reluctance on the part of both the military and the civilians to use military forces to maintain civil law and order, it is inevitable that, in the absence of standby civilian police and law and order experts, the military will have to be used to bridge the public security gap. In Chapter 9, David Marshall's study of the efforts of the UN Mission in Kosovo (UNMIK) to revive the judicial and penal system in Kosovo reveals a curious irony: while a coherent strategy, which included the early introduction of international experts in penal management, was primarily responsible for reviving the legal system, the same mission failed to develop a coherent strategy for dealing with the war crimes trials. He offers a series of suggestions on how this situation might be improved, including the need for a judiciary composed of internationals to resolve alleged violations of international humanitarian law and serious interethnic crime as well as the need to consult relevant local actors in policy and legislative developments. In a similar vein, in Chapter 10 Annika Hansen makes a strong case and a series of concrete proposals for strengthening indigenous police capacity and the rule of law in southeast Europe by not only involving local actors but also tackling the informal indigenous power structures that obstruct reconciliation and economic reconstruction. She concludes that the endeavor might be considered successful if the law and order system is tolerable to the locals, sustainable by the locals, and based on respect for human rights.

Part 4 explores how greater cooperation between the UN and regional actors in Europe would affect the peace and security roles and responsibilities of regional actors in Asia, West Africa, and Latin America. In Chapter 11, Mely Caballero-Anthony, in her examination of the Association of Southeast Asian Nations (ASEAN) and the ASEAN Regional Forum (ARF), notes that these organizations have deliberately focused on conflict prevention mechanisms and processes and, more importantly, on norm building rather than developing robust peacekeeping capabilities, which is an attempt to replicate the OSCE's role in Europe. However, while the East Timor crisis revealed the reluctance of ASEAN to conduct peace operations in one of its member states, the creation of the International Force for East Timor (INTERFET) under Chapter VII of the UN Charter under UN Security Council Resolution 1264 saw ASEAN members (the Philippines, Singapore, Malaysia, and Thailand) contribute forces. This clearly indicated that in Southeast Asia a UN resolution was considered essential for members of the regional organization to take action. In Chapter 12, which focuses on the Organization of American States, Monica Herz argues that while the OAS has become a relevant actor in the security sphere as a result of a new framework generated in the 1990s for the protection of democracy. But the noninterventionist tradition in Latin America, the unilateral policies of the United States, and the organizational fragility of the OAS limit the OAS's new activism. Simultaneously, a new pattern of relationship between the OAS and the UN has been developing, which is a direct consequence of the debate on the reform of the UN in the context of the organization's new activism, of the debate on the reform of the OAS, of the peace process in Central America, and of attempts by the leadership of both organizations to build a new framework for their relationship. In Chapter 13, on the subregion of West Africa, 'Funmi Olonisakin and Comfort Ero examine the first peace operation conducted by a subregional organization (ECOWAS/ECOMOG) in Liberia in 1990. They argue that African states were increasingly prepared to find solutions to crises in their region and that by the time they intervened in Sierra Leone and Guinea-Bissau, West African states had demonstrated their willingness to originate "indigenous" formulas to impose order in their region. This willingness was primarily driven by the growing reluctance among the major powers of the UN Security Council to intervene in African crises and the realization among ECOWAS leaders that they had no choice but to evolve mechanisms and structures aimed at tackling conflicts in the region, however imperfect these capabilities might be. The comparative nature of these chapters is aimed at identifying not only areas of convergence and divergence between the European experience and other regions and regional approaches, but also common trends and common tools to enhance cooperation between the UN and regional actors.

Regionalism as a force for the management of international relations gained a new impetus with the end of bipolarity. The chapters in this book explore the implications of this impulse for peace operations and the balance between the universalism of the UN and the regionalism of organizations that may follow narrower concerns. The developing arrangements are in part a reflection of the difficulties, under conditions of U.S. hegemony so pronounced in the Iraq crisis, of establishing a robust and healthy global institution. An increasing U.S. distrust of multilateral structures and the preference of the Bush cabinet for using ad hoc "coalitions" in military missions when pursuing U.S. interests became apparent from the Kosovo crisis onward. This trend preceded the crisis over terrorism and was more a function of U.S.

domestic politics and the exercise of hegemonic power than the events of September 11, 2001. The UN was to be bypassed and its procedures treated contemptuously in the crusade to remove Saddam Hussein's government from Iraq. Not even NATO, the primary tool of U.S. crisis management in Europe, would be immune from the highly divisive impact of U.S. unilateralism. Although in the short term, institutional multilateralism was significantly damaged, ultimately, the relevance of the UN, of regional security structures, and of UN-regional partnerships is unlikely to depend solely on policies devised in Washington. The reactions of regional states to U.S. unilateralism may bring them closer together to defend the benefits of multilateralism—with or without the United States. In addition, underlying structural change may also create opportunities for greater regional cooperation in trade and economic development that spill over into areas of crisis management. In this regard regionalization should not necessarily be regarded as a perfect panacea for global instabilities but as a useful mechanism in enabling the most powerful "liberal" states to protect their interests and promote their values both within and outside their region while strengthening the global capacity for peace operations in the long term. In the post-Iraq phase the more successful, liberal, multilateral variety of regionalism might also play some role in managing the unilateral tendencies of the world's sole hyper-power.

Notes

1. United Nations Security Council Resolution 1244, June 10, 1999.
2. Boutros Boutros-Ghali, *An Agenda for Peace* (New York: United Nations, 1992), para. 61.
3. United Nations, *Report of the Panel on United Nations Peace Operations,* UN Doc. A/55/305-S/2000/809, August 21, 2000.

PART 1

The UN and Regionalization

1

The Evolving Architecture of Regionalization

Louise Fawcett

Regionalism and regionalization, like globalism and globalization, are contested and much debated concepts. There is no common agreement on what the terms themselves encompass, nor on their significance for the theory and practice of international relations.[1] In this chapter I am primarily concerned with exploring the meaning and content of regionalization, understood here as any activity at the regional level, as opposed to global level, that contributes in some way to the promotion of international peace and security. This definition includes those formal institutions better covered by the term "regionalism," but also different regional models such as ad hoc coalitions, or coalitions of the willing.[2] In particular I am concerned with how regionalization in its different forms fits into the prevailing security architecture. The focus then, in line with the rest of the book, is necessarily on the interactions between regional actors, forces and agencies, and the UN.

While other contributions to the book consider in some detail the relationships between both European and non-European actors and the UN, this chapter attempts to provide a broader analytical and comparative focus, pulling together evidence from different regions and practices to offer an overview of the existing security order and the place of regional actors and agencies within it. There is a temptation to use Europe and the North Atlantic as a constant point of reference. But while Europe *is* endlessly fascinating, it does not, indeed cannot, provide all the answers. Nor is there a single European experience, but rather many, a point underlined by disarray in the EU and NATO over the invasion of Iraq in 2003. This chapter also notes the need to move beyond Europe and focus on, listen to, and learn from regional experiences elsewhere. The African, Latin American, and Asian experiences may offer insights that Europe cannot.

Some would call utopian the search for an evolving security architecture in a world where state interest reigns supreme and international institutions can perform only "modest services."[3] Some remain wedded to a global or regional approach. The assumption made here is that there is such an architecture founded on a shifting balance of global and regional activity. As Ted Gurr highlights: "The emergent norm is that international and regional organizations, and individual states, have responsibilities to mediate internal wars and to engage, using force if necessary, to check gross violations of human rights."[4]

One point to note is that both regionalism and regionalization—in theory and practice—are familiar features of international relations. Their apparent newness lies only in terms of their increased range and scope of activity. A second point is that there is already a legal framework in place as regards regional activity and its relation to the UN. The UN Charter is clear that while Chapter VIII accords primacy to the Security Council, it also legitimizes delegation to member states or regional organizations, provided the Council is kept informed and retains overall authority. The nature, membership, and scope of such groups are undefined.[5] The problem is not which regional actors to empower, but how to determine their remit and relationship to the UN.

If past precedent and the UN Charter provision buttress the current phase of regionalization, evidence of an evolving normative architecture must be sought in the complexity and diversity of present practice. Despite the obvious tensions, the UN and regional actors are intimately and increasingly linked in a common security building project in which a de facto division of labor has emerged. There is a causal and interdependent relationship between robust globalism and robust regionalism: the two are complementary rather than contradictory processes. As regionalism and regionalization increase under a flexible security order, the pressures of international society will bring them closer into line with global processes in such a way that the two are mutually reinforcing.

The chapter starts by examining the phenomena of regionalization. Regionalism and regionalization have a rich if sometimes controversial history, and it is on past experience that present practice is designed and built. After considering the historical context, the focus shifts to the impulses driving regionalism since the end of the Cold War and then to constructing a picture of how regional and global initiatives have interacted and how the partnership has evolved. The chapter then turns to some of the common problems and challenges associated with the present wave of regionalization, before attempting to draw up a balance sheet of the current state of the architecture and associated debates.

Regionalization: A Brief History

When should a history of regionalization begin?[6] Since regionalization is distinguished from a universal "other," one might start in the 1920s by considering the relationship of the League of Nations with different regional groups, treaties, and agencies as the beginnings of the search for regional-global partnership.[7] The 1920s are interesting because they mirror the persisting debates about universalism versus regionalism and supranationality versus sovereignty, raising questions of leadership and of the perceived dilution of global by regional initiatives. Certainly the League did not emerge in practice as a key security provider. Sally Marks notes how, as it turned to "its assigned task of enforcing and preserving the peace, it discovered that the great powers had largely reserved enforcement to themselves and their agencies."[8] This critique is clearly applicable to the UN today.

In terms of formal organization, few regional groups existed outside the Inter-American System. That any international institution could deliver peace and security was a novel idea, and one that dismally failed the test of the 1930s. Security was sought unilaterally, or through alliances and ententes, some of a more permanent, others of an ad hoc nature. This was not subsidiarity or subcontracting; states definitely called the tune. But the League, like the UN, influenced like-minded people and governments to think in somewhat different terms about peace and security. Once embedded, the idea persisted, and the UN sought not only to refurbish it, but also to tackle the thorny question of regionalism. This required a rethinking of the holy grail of universalists, for whom regionalism was at odds with the principle of collective security: making war impossible required the commitment of the entire international community, not selective parts of it.[9]

Regionalism's appearance in the final version of the UN Charter followed representations from states with investments in arrangements like the Inter-American System, the Arab League, and the Commonwealth. It was the Latin American states, fearing the consequences of U.S. hegemony and veto power, who saw in the Organization of American States a vehicle for containment, which pressed for this clause.[10] And in Chapter VIII, Article 52, regional agencies were duly called upon to "make every effort to achieve peaceful settlement of local disputes . . . before referring them to the Security Council." In adopting this stance, the Latin Americans were articulating what would become a common agenda of the third world state faced with difficult choices about types of multilateral action.

What is important here is to reiterate the opportunities that the UN framework established for regional-UN partnership. For even if circumstances, like interpretation and practice, have changed, it is UN Charter principles that have continued to inform decisions about legitimacy and scope of regional action.

The possibility of regional agencies acting with the UN as partners in peace, as envisaged by the UN Charter, was quickly curtailed by the nature and composition of the Security Council and the exigencies of East-West politics. But the region as a unit of analysis and initiator of action became important, partly because of the very difficulties supplied by the Cold War context and also because of the growing assertiveness and self-consciousness of regions themselves. As Stanley Hoffman wrote in the 1980s, one of the realities of post–world war politics was "the division of a huge and heterogeneous international system into subsystems in which patterns of cooperation and ways of controlling conflicts are either more intense or less elusive than those in the global system."[11]

Regional allegiances were defined by the East-West divide (as well as a growing North-South divide), and with the UN system so evidently constrained, peace and security were delivered unilaterally, or regionally, notably through the Warsaw Pact, NATO, and related organizations, or ad hoc coalitions, some more successfully than others. The European Community, for example, played an important role in consolidating a secure and democratic regional community, a model for others to follow. Regionalization, understood in a broad sense, was thus reality.

The empowerment of such regional institutions and actors, and their practices, often without direct reference to the UN, led to a degree of autonomy of action and consequent discrediting of UN purpose that have proved hard to manage and overcome in the post–Cold War era. Bolstered by their reformed security agendas and the exercise of hegemonic power (the United States in the North Atlantic Treaty Organization [NATO], Russia in the Commonwealth of Independent States [CIS], or Nigeria in the Economic Community of West African States [ECOWAS]), but also influenced by the evident limitations of UN capacity in key areas, such groupings, as well as individual states, can sidestep the world organization in ways that are not dissimilar to the days of the Cold War. The role of national interest in governing behavior may be an inevitable feature of international politics; in some cases of UN inaction it may be justifiable. But it is a reminder that the legacy of the Cold War international system (and previous systems) remains and conditions the current security architecture.

Outside the Cold War blocs, the major regional groupings that concern us today had rather a minor role in security maintenance, their Charter VIII–friendly potential notwithstanding. Overall, regional actors did not feature prominently in the UN's new peacekeeping roles. Some exceptions—the Organization of African Unity (OAU) in Chad in 1981, the League of Arab States in Lebanon in 1976,[12] the Commonwealth in Rhodesia/Zimbabwe in 1980—hardly contradict this picture. The Organization of American States (OAS) was seen to be closely bound up with U.S. hegemony in its Dominican Republic involvement in 1965 and in actions elsewhere.[13] In the cases of the OAU and Arab League, it is doubtful that even *without* the Cold War they would have been equipped to deal with the conflicts arising from decolonization and independence, or indeed to achieve consensus across such a diverse membership. Perhaps we should not judge them too harshly. Europe, too, for different reasons failed to supply itself with a viable security dimension, as the demise of the European Defense Community project and subsequent stagnation of the Western European Union showed (though the presence of NATO made the need less pressing).

Many conflicts remained outside the remit of any regional organization or actor. Still, if cooperative actions in the Cold War were few, it would be wrong to write off these years. A precedent had been set and survived. These were important learning years for regional institutions, with lessons for balancing, nonalignment, and autonomy of action, but also more creatively for the construction of "security communities" that would later help inform the contours of regional behavior. Indeed, some of the institutions once described as regional dinosaurs, like the OAU (revamped in 2002 as the African Union), are those at the forefront of regional peace initiatives today.

The later Cold War period also saw the birth of a number of new organizations with subregional rather than regional membership, and often with a more conscious security orientation. They were an attempt to move away from the problems associated with larger "pan"-regional bodies or great power–sponsored alliances. With their more limited memberships and goals, they were an early sign of the new regionalization that would follow the Cold War; they had opportunities to develop their credentials as actual or potential partners in the evolving peace and security architecture. An early example is the Association of Southeast Asian Nations (ASEAN) in 1967. Others are the Caribbean Community (CARICOM) and ECOWAS in 1973 and 1975, the South African Development Community (SADC) in 1980, the Gulf Cooperation Council (GCC) in 1981, and the South Asian Association for Regional Cooperation (SARC) in 1985.[14] In a somewhat different category is the Organization of the Islamic Conference (OIC) in 1969. The first four, and the Organization for Security and Cooperation in Europe (OSCE) in 1986, formerly the Conference on Security and Cooperation in Europe (CSCE), have already had some role to play in broader regional peace and security initiatives; the SARC and GCC have not. None were designed specifically to complement the UN's role (though some have subsequently displayed this potential and are mentioned in Boutros Boutros-Ghali's *An Agenda for Peace*), but rather to engage with specific security concerns at the regional level. However, the potential for collaboration existed, to be later exploited as reflected in the conscious upgrade of organizational remit and capability.

Regionalization and the End of the Cold War

If the Cold War was a period that provided motives and parameters for regional action while hampering collective activity and the prospects of partnership, it was not unreasonable to assume that the end of the Cold War would offer new conditions and incentives to the UN and international organizations. At first, there was indeed a flurry of expectations, even euphoria, about UN capacity, reflected in a spate of peacekeeping and related activity in the late 1980s and early 1990s—in Iraq, Cambodia, Mozambique, Angola, and El Salvador. At first sight this reflected the rediscovery of the hitherto elusive role for the UN as key security provider. The UN moment could not last, however. Failure—starkly exposed by the Rwandan crisis—followed early promise. It soon became clear that the UN was overburdened, underfunded, and incapable of undertaking alone the increasingly complex and diverse range of peace and security operations that the post–Cold War environment presented. At this point, regionalization gains salience.

Already some early post–Cold War activity had seen a limited role for regional organizations and actors in cooperative or preventative missions—in the former Soviet Union in Central America and Africa. Significantly, both membership of regional organizations and interest in what writers dubbed the "new regionalism" were on the increase before the Cold War ended, and this growth continued into the 1990s.[15] There was a trickle-down effect from the UN (and to some extent the EU) as far as empowerment of international institutions were concerned. And, as pressure on the UN mounted, task sharing at different levels with governmental and nongovernmental organizations (NGOs) and coalitions of states became increasingly desirable. Words like "subsidiarity" and "subcontracting" crept into the vocabulary of cooperation, even though neither accurately described many of the new relationships. Moreover, in many ways, as suggested below, the post–Cold War environment both dictated and demanded greater regional involvement in the maintenance of peace and security. Both the possibilities and limitations of UN action have led to a reappraisal of the role of other actors and agencies.[16] The net effect has been that despite the attendant problems, a correspondingly larger space for regionalism and regionalization was opened.

It is partly from these impulses to regionalization that a new security architecture has evolved. At one basic level, regionalization is demand driven. First, the present international environment is far more permissive of intervention. Second, our concept of peace and security has expanded to incorporate a range of issues outside the scope of any single international organization. Third, the sheer number and scale of interventions that have been undertaken since the end of the Cold War would require either a vastly expanded and reformed UN, a massive shift in the direction of global governance, or significant participation of regional and other actors.

This expansion of the concept of security, and consequently what constitutes a peace operation, seems appropriate, since short-termism has proved a serious drawback in the recent experience of intervention—the case of Iraq's Kurds is just one example.[17] But it does present serious problems of capacity, given the clear limits to UN expansion and activity in the post-9/11 climate, particularly in certain crucial areas. Thomas Weiss has noted how the "logic behind Chapter VIII" has been brought back by the UN's "overextension."[18] As our interpretation of security broadens and peacekeeping becomes more multidimensional, the range of actors and instruments required widens.

Cognizant of this problem, in terms of both the limitations on UN action and the desirability of greater regional input, the last three Secretaries-General—Javier Perez de Cuéllar, Boutros Boutros-Ghali (most famously in his *An Agenda for Peace*), and Kofi Annan—have all highlighted the potential role of regional agencies along with the need to revitalize the Chapter VIII provision. They issued calls for greater regional participation at different levels, signaling the desirability of a new global-regional balance. But perhaps deliberately, none have been explicit about the remit of regionally inspired activity (although it is mentioned in relation to the four key areas covered in *An Agenda for Peace:* preventative diplomacy, peacekeeping, peacemaking, and postconflict peacebuilding). Nor have they been precise about the relationship between regional actors and the UN, beyond the general terms laid down in the UN Charter.[19] This reveals the flexibility and inclusivity of the Charter, and the unwillingness to exclude, chastise, or circumscribe regional actors because of actions that may not conform to the Charter provision. Perhaps though, in some fashion, it also reveals the still present and, in certain quarters, unresolved tensions between regional and universal action.[20]

At another level, regionalization is also driven by needs and interests. As bipolar overlay and influence slipped away, regions were not only required but also actively sought ways and means to assert their identity and purpose in the new global environment. The two were not always complementary processes, because regions, unsurprisingly, have their own agendas. While such tensions became apparent in the former Yugoslavia, beyond Europe, in Africa, the experience of the Cold War and evident limitations of the UN (evidenced in the Congo, Sudan, and Ethiopia) contributed to a "crisis of credibility," reinforcing a desire for greater autonomy among Africans and a more assertive regional role.[21] This assertiveness has been true of developing countries generally, many of which felt marginalized by international trends. Regionalism and regionalization provide a way into a Western-dominated "globalizing" order, a means of interaction, influence, even norm creation and agenda setting. As we have seen in developing-country coalitions in different international institutions (the powerful Asian economies are an obvious example), these can act as a check and balance or perhaps give a steer to multilateral initiatives. If this can work for economic regionalism, why not for security regionalism also? Alongside Africa's push for "African solutions to African problems," ASEAN set the tone for a distinct Southeast Asian security community; in Latin American democratization, peacebuilding measures, and preventive diplomacy—as during the anti-Chavez coup in Venezuela—have predominated.

It is increasingly evident that regions want, and have always wanted, more say and representation. In this regard, regional groups expressed disappointment at the single paragraph referring to UN collaboration with regional organizations in the Brahimi Report.[22] Resistance to being part of a U.S.-led global order, or indeed any order where institutions are dominated by strong states and fear being left out, having no place at the negotiating table, have all served both to promote the forces of regionalism and also to demand that they be taken seriously: in any peacemaking project the regional constellation of states cannot be ignored.[23] A common fear among developing countries since the end of the Cold War is that the UN has been hijacked or bypassed by the powerful Western states.[24] This fear was expressed vociferously during the 1991 and 2003 Gulf Wars by many countries, not necessarily Iraq's allies. Regional initiatives can mitigate this fear and provide incentives to collaboration.

Alongside and linked to these pressures from within and without, the debate about regionalization takes place at a time of widespread doubt and questioning about the capacity of the international system to effectively handle the range of global and local problems. This doubt has been reinforced time and again, but perhaps most startlingly by events in September 2001, by the West's evident inability to develop a new approach to international relations after the Soviet withdrawal from the Cold War.[25] Talk of a new world order evaporated as Cold War–type conflicts dragged on alongside the now familiar "new wars" despite or perhaps because of the denial of superpower aid. The UN and related institutions have failed to match expectations and adjust to the new and unfamiliar challenges of intrastate conflict.

This sense of an order that has failed is backed up by a glance through the post–Cold War years. The mixed record of interventions in Iraq, Yugoslavia, Somalia, Cambodia, Rwanda, and elsewhere reveals an urgent need to extract lessons, and to develop a better conceptual framework to guide policy, to create a better model for the future.[26] There is no simple solution: regionalization and subsidiarity may give rise to new problems; some regional crises (Colombia, Palestine-Israel, India-Pakistan) remain "black holes" in terms of cooperative capability. Regionalism is thus no panacea, but it can help overcome the failure of states and the UN hitherto to address what Richard Falk pessimistically calls the "pathological anarchism" of the international system.[27]

Old Institutions, New Agendas?

What results have the push factors yielded, and what has been the response of international organizations and actors to them? It is argued here that we have already witnessed the globalization of regionalism. Apart from the growth of regional activity noted earlier, we have seen attempts at refurbishment of existing organizations, for example in the Western European Union (WEU),

ASEAN, the OIC, ECOWAS, and the OAU, with new commitments to unity and increased tasks and services. We have also seen the adaption and expansion of existing institutions to bring in new members, principally in Europe (EU/OSCE/NATO), but again in Southeast Asia. We have witnessed the launching of schemes like Mercosur, the Arab Mahgreb Union, the Asia Pacific Economic Cooperation Forum (APEC) and the ASEAN Regional Forum (ARF), the CIS, and a range of projects for promoting cooperation in the Black Sea, Baltic, and southern Mediterranean.

One might be forgiven for confusing or forgetting some of these acronyms. A number of the groups and schemes mentioned above are peripheral to our discussion; some have made little impact within their respective spheres. Often their roles are limited, their purposes poorly defined, and they do not as yet play any part in the emerging security architecture, though based on past precedent some at least may come to do so in the future. However, a number of such organizations have responded to the challenges of the post–Cold War period, broadening the scope of their activities, adding new functions—from mediation to conflict management and preventative diplomacy—perhaps going beyond initial Charter purposes. Overall this is a picture of regional empowerment with a role for regionalization in the new security order already staked out. And evidence of the past ten years suggests a steady increase in the number of non-UN peacekeeping actions.[28]

The picture that emerges here, and one that is borne out by the evidence of other chapters, is very diverse, making it hard to discern a common pattern or set of principles. But it does amount to a selection, a menu of regional responses to the new global security agenda, with ways into that agenda provided by new facilitating mechanisms, a relaxation of the norm of intervention, or the adoption of new principles and practices. In this regard one might single out changes in doctrine and organizational capacity as key features.[29] Europe might have led the way in this respect with major changes effected in the aims and purposes of NATO, the OSCE, and the WEU. In the broader European and former Soviet space we should also note the activities of the CIS and the Euro-Mediterranean Partnership, incorporating North Africa and parts of the Middle East.[30] But we should also be cautious about considering Europe's security architecture as the best or only model for export.

Some non-European examples of the above changes are found in the OAU's mechanism for conflict prevention and resolution (1993); the ECOWAS agreement on establishing a conflict resolution mechanism (1998); the SADC's decision in 1996 to create an organ for politics, defense, and security; ASEAN's decision to create the ARF in 1993; and the OAS's Santiago Declaration of 1991. In some cases the emphasis has been on peacekeeping activity, cooperation, and devolution of power to subregional institutions; in others on peacebuilding, with more focus on confidence building and preventative diplomacy. While each organization has chosen to respond or not to respond to peace and security issues in a distinctive way, it is apparent that regions both expect and are expected to provide input into crises of local origins, and that they can and will look to the UN for greater or lesser degrees of direction and cooperation. Burden sharing will necessarily depend on the nature of the conflict and the capacity of regional actors.

Charter change, innovative and far-reaching as it may be, is not enough, and does not guarantee either efficacy or partnership of the sort desired by the UN, where greater cooperation is called for.[31] Particularly problematic has been the NATO/ECOWAS provision for military action without prior Security Council approval.[32] Some commentators are highly critical and would describe recent regional actions as illegitimate, or merely reflective of deep flaws within regional groups or within the UN. One commentator on the intervention of the ECOWAS Ceasefire Monitoring Group (ECOMOG) felt that it should not be regarded as an example or model for other types of regional-UN partnership.[33] In an exchange with Michael Ignatieff, Robert Skidelsky insisted that rather than regarding NATO action against Serbia in a positive light, "the by-passing of the UN by NATO sends a clear message to all countries that force, not law, governs international affairs."[34]

Such criticisms highlight common problems, but perhaps reflect a dismissal of context and a rather too narrow view of what might be expected from a regional organization. It makes more sense to regard the ECOMOG intervention as remarkable for happening at all, and remarkable also, as Chapter 13 points out, for marking the beginning of a learning curve, as the Sierra Leone case subsequently demonstrated. The same could be said for NATO's involvement in the former Yugoslavia. The norm here appears to be to act with a UN mandate where possible, but to reserve the right to waive this condition when circumstances demand.

In this sense it may be helpful to distinguish between "hard" and "soft" peacekeeping. The UN has a long record of success in the latter, but little in the former, and more recently it is regional organizations (like NATO and ECOWAS), or ad hoc coalitions, that have taken the difficult decisions about intervention and enforcement. There may be situations in which "doing nothing" is the best option; in others, "hard" peacekeeping, provided by regional actors, may be preferable to no peacekeeping.[35]

This is not the place to rehearse the arguments about the relative merits of regional as opposed to collective or UN action. These are well covered in different works,[36] and further elucidated by many contributions in this volume. There are obvious advantages and disadvantages to both global and regional approaches, which merely serve to reinforce the importance of complementarity in any emerging architecture, and the cautious but positive note adopted by Thomas Weiss seems to be appropriate here. Both offer important but ultimately different things. However, by way of highlighting some of the new trends and their possible meanings, common problems associated with the new regionalization can be marshaled under four broad headings.

Some Common Objections

Regionalization and Primacy

One legitimate question about the regionalization process is: who drives and does it matter? A UN model would suggest the importance of a clear mandate as regards both devolution of power and appropriate regional actors. Practice is more messy. The evidence of increased activity of regional organizations and actors does not necessarily support a picture of partnership, subsidiarity, and subcontracting, though these may be present in individual cases. On some occasions, the UN appears to defer to regional powers in relations with regional groupings, providing only retrospective recognition. The experience of ECOMOG seems to fit this category, while the evidence from the CIS and NATO is mixed.[37] Yet in these cases regional-global efforts were combined to some success. One cannot say definitely that had such interventions not taken place that the world (or the UN) would be a better place. While in practice the issue of primacy has become diluted, it remains important. UN action provides a seal of approval and legitimacy that may be absent from regional initiatives, and thus is actively sought by regional actors. If any organization or individual state associates itself with unpopular or controversial policy, its reputation can become tarnished. Hence flexibility and sensitivity are required, indeed are essential at the partnership-building stage. Perhaps the East Timor case is a good model for such flexibility. Where the UN and/or regional organizations cannot respond, and when prompt action and great power support are essential, a less restrictive UN mandate may be called for.[38] At a practical level, experience has shown that any cooperative arrangement involving task and burden sharing can quickly become bogged down over the issue of unified command structures. As Boutros-Ghali pointed out (in reference to the case of Yugoslavia), in the absence of any agreed method on who holds operational command, the principle of joint agreement by the different organizations involved is vital.[39]

Sovereignty

Sovereignty has always worked against regional organizations, even the most successful ones, particularly over security issues, as the European case has displayed. It has been the sine qua non of the UN Charter, though now more porous in the case of humanitarian intervention. As Boutros-Ghali has commented, "the time of absolute and exclusive sovereignty . . . has passed."[40] But this is only part of the story. While the principle of noninterference remains a significant obstacle to action for organizations like ASEAN, the UN pattern has been picked up in small ways by Latin American and African organizations in particular. To this extent the UN leads and others follow. But even where the principle of noninterference remains sacrosanct, this does not impede regional groups from playing a role in peacebuilding, in helping to create a secure regional environment. Any activity that promotes regional community such as measures for democracy building, economic integration, or confidence building can contribute to the global security architecture.

Hegemony

Just as regional actors and groups can upstage the UN, so can individual states set the agenda within regions. Bringing in regional organizations or legitimizing regional actors often gives rise to the hegemony issue. We can point here to the ECOWAS-Liberia example (where Nigeria clearly dominated the process and provided the lion's share of ECOMOG's military component). But this has also been replicated to different degrees elsewhere: in NATO, the CIS, and the OSCE, and almost inevitably in any ad hoc coalition. Hegemony is a common problem among regional actors and multilateral forces, whether or not they are acting in concert with the UN. At its most negative, regionalism can be seen as "little more than an occasional instrument for the assertion of hegemonic control, that, depending on circumstances, can be viewed as either legitimated by collective procedures or not."[41] But hegemony cannot be a reason for excluding regional actors; it is an argument for setting clearer guidelines and parameters for action, for making regional organizations conform to certain standards, and for greater institutional democratization. In the controversial case of Russia and the CIS, it can be argued that however overdetermined Russian involvement, the CIS presence in the former Soviet space has helped preserve peace and stability.[42] Indeed, greater cooperation with UN structures, and thus greater accountability, might induce regional actors to modify their behavior, mitigating hegemony rather than just reinforcing it. Regionalization thus may encourage socialization and norm adherence.

Capacity

The limited capacity and resources of many regional organizations, particularly non-Western organizations, is often cited as a major motive for regarding their role as limited and secondary.[43] This may be true, or partly true, in terms of military and institutional capacity and diplomatic leverage. But regional actors may also have both relevant expertise and a level of acceptability in areas where the UN may not, particularly in complex operations and conflict prevention and peacebuilding. Clearly it is unlikely that any regional grouping would go it alone in a multidimensional operation. But where a sustained commitment is involved, as for example in the ECOWAS-Liberia case, states may have to ask hard questions. Generally, where costs are high and resources limited, regional organizations might have to make difficult decisions about which operations to undertake.[44] But capacity problems in some areas are not a reason for inaction in others, merely enhancing the argument for complementarity and global support for regional initiatives.

Some Advantages

Against such problems and difficulties, it is worth reiterating some of the advantages of regional action. Any new architecture will be in part a response to its perceived strengths as well as its weaknesses. Certainly, regional organizations are not uniquely problematic, and many of the difficulties they experience are shared with the UN. Here, a better exchange of information and study of comparative advantage are crucial to dividing labor and allocating tasks effectively.

First, regional organizations and actors have demonstrated an ability and willingness to act where the UN (or relevant regional organizations) may be impeded from doing so. In Africa and the former Yugoslavia, for example, the involvement of regional actors has been beneficial to the overall balance of peace and security.

Linked to the above are the difficulties accompanying types of UN intervention. Despite the UN's greater claim to legitimacy, it could be said that the experience of the 1990s demonstrated that it was unsuited to high-intensity military enforcement operations: regional actors or coalitions of the willing have proved more effective. The same might be said for civilian governance. In East Timor a case could be made for the greater effectiveness of coalition missions in managing a transitional government.[45]

Another obvious impediment to UN action is the inability to quickly respond to conflicts, an obstacle compounded by the lack of a standing force. Certainly the failure of the UN to respond to the Yugoslav crises strengthened NATO determination to act without prior authorization, thereby undermining UN authority.[46] A quick and timely response to conflict is acknowledged to be vital. In the absence of such a UN force, rapid reaction forces can be supplied by regional actors, and again there is experience to draw on here.

Proximity to the conflict, knowledge of the region, shared security dilemmas, and common interests in conflict solutions (and the possibility of "locking in shared norms and values"), as well as the reduced numbers of actors, less complex (perhaps) decisionmaking procedures, and lower costs, may also give regional actors the advantage in some peace operations.[47] They may also be an active preference among involved parties for the deployment of regional actors. Significantly, regional actors may also profit from increased transparency, early warning, more accurate information, and the fact that summitry can be accomplished at the local level. This merely highlights the importance of using the fullest range of different mechanisms of diplomacy and peacemaking at the regional level.[48]

Conclusion: An Evolving Architecture of Regionalization?

What lessons have been learned, and what are the observable trends and patterns? The approach adopted here has been in favor of regionalism, flexibility, and complementarity. It has taken regionalization seriously. Robust regionalism goes hand in hand with robust globalism: this is a common project, not a zero-sum game. Thus renewed interest in regional organizations and actors is not merely the current fashion, nor is it part of the UN's "midlife crisis."[49]

There is little room for utopian universalism or regional triumphalism. The promotion of "intraregional peace" is one starting point, but not the only starting point for the construction of a more stable international order.[50] The goal is an effective partnership, and the challenge is to make both work better, and to work better together within a flexible framework. This means moving beyond debates about leadership and the lingering suspicion and mistrust that seem to persist between regional and global activity. It is illustrative that the Norwegian Nobel Committee continues to favor global over regional cooperation. The 2001 peace prize went to the UN and Kofi Annan, and previously peace prizes were awarded to "peacekeepers" and NGOs, but no regional organization has ever been a recipient.[51] Without a relationship built on cooperation and trust, any new peace and security agenda, with the many demands it imposes, can never be realized.

Peace and security should be accorded utmost priority. Without these basic conditions, other development goals cannot be met, whether political, economic, or social. In this context regional security cooperation must be taken seriously and promoted wherever possible, and in this regard there is much that the international community can do. Developing countries are right to demand more support from international institutions—as their responses to the Brahimi Report demonstrate—but the international system is still, to some degree, a self-help system, and states and regions must also help themselves. Nevertheless, strong global and regional institutions like the EU should make good their oft-promised commitment to help build and support viable institutions elsewhere.

International values, ideas, norms, and principles are not UN property, but part of a shared global project: they can and should be transmitted to all international institutions, making them stakeholders. We have seen a significant "trickle-down" effect in normative practice from the UN to regional organizations, but the traffic can be two-way and the UN might also profitably learn from the experience of regional institutions. Generally, strong institutions are too focused on their own (usually Western) experiences and are unwilling, unable, or perhaps too arrogant to learn from or listen to their weaker counterparts.

Regionalization, understood in the broadest sense, has made significant progress since the end of the Cold War, but it is not a post–Cold War phenomenon. It was facilitated and driven by forces external and internal to regions before, during, and after the Cold War, and it is against this backdrop that we must understand its present progress and future prospects. This then is not a blank slate: the UN must adjust to the role that regional organizations have acquired "beyond the Charter," and regional organizations and actors must reduce their critiques of the world organization and move toward a more cooperative, flexible, and effective burden-sharing approach. To be sure, some progress has already been made, but much remains to be done. Where strong powers are concerned, task sharing and issues of leadership will always be difficult. And here lie some lessons for the NATO alliance.

Despite the controversy attendant on the Yugoslav interventions, NATO has shown a degree of adaptability and flexibility to the new security environment. But when we think about NATO's role and lessons for other groups, it is worth bearing in mind that one of NATO's strengths lies precisely in its Cold War experience. The Cold War provided NATO with the integrated command structure that has so proved vital to success. Unlike most regional organizations, NATO has the tools for action and the ability to use them.[52] In this respect, one can see why coalitions of the willing, in which states rely on their own security apparatus, may prove superior at certain levels of peacekeeping.

This does not, of course, mean that other regional organizations cannot equip themselves in similar fashion, but this is likely to be a very slow process, since none have comparable experience or resources. But by way of analogy we might look at the experience of integration in Europe. Most would agree that the EU has been remarkably successful in relative terms. And other groups have, since its inception, sought to imitate and learn from European Community practice. If the EU can be a model at one level, why not NATO at another? If some regional groups, in Southeast Asia, Latin America, and Africa, have assumed with some degree of success the tasks the EU assigned itself, in terms of bringing down internal barriers and promoting free trade, this is significant progress. And it is encouraging from the security perspective also, because as neofunctionalist theory has taught us, organizations can expand their range of functions, moving from one area to another.

How does this concern our search for a new security architecture for the twenty-first century? As regional organizations increase their range of functions, and we have seen this happening at the security level in the four major regions under discussion here, they become more competent and attractive actors, not only within their own regions, but within regional-global combinations, as partners for peace. Events in Iraq in the spring of 2003 served as a powerful reminder of the need for an effective regional security system in one of the world's most vulnerable areas.

NATO, or variations on the NATO theme, can help shape and define other security agendas for the future. But a note of caution is also needed. NATO is only one of a range of possible models. We have been reminded since the events of September 11, 2001, just how diverse—and controversial—the different modalities of intervention are, whether multilateral, regional, or unilateral, highlighting the need for flexibility, but also checks and balances. At another level, it is important that NATO does not scare off regional groupings as another example of U.S. hegemony dressed as regionalism. NATO and UN activism and strong U.S. unilateralism give rise to real concerns about sovereignty and equality among developing countries. These concerns may be overstated, but perceptions of power and powerlessness are hard to shift and will affect the reputation of peace operations.

It has been said that the use of force for humanitarian purposes has become an established pattern in the post–Cold War international order, and that interventions—such as that of East Timor—are "a barometer for how far the normative structure of international society has been transformed."[53] Is NATO the barometer for regionalization? The answer must surely be no: quite apart from NATO's divisions over the invasion of Iraq, the criteria for measurement are too diverse. Certainly we have the beginnings of normative change, understood as "standard setting, adding to established . . . practice."[54] The UN norm is that regional actors should be encouraged to engage in all types of peace operations, but the remit and authority should derive from the Security Council. For regional actors, the norm is slightly different: they will engage selectively in different types of peace operations, preferably but not necessarily with prior endorsement of and support from the UN. Normative balance, as well as an appropriate division of labor, have yet to emerge. As Kofi Annan has elegantly expressed it, there is an urgent need to forge unity on issues of principle and process.[55]

The effect of such normative change that has occurred has been to enhance the potential for regionalization and cooperative action, as well as to highlight potential problems. It would be too grand to claim a new normative architecture of regionalization, while the practice remains essentially à la carte. Just as threats are different and require different forms of treatment, so are regions and their actors and institutions. For this reason we cannot talk about any overarching framework, or a standard response to securing peace. That some trumping occurs is inevitable. But in a world where global government remains an illusion, there is no option but to but to seek to regional-ize peace and security.

The UN cannot "deliver us from evil," nor indeed can any regional agency.[56] This was a lesson forcefully brought home by the events in Iraq in early 2003. But both the UN and regional actors will continue as security providers within their respective spheres in a flexible, if at times competitive, relationship. The institutional fallout from the Iraq crisis will settle—and there will be other crises—but the processes described in this volume, the regionali-zation of peace and security, however imperfect, are likely to endure. The legit-imacy bestowed on states by participation in and cooperation with international institutions, by the shared pool of common values and norms, still matters: unli-ateralism cannot be a permanent option. The search for a more robust security architecture, engaging an ever-increasing range of actors, must continue.

Notes

1. See, for example, Paul Taylor, *International Organization in the Modern World: The Regional and the Global Process* (London: Pinter, 1993), pp. 7–23.

2. This moves somewhat away from Joseph Nye's definition, which attributes to regions a geographical relationship. Geography may or may not define the composi-tion of an ad hoc coalition; nor can it be said to define, for example, the Common-wealth or the Organization of the Islamic Conference (OIC). See Joseph Nye, *Inter-national Regionalism* (Boston: Little, Brown, 1968), p. vii. For contrast, see Louise J. Cantori and Steven L. Speigel, *The International Relations of Regions: A Comparative Approach* (Englewood Cliffs, NJ: Prentice Hall, 1970); Michael Barnett, "The UN, Regional Organizations, and Peacekeeping," *Review of International Studies* 21, no. 4 (October 1995): 418–419.

3. Stanley Hoffman, *Janus and Minerva: Essays in the Theory and Practice of International Politics* (Boulder: Westview Press, 1987), p. 75.

4. Ted Robert Gurr, "Containing Internal War in the Twenty-First Century," in Fen Osler Hampson and David M. Malone, eds., *From Reaction to Conflict Preven-tion: Opportunities for the UN System* (Boulder: Lynne Rienner, 2002), p. 51.

5. See Danesh Sarooshi, *The United Nations and the Development of Collective Security: The Delegation by the UN Security Council of Its Chapter VII Powers* (Oxford: Oxford University Press, 1999), pp. 1–2, 142–146; Hilaire McCoubrey and Justin Morris, *Regional Peacekeeping in the Post–Cold War Era* (The Hague: Kluwer Law International, 2000), p. 35.

6. Parts of this section draw on my chapter "Regionalism in Historical Perspec-tive" in Louise Fawcett and Andrew Hurrell, eds., *Regionalism in World Politics* (Oxford: Oxford University Press, 1995), pp. 9–36.

7. In Article 21 the League Covenant acknowledged the validity of regional understandings as a basis for maintaining peace.

8. Sally Marks, *The Illusion of Peace* (London: Macmillan, 1976), p. 31.

9. As expressed, for example, by the early functionalist writer David Mitrany in *A Working Peace System* (Oxford: Oxford University Press, 1944).

10. McCoubrey and Morris, *Regional Peacekeeping,* p. 37.

11. Hoffman, "International Organization," p. 293.

12. An ad hoc Western multilateral force was also used in 1982 in Beirut to oversee the Palestinian evacuation. See Clive Archer, *International Organizations* (London: Routledge, 1992), p. 182.

13. See Gareth J. Evans, *Cooperating for Peace: The Global Agenda for the 1990s and Beyond* (St. Leonards, New South Wales: Allen & Unwin, 1993), p. 103; Paul F. Diehl, *International Peacekeeping* (Baltimore: Johns Hopkins University Press, 1993), p. 121.

14. William Tow, *Subregional Security Cooperation in the Third World* (Boulder: Lynne Rienner, 1990).

15. For evidence on the growth of regional organizations, see Taylor, *International Organization,* pp. 24–26.

16. See Thomas G. Weiss, ed., *Beyond UN Subcontracting: Task-Sharing with Regional Security Arrangements and Service-Providing NGOs* (London: Macmillan, 1998).

17. David Keen, "Short-Term Interventions and Long-Term Problems: The Case of the Kurds in Iraq," in John Harriss, ed., *The Politics of Humanitarian Intervention* (London: Pinter, 1995), pp. 167–186.

18. Weiss, *Beyond UN Subcontracting,* p. xii.

19. Boutros Boutros-Ghali, *An Agenda for Peace* (New York: United Nations, 1992), para. 64.

20. See, for example, Marrack Goulding, *Peacemonger* (London: John Murray, 2002), p. 218.

21. See Alex de Waal, "Wars in Africa," in Mary Kaldor, ed., *Global Insecurity* (London: Pinter, 2000), pp. 49–51.

22. See *Refashioning the Dialogue: Regional Perspectives on the Brahimi Report on UN Peace Operations,* www.ipacademy.org/publications, pp. 5, 8.

23. I. William Zartman, "Putting Humpty Dumpty Together Again," in David A. Lake and Ronald Rothchild, eds., *The International Spread of Ethnic Conflict* (Princeton: Princeton University Press, 1998), p. 330.

24. See Mats Berdal, *Wither UN Peacekeeping?* Adelphi Paper no. 281 (London: International Institute for Security Studies, 1993), p. 74.

25. Michael MccGwire, "The Paradigm That Lost Its Way,' *International Affairs* 77, no. 4 (2001): 777–803.

26. See James Mayall, introduction to James Mayall, ed., *The New Interventionism* (Cambridge: Cambridge University Press, 1996), pp. 1–24; Jack Snyder and Robert Jervis, "Civil War and the Security Dilemma," in Barbara F. Walter and Jack Snyder, eds., *Civil Wars, Insecurity, and Intervention* (New York: Colombia University Press, 1999), p. 15.

27. Richard Falk, *Predatory Globalization: A Critique* (London: Polity Press, 1999), pp. 75–76.

28. Michael Pugh, "Maintaining Peace and Security," in David Held and Tony McGrew, eds., *Governing Globalisation* (Cambridge: Polity Press, 2002), pp. 209–233.

29. Michael Doyle, "Discovering the Limits and Potential of Peacekeeping," in Olara Otunnu and Michael Doyle, eds., *Peacemaking and Peacekeeping for the New Century* (Boston: Rowman and Littlefield, 1996), p. 16.

30. Michael Schulz, Fredrik Soderbaum, and Joakim Ojendal, "Key Issues in the New Regionalism: Comparisons from Asia, Africa, and the Middle East," in Bjørn Hettne, Andreas Inotai, and Osvaldo Sunkel, eds., *Comparing Regionalisms: Implications for Global Development* (London: Palgrave, 2001), p. 249.

31. Michael C. Williams, *Civil-Military Relations and Peacekeeping,* Adelphi Paper no. 321 (London: International Institute for Strategic Studies, 1998), pp. 15–17.

32. On the NATO case, see Espen Barth Eide, "Regionalising Intervention? The Case of Europe in the Balkans," in Anthony McDermott, ed., *Sovereign Intervention* (Oslo: PRIO, 1999), p. 81.

33. Clement Adibe, "The Liberian Conflict and the ECOWAS-UN Partnership," in Weiss, *Beyond UN Subcontracting,* p. 84.

34. Michael Ignatieff, *Virtual War: Kosovo and Beyond* (London: Vintage, 2001), p. 75.

35. Dennis C. Jett, *Why Peacekeeping Fails* (London: Palgrave, 1999), p. 57. For a discussion of hard and soft realism as applied to peacekeeping, see Jeremy Ginifer, "How Civil Wars End," in McDermott, *Sovereign Intervention,* pp. 124–126.

36. Evans, *Cooperating for Peace;* Thomas G. Weiss, *The UN and Changing World Politics* (Boulder: Westview, 1994); Weiss, *Beyond UN Subcontracting;* McCoubrey and Morris, *Regional Peacekeeping.*

37. For the Russian case, see S. Neil MacFarlane, "On the Front Lines in the Near Abroad," in Weiss, *Beyond UN Subcontracting,* p. 117.

38. See Moreen Dee, "Coalitions of the Willing and Humanitarian Intervention: Australia's Involvement with INTERFET," *International Peacekeeping* 8, no. 3 (Autumn 2001): 1.

39. Boutros Boutros-Ghali, "Peacemaking and Peacekeeping for the New Century," in Otunnu and Doyle, *Peacemaking and Peacekeeping,* p. 22.

40. Boutros-Ghali, *An Agenda for Peace,* para 17.

41. Falk, *Predatory Globalization,* p. 77.

42. See, for example, Matthew Evangelista, "Historical Legacies and the Politics of Intervention in the Former Soviet Union," in Michael Brown, ed., *The International Dimensions of Internal Conflict* (Cambridge: MIT Press, 1996), pp. 125–127.

43. See Diehl, *International Peacekeeping,* p. 126; Evans, *Cooperating for Peace,* p. 78; Goulding, *Peacemonger,* pp. 217–218.

44. Donald Rothchild and David A. Lake, "Containing Fear: The Management of Transitional Ethnic Conflict," in Lake and Rothchild, *The International Spread of Ethnic Conflict,* p. 221.

45. Jarat Chopra, "The UN's Kingdom of East Timor," *Survival* 42, no. 3 (Autumn 2000): 35–36.

46. Patrick McCarthy, "Reliable Rapid Action for the UN," *International Peacekeeping* 7, no. 2 (Summer 2000): 139–154.

47. Otunnu and Doyle, *Peacemaking and Peacekeeping,* p. 268; Jett, *Why Peacekeeping Fails,* p. 13. See also *"Responsibility to Protect" Report of the International Commission on Intervention and State Sovereignty,* December 2001, http://iciss-ciise.gc.ca, p. 53.

48. See Fen Osler Hampson, "Preventative Diplomacy at the UN and Beyond," in Hampson and Malone, *From Reaction to Conflict Prevention,* pp. 150–151.

49. David O'Brien, "The Search for Subsidiarity: The UN, African Regional Organizations, and Humanitarian Action," *International Peacekeeping* 7, no. 3 (Autumn 2000): 60.

50. Charles Kupchan, "After Pax Americana," *International Security* 23, no. 2 (Fall 1998): 45. But see also the earlier work by Joseph Nye, *Peace in Parts: Integration and Conflict in Regional Organization* (Boston: Little, Brown, 1971).

51. Geir Lundestad, "The Nobel Peace Prize in Its Next Century: Old and New Dimensions," in Geir Lundestad and Olav Njolstad, eds., *War and Peace in the Twentieth Century and Beyond* (Singapore: World Scientific, 2002), p. 226.

52. See Celeste Wallander, "Institutional Assets and Adaptability: NATO After the Cold War," *International Organization* 54, no. 4 (Autumn 2000): 725.

53. Nicholas Wheeler and Tim Dunne, "East Timor and the New Humanitarian Intervention," *International Affairs* 77, no. 4 (2001): 805.

54. Geoffrey Best, *Law and War Since 1945* (Oxford: Clarendon Press, 1997), p. 7.

55. *"Responsibility to Protect,"* p. 3.

56. William Shawcross, *Deliver Us from Evil* (London: Bloomsbury, 2000), p. 16.

2

The World Order Politics of Regionalization

Michael Pugh

In the last decade there has been a debate about the pros and cons of regionalization in the maintenance of peace and security. The purpose of this chapter is to evaluate the potential and limits of regionalization from a macro view of the politics of world order. It presents an alternative construction for considering UN-regional partnerships by critically examining the framework of world order politics, within which the process of regionalization occurs. By considering assumptions that lie behind world order politics, it offers a different but complementary level of analysis to other chapters in this book.

Problem Solving Within the World Order Framework

In broad terms it is possible to speak of a received view concerning the relationship between the UN and regional actors. The dominant outlook in the literature and utterances of academics and practitioners reflects a resurgence of regionalism as a complementary mechanism to the UN in the governance of peace and security.[1] The term "regionalization" is often applied, and is used here to mean a configuration of authority and power devolved in accordance with Chapter VIII of the UN Charter to international organizations that occupy a security space between national and global levels. Under Chapter VIII regional organizations are required to resolve disputes peacefully. Regionalization is marked by intensified diplomatic interaction between the UN and regional bodies, and by multidimensional task-sharing missions in the field. For example, summits on cooperation in maintaining peace and security have been held biennially since 1994 between a variety of bodies and the UN (represented by the presidents of the General Assembly and Security

Council and directors and senior officials of UN departments, agencies, and offices).[2]

The concept of regionalization is hardly new. Regional organizations and coalitions have long been engaged in dispute resolution, peace support operations, and related activities. A British Commonwealth operation demilitarized the factions in Rhodesia/Zimbabwe in 1979. A U.S.-sponsored force began operating in the Sinai after the Camp David Agreement. The Organization of American States (OAS) was already fostering U.S.-approved democratic norms in the 1980s, before acting as partner to the UN in Haiti in 1991. An ad hoc "Contadora group" of Central American states acting outside the OAS eventually helped to bring disputes in Nicaragua, El Salvador, and Guatemala to a close. Inter-African forces attempted to deal with problems in Zaire, Chad, and Mozambique in the 1970s and 1980s, though on an ad hoc rather than institutional basis.

However, regionalization has been promoted with energy by revivalists as a logical response to the structural "realities" of world politics—a paradigm shift that in their view involves "a wide variety of modes, better suited to a diverse and volatile international relations context."[3] Coping with the "realities" and focusing on "what we've got" is justified partly as an adjustment to changes in the balance of institutional competencies for dealing with instability, and partly as a response to "new" wars that seem to demand local solutions to local problems.

This chapter raises the question: does regionalization signify anything more than an adjustment that maintains hierarchical order of global authority and political economy? Indeed, other developments in the global political economy seem to be far more fundamental in their disturbance of the Westphalian interstate order than regionalization. For example, the infusion of nonterritorial webs of state/nonstate interests and shadow economies has led some commentators to conclude that these are the agents in geopolitics rather than geopoliticians.[4] However, like the new balance between regional and global security, the deterritorialized networks may represent new mechanisms for old and new elites within an established pattern of interregional economic exchange, which from a critical theory perspective is marked by growing inequalities, social dysfunction, and conflict.[5] The networks may have altered the territorial stage of international authority and introduced a new cast of actors. But the overarching imbalances between rich and poor in the formal territorial system are not reversed by the new networks. On the contrary, exploitative relations in the shadow economies[6] and the uneven distribution of intellectual and technological property ownership, which sustains networked business,[7] serve to fortify those inequalities.

The argument here draws in particular on the work of Robert Cox and Mark Duffield, and attempts to apply their world order analyses to the issue of regionalization. From Cox's critical theory perspective, the debate should be about whether the new balancing in global security is an approach that takes the world order, and its institutions, as the given framework within which the system can be stabilized.[8] The central argument in this chapter is that the received view is not neutral but serves the purpose of an existing order within which adjustments can occur. The concentration of regionalists on "the doable" and on "working with what we've got" may lead to practical value and benign results—and yield important lessons as exemplified in other parts of this book. This chapter contends, however, that the prevailing wisdom and much of the dissent on the issue do not interrogate the order itself, and, by accepting the order as "reality," they reinforce its underlying values and structures.

Nevertheless, regionalization does contribute to a particular revision of world order, which Duffield designates as "the liberal peace." It recognizes that poverty and underdevelopment is a security issue, and it entails a kind of *mission civiliatrice* to achieve radical social transformation in conflict-prone parts of the world. The mission is based on libertarian concepts of democracy, conflict resolution, and market sovereignty. Whether the vision of a "liberal peace" tests the framework of world order itself or seeks to protect it from unruliness raises questions about the limits of regionalization.[9]

The chapter begins by characterizing the shift in the UN-regional balance as a new orthodoxy, but set within historical and structural limits. Next it considers the objections made by dissenters and offers a critique of the notion that regionalization represents a paradigmatic shift rather than an adjustment within the existing order. Dynamics of the global political economy are then explored to demonstrate that regionalization carries the risk of ghettoizing "undisciplined" parts of the world. The chapter concludes with an argument that the world order problem of excluded peripheries is not adequately addressed by this redistribution of authority.

A New Balancing in Global Governance

Perhaps not as "spellbinding a 'big picture' of world politics" as the Cold War,[10] regionalization of peace and security is certainly offered as one of its successors—a new, intelligible vision of global governance and a radically different world order from Cold War bipolarity.[11] However, in support of the contention that this is more of an adjustment within, rather than a challenge to, the world order, we should note that regionalization was present at the UN's birth. The San Francisco conference on a UN Charter in April 1945 witnessed an "explosive" clash between the seemingly incompatible universal and regional tendencies.[12] Winston Churchill, in particular, favored regionalism to safeguard Euro-Atlantic interests. For him the alternatives were not so much a choice between regionalism or universalism, but between regional balances of power or global control by the big powers.[13] Although the eventual compromise in Chapter VIII encouraged regional initiatives for peaceful resolution of disputes but maintained Security Council primacy in enforcement, the formula left many issues undefined. These included the definition of a regional organization and the role of regional authorities in field operations that moved from Chapter VI peaceful settlement of disputes into Chapter VII enforcement. All the same, the framework established at San Francisco has endured ambiguously and permissively. Chapter VIII did not need to be redrawn to facilitate the new balancing after the Cold War. It simply came into its own, with both regionalism *and* global control by U.S.-dominated arrangements. The "new balancing" in relations between the UN and regional organizations can thus boast historical grounding in liberal internationalism bounded by power politics.

The same framework operated in the radically changed circumstances of the early 1990s. Representing a legacy of elitism in what seemed like a flashback to World War II, the heads of state of the Security Council's five permanent members (P-5) held a summit in January 1992, fresh from a victory against Iraq, to discuss the "new" world order. With the UN seemingly poised to develop its scope, and perhaps autonomy, they instigated a UN review of crisis management and peace operations. Boutros Boutros-Ghali's report, *An Agenda for Peace,* balanced a widening of peace operations (well beyond blue beret peacekeeping) with a spread of mechanisms to achieve them. The report stated that

> regional arrangements and agencies in many cases possess a potential that should be utilized in serving the functions [of] preventive diplomacy, peacekeeping, peacemaking and post-conflict peace-building. Under the Charter, the Security Council has and will continue to have primary responsibility for maintaining international peace and security, but regional action as a matter of decentralization, delegation and cooperation with United Nations efforts could not only lighten the burden of the Council but also contribute to a deeper sense of participation, consensus and democratization in international affairs.[14]

Regionalization thus gained in stature as the P-5 struggled to resolve the dilemmas of defining state interests in a world where the global institution was threatening to assume an ever larger operational role. The UN faced a wide range of crisis management commitments in the western Sahara, Namibia, Mozambique, Cambodia, Angola, Nicaragua, El Salvador, Haiti, Somalia, and the former Yugoslavia. Security Council members had an opportunity after the January 1992 summit to secure and expand the organization to cope with these new demands. But their delinquency in failing to recommend a wholesale review of the rationale and management of peace support operations, or to provide the financial and other means necessary to meet the UN's

role, crippled any potential UN autonomy. Tensions over the Somalia operations then led the United States to become strongly opposed to placing its
forces under a UN commander. The Clinton administration responded to ide-
ological and tactical hostilities toward the UN among predominantly right-
wing members of Congress by issuing a presidential directive, PDD25 of February 1996, that laid down stringent conditions for participation in UN
operations.[15]

Some advances were made in the UN's competence and efficiency, and
various initiatives were undertaken to improve the availability and readiness
of forces at the UN's disposal, notably a database of potentially available
units.[16] The most advanced development was the creation in 1999 of the
Standby High Readiness Brigade (SHIRBRIG) by a group of like-minded
states led by Denmark. Its earmarked units are available at short notice to the
UN, and a headquarters was deployed to the Ethiopia-Eritrea border as a pre-
cursor of the UN Mission in Ethiopia and Eritrea. Nevertheless, SHIRBRIG
is only available for Chapter VI operations.

Paradoxically, regionalization, which under Chapter VIII was originally
envisaged as a mechanism for employing Chapter VI measures, came to be
relied upon for Chapter VII enforcement operations. Where considerable
coercive power has been considered necessary, the chief management device,
beginning in Somalia and Yugoslavia, has been to subcontract to regional bodies and coalitions of the "willing and able." In the context of the crisis in
Bosnia-Herzegovina, Shashi Tharoor, then Kofi Annan's special adviser in the
UN's Department of Peacekeeping Operations (DPKO), referred to

> the deployment of United Nations peacekeepers tasked to mitigate the nature
> and course of an ongoing conflict by limiting the parties' recourse to certain
> military means (. . . interdiction on the use of aircraft for combat purposes)
> or to attacks upon certain cities (protection of "safe areas"), in both cases
> backed by the threat of military force provided by a regional organisation
> [the North Atlantic Treaty Organization (NATO)].[17]

Limitations on the UN's autonomous capacity were also evident in reforms in
the humanitarian field. The Department of Humanitarian Affairs (DHA) was
replaced in 1998 by the Office for the Coordination of Humanitarian Affairs
(OCHA) in a major UN reform package designed to save money and cut
posts. Several states, including the UK and the United States, had frowned
upon the way that the DHA had become a new layer of bureaucracy in the UN
system. OCHA has powerful standing in New York through its responsibility
for chairing the UN's cabinet-style Executive Committee for Humanitarian
Affairs, but it does not have the field presence of relief agencies such as the
Office of the UN High Commissioner for Refugees (UNHCR) or the World
Food Programme.

The Consensus

The consensus and orthodox view of regionalization has come to depend on a rationale that can be distilled into three imperatives. The first emphasizes the overload and/or enfeeblement of the UN's competence to fulfill its duties to universalism in multidimensional operations. This "reality" was adopted in the Brahimi Report as a lesson of post–Cold War peace operations. Although only one paragraph was devoted to the issue, it recommended strengthening cooperation between the UN and regional organizations.[18] But overstretch is a reciprocal function of both resources and commitments. Given that responding to calls for assistance is its job, it can be argued that the recalcitrance of states to provide the wherewithal for the UN to respond effectively, even without a deadlock in the Security Council, justifies the adage that the UN's defects are largely attributable to the way it is managed by the most powerful members.[19] Security Council members have had a tendency to pass resolutions but then fail to provide the means to fulfill them. Most notoriously, the UN's credibility was severely compromised when states provided only 7,000 of the 34,000 troops requested by Boutros-Ghali to protect the "safe areas" in Bosnia.

The second and complementary rationale concerns the evolution of blocs in various degrees of cooperation and integration as a consequence of the demise of bipolarity. For the most part this is portrayed as striking a new balance of responsibility for mitigating instabilities. Proponents point to the buildup of capacities by regional actors and their apparent wish to exert clout. The European Union (EU) is a significant example, on the road to developing its Common Foreign and Security Policy (CFSP). It has been badly split over the invasion of Iraq in 2003 and U.S. unilateralism, but has reached a point where, for example, it is committed to bringing southeastern Europe into the fold. On a smaller scale, a local hegemon, Australia, took over from New Zealand the task of peacekeeping in Bougainville in 1998 and led the protection force in East Timor in 1999.

Third, the localized nature of intrastate conflicts that have dominated the international security agenda is said to require regional knowledge and cultural sensitivities. The overwhelming number of conflicts are not merely intrastate wars. As in West Africa and the Democratic Republic of the Congo, they often spill over into neighboring states and embroil regional actors in what have been termed "regional conflict complexes."[20] From a functional perspective it is politically, culturally, and geographically astute to invoke regional organizations to maintain the peace. Furthermore, Africanization, for example, is represented as the empowerment of regional states.[21] Although in the case of Latin America, the Organization of American States has been viewed historically as a vehicle for U.S. power projection, regionalization can also be constructed as a form of ownership that safeguards against the intrusion of neoimperialist strategic interests.

In summary, the weight of opinion about the new balancing asserts that the "need and rationale for task-sharing and cooperation between the UN and regional organizations is clear."[22] It is a sensible division of labor.[23] Reform proposals develop logically from this functional rationality, seeking, for example, to ensure coordination between partners and to develop regional capacities based on common normative principles.[24] Its ideal managerial relationship is "partnership" involving respect for the UN Charter but allowing variable geometry in a range of peace operations and conflict resolution activities. In peacebuilding the UN is a designated coordinator, not so much because of its field presence, but because of its political status as being "above the fray" of competition.[25]

Dissent

The dissenting regio-skeptics among commentators have been fewer in number, and perhaps marginalized in influence, but their disagreement indicates that the issue of regionalization is neither politically neutral nor a self-evident proposition. First, the global hegemonic power of the United States under the George W. Bush administration has no particular interest in regional organizations per se. The major lesson of Kosovo for the Bush team was that unwieldy multilateral structures such as NATO could not be trusted and could hinder the achievement of U.S. objectives. Thus, in spite of the degree of unity displayed by NATO in regarding the September 11 attacks as an act of aggression under Article 5 of the Washington Treaty, the alliance was simply ignored in the U.S.-led assault on Afghanistan in 2002. Although in 2003, NATO was subsequently delegated to take over the International Security Assistance Force (ISAF), to provide security in and around Kabul, the United States was quite prepared to wreck NATO by pursuing unilateral policies on Iraq. "Partners" willing to follow, or allowing themselves to be bought off, could be chosen on an ad hoc basis and largely for cosmetic political covering rather than for military assistance (which the United States hardly requires). For the flexible warriors in Washington there was no virtue in having missions determined by collective structures, least of all by the UN with its attention to wider issues such as international law. The future of regional security arrangements are therefore significantly dependent on their utility for U.S. policymakers rather than their contribution to conflict management as partners of the UN. Second, the UN's own moral authority is potentially undermined by regionalization, fostering a reordering of legitimacy that dilutes the idealism of universal entitlements. In Sir Marrack Goulding's

view, it is contrary to the ethical vision of universalism for people in a particular region to receive "only the level of peacekeeping that their regional
organization can provide."[26] The universal reach of the UN is questionable, of
course, but decentralization will further fragment security, possibly abandon-
ing some areas of the world to lawlessness, in parallel with the highly differential impacts of economic integration. In this view, deprived areas that are
economically and strategically peripheral will experience the double deficit of
perpetual economic crisis and a "peacekeeping apartheid."[27]

This is related to a third, pragmatic objection concerning the uneven
spread of regional competence. Only the members of the Euro-Atlantic security complex seem sufficiently well equipped and motivated to participate
effectively in decentralization.[28] The political cohesion, infrastructure, and
civilian and military capacity available through NATO, the European Defense
and Security Initiative, and the Organization for Security and Cooperation in
Europe (OSCE) cannot be replicated elsewhere. The Organization of African
Unity, for example, provided little leadership or management in the early
1990s, and the Economic Community of West African States took eight years
to make an impact on the civil war in Liberia, which broke out in 1991.[29]
African states have debilitating problems of their own, though the western P-
5 states emphasize that competence can be built up and supported from outside, exemplified by the U.S., UK, and French peacekeeping training programs in West Africa.[30]

A fourth antiregional argument rests on concerns about the interests and
partiality of regional hegemons, which may often become part of the problem
rather than the solution. Decentralization presents opportunities for ambitious
regional powers to meddle in crises, as Nigeria is accused of doing in Liberia
and Sierra Leone. This may be disingenuous about the supposed universalism
of the UN's role in maintaining peace, which is always contingent on the P-5
in the Security Council and their highly selective à la carte multilateralism.[31]
Nevertheless, the UN's global representation and universal standard setting
may restrict P-5 unilateralism more effectively than in regional organizations.
Such might be an interpretation of the U.S. administration's decision to at least
obtain UN authority for governing Iraq in May 2003 while having taken illegal, unilateral action against Iraq to overthrow the Ba'ath regime.[32] In general,
regional security organizations are more state-centric than the UN, lacking the
world body's multiagency inputs in decisionmaking, and without the level of
consultation and observer status that the UN grants to nonstate groups such as
nongovernmental organizations and, ironically, to other regional organizations.

Finally, because problems arise in the management of the UN-regional
balance, the value of regionalization is conditional on its ability to provide
satisfactory answers to practical issues (as argued by Ian Martin in Chapter 3).
The proregional consensus accepts that the relationship is likely to have more
satisfactory outcomes if certain conditions are met, including:

- agreement on mechanisms for consultation,
- respect for UN primacy,
- prior agreement between the UN and regional organization on the level of support to be expected from one another,
- clearly defined divisions of labor so as not to duplicate efforts, including explicit understandings of each other's activities, and
- consistency of action among participants.[33]

Laying down principles common to all regional bodies, solidifying the terms of UN and regional authority on the basis of the UN Charter, and investment in the management of partnerships will, it is suggested by proponents of regionalism, mitigate tensions between the UN's moral and legal authority and the powers of regional partners. Nevertheless, such demands are sufficiently steep (consistency of action among participants, for example) to tempt the conclusion that panaceas are unlikely to emerge from either the regional or the universal stance in the existing unruly world order.

This chapter does not aim to resolve the debate but to argue that it indicates the political nature of the new balancing. Goulding, for example, queries the political motivation of regionalization: "The real aims of the Western countries that argue for it are to ease the financial burdens placed on them by the post–Cold War proliferation of peace operations and to avoid risking their soldiers' lives in other peoples' wars."[34] The accusation may be partially contradicted by the UK's willingness to send forces to Sierra Leone and Australia's willingness to send troops to East Timor. But like the readiness of the U.S. administration to take risks in removing Al-Qaida and the Taliban regime from Afghanistan and in sending antiterrorist contingents to the Philippines, direct strategic interests or domestic pressures can also be detected in these cases.[35] Generally speaking, the North has been reluctant to send military forces to Africa in particular, preferring to assist the development of African capabilities, though in the short term this reinforces African dependence on external equipment and expertise.[36] Whether burden shedding or burden sharing is the political tendency, however, regionalist and regio-skeptic arguments coexist in a problem-solving, rather than world-order-resolving framework. This can be demonstrated through analysis of key dynamics in the global political economy, starting with the regional approach to international relations itself.

Dynamics in the Global Political Economy

Regional approaches were rather neglected in the Cold War international security literature, with notable exceptions such as Karl Deutsch's concept of "security communities" and Joseph Nye's "islands of peace," where war is ruled out as a dynamic in interstate relations.[37] But by the 1990s regional analysis had become a deservedly important level of security studies, particularly in the hands of European academics, who developed a theory of "security complexes" to reflect a post–Cold War interest in multipolarity and bloc development. "Security complexes" are defined as constellations where state or other units exhibit an intensity of interchange on security issues, such that their securities cannot be considered separately. They embody durable patterns of amity and enmity.[38] The regional level of analysis challenges the dual fixations with global and national security. It is a site not only where national and global security interplay, but also where interstate institutions will sometimes dominate. In this respect, regionalization contributes to the multilayering of global governance.

However, a more refined way of bounding security issues is to give greater weight to what Duffield calls nonterritorial "complex networks."[39] Regional security complexes relate units in a spatial and predominantly statist sense, occupying an arena where the nation state meets the world order. By contrast, complex networks are nonterritorial linkages between disparate units, including humanitarian agencies and private security firms, brought together by common interests in, for example, promoting and protecting a liberal view of the global economy. They are more akin to epistemic communities than interstate authorities.[40] This approach has the merit of making close connections between the political and economic security visions of global governance and of releasing the issue from a dominant military model of security, which in Asia, for example, appears to have limited relevance to regional cooperation. It suggests that the core centers of capital are not engaged in radical transformation of the world order in the spatial sense of being bent on the control of territory, but through nonobservable, nonterritorial network power over social, economic, and political processes.[41]

In this connection, it is intriguing that the new balancing between central and regional competencies is formulated in the authoritative language of economic rationality. The terms commonly employed include "burden sharing," "subcontracting," "cost-effectiveness," "comparative advantage," "partnerships," and a "division of labor."[42] Each designation may refer to a distinctive managerial relationship: subcontracting reflects the supremacy of a central authority, whereas burden sharing implies a more diffuse control. But the terminology is not merely a convenient borrowing from business, inspired by the notion that the new form of governance is analogous with it. It alludes to a synthesis of security with a particular construction of the global political economy.

Far from signaling the integrative process that economic globalization implies, regionalization has deepened the interconnections *within* core regions of the capitalist economy while excluding other regions.[43] However, one must be careful to define this "exclusion" in terms that allow for interaction with the capitalist core. For example, political entrepreneurs commandeer neoliberal processes, such as privatization of utilities, in order to further narrow patrimonial interests. The illiberal governance of traditional elites in excluded areas thus exhibits a hybrid of tradition and modernity.[44] For Duffield, exclusion is a form of managed subordination and transformation. In the absence of adequate international regulation, the interactions also permit an interleaving of legal enterprises with organized criminal activity to connect core and periphery regions.[45]

Within the core areas there is clearly a widespread recognition that poverty and underdevelopment is destabilizing. It is a risk not only to global integration but also to integration of the core areas, through, for example, the eruption of conflict and attendant refugee movements from poor toward relatively wealthy countries. Therefore, "the promotion of development has become synonymous with the pursuit of security," and security has become a prerequisite for development.[46] As Kees van der Pijl shows, a transnational financial and entrepreneurial class of (mainly) "first world" economic planners has continually adjusted the content of the mission to bring corporate neoliberalism to the world.[47] It has done so through a plethora of interconnected groups, represented inter alia by the Bilderberg Group, the Trilateral Commission, and the World Economic Forum. The latest adjustments, widely adopted by international financial institutions (IFIs) and the UK's Department for International Development, for example, include the mitigation of market harshness via poverty reduction and social responsibility programs, under such legends as "Making Globalization Work for the Poor."[48]

This is essentially a technical transformation, a change in the systems and processes for exercising influence to maintain an established order. As Cox points out, the influence is politically subjective and contested, and has divisive as well as integrative impacts. The overall objectives and outcomes remain remarkably conservative: consolidation of the core areas, and exclusion, "poor relief," and "riot control" in the periphery.[49] The IFIs have not changed their macroeconomic conditionalities or provided additional and adequate means to sustain basic social services, employment, and local productive capacity.[50] Furthermore, a commercialization of aid policy and humanitarian assistance is also highly conditioned by the ideals of liberal peace to stimulate outcomes congenial to a particular view of political economy. As Duffield observes: "Rather than requiring the reform of the international system, [aid policy] has been redefined in terms of the radical transformation of excluded societies in order to make them fit into this system."[51] This includes the transmission of democratic/market values and ideals by peacekeepers and peacebuilders in war-torn societies.[52]

Accordingly, the "new" global struggle is not primarily, as some argue, about terrorism and counterterrorism,[53] but about the clash between strategic complexes seeking liberal social transformations on the one hand and socially exclusive, nonliberal zones of conflict, comprising nonstate actors operating through shadow economies and shadow authorities on the other.[54]

However, discourses that draw clear conceptual boundaries between excluded regional conflict formations on the one hand and market democracies portrayed as models of decorum on the other do have great significance. Responsibility is shifted to the excluded areas as the sources of unrest, exempting the liberal mission and its management of transformation from censure.[55] Boundary drawing becomes a form of ghettoization in which the inception of conflict and its management is positioned with the societies most immediately affected. Indeed, although there is no single political view from the world of unrest, it is an abiding concern of many regional actors that the countries promoting the liberal peace are reluctant to commit resources to the UN for operations outside Europe.[56]

Where does the new balance between regional organizations and the UN fit into this depiction of the global political economy? At one level, it favors the status quo because the core centers of the liberal peace will simply continue to exert clout regionally and to keep unruly parts of the world at arm's length by subsidizing regional initiatives. Differentiation in regional competence, and in the demands on that competence, is unlikely to be lessened without a momentous shift in the asymmetries of the global political economy. At another level, regionalization will create new stakeholders in controlling war zones, but without necessarily addressing the issues arising from the existence of networked conflict trades and regional conflict formations. In fact, the current weaknesses in efforts to regulate the trade in goods that feed conflict include both the connivance of regional elites in perpetuating the trades and the absence of regional implementation mechanisms for regulating them.[57] Finally, if security is a development issue, as Duffield and others argue, the developmentalism of the liberal peace needs to be considered at global, regional, and national levels as a possible *source* of problems in world ordering.

Conclusion

Like other world order configurations, regionalization is not a redistribution of authority that can be taken as neutral or even taken for granted. It clearly contributes to a multilayering of authority. But whether it changes the hegemonic strategies of rich and powerful states in a fundamental way or moves the boundaries of inclusion and exclusion seems doubtful. Nor does it appear to change the dynamics of exclusion and conflict, unless perhaps to intensify it. For regionalization may serve the purpose of keeping conflicts at a distance from the sanctuaries of decorum. In effect, regionalization gives authorities in the core areas varied opportunities to express the *mission civiliatrice* of "liberal peace" and to experiment in proxy policing and the exercise of authority. Yet the fragility of the world order framework lies in its deepening of exclusion. As the U.S. preference for ad hoc "coalitions" demonstrates, regional structures do not necessarily provide the only alternative to universalism. In response to this, institutions and policymaking elites continually shift and adjust to reduce the vulnerabilities of the liberal peace, but without addressing its complicity in the structural dysfunctions that make peace operations necessary.

A regional-UN partnership reflects new balances affecting political and military institutions. It may counter the excesses of universalism and thicken the fabric of participation. But at a macro level it does not fundamentally alter the pattern of influence exercised by the core areas of wealth and corporate economic power, whether expressed through the Westphalian state system or Duffield's complex networks. The new balancing shifts authority toward a nuanced and regionally sensitive exercise of conflict management. But it cannot be said to shift the boundaries of political community toward greater inclusion of those among the dispossessed and their "possessed" sympathizers who contest the prevailing world order.

Notes

I am grateful to the fellow book contributors who commented on this chapter and also to Neil Cooper and Mark Lacy of the University of Plymouth's International Studies Centre.

1. See, for example, Report of the Secretary-General on the Work of the Organization, UN Doc. A/46/1, 1991; Kofi Annan, address to the Third UN–Regional Organizations Meeting, New York, July 28, 1998.

2. Meetings are also held at the regional level; for example, officers from the Economic Community of West African States (ECOWAS) have participated in UN interagency assessment missions, and UN representatives have attended ECOWAS meetings.

3. Justin Morris and Hilaire McCoubrey, "Regional Peacekeeping in the Post–Cold War Era," *International Peacekeeping* 6, no. 2 (Summer 1999): 149.

4. Gearóid Ó Tuathail (Gerard Toal), "Postmodern Geopolitics? The Modern Geopolitical Imagination and Beyond," in Gearóid Ó Tuathail and Simon Dalby, eds., *Rethinking Geopolitics* (London: Routledge, 1998), p. 33. See also Mark Duffield, *Global Governance and the New Wars: The Merging of Development and Security* (London: Zed Books, 2001), chaps. 3, 6; Dietrich Jung, ed., *Shadow Globalisation: The Political Economy of Intra-State War* (London: Routledge, 2003).

5. The literature testifying to this is vast, but for a useful summary, see Susan Willett, "Insecurity, Conflict, and the New Global Disorder," *Institute of Development Studies Bulletin* 32, no. 2 (April 2001): 35–45.

6. For example, the value added to "conflict diamonds" in their rough state is appropriated outside the mining areas. Ian Smillie, *Dirty Diamonds: Armed Conflict and the Trade in Rough Diamonds* (Oslo: Institute for Applied Science [FAFO]), 2002), p. 8.

7. Christopher May, *A Global Political Economy of Intellectual Property Rights: The* New *Enclosures?* (London: Routledge, 2000).

8. Robert W. Cox, "Social Forces, States, and World Orders: Beyond International Relations Theory," *Millennium* 10, no. 2 (1981): 128–129. In brief, Cox takes a critical approach to theories and mechanisms that seem designed to cope with instabilities and inequalities within world orders that are themselves dysfunctional. His theory has an underlying goal of emancipating societies by exposing the persistence of injustice that arises from treating theories about the prevailing international framework as incontestable.

9. This issue is explored in Michael Pugh and Neil Cooper, with Jonathan Goodhand, *War Economies in a Regional Context: The Challenge of Transformation* (Boulder: Lynne Rienner, 2004).

10. Gearóid Ó Tuathail (Gerard Toal) and Simon Dalby, introduction to Tuathail and Dalby, *Rethinking Geopolitics,* p. 1.

11. Barry Buzan, Øle Wæver, and Jaap de Wilde, *Security: A New Framework for Analysis* (Boulder: Lynne Rienner, 1998).

12. Only the Inter-American System, the Commonwealth, and the Arab League were in existence as quasi-regional bodies. See Inis L. Claude Jr., *Swords into Plowshares: The Problems and Progress of International Organization* (London: University of London Press, 1965); Boutros Boutros-Ghali, in UN press release SG/SM/4929, February 17, 1993.

13. E. J. Hughes, "Winston Churchill and the Formation of the United Nations Organization," *Journal of Contemporary History* 9, no. 4 (1974): 187, 191–194.

14. Boutros Boutros-Ghali, *An Agenda for Peace* (New York: United Nations, 1992), para. 64.

15. Michael G. MacKinnon, *The Evolution of UN Peacekeeping Policy Under Clinton: A Fairweather Friend?* (London: Frank Cass, 2000), pp. 116–118.

16. Donald C. F. Daniel and Bradd C. Hayes, "Securing Observance of UN Mandates Through the Employment of Military Force," in Michael Pugh, ed., *The UN, Peace, and Force* (London: Frank Cass, 1997), pp. 112–113.

17. Shashi Tharoor, "The Role of the United Nations in European Peacekeeping," in Espen Barth Eide, ed., *Peacekeeping in Europe,* Peacekeeping and Multinational Operations Series no. 5 (Oslo: NUPI, 1995), p. 44.

18. United Nations, *Report of the Panel on United Nations Peace Operations,* UN Doc. A/55/305-S/2000/809, August 17, 2000.

19. Anthony Parsons, *From Cold War to Hot Peace: UN Interventions, 1947–1995* (London: Penguin, 1995), p. x.

20. Peter Wallensteen and Margareta Sollenberg, "Armed Conflict and Regional Conflict Complexes, 1989–97," *Journal of Peace Research* 35, no. 5 (1998): 621–634.

21. Jeremy Greenstock, International Peace Academy (IPA), and Center on International Cooperation, *Refashioning the Dialogue: Regional Perspectives on the Brahimi Report in UN Peace Operations,* report on regional meetings, February–March 2001 (New York: IPA, 2001), www.ipacademy.org/publications, p. 2.

22. Muthiah Alagappa, "Regional Arrangements, the UN, and International Security: A Framework for Analysis," in Thomas G. Weiss, ed., *Beyond UN Subcontracting: Task-Sharing with Regional Security Arrangements and Service-Providing NGOs* (London: Macmillan, 1998), p. 4.

23. Peter Viggo Jakobsen, "Overload, Not Marginalization, Threatens UN Peacekeeping," *Security Dialogue* 13, no. 2 (2000): 167–177.

24. Mary M. MacKenzie, "The UN and Regional Organizations," in Edward Newman and Oliver P. Richmond, eds., *The United Nations and Human Security* (Basingstoke: Palgrave, 2001), p. 165.

25. United Nations, *Report on Third Meeting Between the United Nations and Regional Organizations* (New York: United Nations, July 28–29, 1998).

26. Marrack Goulding, *Peacemonger* (London: John Murray, 2002), p. 218.

27. Anonymous participant in the workshop "The Brahimi Report: Overcoming the North-South Divide," report by Winrich Kühne, Stiftung Wissenschaft und Politik, Sixth International Workshop, Berlin, June 29–30, 2001, p. 15.

28. Goulding, *Peacemonger;* Benjamin Rivlin, "Regional Arrangements and the UN System for Collective Security and Conflict Resolution: A New Road Ahead?" *International Relations* 11, no. 2 (1992): 95–110; Walter Dorn, "Regional Peacekeeping Is Not the Way," *Peacekeeping and International Relations* 27, nos. 3–4 (July–October 1998): 2–4.

29. Roy May and Gerry Cleaver, "African Peacekeeping: Still Dependent?" *International Peacekeeping* 4, no. 2 (1997): 1–21.

30. See Eric G. Berman and Katie E. Sams, "The Peacekeeping Capacities of African Regional Organisations," *Conflict, Security, and Development* 2, no. 1 (2002): 40.

31. See Phyllis Bennis, *Calling the Shots: How Washington Dominates Today's UN* (New York: Olive Branch Press, 1996).

32. "UN Mandate Oils Wheels for Reconstruction of Iraq," *The Guardian* (London), May 23, 2003, p. 1.

33. UN Secretary-General's principles as suggested at a meeting in February 1996, cited in United Nations, *Report on Third Meeting Between the United Nations and Regional Organizations.* For a more extended discussion, see Tonny Brems Knudsen, "Humanitarian Intervention and International Society: Contemporary Manifestations of an Explosive Doctrine," Ph.D. diss., University of Aarhus, June 1999.

34. Goulding, *Peacemonger,* p. 217.

35. The UK faced domestic pressure as a consequence of the Sandline affair, and Australia has an interest in East Timor's stability to advance oil extraction.

36. Eric G. Berman and Katie E. Sams, *Peacekeeping in Africa: Capabilities and Culpabilities* (Geneva: UNIDIR, 2000), pp. 45–61; Eric G. Berman, "The Security Council's Increasing Reliance on Burden-Sharing: Collaboration or Abrogation?" *International Peacekeeping* 5, no. 1 (1998): 13–14; May and Cleaver, *African Peacekeeping.*

37. Karl W. Deutsch, ed., *Political Community and the North Atlantic Area* (Princeton: Princeton University Press, 1957); Joseph Nye, *Peace in Parts: Integration and Conflict in Regional Organization* (Boston: Little, Brown, 1971), chap. 5.

38. Barry Buzan, *People, States, and Fear,* 2nd ed. (Hemel Hempstead: Harvester Wheatsheaf, 1991), p. 190. But note that where war has a regional dimension, the term "regional conflict complex" or "formation" is more accurate. See Wallensteen and Sollenberg, "Armed Conflict"; New York University Center on International Cooperation, *Regional Conflict Formations: Processes of Development and Challenges for Conflict Management,* [n.d.] www.cic.nyu.edu/conflict/conflict_project6.html.

39. Duffield, *Global Governance,* p. 51.

40. As an attribute of functionalism, "epistemic communities" were identified in the work of Ernst Haas as experts engaged transnationally in problem solving. Ernst Haas, *Beyond the Nation-State: Functionalism and International Relations* (Stanford: Stanford University Press, 1964).

41. Duffield, *Global Governance,* p. 34.

42. The terminology is used by practitioners and academics alike; for example, Kofi Annan, address to the Third UN–Regional Organizations Meeting; Edwin M. Smith and Thomas G. Weiss, "UN Task-Sharing: Toward or Away from Global Governance?" in Weiss, *Beyond UN Subcontracting,* p. 227.

43. Duffield, *Global Governance,* p. 3.

44. Dietrich Jung, "Political Sociology of World Society," *European Journal of International Relations* 7, no. 4 (2001): 457; Michael Pugh, "Postwar Political Economy in Bosnia and Herzegovina: The Spoils of Peace," *Global Governance* 8, no. 4 (2002): 86–108.

45. Kees van der Pijl, *Transnational Classes and International Relations* (London: Routledge, 1998), p. 135; Neil Cooper, "State Collapse as Business: The Role of Conflict Trade and the Emerging Control Agenda," *Development and Change* 33, no. 5 (November 2002): 935–955 (special issue on "State Failure, Collapse, and Reconstruction"); Michael Pugh, "Conflict and Transnational Crime," paper for the conference "The New Global Security Agenda in Asia and Europe: Transnational Crimes and Prospects for Asia-Europe Cooperation," Danish Institute of International Affairs (DUPI) and the Asia-Europe Foundation (ASEF), Copenhagen, May 27–28, 2002.

46. Duffield, *Global Governance,* p. 37.

47. van der Pijl, *Transnational Classes,* pp. 129–134.

48. DFID, *Eliminating World Poverty: Making Globalisation Work for the Poor,* White Paper on International Development, Department for International Development, Cm 5006, London, December 1999.

49. Robert Cox, "Critical Political Economy," in Bjørn Hettne, ed., *International Political Economy: Understanding Global Disorder* (London: Zed Books, 1995), p. 41. See also Béatrice Hibou, *The Political Economy of the World Bank's Discourse: From Economic Catechism to Missionary Deeds (and Misdeeds),* Les Études du CERI no. 39 (Paris: Centre d'Études et de Récherches Internationales, March 1998).

50. The joint document, "A Better World for All," issued by the UN, the Organization for Economic Cooperation and Development, the International Monetary Fund, and the World Bank in June 2002, was characterized as constituting an "unholy alliance" that marginalized voices from the South, represented the poor as victims in need of Northern medicine, failed to recognize the role of the IFIs in generating poverty, and disregarded the need for welfare, wealth distribution, and workers' rights. See NGO Caucuses, *NGOs Call on the UN to Withdraw Endorsement of "A Better World for All,"* June 28, 2000, www.earthsummit2002.org/wssd/wssd5ngos.htm.

51. Duffield, *Global Governance,* p. 30.

52. Roland Paris, "Echoes of the *Mission Civiliatrice:* Peacekeeping in the Post–Cold War Era," in Newman and Richmond, eds., *The United Nations and Human Security;* Roland Paris, "Wilson's Ghost: The Faulty Assumptions of Post-Conflict Peacebuilding," in Chester A. Crocker, Fen Osler Hampson, and Pamela Aall, eds., *Turbulent Peace: The Challenges of Managing International Conflict* (Washington, DC: U.S. Institute of Peace Press, 2001), pp. 100–118.

53. John MacKinlay, "Opposing Insurgents in Peace Operations," in Thierry Tardy, ed., *Peace Operations in World Politics After 11 September 2001* (London: Frank Cass, 2003).

54. Duffield, *Global Governance,* p. 15.

55. Ibid., p. 38.

56. Greenstock, IPA, and Center on International Cooperation, *Refashioning the Dialogue,* p. 12; Kühne, Stiftung Wissenschaft und Politik, Sixth International Workshop, pp. 15–16.

57. Neil Cooper, "Peaceful Warriors and Warring Peacemakers," in Jürgen Brauer, Paul Dunne, David Gold, and John Tepper Martin, eds., *ECAAR [Economists Allied for Arms Reduction] Review* (2002): 45–56.

3

Is the Regionalization of Peace Operations Desirable?

Ian Martin

The consequences of the regionalization of peace operations present themselves in very different ways in different contexts. My encounters with differing conflict situations as a practitioner, first in the field of human rights and then in general peace operations in four regions—Haiti in the Americas, Bosnia and Herzegovina in Europe, Rwanda and Ethiopia-Eritrea in Africa, and East Timor in Asia—have been relevant to very different aspects of regionalization. There seems to be a general trend toward considering regionalization as an inevitable factor in the changing balance of the international system. Even if it is inevitable, however, regionalization will only produce desirable outcomes if satisfactory answers are found to the kinds of practical issues that were evident in these divergent cases.

Haiti

In Haiti, the efforts to restore constitutional government after the 1991 coup were left to the regional organization the Organization of American States (OAS) until 1993, when the leading role passed to the UN. This in itself carried a lesson. The diplomatic efforts of the OAS had been backed only by weak regional sanctions and had been undermined by ambivalence on the part of the U.S. administration. The OAS had operationalized its role by sending a small international civilian mission to Haiti, with a rather vague humanitarian and human rights mandate. But the de facto authorities had been able to deny the mission any real freedom of action. President Jean-Bertrand Aristide wanted a UN involvement that could lead to more effective sanctions. The UN was willing to undertake this once the new U.S. administration, under

47

Bill Clinton, appeared serious in its commitment (if only because the administration needed a way out of the president's embarrassing volte-face on the refoulement of Haitian refugees). The OAS was not entirely happy to see the leading role pass to the UN, but it was mollified by a notable innovation: the lead negotiator, Dante Caputo of Argentina, became simultaneously Special Representative of the UN Secretary-General and Special Representative of the Secretary-General of the OAS.

The first achievement of the new negotiator, with U.S. support, was to persuade the de facto regime to acquiesce in the sending of a much larger civilian mission, with a clear and strong human rights mandate. Initially, thought was given to two parallel missions, one UN and one OAS. Fortunately this was rejected in favor of a fully joint mission: the OAS/UN International Civilian Mission in Haiti (MICIVIH). Its human rights observers— 200 at their peak—were recruited and contracted half by the OAS and half by the UN. Ably headed from beginning to end by the executive director contracted by the OAS, with a succession of deputies contracted by the UN, it remained a fully joint mission through the many different stages of peacemaking, peacekeeping, and peacebuilding. It deployed its personnel with no distinction as to the contracting organization. If working with the administrative procedures of two organizations had its problems, it also sometimes allowed the inflexibility of one to be subverted through the other.

Relations over Haiti between the UN and the OAS at the headquarters level were never entirely cordial, but at the operational level cooperation was exemplary. Whatever the overall judgment to be passed on the international involvement in Haiti, MICIVIH was a model of joint action that might usefully be followed elsewhere, at least in the human rights field.

Bosnia and Herzegovina

In Bosnia and Herzegovina, the sequence of responsibility occurred in the opposite direction. Those designing the architecture of international organizations for the implementation of the 1995 Dayton Agreement unfairly viewed the UN as discredited. They turned to the regional organizations: the North Atlantic Treaty Organization (NATO) for security; the Organization for Security and Cooperation in Europe (OSCE) for elections, democratization, and human rights; and the Council of Europe for building legal institutions. However, the UN was the only authority that could be expected to establish an international police task force, and the UN High Commissioner for Refugees (UNHCR) remained a key actor in carrying out its refugee mandate. It is a cardinal rule of effective peace operations that the military must be under civilian political authority in theater. But regionalization in Europe has ensured that this rule can never be followed there, since NATO maintains a contrary policy. That was only the beginning of a nightmare in the Bosnian peace-building process. The civilian mandates cried out for strong, integrated management: what they got was weak coordination through the Office of the High Representative (OHR). Even this was often resisted. Although he ended up with extraordinary powers to dismiss local political actors, the High Representative had no executive authority over the international organizations. The allocation of mandates split functions apart that needed close coordination: policing, the rule of law, and human rights. At the same time, it put together things best kept apart: for example, the OSCE's elections mandate undermined its human rights role. The optimal mission structure is surely the classic UN model of a Special Representative of the Secretary-General (SRSG) with full authority over a Force Commander and all civilian components. Bosnia can be studied as the most dysfunctional international architecture so far devised for any one country. This is not an inevitable consequence of regionalization, even in a region with too many regional organizations, but it offers a dire warning. The Bosnian situation was obviously in the minds of those planning the structure of the transitional administration in Kosovo, where the peacebuilding pillars constituted by different international organizations have come, at least in theory, under the full executive authority of a single head, the SRSG.

In both Haiti and Bosnia and Herzegovina, there were important relationships between the UN and the regional organizations in the phases of negotiation as well as implementation. Rwanda and Ethiopia-Eritrea both raised issues arising from regionalized negotiations (with only a minor UN role) transferring to UN implementation (with only a minor regional role).

The Arusha negotiation between the Rwandan parties was a regional process, mediated by Tanzania for the Organization of African Unity (OAU), with French and U.S. support. The OAU role was operationalized in the form of the Neutral Military Observer Group in Rwanda (NMOG), created to monitor ceasefire agreements. When the final Arusha Accords were agreed in August 1993, the Rwandese Patriotic Front would have preferred the substantial "neutral international force" the agreement envisaged to be deployed under OAU rather than UN authority. But the OAU stated that this was beyond its capability. Critically, but unrealistically, this force was expected to be deployed within thirty-seven days to support the establishment of the new transitional government. Its mandate in the accords was extensive: to guarantee overall security, help ensure the safety of the civilian population, and assist in the search for weapons caches and neutralization of armed bands throughout the country. But when these agreements met the reality of UN decision-making, the mandate was restricted, the troop strength minimized, and the deployment delayed.

Perhaps the subsequent tragic history of Rwanda would have been little different if the organization tasked with operational responsibility for implementing the accords had been more centrally involved in the negotiations, and thereby confronted with political realities. But the most incisive analysis of the Arusha process concludes that a central lesson is clear:

> If the mediation process serves to isolate hard-liners and extremists, then the implementation process must have sufficient military clout to contain them and neutralize their opposition. Alternatively, if there are limited military resources to bring to bear, the mediation process should work on the assumption of bringing the hard-liners into the process. . . . The inconsistency of prenegotiation, mediation, and implementation strategies for dealing with the spoilers doomed the overall peace process in Rwanda.[1]

Thus although the Arusha process seemed a model of regional negotiation accomplishment, neither of these alternatives was achieved—and genocide followed. It has been commonly argued that the UN should not implement agreements it has not itself negotiated. That formulation is perhaps unrealistic, but at least the organization, and others that are expected to play a major role in implementation, should be centrally involved in the negotiations.

Ethiopia and Eritrea

This precept was no more adhered to in the negotiations toward a cessation of hostilities and durable peace between Ethiopia and Eritrea to terminate the interstate war that had broken out in 1998. After the rejection by Eritrea of an initial U.S.-Rwanda peace proposal, these negotiations were formally within an OAU framework. In practice, however, they were led jointly by Algeria on behalf of the OAU, with a U.S. team headed by President Clinton's special envoy, Tony Lake. Ethiopia initially sought to confine the external role to military observers rather than peacekeepers, and to the OAU rather than the UN. By contrast, Eritrea's traditionally frosty relations with the OAU led it to prefer a UN role. Practicalities prevailed: again it was agreed that the UN should take on a role defined by a negotiating process in which it had had only a most limited watching brief. The Agreement on Cessation of Hostilities, signed in Algiers in June 2000, provided in curious language that "a peacekeeping mission shall be deployed by the United Nations under the auspices of the OAU." This mission was deployed as the UN Mission in Ethiopia and Eritrea (UNMEE). The OAU has indeed remained involved in the implementation of the agreement, through a small military observer mission of its own whose head participates in the Military Coordination Commission, chaired by UNMEE's Force Commander, and through strong diplomatic support to the efforts of the SRSG. But no one would pretend that its role on the ground is other than secondary to that of the UN's 4,000-strong peacekeeping mission.

The major difficulties UNMEE faced in implementing the Agreement on Cessation of Hostilities related to issues that were not fully defined in the agreement. The UN had participated in the elaboration of detailed "technical arrangements" for the implementation of a peace agreement. But these were never accepted by Ethiopia, which was in the victor's "driving seat" when the third round of hostilities was halted. The technical arrangements were thus set aside by the negotiators, greatly complicating the UN's task of implementation. In particular, the agreement required Ethiopia to pull back its forces from positions that were not under Ethiopian administration on May 6, 1998. Eritrean forces were then to remain at a distance of twenty-five kilometers from Ethiopian positions, creating a temporary security zone monitored by UNMEE. But the issue of where the line of control existed at the outbreak of hostilities was well known to be a matter of bitter dispute. From the point of view of those who were to implement the agreement, it would have been desirable to have had a line already mapped in the course of the negotiations. However, this could have delayed the cessation of bloody conflict, and so the negotiators left the implementers to wrestle with the issue. Perhaps they were right, but predictably it proved to be the cause of the main difficulties UNMEE experienced in its relations with the parties.

East Timor

Regionalization was a major aspect of intervention in the case of East Timor, yet regional organizations as such played almost no role. Not only had the Association of Southeast Asian Nations (ASEAN) taken no active interest in the East Timor issue, but as one analyst has put it, "the East Timor case illustrates the major deficiency of regional organizations . . . as they generally include interested parties, they cannot act impartially."[2] With the exception of initial abstention by Singapore, ASEAN member countries always voted with Indonesia in UN votes on East Timor. The external pressures on Indonesia to concede autonomy or self-determination to East Timor came from elsewhere, and in the end it was the internal dynamic of post-Suharto Indonesia stimulated by the UN Secretary-General's good offices, Portugal's persistent pressure, and a change of policy in Australia that paved the way to the 1999 referendum.

It was not hard for governments of the region to agree to participate in the UN Mission in East Timor (UNAMET), tasked with implementing the ballot, by sending civilian police and military liaison officers, since it was Indonesia that had decided to offer the choice of autonomy or independence. For the most part regional governments continued to praise Indonesia's cooperation, even as the evidence of Indonesia's failure to fulfill its commitment to security and neutrality during the "popular consultation" mounted and was confirmed by their own personnel on the ground. When the announcement of the vote for independence was followed by killing, destruction, and forcible deportation, the regional governments pressed Indonesia to invite international assistance to restore order, while maintaining that intervention must only occur with Indonesia's consent.

The UN had been planning toward an eventual blue helmet force to maintain security during a smooth transition to independence, which it had unrealistically hoped for. However, it was clear that the task of rapid peace enforcement could only be carried out by a "coalition of the willing." Two forms of regionalization now came into play. The leading members of the Security Council had no intention of committing substantial troops themselves: there had to be a country in the region, with a robust military capability, ready to take the lead. Australia was willing to do so, as long as Indonesia consented, and as long as it was supported by some degree of commitment from Western countries that had key relationships with Indonesia. But if Australia was regional enough for this purpose, Indonesia sought a different kind of regionalization. It wished to minimize the Australian role, and maximize that of Asia, and particularly ASEAN countries, so as to limit the anticipated nationalist backlash.

Indonesia wanted the international force to be headed by an ASEAN commander, whereas Australia was clear that an intervention dependent on its military capability must be under its command. In other respects, however, the Indonesian and Australian preference for maximizing Asian participation was a coincident policy that contributed to the commitments from Thailand (which provided the deputy commander), the Philippines, and Singapore. The funding of Asian contingents came from a trust fund, to which Japan made the most substantial contribution.

Asian regional organizations played no formal role in this mobilization, which was largely undertaken through the intense diplomatic contacts of Prime Minister John Howard of Australia and UN Secretary-General Kofi Annan. Nevertheless, fortuitous timing benefited the mobilization effort in two respects. First, Thailand currently chaired ASEAN, which enhanced the roles its prime minister and foreign minister were able to play in bringing about ASEAN participation. Second, the Asia Pacific Economic Cooperation Forum (APEC) was due to meet in Auckland just as efforts to induce Indonesia's consent to intervention and to mobilize an international force approached their peak. Few regional organizations were less likely to adopt an interventionist political role, and the East Timor crisis was never brought into its formal meetings. But a special ministerial meeting was convened and, despite initial doubts, almost all Asian countries participated, conveying to Indonesia a strong demonstration of the concern throughout the region. By the time heads of government joined their foreign ministers in Auckland, Indonesia's

President B. J. Habibie was on the verge of inviting assistance, and high-level discussions in the margins of the meeting facilitated the assembly of the force.

Conclusion

These very disparate cases do not allow for easy generalization. But they do suggest issues that are relevant to assessing the advantages and disadvantages of regionalization, or of the UN's preeminence. The United Nations cannot possibly do all that is necessary in the name of peace operations in all regions, and there are well-known limitations to its own competence. Both the attention of the Security Council and its willingness to commit resources are dependent on the interests of its permanent members. Within the UN Secretariat is a disjunction between those involved in preventive diplomacy and peacemaking, and those who take on the operational responsibility for peacekeeping. An integrated UN mission under the authority of an SRSG does not guarantee that military and civilians, police and human rights officers, and humanitarians and political officers will work cooperatively toward a common goal. Still less do UN agencies readily subordinate their individual interests to ensure coordination of humanitarian or peacebuilding efforts. UN peacekeepers are not always subject to proper accountability. Lessons are not always learned, nor are they always conveyed to those responsible for later operations.

But the trend to greater regionalization faces even greater challenges in these respects, and the UN's most experienced manager of peacekeeping operations concludes robustly that

> the arguments for regionalization are specious and the arguments against it strong. The real aims of the Western countries that argue for it are to ease the financial burdens placed on them by the post-Cold War proliferation of peace operations and to avoid risking their soldiers' lives in other peoples' wars. . . . There are two main arguments against regionalization. First, no regional organization except NATO has the administrative, logistical and command structures needed to deploy and manage multinational military operations. The peace operations deployed by other regional organizations have been ineffective and/or have been used to advance the interests of the regional superpower. . . . The second argument against regionalization is an ethical one. The United Nations was intended to be a universal organization. Its services are available to all its members on a basis of equality and at the expense of the membership as a whole in accordance with each state's ability to pay. It would be contrary to this vision to insist that member states in a particular region should receive only the level of peacekeeping that their regional organization can provide.[3]

From a practitioner's point of view, the challenge can be summarized in the form of five questions:

1. How can peace operations benefit from the positive commitment and understanding of regional actors for one of their own, rather than suffer from interests and collective self-protection that impede a principled approach?
2. In a world of regionalization, how can it be ensured that those who face the realities of implementing peace settlements have been fully represented in the process of negotiating peace?
3. How can peace operations benefit from the comparative advantage of multiple UN and regional actors within an effectively coordinated effort and avoid competition, duplication, confusion, and inefficiency?
4. How can it be ensured that regional peacekeepers respect international human rights obligations and are properly accountable for their responsibility to do so?
5. With an increasing number of actors, how can the cumulative experience of peace operations be institutionalized and the professionalism of each dimension progressively enhanced?

The trend toward regionalization may be inevitable, but the extent to which it is desirable will depend on the extent to which satisfactory answers are found in practice to these questions.

Notes

1. Bruce Jones, *Peacemaking in Rwanda: The Dynamics of Failure* (Boulder: Lynne Rienner, 2001), p. 170.
2. James Cotton, "Against the Grain: The East Timor Intervention," *Survival* 43, no. 1 (Spring 2001).
3. Marrack Goulding, *Peacemonger* (London: John Murray, 2002), pp. 217–218.

PART 2

The UN, NATO, and European Organizations

4

The UN and NATO: The Logic of Primacy

Dick A. Leurdijk

In 1949, during the negotiations on the establishment of the North Atlantic Treaty Organization (NATO), when the preamble to NATO's treaty was first discussed, the French representative suggested that some reference might be made in it to Chapter VIII of the UN Charter concerning "regional arrangements."[1] The French had always taken the view that the pact was both a regional arrangement within the meaning of Chapter VIII as well as a collective defense system under Article 51. The British objected strongly to any reference whatsoever, fearing that all action taken under the NATO Pact should be subject to the veto of the Security Council. Eventually, it was agreed that any specific reference in the preamble, or in any of the articles of the treaty, to Chapter VIII of the Charter would be omitted. In their public statements, member states should stress the relationship of the Alliance to Article 51.

This episode defined the relationship between the North Atlantic Treaty Organization and the United Nations, but the implications of the decision at the end of the 1940s were not realized until fifty years later. In the fall of 1998, in preparing the conditions under which NATO would start Operation Allied Force in Kosovo, the main formal issue, indeed, was whether the Alliance was legally justified to use force without an explicit authorization of the UN Security Council. In the exchange of arguments among the NATO members, history repeated itself. The debate mirrored the awareness of the founders of NATO that, as a Chapter VIII organization, NATO could lose its autonomy, thereby undermining the very foundation of its existence as a collective defense organization.

In this chapter, I argue that UN-NATO relations since the early 1990s have developed along the lines of two models. Under the so-called subcontracting model, based on Chapter VIII of the UN Charter, NATO's military actions were legally authorized by the UN Security Council, for so-called collective security purposes, in terms of maintaining international peace and security under conditions of both war and peace. Alternatively, Operation Allied Force in Kosovo, executed by the Alliance without a formal authorization of the Security Council, provided a second model, basically reflecting NATO's original character as a collective defense organization primarily concerned with the preservation of its own security. Thus the relationship between the UN and NATO in the years to come will be determined by NATO's "dual-track" policy, summarized as: "with the UN if possible, without the UN if necessary."

NATO

At the time of the UN's establishment in 1945, regional organizations in the European region were nonexistent. It took another four years before NATO was established as a collective defense organization aimed at preserving the territorial integrity of its member states against external threats. Article 5 of the North Atlantic Treaty identified the commitments that the Allies accepted, in exercise of the right of individual or collective self-defense recognized by Article 51 of the UN Charter, stating: "The Parties agree that an armed attack against one or more of them in Europe or North America shall be considered an attack against them all."

The end of the Cold War resulted in a new political and strategic environment in Europe and the world. As the importance of NATO's classical collective defense task diminished, the Alliance adapted from deterring a clearly defined threat to coping with what emerged to be an unpredictable and unstable security environment. This led to a new conception of security risks and the realization that NATO's preoccupation, from then on, might be to contain the consequences of conflicts in Eastern Europe. This was reflected in NATO's "New Strategic Concept," approved in November 1991, which stated:

> Risks to Allied security are less likely to result from calculated aggression against the territory of the Allies, but rather from the adverse consequences of instabilities that may arise from the serious economic, social and political difficulties, including ethnic rivalries and territorial disputes, which are faced by many countries in central and eastern Europe. [The resulting tensions could] lead to crises inimical to European stability and even to armed conflicts, which could involve outside powers or spill over into NATO countries, having a direct effect on the security of the Alliance.

NATO's new security perception required new conceptual thinking to adapt strategic concepts and operational directives, including the identification of missions. At the beginning of the 1990s, peacekeeping became a key concern for the Alliance, mainly as a consequence of the combined effect of two factors: the general policy debates on NATO's future tasks, and the implications for the Alliance of the war in the former Yugoslavia. As part of its reorientation with a view to its future raison d'être, in June 1992 NATO endorsed the principle of its participation in peacekeeping, in particular by making available its assets to the Organization for Security and Cooperation in Europe (OSCE). The modalities of this endorsement remained to be worked out, essentially leading to a debate on NATO's "out-of-area syndrome," given the geographic proximity of the Yugoslav crisis along its borders. Six months later, on December 17, 1992, in responding to a letter from the UN Secretary-General to his NATO counterpart, the Allies officially confirmed their preparedness

> to support, on a case-by-case basis and in accordance with our own procedures, peacekeeping operations under the authority of the UN Security Council, which has the primary responsibility for international peace and security. We are ready to respond positively to initiatives that the UN Secretary-General might take to seek Alliance assistance in the implementation of UN Security Council Resolutions.[2]

In May 1993 the Alliance gave a review of such initiatives "under consideration, under way, or already undertaken" in its cooperation with the UN.[3] Finally, in its 1994 Brussels summit declaration, the Alliance reconfirmed its political willingness to support the UN, thereby upgrading its institutional relations with an operational dimension. In the meantime, the Alliance was confronted with a number of basic questions with respect to its foundations and its relationship with the UN:

Was NATO a regional organization under Chapter VIII of the UN Charter?
Did NATO have legal competence to act "out-of-area"?
Did NATO have competence to engage in non–Article 5 activities ("new missions") if there was no armed attack as mentioned in Article 5, and if so, should the NATO treaty then be adapted?

These issues, however, were never being discussed exhaustively, nor were formal decisions being taken at the level of the North Atlantic Council. Nonetheless, in practical terms the implications for the military of providing support to the UN were far-reaching. The Alliance was forced to make two unprecedented U-turns. First, it had to cooperate for the first time with the UN, by tradition seen as a completely different and "soft" peace organization, under completely new operational circumstances. Second, at a later stage, under conditions of "peacebuilding," it was supposed to work closely with a whole array of civilian organizations under no less exceptional circumstances. In other words, the military no longer had to be prepared for war; it now also had to be prepared for peace. In conceptual terms, the outcome of NATO's transformation after the Cold War led to a two-track policy, with both a collective defense and a collective security dimension.[4]

The emerging cooperation in the former Yugoslavia between the UN and NATO was seen as an illustration of subcontracting to, and task sharing with, regional organizations—based on the Security Council delegating its powers concerning enforcement action.[5]

NATO and the UN in Bosnia and Herzegovina: Subcontracting Before Dayton

A main feature of NATO's involvement in the former Yugoslavia has been its provisional and unplanned character.[6] Taking into account its potential as a functioning military organization, it was felt in the early 1990s, after an initial cautious reaction to the civil war, that its capabilities could be used for so-called non–Article 5 operations. While rejecting any form of automaticity in supporting UN peacekeeping operations and stressing its autonomous position, NATO had expressed its willingness, in principle, to provide assistance on an ad hoc basis, while recognizing the Council's political primacy. In fact, NATO's statement in December 1992 only confirmed the cooperation that was already taking place between the UN and NATO in the former Yugoslavia. It should be stressed that this process was preceded and accompanied by the deployment of the UN Protection Force (UNPROFOR) with its peacekeeping mandate. Its primary task in Bosnia and Herzegovina (BiH) was to support the provision of humanitarian assistance, with the UN High Commissioner for Refugees (UNHCR) acting as the "lead agency," in what would become "one of the worst humanitarian emergencies of our time."[7] Gradually the Security Council's involvement more or less simultaneously led both to a gradual extension of the mandate of UNPROFOR and to NATO's increased involvement, aimed at the achievement of the objectives that the Security Council had determined were necessary for the maintenance of international peace and security: the imposition of economic sanctions, including an arms embargo, the establishment of a no-fly zone, and the declaration of six "safe areas." The implementation of these measures led to new forms of cooperation between the UN and NATO, at sea, in the air, and on the ground, in a hostile environment, in different formats, including mixtures of monitoring, peacekeeping, and peace enforcement.

NATO's involvement in the Yugoslav crisis began at sea on July 16, 1992, with Operation Maritime Monitor. On that day, when for the first time in its history the Alliance was in action, NATO ships entered the Adriatic Sea and began monitoring compliance of resolutions on "a general and complete embargo on all deliveries of weapons and military equipment to Yugoslavia" and on economic sanctions against the Federal Republic of Yugoslavia (Serbia and Montenegro). On November 22 this was upgraded to enforcement of a total embargo on land, at sea, in the air, and on the Danube, with member states being authorized "to use the necessary means commensurate with the circumstances." Three months after initiating its first action at sea, NATO started a similar monitoring action in the air, after the Security Council had established "a ban on military flights in the airspace of Bosnia-Herzegovina." As in the case of the maritime embargoes, the monitoring was followed by an enforcement operation. In March 1993, under Resolution 816, member states, "acting nationally or through regional organisations or arrangements," were authorized to take "all necessary measures in the airspace of BiH, in the event of further violations." In executing Operation Deny Flight, NATO, for the first time in the Yugoslav crisis, had to cooperate closely with the UN, particularly with UNPROFOR. For this reason, liaison officers were exchanged. On February 28, 1994, NATO aircraft shot down four Serbian aircraft that had violated the no-fly zone. It was the first time that NATO planes opened fire over BiH, and the Alliance's first hostilities since it had been founded forty-five years before.

The third variant of subcontracting, NATO's role in implementing the Security Council's "safe-area policy," would in particular cause much confusion. Its dilemmas, legally, politically, conceptually, and operationally, had serious consequences both for the relationship between the two organizations and for the effectiveness of the policy as a whole. To illustrate the point, NATO provided air power for purposes authorized by the Security Council and in support of UNPROFOR in the implementation of its mandate, in terms of both "close air support" under peacekeeping and "air strikes" under an umbrella of peace enforcement. This caused unprecedented problems of conceptual definitions and command and control, such as the "dual-key" arrangement, which effectively meant an operational model with two captains on one ship, each having a veto. In the absence of a precise agreement as to the circumstances justifying the use of force, each organization responded to its own interests and priorities in weighing, for instance, the safety of UN personnel against the lives of those living in the areas; the possible repercussions of the use of force by NATO for the safety of UN soldiers on the ground; and the continuity of the peace talks in which the UN played a mediating role. The carnage in the Sarajevo marketplace in February 1994 forced the UN Secretary-General to ask NATO to authorize air strikes. The NATO Council formulated an "ultimatum" aimed at the withdrawal, or regrouping and placing under UNPROFOR control, of the heavy weapons of both parties located in an "exclusion zone." A similar ultimatum was served to prevent the fall of Gorazde in April 1994. The decision after the fall of Srebrenica in July 1995 that attacks against the remaining safe areas would lead to "a firm and rapid response from NATO air forces" was based on an adaptation of the dual-key arrangement. It proved to be another decisive element of the prelude to Operation Deliberate Force—in which the UN and NATO together determined the terms of the ceasefire, leading finally to the Dayton Peace Agreement.

The UN and NATO After Dayton:
Another Case of Subcontracting

The implementation of the Dayton Peace Agreement added a new dimension to the relationship between the UN and NATO: forms of cooperation under conditions of peace, as part of a "postconflict peacebuilding" effort. After three and a half years of war, on December 14, 1995, the parties signed a general framework agreement for peace in Bosnia and Herzegovina, a document with eleven annexes, divided into a military and a civilian component. This reflected the built-in division of labor between the military authorities, under NATO leadership, and the activities of the organizations involved in the civilian aspects of the peace settlement, under the coordination of the High Representative appointed by the UN Security Council. In December 1995 the NATO Council endorsed the military planning for the multinational Implementation Force (IFOR), stating that the operation would attest to its capacity for new missions of crisis management and peacekeeping. The concept of IFOR was elaborated at NATO headquarters in Brussels, outside the UN framework. Following the ceremonial signing of the peace agreement in Paris, the Security Council, acting under Chapter VII of the UN Charter, authorized the member states acting through or in cooperation with NATO to establish IFOR to assist in the implementation of the territorial and other militarily related provisions of the peace agreement. The following day, December 16, 1996, the North Atlantic Council approved the overall plan for IFOR and directed that NATO commence Operation Joint Endeavor. NATO's Acting Secretary-General spoke of the Alliance's "most challenging operation in its history," adding: "This is indeed a historic moment for the alliance—our first-ever ground force operation, our first-ever deployment 'out-of-area,' our first-ever operation with our PfP [Partnership for Peace] partners and other non-NATO countries." The force would have a unified command and be NATO-led, under the political direction and control of the North Atlantic Council, and operate under NATO rules of engagement.

NATO's principal tasks were related to military aspects (cessation of hostilities, withdrawal of foreign forces, redeployment of forces, prisoner exchanges), regional stabilization, and the interentity boundary line. Halfway through IFOR's mandated term, the purely military tasks were accomplished.

This marked the beginning of the "transition to peace," which made it possible for the force gradually to pay more attention to civilian tasks, to be conducted in close cooperation with a number of other international bodies, such as the High Representative, the UN International Police Task Force (UNIPTF), the UNHCR, the OSCE, and the International Criminal Tribunal for the Former Yugoslavia (ICTY). Thus, in addition to its primary military tasks, IFOR had a number of so-called supporting tasks aimed at the establishment of a secure environment for the conduct by others of civilian tasks associated with the peace settlement, including elections, humanitarian assistance, law enforcement, the return of refugees, and so on.

After the expiry of IFOR's mandate, the Security Council authorized the establishment of a Stabilization Force (SFOR) as the legal successor to IFOR, this time for a period of eighteen months. NATO's initial planning was aimed at progressively reducing the force's presence and eventually effecting its withdrawal in June 1998. This, however, proved to be premature. In February 1998 the North Atlantic Council, acknowledging the fragility of the peace process, decided to establish a new SFOR with the task "to deter renewed hostilities and to contribute to a secure environment for the ongoing civil implementation efforts in order to stabilize and consolidate the peace in Bosnia and Herzegovina." There was consensus that the brunt of the Dayton Peace Agreement still had to be implemented, including elections and the return of refugees and displaced persons in particular. This also explains why, contrary to earlier decisionmaking, no "end date" for the next mission was given. This time, NATO preferred to speak in terms of an "end-state," signaling that the duration of SFOR's presence was made dependent on the realization of specific benchmarks in the implementation of the Dayton Agreement as part of a transition strategy aimed at the transfer of responsibilities to the local and national authorities in BiH.[8] Furthermore, NATO's increasing civilian orientation was underlined by its decision to help promote public order by the creation within SFOR of a Multinational Specialized Unit aimed at enhancing SFOR's ability "to support the local authorities in responding to civil disorder, without engaging in police functions, so as to assist the return of refugees and displaced persons and the installation of elected officials."[9] By adopting Resolution 1174 in June 1998, the Security Council authorized the continuation of SFOR. In December, NATO ministers agreed that an accelerated return of refugees and displaced persons, in particular to minority areas, would be "a key task for 1999."[10] Five years after the signing of the Dayton Agreement, this task still had not been accomplished as originally intended, illustrating the difficulties the international actors, including NATO and the UN, had experienced in implementing the provisions of the peace agreement. Some observers seriously doubted whether the international community would be able to realize its peacebuilding ambitions.[11]

Kosovo: Beyond Subcontracting

Against the background of UN-NATO cooperation in BiH under conditions of war and peace, the thinking about the relationship was further influenced by the dynamics of two coincidental developments in the months leading up to NATO's fiftieth anniversary: the situation in Kosovo and the discussion within NATO on its "New Strategic Concept" for the twenty-first century.

The issue of Kosovo was already on NATO's agenda at the end of January 1998, before the outbreak of violence in the first week of March of that year. NATO's concern about the "potentially explosive" situation in Kosovo, in terms of "a second Bosnia," was related both to the fear of a possible spillover into neighboring countries and to the possible negative consequences for the consolidation of the peace process in BiH. These concerns were reflected in official statements. On March 6, 1998, for example, NATO's Permanent Council declared: "NATO and the international community have a legitimate interest in developments in Kosovo, inter alia because of their impact on the stability of the whole region which is of concern to the Alliance."[12] The Council's recognition that NATO had "a legitimate interest in developments in Kosovo" was the starting point for a discussion on the modalities of a possible military intervention by the Alliance along its periphery—an option that was mentioned publicly in April.[13]

In the fall of 1998 two considerations led to an intensification of the decisionmaking processes both at the UN and within NATO. The first consideration was the prospect of an "impending humanitarian catastrophe," taking into account the estimated number of displaced people (230,000) without shelter and food, as a consequence of the use of force by Belgrade against the civilian population, when winter was approaching.[14] Under these circumstances, the Security Council, on September 23, adopted Resolution 1199, in which it formally confirmed earlier political demands with which President Slobodan Milošević had to comply, including the cessation of hostilities, the withdrawal of troops and special police forces, the return of refugees and displaced persons, access for humanitarian organizations, and international monitoring in Kosovo. Second, concerned about its credibility after so many unanswered cases of defiance of the international community's demands, NATO set in motion the procedure that would culminate, by mid-October, in the issue of activation orders for both a limited air operation and a more substantial and phased air campaign. Five months later these orders formed the basis for what would become Operation Allied Force.

In the meantime, it had become clear to all concerned that at the Security Council a resolution authorizing the use of force by NATO would be vetoed by, among others, the Russian Federation. This made the issue of the legal grounds for military action all the more acute. NATO members were divided and could not agree on an official, common position in this respect. European partners insisted on the need to have UN authority, while the United States argued that NATO action was justified on inherently legitimate humanitarian grounds, which did not require an authorization by the Security Council. The differences of opinion on this issue among NATO's sixteen nations were reflected in consecutive statements stressing the need for a "relevant," an "appropriate," a "sufficient," or a "sound legal" base, while avoiding references to the need for an explicit UN mandate. Finally, the European states consented to the use of force, arguing that Kosovo would be an exceptional case and did not set any precedent. Members thus reached consensus. Secretary-General Javier Solana explained: "All the Allies believe that under these grave circumstances (of 'an impending humanitarian catastrophe') in Kosovo, and in the presence of the provisions of resolution 1199, there are legitimate grounds for the use of force or the threat of the use of force."[15] Unable to reach agreement on the definition of a formal and common legal foundation, the Alliance left it to each individual member state to formulate a separate, national legitimation of the activation orders. The justification in terms of "a sufficient legal base" thus had two functions: it served to cover up the lack of an explicit UN authorization and to cover up the inability of NATO to formulate an official, common legal basis for the planned air operations.

Notwithstanding its contentious formal status, the Milošević-Holbrooke "agreement," signed at the end October 1998, provided the basis for the establishment of a verification regime consisting of two components: an OSCE mission of 2,000 unarmed "verifiers," and a NATO air verification mission with noncombatant reconnaissance platforms. The aim of both was to verify the compliance of Yugoslavia, and of "all others concerned in Kosovo," with Resolution 1199. By adopting Resolution 1203 on October 24, 1998, the Security Council formally authorized both missions, including NATO's role.

A series of incidents on the ground culminated in a massacre at Račak on January 15, 1999. The Contact Group summoned both parties to the conflict to Rambouillet to begin negotiations on a political settlement for a transitional period of three years, providing for "a substantial autonomy for Kosovo" while preserving the territorial integrity of the Federal Republic of Yugoslavia. NATO lent its full support to this strategy by repeating its threats of using force, in line with the activation orders of mid-October 1998.[16] The talks failed to reach a breakthrough. After a last mediation effort by Richard Holbrooke, NATO finally started Operation Allied Force on March 24, 1999—the execution of air strikes in line with the activation orders. Only then did the public debate start on the political, military, and international legal implications of the use of force by NATO, in terms of its legitimacy, proportionality, and effectiveness—a debate that coincided with the discussion on NATO's New Strategic Concept. Unsurprisingly, the extraordinary summit of the Alliance was dominated by NATO's performance in Kosovo.

NATO's New Strategic Concept

It was against the background of its experience, gained both before and after the signing of the Dayton Peace Agreement, that NATO, anticipating its fiftieth anniversary in May 1999, started its deliberations on the formulation of its main policy document for the twenty-first century, the New Strategic Concept. The process was of course further influenced by NATO's involvement in the Kosovo crisis, especially since the start of Operation Allied Force in March 1999.

After an initial discussion during NATO's ministerial meeting in Luxembourg in June 1998 on the adaptation of NATO's Strategic Concept, U.S. secretary of state Madeleine Albright summarized the U.S. position as follows: "NATO's fundamental mission will always remain collective defence against aggression. At the same time . . . we have always had the option to use NATO's strength beyond its borders to protect our security interests. If joint military action is ever needed to protect vital Alliance interests, NATO should be our instrument of choice."[17] She quoted President Clinton, who on an earlier occasion had said: "Tomorrow's NATO must continue to defend enlarged borders and defend against threats to our security from beyond them—the spread of weapons of mass destruction, ethnic violence and regional conflict." Albright in this context alluded to some of the problems that still had to be solved, including the question whether there should always be a UN authorization for NATO to act. U.S. secretary of defense William Cohen, arguing along the same lines, did not think it necessary for NATO to subordinate its security to the UN, emphasizing NATO's own autonomy in taking decisions. The European allies said that they would not approve the use of force by NATO without a UN mandate, arguing that this would be against international law and the UN Charter, and fearing both the risk of alienating the Russians and/or the Chinese and the consequences that such a "precedent" could set for others in the future. In the meantime the developments in Kosovo underlined the need to reach consensus among NATO's membership. In September 1998, Secretary-General Solana stressed that, for him, the issue was "political," adding: "We must not enter into a legalistic debate" on this.[18] It was indeed in this spirit that NATO took its decisions on the activation orders, based on a consensus to "agree to disagree." NATO still had to find a legal formula for any "future Kosovos" in its New Strategic Concept. After lengthy discussions, it was agreed to identify NATO as "an Alliance of nations committed to the Washington Treaty and the United Nations Charter" for the performance of a series of fundamental security tasks, including crisis management, in the "Euro-Atlantic area."[19] NATO's commitment to both documents seems to suggest the juxtaposition of NATO and the UN, rejecting any form of hierarchy or submission—in line with the intentions of NATO's founding fathers to escape the subordinate status that was sought by the makers of the Charter.

NATO underlined, more explicitly than it had fifty years before, that it wanted to keep all its options open. It may place itself at the service of the UN, but at the same time it would retain its right to act without an explicit authorization of the Security Council under conditions to be determined by NATO itself (probably, in exceptional cases, should vital Alliance interests along the periphery of NATO be at stake, or in cases of humanitarian emergencies).

The Kosovo Model: A Transitional Arrangement

While NATO's air attacks were heavily contested on international legal grounds, in the aftermath of Operation Allied Force NATO acted again within the framework of the UN as part of the transitional arrangement as established under Security Council Resolution 1244. President Milošević's compliance with the list of political demands as contained in Resolution 1199, the main purpose of Operation Allied Force, brought a termination of the air strikes. It also paved the way for a new phase in the Kosovo crisis: the establishment of a UN administration for a transitional period, pending a definitive settlement of the status of Kosovo, with key roles for both the UN and NATO. This "Kosovo model," which was inspired by the Dayton Agreement, provided for an interim arrangement in a similar attempt at postconflict peacebuilding. The matter of the presence of NATO forces on the ground in Kosovo proved to be one of the main obstacles for President Milošević. The final formulation on the stationing of an "international military presence" (KFOR) with "a substantial participation" of NATO "under unified command and control" offered ample room for meeting the demands of all concerned. NATO wanted an operation led by a NATO commander, with the North Atlantic Council providing political guidance, while Milošević wanted the international force to be embedded in the framework of the UN Security Council, guaranteeing Moscow's formal involvement in the adoption and implementation of the provisions of Resolution 1244. KFOR's main tasks, executed under Chapter VII enforcement powers, were purely military and civilian. The military tasks related to enforcing a ceasefire, withdrawing (para)military forces, and demilitarizing the Kosovo Liberation Army (KLA). The civilian tasks were aimed at establishing a secure environment in which humanitarian aid could be delivered, refugees and displaced persons could return home, the international civil presence could operate, and a transitional administration could be established.

Pursuant to Resolution 1244, the UN Secretary-General, "with the support of relevant international organisations," was entrusted with the task of establishing an interim administration for Kosovo. This constitutes the main task of the UN Mission in Kosovo. The Security Council authorized UNMIK with the exercise of authority over the territory and its inhabitants. It thus delegated to the mission all legislative and executive authority, including the exercise of the judiciary and the deployment of a police force with executive powers. In his capacity as Special Representative of the Secretary-General (SRSG), the UN administrator is responsible for "supervision of the implementation of the international civil presence" and is entrusted with coordination of the activities within the civil component as well as between this sector and KFOR. As such he is the counterpart of KFOR, though both, of course, had to develop their working relationships with the other international organizations involved as well.

Thus, like SFOR, KFOR was tasked with both specifically military and so-called supporting roles, which established direct operational links between KFOR and the civilian components: the UN as the lead agency for the civil administration, the UNHCR for humanitarian aid, the OSCE for democratization and institution building, and the European Union for reconstruction.

The Logic of Chapter VIII and Beyond

On the basis of the experience of the last decade in the Balkans, the relations between the UN and NATO have developed along the lines of two models: the subcontracting model, fitting within the logic of Chapter VIII, and the non–Chapter VIII model. What makes the UN-NATO relationship so special is that NATO, while being the only regional organization with the capability to carry out military enforcement action, retains its right to act militarily both within and outside the structure of Chapter VIII, stressing under both conditions its autonomous position with respect to the UN.

The Subcontracting Model

The cooperation between the UN and NATO in the former Yugoslavia has been generally interpreted as an illustration of subcontracting, whereby the Security Council, under the UN Charter, delegates its powers for the use of force to regional organizations. The Council, entrusted with the primary responsibility for the maintenance of international peace and security, not only has the competence to decide "measures involving the use of force" (under Chapter VII of the UN Charter), but also has the competence to delegate, or subcontract, the implementation of such enforcement action to, among others, regional organizations (under Chapter VIII). Article 53(1) of the UN Charter gives the Security Council the competence to "utilize" regional organizations "for enforcement action under its authority." In legal terms, this authority of the Council requires a number of conditions in order to make the delegation lawful: an explicit prior authorization by calling upon member states and/or regional organizations for military enforcement action; the identification of a clear objective or goal by the Security Council; and compliance by regional organizations with a reporting requirement (under Article 54).[20] At the same time, however, it should be clear that the Security Council cannot impose an obligation on regional organizations to carry out military enforcement action. This is a decision that is to be taken by the regional organization itself, taking into account the organization's own constitutional limits and political motivations. It was against the background of this institutional framework that the relationship between the UN and NATO in the former Yugoslavia would develop.

The development of the relations between the UN and NATO, both in BiH and Kosovo, provided a number of cases of subcontracting. Under these conditions, NATO committed itself to the attainment of political goals, as defined by the Security Council. The involvement of the international community in the two operation areas was aimed at both establishing the peace and assisting in implementing ensuing peace settlements. In both time scales several models of subcontracting or "burden sharing" have been applied: the execution of specific tasks, and more general "peacebuilding" efforts. In regard to the implementation of the more specific tasks, such as the enforcement of an economic embargo, a no-fly zone, and the security of safe areas (before the signing of the Dayton Agreement) and NATO's participation in a verification mission in Kosovo, NATO acted on the basis of authorizations by the Security Council with explicit requests directed at member states acting nationally or through regional organizations or arrangements.

The most characteristic feature of the current relationship between the UN and NATO is its operational and ad hoc basis, given cooperation in the field in implementing peace settlements in BiH and Kosovo. In both cases, the UN was not involved in the talks on the peace settlements, and the role of the Security Council was essentially limited to rubber-stamping the deployment of SFOR and KFOR and, while acting under Chapter VII, giving them enforcement powers. Both "peacebuilding" models are based on a division of labor along civil-military lines, with NATO taking the lead in implementing the military components, and the UN taking a more complex position. In BiH the UN played a relatively minor role with its police task force before handing it over to the EU at the start of 2003, while in Kosovo UNMIK has a key role in providing for the transitional administration of the area.

In operational terms both organizations have developed close working relations based on the provisions of the peace settlements. It is clear that coordination is of utmost importance for success. In each mission we have seen the institutionalization of different mechanisms to ensure the necessary coordination. The Dayton Peace Agreement provided for a joint military commission and a joint civilian commission, which implied only a relatively loose form of cooperation. In Kosovo, under Resolution 1244, the SRSG was invited to "coordinate closely with the international security presence [KFOR] to ensure that both presences operate towards the same goals and in a mutually support-ive manner." Former KFOR commander General Klaus Reinhardt noted that in Kosovo "an unprecedented level of integration and cooperation between civil and military organizations" has been achieved, where the leaders of KFOR, UNMIK, and the four pillars acted as a joint planning team, a situation that he described as "unique in the history of civil-military cooperation."[21]

NATO's role in "peacebuilding" confirmed its original position with respect to the UN. Its initial performance in the former Yugoslavia before the signing of the Dayton Peace Agreement was generally interpreted as falling in line with the UN Charter, according to which the Security Council subcon-tracted its authority to use force to NATO as a regional organization, which was considered by some observers as perfectly fitting within the framework of Chapter VIII: "The combination . . . of the Council delegating tasks in the area of peace and security to NATO and the self-redefinition of NATO to carry out tasks which are in addition to its original mandate under the NATO Char-ter, allow it to fit within the rubric of a Chapter VIII regional arrangement."[22]

NATO's role in peacebuilding in Bosnia and Kosovo also fitted in the subcontracting model of Chapter VIII inasmuch as the deployments of IFOR/SFOR and KFOR were authorized by the Security Council, albeit at the request of the signatories of the peace settlements. At the same time, however, NATO would never agree with the interpretation of its role "as a Chapter VIII regional organization." Such an interpretation overlooks the fact that the Alliance's willingness to undertake enforcement action at the request of the Security Council has always been conditional. In responding to concrete requests for support to the UN and while accepting the Security Council's political primacy and primary responsibility for international peace and secu-rity, NATO always stressed that this recognition was not unqualified. This explains why the Alliance, from the beginning, made a number of explicit reservations with respect to its willingness to cooperate with the UN, saying it was, *in principle,* prepared to respond positively; stressing there would be *no automaticity* in responding positively (fearful of setting precedents); and saying that its performance would take place according to its *own procedures.* In this way, the Alliance tried to underline its autonomous position vis-à-vis the UN.

In practical terms, the subcontracting concept itself can be subdivided into two models. In the first model NATO conforms to explicit requests for military action from the Security Council or the Secretary-General in order to conduct specific tasks as defined by the Security Council. Under the second ("peacebuilding") model, NATO was closely involved in the talks preceding the agreements on peace settlements, which guaranteed involvement in defining the modalities of the military presences of IFOR/SFOR and KFOR, respectively. This contributed to a growing political significance of the role of the North Atlantic Council as an instrument of international policymaking. Before the Dayton Agreement, for example, the Council became closely involved in the formulation and implementation of parts of the safe area policy, including ultimata and exclusion zones. At a later stage, it provided political guidance to SFOR, for example, in determining SFOR's policy with respect to the apprehension of indicted war criminals and response to "public security issues." This development was further strengthened by a similar role for the North Atlantic Council under Resolution 1244 (in determining the response to unrest in the "ground safety zone" along Kosovo's border with Serbia proper and Macedonia).[23]

The Second Model: Beyond Chapter VIII

The second model that determines the relations between the UN and NATO might be described as "NATO issuing its own mandate." The lesson of NATO's Operation Allied Force has been that the Alliance emphatically wanted to keep the option open for the use of force outside the framework of Chapter VIII for so-called non–Article 5 operations. Although, formally speaking, the aim of the air attacks was to enforce President Milošević's compliance with a package of political demands, as contained in Resolution 1199, in applying the use of force NATO acted without a formal and explicit Security Council authorization. This has made clear, once again, that the subcontracting model is inadequate to describe the relationship between the UN and NATO. In adopting the activation order, NATO confirmed that there is another logic beyond Chapter VIII of the UN Charter.

By adopting the activation order on October 13, 1998, NATO effectively created a precedent for its conduct of non–Article 5 operations outside the framework of Chapter VIII. Because in this situation NATO "issued its own mandate," with no authorization from the Security Council, it is relevant to learn what formal legal base was given for its decision. While the members could not agree on a formal and common legal justification, one can argue that at least a combination of considerations laid the basis for the activation order: security concerns for the stability in Europe as a consequence of potential spillover effects of a conflict in the Balkans, humanitarian concerns in light of an "impending humanitarian catastrophe," concerns for the credibility of NATO as a forceful military alliance, and enforcement of compliance with political demands.[24] If this is true, then Operation Allied Force would have provided an illustration of the modern "dual-track" policies of NATO, combining collective defense and collective security considerations in its decisionmaking processes. Together with its role under the subcontracting model, the implication would be that NATO thus presents itself as being at the service of the UN system of collective security in two functions. It does so in its role as an actor implementing UN Security Council resolutions, as well as in its role as guarantor of upholding collective security values, such as enforcing Security Council resolutions and the respect of international human rights. (The latter role, however, is heavily contested, as was made clear by criticism from many sides that Operation Allied Force was unjustified in terms of a "humanitarian intervention"—see Chapter 1 in this volume.) As far as the relationships between the UN and NATO are concerned, the conclusion must be that both models will coexist and provide the parameters within which working relationships will be established. There is no alternative from the viewpoint of the UN than to accept the position of NATO that it will never unconditionally "subcontract" itself to the UN, while it retains its right to act both within and outside the parameters of Chapter VIII in executing non–Article 5 operations. Paraphrasing former U.S. president Bill Clinton's foreign policy line with respect to the UN, as noted at the outset of the chapter, this NATO policy can be summarized as: "with the UN if possible, without the UN if necessary."[25]

Within thirty-six hours after the unprecedented terrorist attacks on the United States on September 11, 2001, the North Atlantic Council adopted the statement that "if it is determined that this attack was directed from abroad against the United States it shall be regarded as an action covered by Article 5 of the Washington Treaty, which states that an armed attack against one or more of the Allies in Europe or North America shall be considered an attack against them all." On October 2, after a classified briefing, the North Atlantic Council, concluding that "the information presented points conclusively to an Al-Qaida role in the 11 September attacks," took the historic decision to formally invoke Article 5. Nonetheless, it soon became clear, for the time, that the United States, in taking the lead in the "war on terrorism," was not seeking an active involvement of NATO in Operation Enduring Freedom in Afghanistan. This marginalization, followed by disarray driving the Iraq crisis, immediately raised questions about NATO's credibility as an effective military alliance, and even about its future. At the same time, however, NATO started a process of adaptation, trying to identify its role in the "new security environment" and opening up the prospect of acting as a global player involved in the "war on terrorism." The adaptation phase was finalized at NATO's summit in Prague in November 2002, with the adoption of relevant decisions, among them the establishment of a Response Force.

Thus NATO wants to keep all its options open under all circumstances. This also explains why, contrary to what some in the past have argued, NATO probably is not interested in a further formalization of its relationships with the UN beyond the existing institutional framework and beyond the ad hoc operational "peacebuilding" frameworks in the field in BiH and Kosovo.

Notes

1. This paragraph is based on Sir Nicholas Henderson, *The Birth of NATO* (London: Weidenfeld and Nicholson, 1982), pp. 101–105.

2. *Final Communiqué,* Ministerial Meeting of the North Atlantic Council, NATO Headquarters Brussels, December 17, 1992; *Atlantic News* no. 2484 (annex), December 19, 1992.

3. United Nations, *An Agenda for Peace: Preventive Diplomacy, Peacemaking, and Peacekeeping,* Report of the Secretary-General, UN Doc. S/25996, June 15, 1993.

4. David S. Yost, *NATO Transformed: The Alliance's New Roles in International Security* (Washington, DC: U.S. Institute of Peace Press, 1998).

5. Thomas G. Weiss, ed., *Beyond UN Subcontracting: Task-Sharing with Regional Security Arrangements and Service-Providing NGOs* (London: Macmillan, 1998).

6. For more details, see Dick A. Leurdijk, *The United Nations and NATO in Former Yugoslavia, 1991–1996: Limits to Diplomacy and Force* (The Hague: Netherlands Atlantic Commission and Netherlands Institute of International Relations [Clingendael], 1996).

7. United Nations, *Report of the Secretary-General Pursuant to Security Council Resolution 757, 758, and 761 (1992),* UN Doc. S/24263, July 10, 1992.

8. These benchmarks could include the return of refugees, the fight against corruption, the arrest of war criminals, the success of the new police forces, and the degree of democratization. *Atlantic News* no. 3007, May 6, 1998.

9. "Statement on Bosnia and Herzegovina: Issued at the Ministerial Meeting of the North Atlantic Council Held in Luxembourg on 28th May 1998," *Atlantic News* no. 3013 (annex), May 29, 1998.

10. "Statement on Bosnia and Herzegovina: Issued at the Ministerial Meeting of the North Atlantic Council Held at NATO Headquarters, Brussels, 8th December 1998," *Atlantic News* no. 3065 (annex), December 10, 1998.

11. See, among others, Ferdinando Riccardi, "A Look Behind the News," *Bulletin Quotidien Europe* no. 7959, May 7–8, 2001.

12. *Bulletin Quotidien Europe* no. 2994, March 6, 1998.

13. *International Herald Tribune,* April 28, 1998.

14. The number of over 230,000 displaced persons, as mentioned in Security Council Resolution 1199, adopted in September 1998, was based on the estimate of the Secretary-General in his report to the Council. S/RES/1199, September 21, 1998.

15. *Atlantic News* no. 3049, October 14, 1998.

16. Ibid., no. 3078, February 3, 1999.

17. Ibid., no. 3016, June 5, 1998.

18. Ibid., no. 3043, September 30, 1998.

19. "The Alliance's Strategic Concept," *Atlantic News* no. 3105 (annex), May 5, 1999.

20. This formal requirement, however, can hardly be taken seriously in terms of accountability. In practice, NATO provided the Security Council only with reports of a few pages in length.

21. Klaus Reinhardt, "KFOR and UNMIK: Sharing a Common Vision for Kosovo," *NATO's Nations and Partners for Peace,* No. 1, 2000.

22. Danesh Sarooshi, *The United Nations and the Development of Collective Security: The Delegation by the UN Security Council of Its Chapter VII Powers* (Oxford: Oxford University Press, 1999), p. 251.

23. Similarly, an issue that deserves more attention is the relationship between the Security Council and other international decisionmaking bodies, such as the Group of Eight, the Contact Group, and the Peace Implementation Council.

24. Dick Leurdijk and Dick Zandee, *Kosovo: From Crisis to Crisis* (Aldershot: Ashgate, 2001).

25. In an address on January 4, 1992, then–presidential candidate Clinton said: "I will never turn over the security of the United States to the United Nations or any other international organization. We will never abandon our prerogative to act alone when our vital interests are at stake. Our motto in this era will be: 'Together where we can; on our own where we must.'" Quoted in Dick A. Leurdijk, "The United States and the United Nations: An Uneasy Relationship," in Marianne van Leeuwen and Auke Venema, eds., *Selective Engagement: Foreign Policy at the Turn of the Century* (The Hague: Netherlands Atlantic Commission and Netherlands Institute of International Relations [Clingendael], 1996), pp. 75–94.

5

The Role of the OSCE and the EU

Nina Græger and Alexandra Novosseloff

The issue of cooperation and coordination between the United Nations and the European regional security organizations as well as between the regional organizations themselves is currently taking on new dimensions. It is the purpose of this chapter to analyze how the recent developments in the Organization for Security and Cooperation in Europe (OSCE) and the European Union (EU) affect this issue. The building of capacities for civilian and military action by the EU reflects its political desire to assert its profile on the international scene and influence on world politics. Furthermore, it appears that multidimensional peace operations as in Kosovo cannot be efficiently dealt with by one international organization alone. In Europe, the development of the European Security and Defense Policy (ESDP) and the EU enlargement process raise questions about the relationships with the other organizations of the continent, such as the OSCE, the North Atlantic Treaty Organization (NATO), and the Council of Europe. Not only the EU but also NATO and the OSCE are taking on new, civilian tasks that extend their original mandates, especially with regard to peace operations.

This chapter first reviews the legal grounds and the institutionalization of existing and future cooperation between the UN and regional organizations in Europe in general and in peace operations in particular. Next it examines the practice and prospects for cooperation between the regional organizations within Europe, focusing on EU-NATO relations and EU-OSCE relations. Finally, the chapter analyzes the implications of ESDP and the emerging European forces' posture for the future cooperation between the UN and the EU.

Legal Bases and Principles for Cooperation Between the UN and Regional Organizations

The UN is and remains the only legal resort for coercive action. The primary responsibility of the UN Security Council in authorizing the use of force and in maintaining international peace and security is recognized by the founding texts of European regional organizations (the North Atlantic Treaty and NATO's 1999 Strategic Concept, the Treaty on European Union, the Helsinki Final Act, and the Charter for European Security).

The extended conception of the notion of a regional arrangement allows the UN Security Council to call on a diversity of institutions. The practice of the Security Council could lead one to consider all regional organizations used or mandated by the Council as regional arrangements consistent with the provisions of Chapter VIII.[1] However, the wording used in Council resolutions shows a reluctance to name the regional organizations it mandates or uses when they have mainly military functions. This was the case for NATO and the Western European Union (WEU),[2] which were rarely named by Council resolutions.[3] The most common phrase used concerns states acting "nationally or through regional agencies or arrangements," and "when NATO acts for the United Nations, it is not the organization which is mandated but its Member States."[4] In contrast, the Security Council has very often expressly named the Organization of African Unity (OAU), the Organization of American States (OAS), and the OSCE (regional arrangements recognized as such by the General Assembly) in the text of its resolutions. The Security Council therefore draws a distinction between the organizations formally recognized by the General Assembly and the others, and between civilian organizations and military alliances. In practice, however, the Council uses the regional organizations that are most able to fulfill the tasks it assigns to them.

Among the European organizations, the status of the EU is less clearly established or defined.[5] The EU does not yet have a legal personality, but this does not impede its recognition as a regional arrangement. The same is true for the OSCE. The EU was indeed mandated by the Security Council to send troops to Ituri in northeastern Congo in May 2003. Within the UN, the EU functions as a regional group that takes common positions in the debates of the General Assembly. The development of the Common Foreign and Security Policy (CFSP) is likely to change this. The political will to give the EU military and nonmilitary capacities for crisis management allows it to act, with a Security Council mandate, on the continent and at its borders (the Treaty on European Union does not define the geographical scope of EU action in the framework of CFSP).

Institutionalization of Cooperation
Between the UN and the European Security System

Due to the vagueness of the texts, the institutionalization of cooperation between the UN and regional organizations has evolved on a case-by-case basis, as circumstances and necessities allowed.[6] Should the development of European institutions lead to an institutionalization of the existing cooperation? Should existing informal partnerships be included in the texts? Is it necessary to abandon some flexibility for the sake of a more binding but perhaps slower or less reactive system? This cooperation between the UN and regional organizations is first of all the result of a voluntary process. Because states seem to prefer a light and progressive institutionalization to a formal and binding one, these relationships are more likely to evolve informally, out of high-level political decisions. Relations also reflect contradictions and ambiguities about how organizations should cooperate without constraining each other.

Nevertheless, cooperation between all the international organizations is strongly recommended by numerous official documents and declarations issued by European or transatlantic summits.[7] Despite the declared need for cooperation and coordination, however, the implementation of these documents and declarations is slow to take effect. The UN and the regional organizations acknowledge the need for a soft institutionalization (in place of ad hoc arrangements) based on high-level meetings and varied consultations. As underlined by Céline Chamot, "the 'model' of cooperation between the UN and regional organizations that is emerging for the future is a cooperation which is softly institutionalized, targeted and pragmatic."[8]

In any case, institutionalization should not be privileged to the detriment of objectives—the building of a true common political project. This project of cooperation between international and regional organizations could be achieved through decentralization. Such a decentralization would require a genuine coordination in the identification of needs, competencies, and capacities for action in the economic, social, political, policing, and military fields, instead of separate microprojects without any overarching strategic plan. The complex nature of crisis management will make such cooperation essential in both the civilian and the military fields.

The high-level meetings between heads of organizations currently represent the most privileged meeting place for cooperation and coordination of these organizations' activities and projects. Increasingly, the NATO Secretary-General, the EU High Representative, and the OSCE Secretary-General address the Security Council on specific topics. The UN Secretary-General and his deputy participate in the most important OSCE meetings but only rarely in NATO's meetings. The UN has now established two high-level meetings a year with the EU. This cooperation also evolves during the periodic meetings held in New York between the UN organs and all the regional organizations (see the Introduction in this volume).

At a lower level, exchanges of personnel and training courses could also improve cooperation, and coordination could be strengthened through the systematic creation of representation bureaus or liaison officers of European regional organizations to the United Nations and vice versa. The European Commission and the European Council have separate representation bureaus in New York, but they are external to the UN (like an embassy). We suggest that in addition to this, a liaison office of the European Council should be established within the UN Department for Peacekeeping Operations (DPKO). The UN has no liaison office in the Secretariat of the European Council, but in January 2002 the UN Secretary-General decided to establish a UN bureau in Brussels to strengthen cooperation with the EU and NATO. As a follow-up, we suggest that the European Council opens bureaus at the OSCE and at the UN's office in Vienna. Regarding the OSCE, in October 2001 the OSCE Permanent Council supported a British proposal to create liaison offices of the OSCE at the EU and at NATO in Brussels.

Cooperation Between the UN and European Regional Organizations in Peace Operations

At the strategic level, cooperation between organizations primarily results from diplomatic exchanges, with the presence of observers at the plenary meetings of the different organizations and informal consultations at different levels. High-level meetings or seminars are held to assess or further strengthen existing coordination. The UN convenes an annual meeting with most of the regional organizations. Some regional organizations also invite representatives of the UN to their seminars or meetings, which allows an exchange of information (as recommended by Article 54 of the UN Charter). Beyond declarations of good intentions, few concrete steps come out of these meetings. Calls in favor of stronger cooperation between the UN and European security organizations are made or repeated each year, but have not led to genuinely institutionalized cooperation within crisis management. Instead, this cooperation has developed under the pressure of circumstances, as a result of practice rather than of principles and adopted policies.

At the operational level, the UN and regional organizations may cooperate in the pacific settlement of disputes or in peace enforcement operations by joint action, delegation, or simple authorization. In the event of the latter, the regional organization acts as the military arm of the UN as provided for by Article 53. Before the crises and conflicts in the Balkans, this cooperation was only sporadic and limited, where the UN asked for the help of regional organizations in the pacific settlement of regional disputes or conflicts, and for the implementation of an economic embargo. During the Gulf War of 1990–1991 and in support of UN Security Council resolutions, the WEU participated in the coordination of naval operations commanded by each state nationally.[9] In the early phase of the Yugoslav crisis, the WEU participated in the maritime monitoring of the embargo against Serbia and Montenegro in 1992–1996 (Operation Sharp Vigilance and Sharp Guard).

The UN and NATO cooperated, but with difficulty, in the UN Protection Force (UNPROFOR) operations. In Bosnia and Herzegovina, the two organizations cooperated through the Multinational Specialized Units of the Alliance and the UN Police International Group. In 1997, Operation Alba, led by Italy, was authorized by the Security Council and formally approved (prior to the UN resolution) by the Permanent Council of the OSCE. Operation Alba, the peacekeeping operations in Georgia and Tajikistan (where the UN cooperated with the OSCE and the Commonwealth of Independent States [CIS] in the field), and the OSCE police mission in Eastern Slavonia, a direct continuation of the UN mission (the UN Transitional Administration for Eastern Slavonia, Baranja, and Western Sirmium [UNTAES] and the UN Police Support Group [UNPSG]), are widely considered to have been successful. During the Kosovo crisis, the Security Council supported the OSCE Verification Mission (S/RES/1203), which was backed by NATO air power and a contingency extraction force. NATO and the OSCE are now cooperating in the UN Mission in Kosovo (UNMIK): Kosovo Force (KFOR) on security matters and (OMIK, the OSCE's mission in Kosovo) on institution building and the organization of elections.[10] The OSCE is also responsible for the Police Service School of Vucitrn, whose objective is to train 3,500 Kosovar policemen in the skills of nondiscriminatory and efficient police activities. Despite the leading role of the UN, however, the Special Representative of the Secretary-General (SRSG) has no competence to coordinate the EU and the OSCE pillars.

The cooperation between the UN and the European regional organizations in relation to the violent conflicts in the Balkans has occurred in a very selective way. The Security Council has authorized a regional organization to act on its behalf and to report back about its actions on a periodic basis, according to the "subcontracting" model.[11] This form of cooperation has functioned satisfactorily when the regional organizations are focused on the pacific settlement of disputes and preventive diplomacy, like the preventive diplomacy conducted by the UN Preventive Deployment Force (UNPREDEP) and the OSCE in the former Yugoslav Republic of Macedonia (FYROM) in the 1990s. The UN and the OSCE have had an agreement to coordinate their activities since May 1993, which reflects a political will to develop consistency and continuity in their cooperation.[12]

Practice and Prospects for Cooperation
Between European Security Organizations

The building of ESDP is not only changing the EU's relations with the UN, but also those with NATO and the OSCE. The EU is currently developing military and civilian capabilities for crisis management that intensify the problems of duplication, overlapping, and influence between the three main organizations on the continent. The development of ESDP tends to put into question the idea of comparative advantage. This idea assumes that military matters should be dealt with by NATO, economic matters by the EU, and democratic and human rights matters by the OSCE. The tacit division of labor, under which the EU and to some degree also the OSCE were responsible for "soft security" issues and NATO was responsible for the use of "hard power," is no longer valid. To an increasing extent, NATO has engaged in the protection of humanitarian aid, for instance, while the EU is developing "hard power" through the emerging ESDP.

EU-NATO Cooperation: The Risk of Duplication

The emerging EU military capability should also be seen in the context of EU-NATO and Europe-U.S. relations. Regarding EU-NATO cooperation, the core question is the assessment of intervention capabilities. One way of dealing with the issue of duplication and interoperability would be to define a set of standards aimed at strengthening the military performance of the Alliance as a whole, and another aimed at developing that of the EU.[13] According to the Helsinki Headline Goals and the Göteborg European Council, EU-NATO cooperation should rest on a regular dialogue with permanent arrangements for consultation and cooperation between the two.[14] The statement from the EU summit in June 2001 also emphasized coordination, transparency, and the fullest possible participation of the non-EU European allies in the emerging EU crisis management capabilities.[15]

Political statements cannot disclose, however, the sense of competition that exists between the two organizations. The EU military posture under development is likely to reduce the degree of dependence on U.S. forces in the management of crises in Europe's periphery. In spite of the divisions opened up by the Iraq crisis in 2003, the EU is one of the few institutions that can be developed in order to balance U.S. world dominance. How much room there is for an autonomous European crisis management capability after NATO defined crisis management as one of its core functions has become a question of cooperation as well as of competition.[16] Although the EU has access to NATO forces for an EU-led operation when the Alliance as a whole is not engaged, the necessary quantitative and qualitative U.S. national assets may not be available if, for example, the United States is engaged in a crisis elsewhere.[17] And in any case, the United States would expect to be consulted before the EU initiates an operation. In that event, the United States might grant access to its national assets on the condition that it obtains some influence. The latter scenario is less probable in the case of a major crisis. Even when such access is granted, Europe may want an operation to be less dependent on changes in U.S. defense budgets or a shift in U.S. public opinion that could lead to troop withdrawals in the middle of a mission. Whether or not the EU could legitimately initiate an operation without involving the United States in this decision remains an issue for debate.

In March 2001 EU-NATO cooperation was faced with a practical challenge that required cooperation: finding a political solution to the crisis in Macedonia. Secretary-General Lord Robertson, High Representative for the CFSP Javier Solana, and John Pardew for the United States paid several visits to the region and led the negotiations with the government of FYROM and the representatives of the Albanian community. In the subsequent operation, Amber Fox, NATO provided security for EU monitors who supervised the return of refugees who had fled their towns and villages during the fighting. In April 2003, the EU took over from NATO in FYROM, thereby establishing its first military mission (Concordia).

EU-OSCE Cooperation: A New
Geographical and Functional Division of Labor?

The OSCE is the only pan-European security organization that has both a Euro-Atlantic and a Euro-Asian dimension ("from Vancouver to Vladivostok"). It is also the most important norm-building organization in Europe. The tasks of the OSCE are threefold (known as the Helsinki "baskets"): security issues; economic, scientific, technology, and environmental issues; and human-dimension issues.[18] OSCE member states have managed to imprint the development of a political community by contributing to the building of civil societies in the former Eastern bloc through political dialogue and a liberal normative structure.[19] Besides, while crisis management is hampered by strategic considerations and limited by the "out-of-area" *problématique,* norms can travel. For instance, NATO seems to have been heavily inspired by the OSCE norms in its partnership strategy as well as in its enlargement strategy. The earlier and more thoroughly that states adhere to the liberal norms (human rights, pluralism, the rule of law, democracy, market economy) of domestic and international conduct, the earlier they will become NATO and EU members.[20]

The OSCE disposes of a set of institutions and mechanisms to promote respect for its democratic norms. Under the commitments known as the "human dimension," these institutions are the High Commissioner on National Minorities (HCNM), the Office for Democratic Institutions and

Human Rights (ODIHR), and the Representative on the Freedom of the Media. OSCE conflict prevention efforts also include security-related economic, social, and environmental issues, reflected in the establishment of the OSCE Coordinator for Economic and Ecological Activities in 1997. In 1994 the Budapest summit adopted the "Code of Conduct on Political and Military Aspects of Security." The OSCE is first and foremost a civilian organization dealing with "soft security." Its member states have been reluctant to cross that border.

The first occasion when the OSCE stretched this principle in practice was the Kosovo Verification Mission (KVM), which entailed the deployment of approximately 1,600 unarmed civilian verifiers (the goal was 2,000) throughout Kosovo starting in December 1998. The KVM was mandated to verify compliance with the agreement between the OSCE and the Federal Republic of Yugoslavia (FRY) of October 15, 1998, which came about as a result of NATO's activation order for air strikes on Serbian military targets issued on October 13. Noncompliance with the OSCE-FRY agreement would imply that the activation order would enter into force. After several violations of the agreement and futile mediation efforts, the KVM was terminated and NATO started the air campaign against the FRY. Thus, although OSCE peacekeeping capacities are limited, the OSCE Chairman-in-Office (rotating on an annual basis) may appeal to organizations like NATO or the UN (and now the EU) to enforce sanctions on OSCE member states that deliberately and repeatedly violate OSCE norms and agreements.

Partly in response to the shortcomings of the KVM, the Istanbul summit in 1999 gave the OSCE some capacities in the field of peacekeeping, such as the Operation Center within the Secretariat for planning and implementing OSCE field operations and the REACT (Rapid Expert Assistance and Cooperation Teams) mechanism. The latter was established to facilitate and improve the selection and the recruitment of personnel for field missions. The OSCE currently runs eight missions throughout Europe and heads five centers in Central Asia. The consensus rule in the OSCE Permanent Council,[21] and the rule of consent of the host country in establishing operations, limit the type of action conducted by the OSCE.[22]

The OSCE is currently facing three major problems: the place of Russia within the organization, the reform of its institutions, and the building of (potentially competitive) EU civilian capacities, such as policing. The OSCE is the only security organization in Europe in which Russia enjoys full membership rights. The Budapest OSCE summit in 1994 launched a debate on a common and comprehensive security model for the twenty-first century based on OSCE principles and commitments. The idea was to launch "a broad and comprehensive discussion on all aspects of security," which would culminate in a European security pact that could define the European security architecture and the role of the OSCE within it.[23] The Russian government promoted a security model that could provide it with a more prominent place in European security cooperation. Russian authorities have found that the OSCE is focusing too much on the human dimension and have stressed the need to restore the balance between the three "baskets." According to Russian officials, by making the OSCE an instrument of preventive diplomacy instead of using existing OSCE mechanisms, the United States and other NATO members have made the OSCE a vehicle of Western ideas of democracy, to the detriment of Russian interests. Officials have claimed that NATO has impeded work on the Charter for European Security in an effort to make it "a sort of a supplement to the NATO strategic conception adopted in Washington."[24] Due to the disagreement between Russia and the major Western OSCE member states on this issue, the charter implies a less ambitious role of the OSCE in European security than first proposed by the Russian authorities.

The reform proposals of the Romanian Chairman-in-Office in 2001 aimed at creating three committees, corresponding to the three "baskets," under the Permanent Council, partly to meet some of Russia's criticisms, but mostly to create clearer lines of authority between the organs. These proposals also included the strengthening of the Secretariat, which could increase the institutional memory and the political continuity of the organization and also lead to the establishment of a "lessons-learned" capacity. Since the increasing tasks and missions of the OSCE are reducing the ability of the Chairman-in-Office to follow up OSCE commitments and activities, more resources should also be given to the Conflict Prevention Center.

The EU claims that the scope of civilian capacities for prevention and peacebuilding under ESDP covers the whole area of the EU and its partners. Consequently, the geographical scope of OSCE activity might become focused on the Caucasus and Central Asia, whereas the functional scope of OSCE activity might become more focused on the activities of the human dimension (the latter trend was reflected by the ninth OSCE Ministerial Council in Bucharest in December 2001).[25] This does not exclude OSCE intervention in other parts of Europe, but this would most likely be at the request of the EU.

Perspectives for Cooperation
Between the UN and the EU

The development of the political and military capacities of the European Union opens new perspectives for cooperation between international organizations. At the opening of the fifty-fifth session of the General Assembly, the Chairman-in-Office of the European Council, French foreign minister Hubert Védrine, considered it "vital [that the EU] establishes working ties with the UN" in crisis management.[26] At the Göteborg summit, the Swedish EU Presidency considered that "the European Union's evolving military and civilian capacities provide real added value for the UN crisis management activities."[27] This includes conflict prevention and peacebuilding, but the declaration also shows that the member states already see the EU as a regional organization capable of assisting the UN in crisis management. But will the European group at the UN, after the establishment of its military tools, also act as a military arm of the Security Council?

The Various Tools at the EU's Disposal

The EU (the European Council together with the European Commission) has created various tools in order to deal with the whole spectrum of crisis management. The EU will become the sole regional institution in Europe to possess the whole range of civilian and military mechanisms and tools for managing a crisis from its latent (preconflict) stage to its escalation (conflict) stage to its postconflict (peacebuilding) stage.[28]

The EU has built, under the strategic control of the Political and Security Committee (PSC), a number of civilian and military crisis management structures: a Civil Crisis Management Committee, a European Military Staff, a Military Committee, a Situation Center, a Satellite Center, a Committee of Contributors, and an ESDP budget.[29] The competence in civilian crisis management is shared between the European Council and the European Commission. The Commission has built structures for conflict prevention, such as the European Union Monitoring Mission (EUMM), which is conducting border monitoring in southeastern Europe and also monitors political and security developments, including interethnic issues and refugee returns. In February 2001 the Commission created an EU Rapid Reaction Mechanism, aimed at allowing the EU to mobilize existing instruments to be deployed and to disburse funds quickly in response to crises or emerging crises. The Commission's nonmilitary assistance program works on the premise that development assistance is the best form of conflict prevention.[30] The Commission finances numerous UN agencies, contributing, for example, 25 percent of the total budget of the UN High Commissioner for Refugees (UNHCR). Therefore, financial aid under the integrated pillar (Pillar I) forms part of EU "foreign" action. The Commission has been engaged in a major reform to mainstream its assistance across the EU's external relations in order to ensure that conflict prevention is consistently taken into account in all its relevant aspects, including ESDP, development cooperation, and trade.[31] The Göteborg summit in June 2001 endorsed the EU Program for the Prevention of Violent Conflicts, which will improve the EU's capacity to undertake coherent early warning, analysis, and action.

Regarding civilian and peacebuilding capacities, the EU Feira summit in June 2000 adopted a civilian headline goal of 5,000 police personnel by 2003, of whom 1,400 should be available for rapid deployment within thirty days. In

January 2003, 469 officers were deployed as the EU Police Mission in Bosnia and Herzegovina. The EU is also working on capability initiatives regarding the deployment of judges, prosecutors, prison chiefs, and the like, in the postcrisis stage of peace operations. The military headline goal adopted by the 1999 Helsinki European Council involves the deployment (from 2003) of 50,000 to 60,000 combat troops within sixty days and sustainable for at least twelve months. The EU declared itself operational at the Laeken European summit in December 2001, tested this operationality in Macedonia, and envisions taking over the NATO Stabilization Force (SFOR) in BiH in 2004. The EU is not building a "European army" but a collective military capacity capable of conducting the full range of Petersberg tasks.[32] Each member state will participate in the military operations according to its own interest,[33] and will have a voice in the decisionmaking process accordingly (the rule of constructive abstention implies that member states who choose not to participate in a given action cannot stop the action from taking place). It is worth mentioning that the EU may conduct military operations with the participation of non-EU countries. Norway and Turkey have designated forces to the EU and, provided that their contribution is considerable, will participate in the committee of contributors responsible for the daily running of a potential EU-led operation.

EU military capacity has three main objectives: to provide the EU with a "stick," or a capacity for action to ensure that the common foreign policy decisions of the EU are respected; to preserve the autonomy of EU decisions; and to avoid confining the EU as an economic and financial instrument for actions led by others. These tools do not in themselves lead to a common European vision for crisis management, but the building of an ESDP within CFSP should lead toward that goal. ESDP first of all provides common principles for action. A military capability also forms part of the development toward "an ever closer union" and is a logical step after the establishment of a common monetary policy through the creation of the euro. These steps contribute to reinforcing the European integration process,[34] and will help the EU to fully take its place on the international scene. The various instruments at the disposal of the EU also question the issue of coordination between the policies led within the EU (between the Commission, the High Representative, the Committee of Permanent Representatives [Coreper], and the PSC), and between those led by the EU and its member states within the UN system and in other international organizations.[35] Lack of such coordination represents a potential obstacle to the EU force projection capacity.

The European Union at the UN:
A Lobby and a Group of Influence

At the UN, the European Union is currently a lobby group, equivalent to the nonaligned or Group of 77. The European group is organized around the EU

Presidency, talking on behalf of the EU member states and also on behalf of central and eastern states associated with the EU, of EU candidates, and of European Economic Agreement (EEA) member states if they want to join the declaration or statement in question. The weekly meetings (daily during the debates on Iraq between January and March 2003) at the ambassadorial or expert level are aimed at elaborating common positions for all UN working groups, commissions, and committees on issues that are on the agenda of the Security Council, and at preparing the speeches of the EU Presidency within those organs for public debates of the General Assembly or during official meetings of the Security Council. Each year the EU Presidency gives a speech at the opening session of the General Assembly.

Whenever a common position or action is adopted, the EU member states, including the permanent members of the Security Council, must support it. According to Article 19 of the Amsterdam Treaty, member states should "coordinate their action in international organizations and at international conferences: Member States represented in international organizations or international conferences where not all the Member States participate shall keep the latter informed of any matter of common interest." This also holds for those EU states that are members of the Security Council. Moreover, "Member States which are permanent members of the Security Council will, in the execution of their functions, ensure the defense of the positions and the interests of the Union, without prejudice to their responsibilities under the provisions of the United Nations Charter."

However, one must distinguish the Security Council debates from the General Assembly debates. Despite the provisions of the Amsterdam Treaty, the speeches of the EU Presidency at the Security Council are rather rare (in 1999, 15 out of 123 official meetings), although they are the rule within the General Assembly. In the specific case of the work in the Security Council, national positions and points of view still dominate. European statements weigh more when spoken for and are defended separately by France and the United Kingdom. In any case, despite the share of financial contributions borne by the Europeans (36 percent compared to 22 percent by the United States), they have not managed to transform financial strength into political leverage, which could provide the EU with greater weight in the debates of the UN institutions.[36]

The Modalities of a Future Cooperation: The European Union at the UN's Service?

The Göteborg summit identified different types of operations involving the EU and other international organizations:

> EU Member States can contribute nationally to an operation led by international organizations without any EU coordination; EU Member States can

contribute nationally to such an operation but following EU consultations; a coordinated EU contribution could be provided to an operation led by an international organization; the EU could provide and lead a whole component (e.g., police) in an operation under the overall lead of an international organization; the EU could lead an operation but with some components provided by international organizations; the EU could lead an autonomous operation.[37]

These scenarios raise two interconnected questions: the geographical scope of EU action, and the mandate of any EU military operation within or outside that scope.

EU civilian and military means would primarily be used for crises emerging on the territories of the EU member states and EU partners. According to current international law, the Security Council is the only body that can provide legal authorization for the use of force. Article 53 of Chapter VIII of the UN Charter requires that "no enforcement action shall be taken under regional arrangements without the authorization of the Security Council." In the case of a military crisis in Europe that threatens international or regional peace and security, the EU will have to seek this mandate, and even more so since Russia, a permanent member of the Security Council, belongs to the architecture of European security. However, NATO justified the air campaign in the FRY during the Kosovo conflict in 1999 with reference not only to the need to stop human rights atrocities and "human suffering" but also to the need "to bring stability to the region" and "to prevent instability spreading in the region."[38] The question of whether or not NATO had a sufficient UN mandate for the campaign was highly controversial in a number of NATO countries. The question is whether this will become a precedent for enforcement actions undertaken by the EU.

According to Javier Solana, the quality and interoperability of the EU forces and the complementary nature of its contingents could strengthen UN peacekeeping capacities, and Western states could again be involved in UN peace operations under satisfactory conditions. The High Representative has defended the possibility that EU rapid intervention forces can assist the UN in managing crises similar to the UN operations in Sierra Leone and in the Great Lakes region.[39] The EU could have taken over command of the International Security and Assistance Force (ISF) in Afghanistan but chose not to and NATO filled the role instead. The EU will possess military means that could be projected, if the UN Security Council deemed it necessary, outside the European continent, for example in Lebanon or Palestine. The EU would thus be able to contribute to world stability and to participate in UN peacemaking. According to Roland Galharague, "ESDP could allow to provide more than isolated units; it could provide a package of capacities, or even the entire structure of an operation."[40] Despite its readiness to put its civilian and military means at the disposal of the UN, the EU will want to retain the control of the operation. To that end, specific mechanisms for decisionmaking (relations between the UN Security Council and the EU Political and Security Committee and/or the Ministerial Council) and operational conduct (relations between the DPKO and the EU Military Committee) would have to be established.

Conclusion

This study on the place of European regional institutions in crisis management has raised several new questions. Is there a complementarity between the universal (UN) and the regional level? Which principles should guide the cooperation between the UN and regional organizations: comparative advantages and strengths or geographical scope? How is the European security architecture likely to be shaped in the near future? The answers to these questions have essential strategic, tactical, and operational implications that need further research.

It seems today that the structuring of regionalism does not prejudice universalism. On the contrary, in many cases cooperation allows for a strengthening of the maintenance of universal peace and security. Multilateral institutions do not necessarily constrain the individual action of states in the case of a crisis. However, states often prefer ad hoc multilateralism, in the manner of informal groups of negotiation or coalitions of the willing, to institutional multilateralism. In these circumstances, cooperation between the UN and regional organizations does not follow a linear track but is evolving around specific actions or operations and takes the form of informal consultations between heads of organizations, joint seminars, working groups, and the like. This approach and behavior allows states to progressively agree on common concepts and working procedures, as well as on common capacities for action. In turn, this may contribute to bringing about greater convergence between national policies, to reaching joint decisions, and to improving interoperability. The UN is the highest level where states can make visible the efforts undertaken at a regional level. Being heard at the General Assembly or at the Security Council makes a regional organization visible at the world level. It is in these arenas that the EU will be able to give the greater echo to the achievements of its common foreign policy. It is also through the UN that the EU will be able to seek legitimacy for actions conducted to stabilize its borders.

The myriad of tasks involved in contemporary peace operations will undoubtedly provide international organizations with ample workloads that could be distributed among them, but on which grounds? Comparative strengths give few clues, since all the organizations have similar capacities at their disposal. NATO wants to increase its civilian capacities and has elaborated a civil-military cooperation concept. A geographical division of labor in civilian matters could be feasible between the OSCE and the EU. Both organizations may contribute to conflict prevention and postconflict peacebuilding by acting as gatekeepers as well as exporters of international norms, but in different regions. The OSCE could also become a subcontractor for the EU, conducting specific tasks, most likely in the civilian domain, in the EU area. At the same time, regional organizations like the EU and the OSCE pursue their own agendas and goals and are not waiting for others to define their roles. Finally, the politics of choice by the United States and by the major European powers, which have been clearly visible in the division of roles between the international organizations in the conflicts in former Yugoslavia, are also likely to have an impact in the future. In practice, international and regional organizations often function as instruments in the hands of the participating states.

The European continent covers a series of geographical areas (western Europe, central Europe, eastern Europe, Balkan Europe, Mediterranean Europe, and Nordic Europe) and several international organizations and cooperation processes.[41] The EU is a unique international actor with great power ambitions aimed at ensuring stability on the whole continent and beyond. However, the OSCE is the only regional organization in Europe in which both the United States and the Russian Federation are members.

To conclude, the civilian and military management of complex crises remains the main challenge for cooperation between the UN and regional organizations. Cooperation and coordination must take place at all levels and all stages of a crisis, involving an exchange of information and distribution of responsibilities between each organization. The value of this cooperation lies in the fact that each organization is bringing to the other its experience, its expertise, and its lessons learned for the benefit of wider security.

Notes

1. "According to the practice of the Security Council, any particular arrangement, regardless of its membership, its mandate or its scope of action, is able to be considered as a regional arrangement according to the provisions of Article 52§1, as long as its action concretely corresponds to the wide notion of maintenance of international peace and security." Jorge Cadona Llorens, "La Coopération entre les Nations Unies et les accords et organismes régionaux pour le règlement pacifique des affaires relatives au maintien de la paix et de la sécurité internationales," in Boutros Boutros-Ghali, *Paix, développement, démocratie,* vol. 1 (Brussels: Bruylant, 1998), p. 264. See also Danesh Sarooshi, *The United Nations and the Development of Collective Security: The Delegation by the UN Security Council of Its Chapter VII Powers* (Oxford: Oxford University Press, 1999), pp. 251–253.

2. According to Luisa Vierucci, the "WEU has never declared itself to be a regional organization in the strict sense of chapter VIII of the charter of the United Nations, in order not to create confusion in the mind of the public on the autonomy of

action it has by virtue of Article 51 and Article 48." Luisa Vierucci, *WEU: A Regional Partner for the United Nations,* Chaillot Paper no. 12 (Paris: WEU Institute for Security Studies, December 1993). According to Danesh Sarooshi, "the combination of the Council delegating tasks in the area of peace and security to NATO and the self-redefinition of NATO to carry out tasks which are in addition to its original mandate under the NATO Charter, allow it to fit within the rubric of a Chapter VIII regional arrangement." Sarooshi, *The United Nations,* p. 250. However, this interpretation is recent. At the beginning, the drafters of NATO did not consider it a regional arrangement of Article 52, since the actions undertaken through NATO were based on the natural right of collective self-defense (Article 51). See Djamchid Momtaz, "La Délégation par le Conseil de sécurité de l'exécution de ses actions coercitives aux organisations régionales," *Annuaire Français de Droit International* 63 (1997): 107–108.

3. The annex of Resolution 1244 is the only one that expressly mentions NATO. The resolutions authorizing the deployment of IFOR and SFOR only mention "Member States acting through or in cooperation with the organization referred to in Annex 1-A of the Peace Agreement." However, it is obvious that the authors of the resolutions on the conflicts in the former Yugoslavia were implicitly mentioning NATO considered as the military arm of the Security Council.

4. Speech by Roland Galharague, deputy director of the Analysis and Prevention Center of the French Foreign Ministry, seminar on "The United Nations, Europe, and Crisis Management," WEU Institute for Security Studies, October 20, 2000.

5. According to Roland Galharague (ibid.), "the European Union is not and will not be a regional organization of collective security of Chapter VIII of the UN Charter. However this does not prevent it from contributing to the actions of the United Nations."

6. Among others: Resolution 503 (VI) of the General Assembly of January 12, 1952; Agenda for Peace of 1992; Declaration on the Enhancement of Cooperation Between the United Nations and Regional Arrangements or Agencies in the Maintenance of International Peace and Security, of the General Assembly of December 1994 (A/RES/49/57); and more recently, the Brahimi Report of August 2000.

7. For example, NATO's 1999 Strategic Concept states in paragraph 14 that "the UN, the OSCE, the EU and the WEU have made distinctive contributions to Euro-Atlantic security and stability. Mutually reinforcing organizations have become a central feature of the security environment."

8. Céline Chamot, "Vers un partage des responsabilités entre les Nations Unies et les organisations régionales dans le maintien de la paix?" *L'Observateur des Nations Unies* no. 5 (1998): 57.

9. See Vierucci, *WEU,* for further details on the UN-WEU cooperation during those operations and the Yugoslav conflict.

10. The head of OMIK attends UNMIK daily Executive Committee meetings and is a member of the Interim Administrative Council and Kosovo Transitional Councils. The OSCE is also part of the UNMIK Joint Planning Group. See United Nations, *Report of the Secretary-General on Cooperation Between the UN and the OSCE,* UN Doc. A/56/125, June 29, 2001.

11. See Michèle Griffin, "Blue Helmet Blues," *Security Dialogue* 30, no. 1 (March 1999): 43–61.

12. A/RES/48/5, October 13, 1993. The OSCE defined itself as a "regional arrangement" of Chapter VIII, which implied the recognition of the legal, political, and moral authority of the UN. The OSCE concluded an agreement for cooperation and coordination with the UN (May 26, 1993) that committed both organizations to "ensure the coordination and the two-fold complementarity of planning and imple-

mentation of activities, to avoid overlapping and help one another," especially in the field of prevention and peaceful settlement of disputes.

13. François Heisbourg, *European Defence: Making It Work,* Chaillot Paper no. 42 (Paris: WEU Institute for Security Studies, September 2000), p. 6.

14. European Union, *Presidency Conclusions,* Göteborg European Council, June 15–16, 2001, chap. 5, para. 49.

15. Para. 6 in the Göteborg statement. In the *Presidency Conclusions* of the Göteborg European Council, however, participation is granted to non-EU European NATO members and other states *that are candidates to EU accession.*

16. Although not made explicit, the effective sidelining of collective defense and non–Article 5 tasks is expressed in several paragraphs of *The Alliance's Strategic Concept* (see, e.g., pt. 1, para. 6.), adopted at the North Atlantic Council meeting in Washington, DC, on April 23–24, 1999.

17. Arrangements for the assured EU access to NATO military planning capabilities for EU-led operations and the presumption of preidentified NATO capabilities and common assets available to the EU for use in such operations were agreed upon in December 2002.

18. The Helsinki Final Act, adopted by the CSCE in 1975, sets out ten principles in a "decalogue": sovereign equality of states; nonuse of threat or force; inviolability of borders; territorial integrity of states; peaceful settlement of disputes; nonintervention in internal affairs; respect of human rights and basic freedoms including freedom of thought, of conscience, of religion or conviction; equality in the rights of peoples and right to self-determination; cooperation between states; and implementation of obligations according to international law. Several of the OSCE norms are contradictory, such as, for example, the principle of territorial integrity of states, the right to self-determination, nonintervention in internal affairs, and respect for basic human rights and freedoms. A dilemma between two or more of these principles is often present in the areas in which the OSCE is involved, as in Chechnya and Kosovo.

19. Emmanuel Adler, "Seeds of Peaceful Change: The OSCE's Security Community-Building Model," in Emmanuel Adler and Michael Barnett, eds., *Security Communities* (Cambridge: Cambridge University Press, 1998), p. 121.

20. Frank Schimmelfennig, *NATO's Enlargement to the East: An Analysis of Collective Decisionmaking,* EAPC-NATO Individual Fellowship Report, 1998–2000, www.nato.int.

21. Consensus-minus-one was introduced in order to suspend Yugoslavia from the OSCE in 1992 but has not been used since.

22. For example, a fact-finding mission to Chechnya established by the OSCE Istanbul summit was denied access to the conflict area by Russian authorities shortly after the summit. The OSCE Assistance Group to Chechnya, closed down in 2000, was not allowed to return until June 2001.

23. Organization for Security and Cooperation in Europe, *Towards a Genuine Partnership in a New Era,* chap. 7, "A Common and Comprehensive Security Model for Europe for the Twenty-First Century," Budapest, 1994, www.osce.org/docs/english/1990-1999/summits/buda94e/htm.

24. Boris Kazantsev, "NATO: Obvious Bias to the Use of Force," in *International Affairs* (Moscow: Russian Ministry of Foreign Affairs, 1999). Kazantsev is deputy director of the European Cooperation Department of the Ministry of Foreign Affairs.

25. See European Union, *Statements by the Ministerial Council,* MC(9).DEC/2, December 4, 2001.

26. Speech at the fifty-fifth session of the General Assembly, September 12, 2000.

27. European Union, *Presidency Conclusions,* Göteborg European Council, June 15–16, 2001.

28. As the CFSP High Representative said, "establishing a military capability is an important element of a properly functioning CFSP. But it has to go hand-in-hand with the development of adequate civilian capabilities. . . . If we are serious and effective in creating enhanced civilian capabilities, the EU will be able to play a unique role across the full range of humanitarian and peacekeeping tasks." Javier Solana, speech at the Danish Institute of International Affairs, Copenhagen, February 11, 2000.

29. This budget concerns only the "administrative" part of ESDP (the running of ESDP structures). In a EU-led operation, each state will pay its military contribution. On the structures of the EU, see Jean Dufourcq, "L'Engagement européen dans la gestion des crises: Un point de situation militaire," *Annuaire Français de Relations Internationales* 3 (2002): 480–485.

30. Scholars and practitioners generally accept the linkage between development, poverty, and conflict. See, for example, Dan Smith and Nina Græger, eds., *Environment, Poverty, Conflict,* PRIO Report no. 2/94 (Oslo: Peace Research Institute, 1994). This was more recently confirmed in Kofi Annan's *Millennium Report:* "Every step taken towards reducing poverty and achieving broad-based economic growth is a step toward conflict prevention." United Nations, *The Role of the United Nations in the Twenty-First Century: The Millennium Report,* UN Doc. A/54/2000 (New York: UN Department of Information, 2000), p. 45. The EU contributes to conflict prevention, first and foremost, by projecting its civil and economic powers of attraction to the east and to the south through a differentiated enlargement process. The EU has a disciplinary effect on its "near abroad" by demanding that states abide to a set of common rules and principles (the *acquis,* the rule of law, the human rights charter, etc.) in return for substantial financial transfers, regional assistance programs, access to the internal market, and eventually full membership.

31. The reform includes the decentralization of the assistance program to enable the Commission to take the majority of decisions on the spot. Furthermore, a new body, EuropeAid, is responsible for the implementation of the whole life cycle of aid projects and manages about 80 percent of all EU assistance. See "Enhancing the EU's Response to Violent Conflict: Moving Beyond Reaction to Preventive Action," *Conference Report and Policy Recommendations,* p. 12. See also European Union, *Presidency Conclusions,* Göteborg European Council, June 15–16, 2001, par. 52.

32. The Petersberg tasks include humanitarian and evacuation missions, peacekeeping missions, and combat-force missions for crisis management, including missions to restore peace.

33. Finland is one obvious case, where participation in peace enforcement is prohibited by legislation. Also, Denmark does not take part in issues related to security and defense under Pillar II of the Treaty on European Union. See Heisbourg, *European Defence,* an analysis of the different approaches of member states regarding military operations.

34. "[T]he progress made towards a European defense . . . is part of a deep-seated and more general trend towards European integration," as pointed out by President Jacques Chirac. Address to the Special Meeting of the North Atlantic Council, with the participation of heads of state and government, Brussels, June 13, 2001, quoted in *Bulletin Quotidien Europe* no. 7983, June 14, 2001, p. 4.

35. The EU Helsinki summit established a Coordinating Mechanism in the Council Secretariat, which interacted closely with Commission services to examine the nonmilitary crisis management tools at the EU's disposal. But coordination remains the key challenge for the various structures of the EU. See Michael Matthiessen, *Enhancing the EU's Response to Violent Conflict: Moving Beyond Reaction to Preventive*

Action, Conference Report and Policy Recommendations (Brussels: International Security Information Service [ISIS] and Heinrich Böll Foundation, December 2000), p. 16.

36. The European Union is the biggest financial contributor to the UN system. With 30 percent of world gross national product, the EU contributes 36 percent of the UN budget, 39 percent of the peacekeeping budget, 50 percent of the budget for UN funds and programs, and 54 percent of world public development aid. These figures are "extraordinarily in discrepancy with the political influence" of the EU. Afsané Bassir Pour, "A l'ONU, le poids politique de l'UE reste en deçà de son poids financier," *Le Monde,* September 17–18, 2000.

37. *Presidency Report to the European Council of Göteborg,* annex 5, "EU Cooperation with International Organizations in Civilian Aspects of Crisis Management."

38. Press statement of Javier Solana, Secretary-General of NATO, March 23, 1999, NATO Press Release (1999)040, www.nato.int.

39. "Javier Solana Pleads for a European Intervention Force That Cooperates with the UN in World Crises," *La Vanguardia,* May 18, 2000.

40. Galharague, speech at the seminar on "The United Nations, Europe, and Crisis Management," WEU Institute for Security Studies, October 20, 2000.

41. For example, the Barcelona Process in the Mediterranean, the Kiel Process in the Nordic region, and the Stability Pact in the Balkans.

6

Russia, the UN, and NATO: Prospects for Cooperation

Emily Metzgar and Andrei Z. Zagorski

Practical interaction between the United Nations and the North Atlantic Treaty Organization (NATO) has been a growing phenomenon since the mid-1990s, mainly in the context of the peace operations in Bosnia-Herzegovina and in Kosovo (Yugoslavia). There, a variety of UN representatives work hand in hand with NATO troops, as well as with other international organizations and institutions to implement the work prescribed by the international agreements adopted by, or put under the general auspices of, the UN Security Council.

Despite this trend, there is no explicit Russian discourse on UN-NATO cooperation, almost as if this phenomenon were nonexistent. This is due in part to the uneasy relationship between Russia and NATO, especially with regard to the role of the latter in the Balkans in the late 1990s. Lack of analysis of this trend is also due to implicit and explicit Russian foreign policy discourse, both inherited from Soviet times and that emerged from evolving Russian views of international politics through the 1990s.

Instead of searching for a nonexistent Russian discourse on UN-NATO cooperation, this chapter seeks to extract relevant implications for that cooperation from the perspective of Russian foreign policy makers focusing on the European security environment. It begins with a discussion of the context of Russian foreign policy and the evolution of both UN and NATO discourses in Russian foreign policy during the last decade. It continues with a more detailed analysis of Russian perceptions of the roles of the UN, NATO, and other European institutions, and of cooperation between them in post–Cold War Europe. Russian approaches to the evolving cooperation between the UN and NATO are then discussed. Finally, examples of and prospects for Russia-

NATO cooperation are considered. In the conclusion, implications of Russian policies for future UN-NATO cooperation are discussed.

Russian Foreign Policy in Context

Russia seeks to maximize its international leverage in the context of international institutions and understands that its influence is maximized when other nations, particularly the United States, are forced to follow the rules of the institution, instead of being free to pursue their interests unilaterally. Given diminished resources and influence, Russia uses institutions as a means of acquiring and sharing information, setting terms for negotiations, establishing norms of behavior, and limiting the costs of conducting international affairs. With Russia's precipitous decline in international influence since the end of the Cold War, it is not surprising that Russian foreign policy places an emphasis on multilateral institutions with binding rules that, in theory, help constrain the actions of more powerful states.

Russia also devotes attention to nurturing relationships with non-Western regional powers. While it is easy to overstate the importance of Russia's relationship with both India and China, any fair assessment of Russian foreign policy must acknowledge the improving cooperation among the three, particularly since the NATO air strikes in Yugoslavia and the U.S. invasion of Iraq. Shared concern about Islamic fundamentalism, hopes for a strengthened UN and an alternative to the U.S.-centered international system, increasing trade relations, and Russian arms sales to India and China form the basis of these growing relations. The commonalties of Russian and Chinese positions on UN Security Council votes related to Kosovo intervention reflect a further coincidence of interest between the two on matters of national sovereignty and territorial integrity.

Russian opposition to intervention should be seen as geopolitically, rather than ideologically, motivated. As Ekatarina Stepanova has suggested, "The key to understanding Russian policy on the conflict between Serbs and Albanians in Kosovo, as well as Russia's opposition to NATO air strikes against Yugoslavia, is realizing that it is only remotely related to the conflict itself."[1] Russia's position that only the UN has the authority to intervene in internal crises is likely to remain a theme of its relations with the West for the foreseeable future.

Russia's foreign policy in 2000 focused on rebuilding Moscow's relations with the West, both bilaterally and with organizations such as NATO and the European Union (EU). Russia is a participant in the NATO-led Kosovo Force (KFOR) peacekeeping operation enacted after the air strikes ended. Similarly, Russia-NATO Permanent Joint Council (PJC) meetings, which Russia suspended with the initiation of air strikes in Kosovo in 1999, have now resumed.

This cooperation is at least partially attributable to Russian pragmatism. Recognition that Russia relies on Western aid and trade results in practical policies that supersede lingering rhetoric.

Evolving Russian Views of International Politics

Russian discourse on international politics, the emerging post–Cold War world order, and visions of Russia's role have undergone a profound evolution over the last decade. Two aspects of this change are of particular importance in developing an understanding of Russia's relationships with the United Nations, NATO, and other international institutions.

From Romanticism to Multipolarity

The early 1990s were marked both by the inertia of foreign policy thinking in the late Gorbachev era and by what is now referred to as the political "romanticism" of the early democratization period after the collapse of the Soviet Union. Continuing the tradition of superpower politics from the second half of the twentieth century, the former Soviet political elite expected closer U.S.-Russian cooperation in maintaining a new world order after the Cold War. The institutions for cooperation were to be developed, inter alia, through realizing more effectively the potential of the UN Security Council in concert with the United States and other Western countries and through the progressive institutionalization of the Organization for Security and Cooperation in Europe (OSCE). Meanwhile, initiation and expansion of cooperative ties between the former Soviet Union and NATO would replace military confrontation in Europe.

This late-Soviet view of the new world order was not, however, aggressively pursued before the collapse of the Soviet Union. In retrospect, only a few examples of this approach can be identified. They include the Soviet Union's consent to UN Security Council efforts to control Iraqi aggression against Kuwait, the NATO London Declaration of July 1990, the Charter of Paris of November 1990, and early efforts to engage the Soviet Union with the Group of Seven (G7).

While retaining the expectation that both the UN and the OSCE would become major pillars of cooperation with the West in the post–Cold War world order, Russian leadership under Boris Yeltsin put much greater emphasis on parallel integration of Russia into the most relevant Western multilateral institutions. The desire to complete the transformation of the G7 into the G8, the desire to join the World Trade Organization, OECD development, institutionalization of relations with the European Union, and even early discussion of Russian membership in NATO were given priority in Russian foreign policy in the early 1990s. The ultimate goal of this policy was for a democratic Russia to become a full member of the transatlantic community.

This discourse began to change in the mid-1990s when Russian policymakers sensed increasing alienation from the transatlantic community. Controversy over NATO's eastward extension was one of the most important causes. The Russian policy elite began to think increasingly in geopolitical terms. When Evgenii Primakov became foreign minister in 1996, preferences shifted toward building a multipolar world, rather than the unipolar Pax Americana. Under this multipolar world view, the preference was to serve as an independent pole in international politics, rather than as an integral part of the transatlantic community. This would be achieved largely by exercising an assertive integration policy within the Commonwealth of Independent States (CIS) as well as by expanding Russian room for maneuver by intensified cooperation with China, India, or even Iran.

No part of this "multivector" policy was ever perceived by the Russian government as an alternative to close cooperation with the transatlantic community. However, it underlined a distinct identity and national interest that was to limit the extent to which Russia was prepared to engage in institutionalized relations with the West.

The Kosovo crisis, without directly challenging Russian foreign policy interests, highlighted the limits of Russia's intended cooperation with the West. In the aftermath of the crisis, the Russian midterm strategy toward the European Union made these limits explicit. By dismissing the option of eventual membership in the EU, an important strategy paper, handed over to the EU in October 1999, explained why:

> The Russia-EU partnership in the period in question is going to be based on contractual relations, i.e. without officially envisaging the goal of Russia's accession to or association with the EU. Being a world power located on two continents, Russia must maintain freedom of choice and action in her domestic and foreign policy, her status and privileges of a Euro-Asian state and those of the biggest country of the CIS, it must maintain the freedom of position and action within international organizations.[2]

Limits to Russia's Great Power Role

Parallel to the emphasis on maintaining freedom of action in international politics was an increasing recognition by the Russian political elite of the limits imposed on Russian politics by diminished resources. Although nostalgia for the superpower role of the former Soviet Union is still strong in the Russian elite (and largely within the society), it became increasingly evident that Russia was no longer able to perform as a global player. While great power rhetoric is still present in the public statements of Russian leaders, pragmatism became the leading characteristic of Russian foreign policy through the 1990s. This is increasingly so today.

The Russian political elite learned, especially in the second half of the 1990s, that Russian ability to shape developments even in close geographic areas, not to speak of the remote ones, had been drastically diminished. In pursuing its foreign policy objectives, Moscow has become dependent on the cooperation of other regional players. Developments in the 1990s clearly revealed Russia's inability to reach important foreign policy objectives whenever the major, or often even minor, actors went down another path.

Although Russia was successful in obtaining membership in the G8, this has not resulted in a substantial increase of influence. Moscow has been unable to pursue transformation of the OSCE into a regional security organization and has accepted the conception of a multi-institutional, nonhierarchical architecture for European security. It lost the battle against NATO's eastward expansion and was forced to adjust to the new environment by developing the Russia-NATO Founding Act of 1997.[3] Moscow learned that its resources were insufficient to consolidate the Russia-led CIS. Furthermore, Russian attempts to achieve goals set in the mid-1990s have not only been ineffective, but have also drawn on Russia's resources without increasing them and have contributed to the cooling of relations with the West, especially with the United States and United Kingdom on the issue of Iraq.

At the beginning of the twenty-first century, Russia retains only two attributes of a great power: the permanent seat and veto power within the UN Security Council, and a nuclear potential. Even those attributes, however, cannot guarantee Russia its desired position in the new world order, even as the old world order continues to erode.

Russian attempts to block Security Council decisions on Yugoslavia and Iraq, instead of increasing Russian importance, resulted in increasing circumvention of the Security Council by the United States and the UK. Such circumvention diminishes the role of Moscow. NATO air strikes against Yugoslavia in 1999 upset the Russian elite because the decision removed Russia from the joint decisionmaking process and rendered Russian positions irrelevant. Since then, most of Russia's efforts have been directed toward restoring the old world order, whereby the UN Security Council and its permanent members play the central role in maintaining international peace and security. This largely defensive approach was articulated in the May 2000 Foreign Policy Concept of the Russian Federation: "The United Nations Organization must remain the main center for the regulation of International Relations in the 21st Century. The Russian Federation will decisively oppose any attempts to diminish the role of the UN, and of its Security Council in the world politics."[4] Russia's status as a nuclear power is an increasingly important component of its great power role. With the disappearance of the Cold

War's bipolar standoff, there are relatively few political benefits to be extracted from a large arsenal of nuclear weapons. They are instead a deterrent and an option of last resort in the highly unlikely case of aggression against Russia. It has become increasingly difficult for Russia to orchestrate its remaining great power attributes to achieve its foreign policy objectives.

Russia in the United Nations

Russian foreign policy discourse admits the possibility of closer cooperation, or delegation of UN tasks in maintaining international peace and security to regional organizations or arrangements, according to Chapter VIII of the UN Charter. The need for such cooperation and delegation is especially acute in the post–Cold War era, when regional and local conflicts have clearly exceeded the capacity of the UN to deal with them.

Particularly since the NATO air strikes against Yugoslavia, Russian foreign policy places priority on strengthening of the role of the UN and of the Security Council. "In the 21st Century, the UN shall continue playing the role of the leading mechanism for the collective regulation of international relations, and the emerging multi-polar world order shall be based on the principles of the UN Charter and on the norms of the International Law."[5] To attain this stated goal, Russia's Foreign Policy Concept calls for the following:

The basic principles of the UN Charter, including the maintenance of the status of the permanent members of the Security Council, shall be strictly observed.

The UN should be reformed in a "rational" way, so that its ability to react rapidly to international developments, and its ability to prevent and resolve crises and conflicts, are enhanced.

The efficiency of the UN Security Council should be improved by making its composition more representative, but without questioning the veto power of its permanent members.[6]

The Russian program calls for strengthening the role of the UN instead of NATO. Russia hopes to prevent recurrence of a situation in which NATO acts to enforce peace without being sanctioned by the UN Security Council. The Russian proposal suggests:

The principle of nonuse of force or threat of force in international relations should be reconfirmed.

The UN Security Council should retain the exclusive authority to approve military enforcement measures by the international community, and such measures should be considered means of last resort in crisis management.

The UN should increasingly cooperate with regional and subregional organizations and arrangements in peacekeeping based on the provisions of Chapter VIII of the UN Charter.

In any case, the UN Security Council should provide tough political control of any military enforcement operation sanctioned by the Council and implemented by individual countries, a coalition of the willing, by regional or subregional organizations or arrangements.

Both human and material resources of the UN must be increased for it to cope with increasing challenges in the field of peacekeeping and peace enforcement.

The Military Staff Committee should play a more active role in UN peacekeeping.[7]

These suggestions belie Russia's desire to substantiate the exclusive right of the UN Security Council to make decisions about military measures. By extension, the Russian position calls for the enhancement of the Council's political capacity to lead such operations, while at the same time protecting the exclusive veto rights of all the Council's permanent members. While recognizing the reality of both political and physical overreach of UN peacekeeping, Russia also favors further development of cooperation between the UN and regional organizations and arrangements, not least in order to ensure political control over regional peacekeeping by the Security Council.

There are two important caveats to this potentially positive message for Russia's ideas about institutionalizing cooperation between the UN and NATO. First, NATO is almost explicitly excluded from Russian propositions for developing institutional cooperation with the UN. A thorough study of statements of Russian representatives on the issue clearly indicates that NATO is ignored in that context. It is only the CIS (most often) and the OSCE (in a few cases) that are mentioned in that context with regard to European security.

Politically, NATO is seen as the main challenger to the UN. Legally, NATO is regarded not as a regional security organization in the understanding of Chapter VIII of the UN Charter, but rather as a collective defense alliance under Article 51. Thus it would not be regarded as eligible for arrangements envisaged in Chapter VIII.

Second, apart from the exclusive rights of Russia as a permanent member of the Security Council, Moscow's weight and role within the UN beyond decisionmaking have substantially diminished since the end of the Cold War along with its weight in international politics in general. Once Russia agrees to a NATO-led operation under UN auspices, it would find events quickly developing beyond its control.

The primary objective of Russia's UN discourse is to ensure the continued role of the UN Security Council in maintaining international peace and security and Russia's privileges as a permanent member. It would be an uncomfortable development for Moscow if that role were to evolve toward increasing institutionalization of UN-NATO cooperation, unless Moscow's relationship with NATO were to improve significantly.

The United Nations as a Russian Foreign Policy Tool

Russia seeks to maximize its international leverage in the context of the UN Security Council. Russia believes that its influence is maximized if the United States is dragged into the Council and made to follow its rules, rather than left free to pursue its own interests unilaterally.

The United Nations in Russian Foreign Policy

In a March 2001 speech, Russian foreign minister Igor Ivanov spoke of the priority Russia places on enhancing the role of the United Nations, calling it "the leading multilateral instrument combining the efforts of states to ensure international security in all its dimensions."[8] He also referred to the need to enhance the UN's international role, since Russia is a permanent member of the Security Council and doing so would allow Russia to "uphold its national interests and directly participate in major international processes."[9]

The multilateral nature of the United Nations and other international institutions is an opportunity for countries like Russia. For many nations, the challenge is getting the United States to be subject to the rules of the international body. The frustration at failing to do so is particularly acute for Russia, as demonstrated in NATO's decision to launch air strikes against Yugoslavia and the U.S. invasion of Iraq without the sanctioning of the Security Council. Russia certainly ascribes to Celeste Wallander's view that "the UN may be more cumbersome than NATO for U.S. policy, but because the Security Council includes all the major powers, once it has resolved upon policy it has a legitimacy that NATO does not."[10]

Russia believes that the use of force as a response to humanitarian crises, while sometimes necessary, should only be carried out under the auspices of the Security Council, with proper consideration first given to issues of territorial integrity and state sovereignty. Russia further emphasizes the potential role of regional organizations in such UN interventions and suggests that regional organizations should strive to play a more active role in preventive diplomacy, postconflict peacebuilding, and peacekeeping. Russia has called for the "rational" distribution of responsibility between the UN and regional organizations.[11]

Russia's Security Council Membership:
Rights and Responsibilities

In the 1970s, the five permanent members of the UN Security Council were the top contributors to the UN's operating budget, but this is no longer the case. In the last twenty-five years, Russia's rank has slipped from being among the top six donor countries to tenth. There has been a similar decline in Russia's contribution to UN peacekeeping operations. And yet Russia does not hesitate to cast its vetoes in the Security Council.[12]

There is growing concern about the discrepancies between Russia's contributions to the UN and the privileges it retains as a permanent member of the Security Council. Such concerns have the potential to lessen Russia's influence and could lead to resentment by other member states and the belief that Russia's views can somehow be overlooked. Failure to meet the obligations of privileged membership has the potential of becoming a growing liability for Russia as it tries to promote its views of the world and retain its influence within the UN. Russia would do well to nurture its image as a "team player" with respect to its roles in the United Nations. The scuffle over intervention in Kosovo offers mixed results of Russia's efforts to exert influence in an institutional setting.

Russia's failed attempts to prevent NATO action in Kosovo and U.S.-UK action in Iraq are evidence of how multilateral organizations can be side-stepped by other institutions with the political will to act. The Security Council, the institution widely regarded as having the legal authority to intervene in Kosovo, was prevented from taking action by a small group opposed to such action for primarily domestic political reasons. NATO, armed and ready, stepped into the breach. For critics of the UN, this was another example of that organization's inability to act when it is most necessary. For critics of NATO, this was an example of its imperialistic ambitions. The Kosovo Report, the result of an investigation by the Independent International Commission on Kosovo, reads: "The war will be remembered as a turning-point: a compelling collective armed intervention for the express purpose of implementing UN Security Council resolutions but without UNSC authorization."[13]

Learning to Live with the Alliance

Russia's relationship with NATO has been troubled since discussion about expansion of the alliance began several years ago. Russia had long been opposed to NATO expansion and failed to swallow the U.S. argument that NATO's enlargement is about defense, not offense. Seeing NATO conducting air strikes over Yugoslavia showed Russia the true offensive ability of an alliance originally created to counter Soviet power. Russia is suspicious of

NATO's continued development and is concerned about its ability to deploy to areas ever closer to Russian borders, particularly in Central Asia. The fact that NATO's enlargement brings it ever closer to Russian borders is merely a physical representation of the threat Russia perceives.

There is consensus that disagreement between Russia and the West on NATO air strikes to resolve the Kosovo problem in 1999 forced a turning point in Russian foreign policy. There is disagreement only about the implications of this development. Some argue that Russia has now been irrevocably turned away from the West and that its incentives for cooperation with the United States and Europe on a variety of issues have been greatly diminished.

Others believe that although disappointed with NATO's unilateral decision to act, Russia has chosen to nurture its reputation as an independent thinker separate from the West, but not consistently in opposition to it. This is a fundamental distinction with a tremendous difference. In the worst-case scenario, Russia would choose to sacrifice the benefits of cooperation with the West in order to spite the United States and its partners and would pursue close cooperation with partners to the East, selling arms and disregarding the norms established through multilateral relations. In the more optimistic scenario, Russia would develop its own identity, but not necessarily an anti-Western one, forging links with European states that stand up to the United States.

Despite the strong language of Russia's Foreign Policy Concept of 2000, Russian cooperation in the peacekeeping operation implemented after the end of NATO air strikes in Kosovo seems to indicate Russia's preference for the less destructive scenario.[14] This should be good news for the West.

The Kosovo Report neatly summarizes the dilemma presented by Russian disagreement with NATO on military intervention in Kosovo: "Negotiation premised principally on ultimate and credible threats of military force depended either on Russia's approval (which the USA pushed for behind the scenes) or its exclusion (by relying on NATO over the UN), since such threats could not be credible as long as the FRY could count on a Russian veto."[15]

NATO made the decision for air strikes for a variety of reasons. Russia was reluctant to endorse the strong measures promoted by NATO members in the Contact Group and in the G8. At the same time, Russian opposition to military intervention had stymied the UN's ability to move beyond political options for settlement of the Kosovo issue. In March 1999, when NATO air strikes began, Russia froze its relations with NATO in the PJC and condemned the air strikes in the Security Council. NATO governments determined that military intervention not subject to Council vetoes was necessary to restore autonomy to Kosovo and to attain Council-determined goals.

Throughout the Kosovo crisis, the Russian government was especially concerned about the growth of U.S. influence in the Balkans. Many argue that Russia's willingness to participate in KFOR after air strikes ended was largely the result of a desire to counterbalance NATO's role on the ground. Russia felt threatened by U.S.-led NATO activity in a region hitherto considered, by Russia at least, part of the Slavic brotherhood.

NATO activity was also of concern to a nation already worried about NATO's expanded membership and the potential for additional expansion bringing NATO ever closer to Russia's borders. Furthermore, intervention in what Russia called an internal affair was protested for the precedent it could set, possibly leading to future action curbing Russian behavior in Chechnya, something Russia still considers a strictly internal affair.

Nascent Cooperation: A Hopeful Sign

Russia's KFOR Experience

Despite Russian condemnations of NATO's actions, Russian foreign minister Igor Ivanov referred to Russian cooperation with NATO forces in KFOR as "not bad" and as being suggestive of the potential further cooperation between the two parties.[16]

Although it condemned NATO's military intervention, Russia did play a role in the process of attaining peace in Kosovo. As a member of the Contact Group in 1998 and 1999, Russia worked diplomatically to promote a political solution in Kosovo, but refused to approve a Security Council resolution allowing forceful intervention. There was little disagreement among members about the desired end-state of affairs in Kosovo; the issue was instead one of method. The problem facing the Contact Group as it tried to promote a peaceful solution in Kosovo was that even though Russia was the most likely means of communication between the Contact Group and Slobodan Milošević, Russia's public opposition to the use of military force if a political solution could not be found undermined the international community's threat of the use of force as a last resort to compel Milošević to change his policies.[17]

Russia's Foreign Ministry issued the following statement on the second anniversary of NATO's initiation of air strikes against Yugoslavia. The Russian view of those events remains unchanged: it was "the first 'experiment' in the application of the concept of so called 'humanitarian intervention' as an instrument of interference in the internal affairs of other states. The desire to use the . . . Balkans for establishing a NATO-centrist model of European security were . . . revealed. Thanks to Russia's diplomatic efforts, the bacchanalia of NATO violence was eventually stopped, and the problem of Kosovo settlement channeled back into a political process based on UN Security Council Resolution 1244."[18]

Reservations about the manner in which NATO executed its intervention notwithstanding, Russia nevertheless contributed troops and participated in the follow-on peacekeeping operation. With the end of NATO air strikes, KFOR was deployed in June 1999. Russia initially challenged KFOR's role as the international force implementing UN Resolution 1244 by rushing to the airport in Pristina. This was short-lived, as Bulgaria, Hungary, and Romania were asked by NATO to deny Russian access to their airspace, thus cutting off Russian troops from resupply. With an agreement signed soon thereafter in Helsinki, Russia's role in the international peacekeeping force was agreed upon.[19] Although Russia was not allotted its own sector to police, its force of 3,600 was integrated into the German, U.S., and French sectors, with Russian troops under NATO's tactical control. This was no small feat given that Russia had frozen its relations with NATO to protest the initiation of air strikes.

Applying Lessons from SFOR

Russia's cooperation with KFOR built upon the experience of the Stabilization Force (SFOR) in Bosnia. This cooperation, although more symbolic than substantive, was evidence of an improving Russia-NATO relationship in the years before Kosovo, when the growing partnership was disrupted. In June 2000, Russia abstained from a vote extending SFOR for a twelve-month period because, although Russia has been one of the main participants in the Bosnia settlement, "the Russian Federation cannot [pass this resolution] because Russian amendments have not been taken on board."[20] Again, in NATO-led peacekeeping operations, Russia chafes at symbolic contributions it views as devoid of real responsibilities (and rights).

In December 1996, SFOR was authorized to stabilize the peace in Bosnia and Herzegovina under UN Security Council Resolution 1088. SFOR was and continues to be led by NATO, but like KFOR it included participation from non-NATO nations. Indeed, this is the genesis of Russia-NATO cooperation in the peacekeeping context and serves as an example of how the two can learn to work together. Russia's participation in SFOR seemed a natural development since it was one of five countries composing the Contact Group, the collection of states that had helped push for peace in Dayton in 1995.

Lessons learned from SFOR seem to have been at least indirectly applied in the implementation of KFOR. Russia actually began its NATO cooperation with the operation preceding SFOR (the Implementation Force [IFOR]) and continued to participate as the operation evolved from one of peace implementation to peace stabilization. It is clear that SFOR provided an opportunity to break down "enemy stereotypes" between NATO members and Russian counterparts in the peacekeeping operation. The value of this experience should not be underestimated.

Reassessing the Russia-NATO Relationship

Although Russian rhetoric condemned NATO action in Yugoslavia, there were nevertheless encouraging signs that Russia's relationship with the West had not been permanently damaged. This was far from guaranteed when NATO air strikes began in 1999. Russia's early objections to NATO expansion were met with assurances that NATO was a purely defensive organization. Air strikes in Yugoslavia looked offensive to Russia and threatened to derail its hopes for developing a cooperative relationship with its former enemy. NATO's unilateral decision to launch attacks diminished Russia's ability to influence the course of events and rendered the future of Russian security cooperation with Europe uncertain.

Russia-NATO cooperation within the PJC grew again. Since the ministers agreed on a comprehensive work program in May 2000 in Florence, Russia-NATO relations underwent a steady process of rehabilitation, which was bearing fruit by the beginning of 2001. The agenda of PJC work expanded to embrace a wide range of issues, from the situation in the former Yugoslavia to strategy and doctrine, arms control, proliferation, military infrastructure, nuclear weapons issues, theater missile defenses, the retraining of discharged military personnel, and search and rescue at sea, among others. Both sides praised good cooperation between Russian and NATO forces in Kosovo and Bosnia. The involvement of Russian officers at Supreme Headquarters Allied Powers Europe (SHAPE) in the planning of joint operations significantly improved. However, underlying differences over the future of the European security organization persist and have not narrowed since the Kosovo crisis. The expanding list of agenda items on the PJC work program seem to indicate the rough-outline bargaining positions, rather than the framework of a functioning partnership.

Establishment of the PJC was seen by many in the Russian elite as a damage-reducing measure in the context of the first wave of the NATO expansion eastward. Moscow sought to prevent eventual deployment of nuclear weapons, the extension of NATO's military infrastructure, or the deployment of foreign troops to the new member states in east-central Europe. For their part, NATO countries have largely regarded the Russia-NATO Founding Act as a deal to make NATO expansion as comfortable for Russia as possible.

At the same time, the Founding Act envisaged an ambitious goal. The PJC was supposed to "provide a mechanism for consultation, coordination and, to the maximum extent possible, where appropriate, for joint decisions and joint action with respect to security issues of common concern." The declared "shared objective of NATO and Russia" was "to identify and pursue as many opportunities for joint action as possible."

For whatever reasons—and Russia and NATO had a different understanding of why—the anticipated joint decisionmaking process did not work. The dialogue was largely reduced to consultation, and even that was rendered mostly symbolic from Moscow's perspective with the beginning of air strikes against Yugoslavia. Both sides have notably different concepts of European security, and these have diverged even further since the Kosovo crisis. The differences may not be irreconcilable, but they do make it more difficult—and less likely—that substantial progress can be made until this early bargaining phase of the relationship is over.

One of the PJC's objectives when it was set up in 1997 was to clarify questions pertaining to European security from the NATO and Russian perspectives. The Russians have complained that the forum is consultative only in theory and that its primary purpose is one of window-dressing. Russia was in fact excluded from the decisionmaking process leading to the NATO air strikes over Yugoslavia in 1999.

Of all official Russian documents, the Russian Foreign Policy Concept is most explicit in its critique of NATO:

> Realistically assessing the role of the North Atlantic Treaty Organization (NATO), Russia proceeds from the recognition of the importance of cooperating with it in the interests of maintaining security and stability on the Continent, and *is open to constructive collaboration.* The necessary foundation for this is laid down in the Founding Act on Mutual Relations, Cooperation and Security Between the North Atlantic Treaty Organization and the Russian Federation of 27 May 1997. The intensity of cooperation with NATO depends on the implementation of the key provisions of that document and, in the first instance of those concerning nonuse of force or threat of force, nondeployment of groups of conventional forces, of nuclear weapons and of means of their delivery on the territory of the new member states.
>
> At the same time, with the view of the number of features, *the current political and military postures of NATO do not coincide with the security interests of the Russian Federation, and sometimes even run contrary.* This concerns, in the first instance, the provisions of the NATO new strategic concept which does not exclude coercive operations out of the area of application of the Washington Treaty without a mandate of the UN Security Council. Russia maintains its negative approach to the extension of NATO.
>
> Dense and constructive cooperation between Russia and NATO is only possible on the basis of appropriate acknowledgment of the interests of both sides and of unequivocal adherence to mutual obligations entered into.[21]

Russia's uneasy attitude toward NATO is political in nature. It has less to do with NATO itself or with its particular policies, but rather with the diminishing role of Russia. From the Russian perspective, the fundamental difference between NATO and the UN is that Moscow has a voice and veto in the latter, while it is not even a member of the former and therefore cannot affect its decisionmaking process. This means that NATO is unlikely to be accepted by Russia as the central security institution in and for Europe.

Despite the limitations described above, other imperatives balance the rather pessimistic picture of prospects for growth in the Russia-NATO relationship. These positive imperatives suggest that the existing, roughly cooperative relationship is not threatened unless Russia sees its core security interests are at stake. Furthermore, already-existing cooperation can continue to grow, if only to a certain point. Although Russia-NATO interaction is unlikely to reach a level of genuine partnership in the foreseeable future, it will still be interaction characterized by constructive, pragmatic, and selective ad hoc cooperation rather than raw hostility.

The still uneasy relationship between Russia and NATO suggests that institutionalizing cooperation between NATO and the UN in peacekeeping and peace enforcement is unlikely to be supported in Moscow until the situation changes. At the same time, practical ad hoc cooperation between both is and will likely remain tolerated by Russia when it is feasible politically.

Russia and Other European Institutions

Without maintaining illusions as to the extent to which the OSCE could take on peacekeeping and peace enforcement tasks in Europe and thus make the role of NATO as the only robust security organization relative, Russia certainly would prefer that NATO does not remain a lonely player in the field. Without neglecting in principle the possibility that NATO could contribute to European security on the basis of consensus, Russia would like to have a wider choice of options for action if needed. The emerging European Security and Defense Identity (ESDI) is increasingly considered as such an option.

After many years of ignoring the political and security dimensions of integration within the EU, the Russian Foreign Policy Concept of 2000 explicitly attends to ESDI.[22] Issues of European security have been continuously included on the agenda of the EU-Russia political dialogue since 1998. At the semiannual summit meeting in October 2000, Russia and the EU signed a joint declaration to strengthen dialogue and cooperation on political and security matters in Europe.[23] The declaration includes statements in support of:

- instituting specific consultations on security and defense matters at the appropriate level and in the appropriate format;
- developing strategic dialogue on matters, particularly with respect to security, with implications for the Russian Federation and the European Union;
- extending the scope of regular consultations at the expert level on the issues of disarmament, arms control, and nonproliferation; and
- promoting cooperation in operational crisis management.

The modalities and substance of this cooperation are a work in progress. Most notably, in March 2001 it was the EU and not NATO that came together at the summit level, with the participation of Russian president Vladimir Putin, to discuss action needed under the circumstances of the emerging crisis in Macedonia.

However, although the Russian preferences are clear, Russia not only remains cautious, but it also sees limits on the ability of the EU to become a relevant security player in Europe comparable to NATO. The limits Russia recognizes include:

- The establishment of the institution of EU High Representative for Common Foreign and Security Policy (CFSP) and the invention of ESDI have not yet produced the desired effect—that is, to enable the EU to speak with one voice. It is yet another voice added to the fifteen, and this limits the ability of the EU to perform as a single actor.
- The decisionmaking process within the EU, especially in the field of CFSP, is based on the principles of an intergovernmental conference and sets clear limits on quick action. This is especially important in the field of ESDI, where "rapid reaction" of the EU would require lengthy and controversial procedures within national parliaments with uncertain outcomes. Unless the EU transcends its current intergovernmental nature and develops a more straightened mode of decisionmaking, it will remain a weak partner. The December 2000 failure of the European Council in Nice to send a clear message on the subject once again emphasized this weakness of the EU.
- The development the EU's own power projection capacity will take a long time, exceeding the horizon considered here.

These considerations suggest that, provided developments in Europe or in the adjacent areas require common military action, and provided Russia decides to participate in such an action, NATO remains, for the foreseeable future, the single most important partner for Russia.

Conclusion

Russia has acknowledged its need for engagement with the West. European states and the United States agree that Russia should be encouraged to play a cooperative role in the broader transatlantic international community. Nevertheless, the West has failed to effectively engage Russia over the last decade and the United States and Europe have struggled largely unsuccessfully to fashion a strategy to assist Russia in playing such a role. These difficulties are fundamental to understanding Russian positions on international institutions, Russia's role within them, and the institutional mandates that Russia may or may not support.

Despite encouraging signs that Russia does in fact desire a cooperative relationship with Europe and the United States and the institutions they promote, there is still debate about the potential end-state for Russia's relationship with the West. Idealists hope for the day when Russia will truly become a part of the broader transatlantic community, become a member of its institutions, and identify itself and its interests with the West. A more pragmatic view, one more likely to have the support of today's Russian leadership, embodies a more independent Russia, but one that is favorably disposed toward cooperation with the United States and Europe based on shared norms and interests.

This chapter has suggested that there are reasons for optimism in building cooperative relations between Russia and a variety of Western institutions. Russia's participation in NATO-led, UN-sanctioned peacekeeping operations like SFOR and KFOR bodes well for the future. This chapter has also provided a context for understanding how Russia sees the evolving international environment. Discussion of Russian views of international institutions, particularly the United Nations and NATO and Russian participation within or alongside them, provides insight into possibilities for Russia's future roles. It is hoped that the broader picture, as presented here, will lead to the development of realistic expectations for Russia's cooperation with the UN, NATO, and other regional institutions.

Notes

1. Ekaterina Stepanova, "Explaining Russia's Dissention on Kosovo," Harvard University Center for Strategic and International Studies, Program on New Approaches to Russian Security, Policy Memo no. 57, March 1999.

2. Russian Federation, *Strategiya razvitiya otnoshenii Rossiiskoi Federatsii s Evropeiskim Soiuzom na srednesrochnuiu perspektivu (2000–2015 gg.)* [The strategy of developing relations between the Russian Federation and the European Union in the midterm perspective (2000–2015)] (Moscow: Russian Federation, 2000), p. 3.

3. *Founding Act on Mutual Relations, Cooperation, and Security Between the North Atlantic Treaty Organization and the Russian Federation,* sec. 2, www.nato.int/docu/facts/2000/nato-rus.

4. Russian Federation, *Kontseptsiya vneshney politiki Rossiiskoi Federatsii* [Foreign policy conception of the Russian Federation], May 2000, www.mid.ru.

5. Vystuplenie zamestitela Ministra inostrannykh del Rossii S. A. Ordzhonilidze "OON v novom tysacheletii" na konferentsii po mezhdunarodnomu pravu 31 yanvara 2001 goda, Moskva [Statement by Deputy Foreign Minister S. A. Ordzhonilidze, "The UN in the New Millennium," at the conference on international law, Moscow, January 31, 2001], www.in.mid.ru/website/ns-dp.nsf.

6. Russian Federation, *Foreign policy conception* (endnote 4).

7. See Statement by Deputy Foreign Minister of Russia S. A. Ordzhonilidze (endnote 5); and Statement by the Director of the International Organizations Department of the Russian Foreign Ministry, Yurii Fedotov, at the conference "Entering the Twenty-First Century: Towards the Rule of International Law," "Realizatsiya potentsiala OON kak katalizatora i koordinatora peremen v mirovykh delakh: pravovye osnovy I rol' OON v mezhdunarodnom krizisnom reagirovanii" [Realization of the UN potential as a catalyst and coordinator of change in the world affairs: Legal

grounds and the role of the UN in the international crisis management], www.in. mid.ru/website/ns-dmo.nsf.

8. Speech by Minister of Foreign Affairs of the Russian Federation Igor Ivanov at a Reception on the Occasion of the Forty-Fifth Anniversary of the Russian Associ- ation for the United Nations, March 28, 2001, unofficial translation, www.in.mid.ru.

9. Ibid.

10. Celeste Wallander, "International Institutions and Russian Security Coopera- tion," Harvard University Center for Strategic and International Studies, Program on New Approaches to Russian Security, Policy Memo no. 48, November 1998.

11. Statement by Representative of the Russian Federation Gennady M. Gatilov at the Session of the Special Committee of the United Nations on Peacekeeping Oper- ations, February 15, 2000, www.un.int/russia.

12. Although according to one senior Russian diplomat, Russia has been more constrained in the use of its veto in comparison to the other permanent members in the post–Cold War era.

13. Independent Commission on Kosovo, *The Kosovo Report: Conflict, Interna- tional Response, Lessons Learned* (Oxford: Oxford University Press, 2000), p. 19.

14. With respect to the New Strategic Concept, Mark Kramer writes, "The per- ceived slights on NATO's part, combined with the displays of Western air prowess, prompted a major reassessment in Moscow of the country's strategy. This was the immediate catalyst for the drafting which began . . . at the height of the Kosovo crisis. The Russian government's harsh response to the crisis . . . inevitably affected the draft- ing of the Concept." Mark Kramer, "What Is Driving Russia's New Strategic Con- cept?" Harvard University Center for Strategic and International Studies, Program on New Approaches to Russian Security, Policy Memo no. 103, January 2000.

15. Independent Commission on Kosovo, *The Kosovo Report,* p. 146.

16. Remarks by Foreign Minister Igor Ivanov at the Press Conference on the Results of the Meeting of the Russia-NATO Permanent Joint Council, December 15, 2000, www.in.mid.ru.

17. The Contact Group was initially formed in 1994 to address issues related to settling conflict in the Balkans. The Consultative Group on Kosovo was composed of representatives from the United States, Russia, Britain, France, Germany, and Italy.

18. Statement by Russia's Ministry of Foreign Affairs in Connection with the Second Anniversary of NATO's Aggression Against the Federal Republic of Yugoslavia, March 23, 2001, www.in.mid.ru.

19. KFOR's mission: "Under the mandate of UNSCR 1244 . . . KFOR will deploy to establish a secure environment for the return of refugees and internally displaced persons and to monitor, and if necessary, enforce, compliance with the Military Agree- ment and the demilitarization of the KLA." "Agreed Principles for Russian Participa- tion in the International Security Force for Kosovo, as Determined by the Helsinki Agreement," June 18, 1999, www.kfor.online.

20. "UN Renews Bosnia Mission, Russia Abstains from Voting," *People's Daily* (Beijing), June 22, 2000.

21. Russian Federation, *Foreign Policy Conception* (endnote 4), emphasis added.

22. Ibid.

23. Joint Declaration by President of the Russian Federation V. V. Putin, President of the European Council J. Chirac, Assisted by the Secretary-General of the Council of the EU/High Representative for the Common Foreign and Security Policy of the EU J. Solana, and the President of the Commission of the European Communities R. Prodi, on Strengthening Dialogue and Cooperation on Political and Security Matters in Europe, October 2000, europa.eu.int/comm/external_rela...russia/summit_30_00/ stat_secu_en.htm.

PART 3

Peace Operations in Europe: Security Sector Reform

7

Joint Action on Security Challenges in the Balkans

John G. Cockell

The complex environments in which peace support operations have to function often pose difficult internal security challenges, such as the demilitarization of nonstate militias, control and seizure of heavy and light weapons, protection of humanitarian aid zones, deterrence of anarchy and crime in situations of state collapse, prevention of interethnic violence, and control of porous and contested borders. Security sector reforms have been central to the mandates of peace operations in the Balkans, but difficulties in responding to specific security challenges have often led to operational setbacks in the field. Effective management of such challenges has thus been an increasingly important priority for the United Nations and European security organizations, such as the North Atlantic Treaty Organization (NATO) and the Organization for Security and Cooperation in Europe (OSCE). But while NATO can provide the requisite forces for a strong military deterrent, it cannot contribute the political, administrative, legal, and economic elements necessary for effective security sector reform. Joint action by both military and civil actors is necessary for successful management of the security sector. And successful security sector management is in turn central to the broader strategic goal of fostering a sustainable peacebuilding dynamic.[1]

This chapter compares the experience of civil-military responses to security sector issues in two Kosovo missions—the UN Mission in Kosovo (UNMIK) and the Kosovo Force (KFOR)—against other missions in the Balkans: the UN Protection Force (UNPROFOR), the UN Mission in Bosnia and Herzegovina (UNMIBH), and the Implementation Force (IFOR) and Stabilization Force (SFOR) in Bosnia and Herzegovina (BiH); and the UN Transitional Administration for Eastern Slavonia, Baranja, and Western Sirmium (UNTAES) in Eastern Slavonia (Croatia). UNMIK and KFOR have undoubtedly been the most successful complex Balkans operations to date for interorganizational action, and have demonstrated that many lessons were effectively applied in the international peacebuilding response to the Kosovo conflict in 1999. A comparison of evolving Balkans security sector action, from BiH and Eastern Slavonia to Kosovo, suggests that the civil-military interface should move from cooperative relations to coordinated unity of effort. In comparing the situation in Kosovo to the wider Balkans context, however, it is important to stress that Kosovo is not in a truly "postconflict" condition. The key elements for such status—a peace agreement and/or determination of a final end-state for the territory—are glaringly absent in Kosovo, and have been since the arrival of international actors in the contested province. Indeed, Kosovo's indeterminate political status is at the root of many of its most intractable threats to public security, including endemic violence against ethnic minorities, particularly Serbs, and the consequent emergence of polarized ethnic enclaves.

Civil-Military Interaction and the Imperative for Coordination

The inherent complexity of the Balkans conflict environments has demanded interaction between NATO's military forces and civilian organizations, such as the UN and the OSCE, also active in addressing security sector issues. The serious security challenges in Bosnia, which led by December 1995 to the termination of the UNPROFOR mission, inclined many analysts to conclude that the UN lacked the capacity to successfully field complex peace support operations in situations of protracted ethnic conflict. The UNTAES mission (1996–1998) in Eastern Slavonia soon demonstrated, however, that this was not necessarily the case. But the capacity of the organization is challenged where deterrent military force is needed in a rapid and massive manner.[2] This need has been the norm for the Balkans, with BiH and Kosovo both requiring tens of thousands of well-equipped forces able to project a credible war-fighting face. The fact that NATO is the only organization in the region with the capacity to mount such missions was recognized early on by Kofi Annan. In 1993 he advocated UN-NATO cooperation in the delivery of missions that needed "peacekeeping with teeth," noting that their size and complexity makes it "imperative to explore new avenues of cooperation with regional organisations such as NATO."[3]

The interrelated nature of security challenges in these missions has also meant that what used to be understood as a clear distinction between military and civil roles has become increasingly indistinct. While NATO has taken some concrete steps to institutionalize aspects of civil-military interaction in the field, these have generally only been to the extent of formalized *coopera-*

tion. Military and civil actors, however, increasingly must address security sector issues in an overlapping and interdependent manner. In this context, a growing strategic interest for both civil and military organizations is to determine and apply comparative advantage in mission roles, a goal that implies the *coordination* of joint operational and tactical action to achieve shared objectives in the field. Coordination of joint action, in turn, requires a qualitative shift in civil-military interaction toward integrated planning and shared operations, with all the compromises implicit in loss of autonomy on both sides.

Coordination of joint civil-military action should ideally be pursued at three levels: strategic (i.e., between the organizations' headquarter decision-making bodies and secretariats); operational (i.e., theater-level headquarters for the mission area); and tactical (i.e., in field-level operations for mission components).[4] Most structured civil-military interaction in the Balkans has been at the middle, or operational, level. Tactical coordination is increasingly common, but is more subject to ad hoc arrangements and variations. Least explored to date has been strategic coordination between headquarters in New York/Geneva, Brussels/Mons, and Vienna. These three levels of security sector management, and the imperative for coordinated civil-military action in each, will be considered in turn below.

Strategic Coordination:
Mandates and Mission Planning

One of the commonly noted differences between military and civilian organizations is that military planners tend to prepare for potential missions and plan resource allocations in advance. In contrast, many civilian organizations still tend to plan missions after the mandate has been set by their relevant decisionmaking body (e.g., UN Security Council, OSCE Permanent Council). As a result, the potential for strategic coordination of mandates and planning to occur in advance of the deployment of combined civil-military assets on the ground has been largely unrealized, hampered in part by persistent differences in institutional cultures and resources, and by a lack of transparent interaction. For example, officials in the UN Secretariat have been largely unable to undertake more than preliminary mission planning, because there are budgetary restrictions on spending in advance of an explicit authorization by the Security Council. This has prevented the use of advance assessment missions to the area, recruitment of staff, and procurement. Secretariat reforms have, however, led to the dedication of new funds for the financing of mission planning.[5]

Recent trends toward greater civil-military interaction in complex operations should incline mission planning staff in both military and civilian organizations to coordinate on mandates and mission structures in advance of final political decisions being taken. This could improve the likelihood that complex operational needs would be identified and addressed with accurate personnel and resource allocations in advance. These requirements could be expressly stated to decisionmaking bodies, and mandates could then be finalized in the light of more detailed and situation-specific information.[6] While mandates should be as clear as possible in stating consolidated objectives for both military and civil actors, they should not be so specific as to restrict flexibility in the field. Unanticipated challenges, particularly as regards the need for military forces to provide various forms of support to civil authorities, are best confronted when mission managers/commanders have the freedom to quickly forge new arrangements in the field. KFOR, for example, has shifted from an initial concept of operations involving the outward deterrence of Serb-dominated Yugoslav security and paramilitary forces, to the inward protection of Serb minority enclaves and deterrence of Kosovar Albanian attacks on Serbs.

For improved strategic coordination, one study has proposed that integrated civil-military implementation staffs could provide a structured interface for the coordination of joint action on the planning and implementation of peace operations.[7] An established strategic interface could undertake joint contingency planning to meet such operational challenges as the security gap caused by the collapse or withdrawal of state security forces (as was the case in both BiH and Kosovo). While the use of integrated mission task forces has recently been initiated within the UN, they have yet to be fully implemented in the manner recommended by the Brahimi panel, and have not featured the involvement of non-UN military staff.[8] Such an interface should also extend to intelligence, which military forces often obtain from their own national agencies. Civil authorities are usually unable to obtain the use of such intelligence, as national contingents and force commanders feel unable to pass classified information outside of NATO (or even national) structures. But such information could be of considerable help to civil authorities, particularly police forces trying to combat organized crime, and strategic coordination should endeavor to establish formal agreements to facilitate sharing of field intelligence between military and civil organizations.

Other suggested improvements in this area include routine exchanges of planning staff officials, permanent liaison offices, and joint training programs. As well, such strategic coordination could effect improved mutual understanding on crucial elements such as the role and responsibilities of civil police and their relationship with military forces.[9] The issue of strategic civil-military coordination between the UN and regional organizations also raises the related issue of determining comparative advantage. Ideally, some agreed determination of situation-specific comparative advantage would be included in the drafting of mission mandates that involve multiple organizations. But applying a comparative advantage principle to mandates implies not only strategic but also in-theater operational coordination in the realization of inter-related peacebuilding objectives. Indeed, it would suggest that the various organizations involved have a shared understanding of their respective objectives and responsibilities on the ground.

Operational Coordination: Theater Mission Structures

In Kosovo, operational cooperation and coordination between civil and military organizations at the theaterwide level has been enhanced by three important structural features: (1) the effort by KFOR and UNMIK to use routinized processes for coordination of military support to civil authority; (2) the cross-organizational acceptance of a unified five-region geographic plan for operational organization; and (3) the advent within UNMIK of a unified mission structure for all major civil components. These three features represent clear progress and organizational learning over the past experience in BiH, particularly the necessity of a theaterwide civil-military interface.

Military Support to Civil Authorities

If military organizations such as NATO are better at strategic planning in advance of missions, then civil organizations such as the UN and OSCE are often better at responding flexibly to operational uncertainty on the ground, perhaps by virtue of their less hierarchical decisionmaking processes. In Bosnia, NATO aversion to "mission creep" contributed to an overly sharp division between civil and military roles. In 1996 this caused reluctance in IFOR to assist civil authorities, contributing to a security gap that was particularly evident in the area of policing. The lawlessness that followed proved to be beyond the ability of the local police forces to handle effectively. IFOR commanders in Bosnia chose not to use their troops to carry out civil policing duties, even though this would have been desirable in areas where the local police were unable to carry out such functions and the International Police Task Force (IPTF) was not yet able to provide support. The IPTF, established in late 1995 as a component of UNMIBH, is an unarmed force of observers with a mandate to monitor existing local police forces and assist in the reform of their law enforcement capacities. In Eastern Slavonia, in contrast, UNTAES enjoyed a fully integrated mission structure that unified humanitarian, civil, and military components under a single UN command. This integrated structure allowed UNTAES to ensure effective coordination between UN military forces, the UN Civilian Police (UNCIVPOL), and the local involvement of the Transitional Police Force (TPF).

    The current situation in Kosovo is somewhere between these two experiences, and has perhaps applied lessons learned from both. While KFOR is outside of the UNMIK mission structure, it has been reasonably proactive in providing assistance to civil authorities.[10] A high level of effective UNMIK-KFOR interaction was established in June 1999 between the Acting Special Representative of the Secretary-General (SRSG), Sergio Vieira de Mello, and Commander KFOR (COMKFOR) General Mike Jackson, and this has been maintained by their respective successors. Indeed, it has been the usual practice for COMKFOR and the SRSG to meet on a daily basis for coordination purposes. As General Jackson himself remarked in October 1999: "My aim has been to support UNMIK in every way. Mission creep—the concern that the military is drawn into unforeseen tasks—is a meaningless term in the circumstances that we have found ourselves. We share . . . one goal. It has been a joint effort."[11]

Theaterwide coordination on security operations has been steadily increased through routine processes such as the weekly Joint Security Executive Committee (JSEC) meetings. Established in August 1999, the JSEC acts as a functional mechanism for action on all security issues, including policing, weapons control, and protection of minority communities.[12] Joint operational control on security was deemed to be so important that this committee was established to make decisions on specific operations and programs that COMKFOR and the SRSG were unable to address in their daily strategy meetings. At the regional level, KFOR and UNMIK police often conduct joint patrols in areas where KFOR still has full tactical policing authority, with the civilian officers acting as advisers. These coordinated "joint security operations" have been effective in combining UNMIK police expertise with KFOR security capabilities. There are also joint weekly security meetings between UNMIK region/station police commanders, UNMIK regional/municipal administrators, OSCE field staff, and KFOR brigade and battalion commanders. In most of Kosovo's thirty municipalities, UNMIK police and local KFOR battalions have established good levels of tactical coordination, and in some areas (notably in Pristina) joint operations rooms have been established. As in Bosnia, civil-military cooperation (CIMIC) centers are built into the KFOR mission structure, and have facilitated cooperation with the UN (particularly the UN High Commissioner for Refugees [UNHCR]). Most major population centers in Kosovo now have KFOR CIMIC centers. But while CIMIC has undoubtedly aided the general level of tactical cooperation in the field, it also tends to structure this cooperation in a "hegemonic" manner that prioritizes the operational effectiveness of the military.[13] The trend in Kosovo, then, has been to move beyond CIMIC by establishing joint action procedures for routine military support to civil authorities.

As called for under UN Security Council Resolution 1244 (1999), KFOR has performed police duties in areas where the UNMIK police had yet to be established in sufficient numbers to take over executive policing. UNMIK police now have full tactical primacy in four of five regions, and command staff have been reluctant to take on more authority for executive policing than their understaffed capacity can handle: they are having to conduct nonpolice duties such as guarding banks, escorting prisoners, and providing close protection details.[14] KFOR has been anxious, however, to hand over more civil policing tasks to UNMIK as soon as possible. By mid-2000, COMKFOR general Klaus Reinhardt had observed that the main security challenges for Kosovo were continuing ethnic violence and organized crime, challenges that his soldiers were not trained to confront.[15] KFOR, in particular, would like UNMIK police to do more static guard duties. UNMIK police would prefer, in turn, that KFOR leave community tasks such as foot patrols to the police, in order to promote the ethic of democratic, civilian policing with the local population.[16] The operational interface between KFOR and UNMIK police is indeed the key security coordination issue between the two missions at present. A special joint security initiative was established in April 2001 to devise consistent and structured procedures for operational coordination of KFOR-UNMIK police (e.g., on tasking), such that these procedures will remain in place regardless of the regular rotation of KFOR commands.[17]

KFOR and Five Multinational Brigade Sectors

In a major improvement over the situation in BiH, the UN and the OSCE organized their field structures so as to be congruent with the five multinational brigade (MNB) sector boundaries established by KFOR in June 1999. In addition to these sectors (Pristina, Pec, Mitrovica, Prizren, and Gnjilane), there is also full correspondence of a three-level theater mission structure: KFOR main headquarters to UNMIK headquarters, KFOR brigades to UNMIK regional administrations, and KFOR battalions to municipalities. The five-MNB operational structure for KFOR has not, however, been entirely positive for the coordinated management of security sector challenges at the tactical level. As with SFOR before it, a major structural drawback of KFOR is its decentralized force structure, a feature driven by NATO's long-established standing arrangements for troop-contributing member states.[18] Each MNB command has a large degree of discretion over the operational modalities used to establish a safe and secure environment within its area of responsibility. This discretion includes rules of engagement for MNB contingents, as well as wide latitude to decide on the duties and actions required for that region by the KFOR mandate.

In practice, this has meant significant restrictions on the ability of KFOR's main headquarters in Pristina to establish Kosovo-wide standards for the management of security sector challenges in each sector. This is particularly true where those challenges may put KFOR contingents at risk of physical harm. It has also meant that the projection of a deterrent level of military force, a key aspect of NATO's operational comparative advantage, varies in its salience from one sector to the next. For example, the British-led MNB center has been proactively effective in locating and seizing significant arms caches in its sector. This type of operation, clearly helpful for the overall security environment, is either not undertaken or not undertaken to the same extent as in the other MNBs, due to different calculations of risks to force protection. Finally, this decentralization accentuates the differences between national contingents on the imperative for civil-military coordination. Some contingents are markedly less inclined to engage with civil actors in a proactive manner.[19] In contrast, the UN and OSCE components of UNMIK have relatively centralized mission structures, and it is generally understood that policies decided in Pristina are to be executed by regional and municipal administrations and field offices. This is also true for UNMIK police, whose headquarters has effective control over the Kosovo-wide operations of both UN international and Kosovar police officers.

This divergence in mission structures between KFOR and UNMIK can create problems in the maintenance of a safe and secure environment in the face of security challenges. Nowhere has this been more damaging for the overall peacebuilding process than in the tactical management of security challenges in the divided town of Mitrovica, which falls in the MNB north sector and thus under the responsibility of French KFOR. North Mitrovica is now populated almost entirely by Serbs, who are in general hostile to the presence of UNMIK. The UNMIK police station in the north has been attacked and damaged, and several UNMIK vehicles have been burned at various times. More difficult has been the rise since late 1999 of quasi-political Serb gangs of public-order vigilantes, called "bridge-watchers," who purport to monitor the movement of people and vehicles from the south side of the Ibar river into the north. These groups have been linked to prominent political leaders of the Serb community in the north. In this situation, UNMIK police have largely been prevented from carrying out normal police patrols north of the Ibar, a long-standing dilemma that they blame largely on the inability of French KFOR to establish a safe and secure environment for regular policing. Such incidents in Kosovo (and similar problems in BiH with SFOR) suggest that the decentralized NATO structure prevents force commanders from ensuring a consistent level of coordinated security support to civil authorities in all sectors of the theater.

UNMIK and the Four-Pillar Mission Structure

One of the widely recognized shortcomings of the situation in BiH is the absence of effective coordination between the Office of the High Representative (OHR) and other civilian organizations such as the UN, OSCE, and EU. While the OHR is supposed to be the coordinating node for civil efforts in BiH, this has not always been consistently effective in all areas, in spite of twice-weekly meetings of the various missions' "principals." The mission structure eventually established for UNMIK by June 1999 was significantly improved over the situation in BiH, though as late as the Rambouillet negotiations of February 1999 there was the intention of applying a revised OHR-style model to the administration of Kosovo.[20] UNMIK sets the important precedent of bringing various civil organizations together under one mission head, in this case the UN SRSG. The four major organizations involved in civil tasks in Kosovo at the start of the mission were the UN, the UNHCR, the OSCE, and the EU. Each has formed a distinct "pillar" of the mission, headed by its own Deputy SRSG. Effective interpillar coordination has been promoted, in part, through the convening of daily morning meetings of all pillar Deputy SRSGs with the SRSG. This structure has continued, with the exception that the UNHCR withdrew from UNMIK in mid-2000, as its humanitarian and refugee return objectives had been achieved.

The four-pillar structure has thus ensured that the contributions of the OSCE and the EU would be specifically designed to complement the role of the UN in administering Kosovo. Within UNMIK, the UN is responsible for the Office of the SRSG (with its executive legislative role), as well as for providing the various departments of civil administration (including executive policing, the judicial and penal systems, and municipal administration). Based on its comparative advantage, the OSCE has been given the lead task of institution building (including democratization, human rights monitoring, legal reform, police training, and elections), and the EU has been given the task of organizing economic reconstruction (including running the Central Fiscal Authority and coordinating donor inputs). Perhaps more important is the fact that by combining forces within a single mission under one head, these civilian organizations have significantly enhanced the degree to which the international community speaks with one voice to the major political actors in the conflict. UNMIK has thereby largely avoided the fate that befell the OHR in BiH, where various ethnic political parties and entity governmental actors have been able to play one international organization against another, capitalizing on the inability of the OHR to establish an authoritative line.

With this structure, UNMIK has also been able to forge a close connection between security sector reform areas, such as civil policing, local police training, judicial and penal services, and legal reform. All of these interdependent security issues are managed in a manner more directly informed by the ongoing politico-administrative process than has been the case in BiH, with the SRSG providing overall legislative and decisionmaking authority. Since UNMIK has executive authority for civilian security forces in Kosovo, this unity of civil effort has also been important for establishing the clear subordination of such forces to unified and coherent civilian control.[21] The importance of ensuring that civil policing and rule of law are fully integrated into the UNMIK mission structure at the highest level led in May 2001 to the mission forming a new fourth pillar: police and justice. Its establishment was a reflection of then-SRSG Hans Haekkerup's intention to "provide greater focus, centrality, and coordination" for the law enforcement and criminal justice system in Kosovo.[22]

If, however, there are to be more UNMIK-style integrated interorganizational missions in the future, it will be important for them to have recruited and established basic headquarters structures prior to deployment.[23] In spite of this being a lesson of past UN operations, it was not applied in the case of UNMIK, and this led to some problems of logistics and coordination in the early days of the mission (particularly between the UN and the OSCE). Perhaps more significant, this has meant that the OSCE and the UN, as the two largest UNMIK pillars, have never had an integrated headquarters in Pristina. Coordination is more ad hoc, in specific areas that demand regular policy and operational contacts such as elections and the Kosovo Police Service (KPS). The UN and the OSCE also have separate logistics, radio nets, movement control, and administrative departments, as is the case in BiH and Croatia. The term "pillar" in this sense is apposite: the organizations are bridged at the very top, but have little structured contact below that level.[24] Better operational coherence between the UN and the OSCE may have been achieved if the importance of this had been stressed, at the strategic level, to an integrated UN-OSCE-EU headquarters team in advance of deployment.

Tactical Coordination: Management of Security Challenges

In Kosovo, the management of security challenges at the tactical level has been more complex than in any previous Balkans theater. Three areas stand out as illustrations of the degree of coordination achieved by military and civil organizations in the tactical management of specific security challenges: (1) demilitarization and demobilization of the Kosovo Liberation Army (KLA); (2) building a local capacity for civil policing; and (3) responding to insecurity caused by organized crime. Demilitarization, policing, and crime are three of the most commonly cited priorities for security sector management in peacebuilding, and in Kosovo the responses by NATO, the UN, and the OSCE have evinced both achievements and dilemmas in the coordination of joint action.[25]

Demilitarization and Demobilization: Transforming the KLA into the KPC

In their shared efforts to achieve mission objectives in Kosovo, on no issue have KFOR and UNMIK coordinated joint action more successfully (and crucially) than in the demilitarization and demobilization of the KLA. Their success in the rapid dismantling of the former sword arm of Kosovar Albanian nationalism was a genuinely shared one, and merits closer examination. The complexity of connecting demilitarization with demobilization in this case demanded of both organizations not simply cooperation, but concrete, tactical coordination and unity of effort. In BiH, various organizations have been involved in the reform of the three armed forces, but in a cooperative (i.e., less coordinated) manner. SFOR is involved in efforts to restructure these forces by reducing their size, and helps with the screening of officers to ensure apolitical professionalism. The OHR is assisting in the development of a Standing Committee on Military Matters, and the OSCE continues to promote confidence building and arms control.[26] The lack of coordination (and absence of executive authority) may have contributed to the sad fact that five years after Dayton, the three ethnic armed forces remain politicized and largely unintegrated.

The demilitarization of the KLA was central to KFOR's mandate to enforce a safe and secure environment in Kosovo. But demilitarization could not have been achieved without providing a transformative demobilization process for the thousands of KLA militants who had fought to achieve the national liberation of Kosovo. In June 1999 a voluntary undertaking by the KLA to demilitarize and demobilize was signed and presented to COMKFOR by Hashim Thaçi, then commander in chief of the KLA.[27] In close consultation with UNMIK, KFOR developed the concept for a civilian emergency response service modeled on the Sécurité Civile of France. SRSG Bernard Kouchner then signed an UNMIK regulation authorizing establishment of the Kosovo Protection Corps (KPC).[28] This innovation was seen as a way of absorbing former KLA manpower while also directing the aspirations of many of its members to form a standing army. The regulation states that KPC members cannot hold public office, cannot actively engage in political affairs, and cannot play any role in defense, internal security, or law enforcement. Recruiting to the KPC was handled by KFOR together with the senior KPC leadership, but UNMIK was the final arbiter on the recruiting process and could veto applications.

The KPC is thus very much the joint creation of KFOR and UNMIK, and both have substantial and ongoing roles in its operational management. The UNMIK Department for Civil Security and Emergency Preparedness is now responsible for the civil administration of the KPC, and makes all planning decisions concerning KPC funding, policies, and priority functions in Kosovo. KFOR, in turn, provides day-to-day supervision of the KPC, and also has dedicated liaison officers assigned to KPC general staff and the regional task groups.

An important civil role in the transformation of the KLA into the KPC has also been played by the International Organization for Migration (IOM). IOM was assigned responsibility by UNMIK and KFOR for interviewing and screening some 18,500 former KLA applicants to the KPC, and for coordinating training programs for new KPC personnel in both vocational skills as well as various emergency and disaster preparedness tasks. Through its information, counseling, and referral service, IOM has also developed income-generation programs for registered non-KPC former KLA personnel (including now the 2,000 KPC reservists), and facilitates their finding civilian employment.[29] It is noteworthy that KFOR does not provide this training, and this unusual role for IOM has been important in reinforcing the explicitly civil nature of the KPC's role in UNMIK-administered Kosovo.[30] Effective demobilization, however, requires secure funding, and here the international community has been notably reluctant to bolster the advent of the KPC. This lack of support has threatened the security gains made by establishing the KPC as a uniformed service for former combatants. As KPC commander Agim Çeku has noted, the acute lack of resources is a "critical issue," and "without equipment we cannot train effectively or . . . continue to develop as an organisation."[31]

Nevertheless, the terms of the transformation process allowed for the KPC command structure to be built on the old KLA framework. For example, unlike the five-sector mission structure shared by UNMIK and KFOR, the KPC regional task groups are based on the previous six-zone structure of the KLA (which made the Drenica valley, the KLA heartland, its own zone of operations). Commander Çeku, previously the KLA chief of staff, and most of the old KLA zone commanders were made commanders of regional task groups. Çeku and the rest of the KPC command structure openly regard the KPC as a foundation for the future army of an independent Kosovo. There have also been instances, though few, in which KPC commanders have used their position and men to exert overt political intimidation on the Democratic League of Kosova and other political competitors of Hashim Thaçi's Democratic Party of Kosova. More serious have been a series of incidents in which KPC personnel have been involved or implicated in acts of murder, kidnapping, torture and interrogations, and illegal policing and taxation.[32] While these abuses may not be endemic, UNMIK considers it to be KFOR's responsibility to address such problems of KPC supervision. Improved working-level coordination between UNMIK and KFOR on KPC issues, instead of the current system in which coordination is handled only by senior management, would put both sides in a better position to address these dilemmas.[33] This would suggest that complementarity of civil-military roles should be ensured through careful tactical coordination and monitoring, backed up with political support from organizational headquarters for unity-of-effort arrangements made at the mission level.

Whether demobilization has in fact successfully "transformed" the KLA has also become more problematic over the past two years, with the rise of the Liberation Army of Presheva, Medvegja, and Bujanoc (UCPMB) in southern Serbia in February 2000, and of the National Liberation Army (NLA) a year later in Macedonia.[34] In Kosovo, the extreme nationalist People's Movement of Kosova, which had played a central role in the establishment of the KLA in the early to middle 1990s, used the safety of Kosovo to promote these new militant formations, which were essentially updated versions of the KLA. In April 2001 General Çeku found it necessary to dismiss his chief of staff and fourteen other KPC members when intelligence reports indicated that they had been directly involved in the armed actions of the NLA. Çeku stated: "We want to cut any relation with them. . . . There is no home for them in the KPC."[35] This brings home the lesson that demobilizing the apparent "public" structure and membership of a militia may well leave the preexisting political forces that fostered its creation untouched. Political and legal sectors must therefore address the potential for continuing organized political (and criminal) support for armed militancy.

Building Indigenous Police Capacity: Creating the Kosovo Police Service

In both BiH and Eastern Slavonia, established police/paramilitary units formed the basis for postconflict police forces, which were then advised by UN international police monitors. The United Nations IPTF in BiH has had as part of its mandate the reform of the Federation police and the Republika Srpska police, such that they are reduced in size, less militarized, and more oriented to civil police work.[36] But this reform process has had to be pursued in the absence of the IPTF having any executive authority for policing BiH entities. In practice, these police forces have resisted wholesale reform, and by mid-1997 SFOR took stronger steps to support IPTF reform efforts: inspecting hundreds of police stations, confiscating thousands of weapons, and removing unauthorized police checkpoints.[37] In Eastern Slavonia, UNTAES established an innovative Transitional Police Force, to be composed of both Serbs and Croats. At the outset of the mission, the local Serb militia was essentially merged into the TPF, with little change to its structures; Croats were gradually recruited thereafter. Uniforms were changed and the TPF was put under the direct authority of the UNTAES police commissioner. Direct UN control over the TPF is generally considered to have been a key to this success, relative to the experience of the IPTF in BiH. In January 1998 the TPF was integrated into the regular Croatian police force.

In Kosovo, the executive police authority given to UNMIK allowed the mission to take a more fundamental approach to building local police capacity than had been possible in either Bosnia or Eastern Slavonia. Serb-dominated police forces in Kosovo were withdrawn under the terms of the Military Technical Agreement, and the Kosovo Police Service has since been built from scratch. The KPS carries out its duties within the operational structures and under the full command of the UNMIK police.

Training of KPS recruits is handled by a new Kosovo Police Service School (KPSS), run by the OSCE's Pillar III Department of Police Education and Development. Assessment of potential candidates for the KPS is coordinated between the UNMIK police and the KPSS staff. In a province where the local populace has had little faith in the state and its institutions, the new KPS has had an impressive number of applicants. In the initial months of the school, it was understood that as much as half of the intake for the school would come from demobilized former KLA members. In this manner, the KPS has been an integral element in a multipronged effort to demobilize the KLA's military personnel. However, the KPSS has also used basic minimum requirements for vetting applications, and has been very successful in achieving proportional representation for women and ethnic minorities.[38] Upon successful completion of a basic nine-week training course at the school, each recruit is then assigned to an UNMIK police station to undertake a further seventeen weeks of field training, interspersed with eighty hours of follow-up KPSS classroom instruction. This system demands daily coordination between the UNMIK police and the OSCE-run KPSS, and the resulting joint reform process has been a substantial success.

However, behind the basic training of some 4,500 recruits to date lie certain structural difficulties. One of these relates to the pace with which UNMIK police are sent 250 new KPSS graduates every four to five weeks. The international staff of UNMIK police, representing some fifty countries, are hard-pressed to provide effective field training to this number of new KPS officers in a manner consistent with basic standards of Western democratic policing. Another dilemma in building capacity is the very low salary (DM350 per month) paid by UNMIK to KPS officers. The concern is that KPS officers will eventually be unable to resist the lure of corruption, particularly in an area where organized crime is rife. However, the basic training run by the KPSS has provided the basis for an apolitical, multiethnic police force, in contrast to the continuing politicization of BiH police and armed forces (or indeed of the KPC).

Confronting Organized Crime: The KFOR Multinational Specialized Unit and UNMIK Police

In spite of international efforts to provide a safe and secure environment for societies ravaged by war, including police monitoring, reform, and (in Kosovo) executive policing itself, organized criminal activity often becomes a persistent threat to public and personal security. In the conflict areas of the Balkans, organized crime has flourished, including prostitution, racketeering, trafficking in illegal immigrants, and the smuggling of drugs, weapons, petrol, and cigarettes. Criticism of the IPTF in Bosnia for not preventing the 1996 gap in public law and order led to an increase in coordination between SFOR and the IPTF from 1997 onward. This coordination has been manifested in operations such as joint checkpoint policies, joint patrolling, and other joint initiatives such as the disarming of the local special police. Some SFOR battalions have also used IPTF officers as advisers when SFOR troops have had to perform functions such as crowd control.[39] The security gap also led, however, to the introduction of a multinational specialized unit (MSU) to the SFOR mission. The MSU is composed of military/special police from countries that have such forces, such as Italy's Carabinieri and Spain's Guardia Civil. In BiH, the MSU added to the capacity of SFOR to handle civil security challenges without having to use regular soldiers.

MSU contingents have also been raised as part of KFOR. Italy has provided almost all of the MSU personnel in Kosovo by sending in a 300-strong Carabinieri regiment. In Kosovo, MSU personnel have conducted specialized policing operations such as the seizure of illegal drugs from transshipment locations, raids on brothels, and seizure of weapons. These operations have been directed at confronting organized crime rings, and MSU includes law enforcement and counterterrorism within its mandate. As in BiH with SFOR, the MSU is a dedicated KFOR asset, and its command reports directly to COMKFOR. This means that while the MSU is deployed throughout Kosovo and has a theaterwide remit, its personnel are not part of any MNB command structure. This has led to an absence of coordination between MSU detachments and UNMIK police operations. The Carabinieri insist on conducting their operations independently, with minimal prior notification to UNMIK police, and no criminal intelligence or investigations on Kosovar organized crime is shared.[40] These problems highlight the larger need for continuing efforts by both KFOR and UNMIK to improve tactical coordination between KFOR assets/contingents and local UNMIK police stations. The imperative to prevent security gaps is underlined by the fact that regional organized crime rings exploited the first year in which neither KFOR nor UNMIK had the necessary capacity to deter such determined illegal activity.

Conclusion: Ten Lessons on Civil-Military Coordination

In light of this comparison between Kosovo and earlier Balkans peace support operations, perhaps ten lessons (both positive and negative) can be drawn for improved modalities of future security coordination at strategic, operational, and tactical levels.

Strategic Coordination

Lesson 1: Military and civilian organizations should endeavor to plan mission mandates and requirements further in advance. Routine interorganizational contacts would aid such forward planning and promote mutual understanding of needs and resource sharing. Strategic partnerships and mechanisms to approve operational sharing of intelligence, particularly from national and military sources, should also be pursued.

Lesson 2: Mission mandates should clearly express the tasks required of both international military and civilian organizations. Clarity on roles should not, however, prevent proactive flexibility in theater, particularly where this involves military support to civil authority and even a fundamental de facto shift in mandate. Integrated multiorganizational missions should have their core headquarters management team formed in advance of deployment, so as to foster positive commitment to coordination and an integration ethic within the mission.

Lesson 3: When civilian police forces cannot be built up in sufficient numbers to handle executive policing, the lack of capacity can lead to tensions with military forces on specific roles (e.g., organized crime investigations). Delays in police deployment should be anticipated and built into the military operational plan so as to determine what policing roles (and their projected duration) will be required of military assets and thereby prevent later gaps in public security. Wherever possible, advance police and legal advisers should accompany the initial deployment of military forces.

Operational Coordination

Lesson 4: Once in theater, military forces should be used flexibly for police roles. Procedures should be established to review the evolving balance of military versus civilian police assets for these roles, and changes should be made on a flexible basis that will ensure public security while promoting civilian, democratic policing.

Lesson 5: Civil-military coordination is best achieved with full mission integration and co-location of components under a UN SRSG. Where force requirements preclude full integration, coordination can be established through integrated processes such as joint operations centers and joint planning committees. Such joint action cannot be organized through CIMIC centers, as these are established by military forces to meet their own civil cooperation needs.

Lesson 6: Where multiple civil and military organizations have to coordinate operations, congruence of sector boundaries (particularly regional and municipal areas of responsibility and their command/administration centers), and correspondence of mission levels, management is crucial to providing a mutual framework for efficient coordination. This framework can be undermined, however, when individual military sectors have autonomous authority that allows them to set differential policies on support (e.g., riot control) to civil organizations. Joint action on security issues should be mandated from the central command or administration of each organization's mission, and applied consistently across the entire theater of operations.

Lesson 7: Coordination of civil operations between the United Nations and regional civilian organizations is best effected within a single, integrated mission structure under the authority of an SRSG. Regional organizations should strive to merge all aspects of their operations, including logistics and communications, into the single structure. An integrated mission allows for comparative advantage to be coordinated in a clear manner, and places international police under a single civilian authority. It also ensures that the international presence speaks with a single voice to the local actors.

Tactical Coordination

Lesson 8: Demobilization of militias can be effectively managed by civil organizations (e.g., UN, OSCE, IOM) with a multitrack, transformative approach that will direct as many former combatants into productive public service as possible. New security authorities (e.g., Kosovo Protection Corps, Kosovo Police Service) should effect such transformation through rigorous basic training programs, to foster new esprit de corps, and all previous militia structures should be fully dismantled. Such a transformative approach to demobilization requires secure, dedicated budgetary support, however, and should be a central component of mission planning from the outset. This approach, moreover, can only succeed when coordinated with an integrated civil-military plan for effective demilitarization, a task best handled by military actors.

Lesson 9: Coordinated demilitarization and demobilization of militias is unlikely to be effective in ending nationalist militancy in the absence of complementary action by civil authorities to address the political sources of militancy with an effective political process. The political context for militancy may also require the adoption of a regional strategy to confront the potential for militant activity beyond the mission theater. Such a strategy should also incorporate effective measures to deter the links between regional organized crime and militant organizations.

Lesson 10: Civil-military coordination can be significantly undermined where mission administrators and commanders cannot prevent exceptionalism for certain mission programs and assets or national contingents. In particular, civil authorities rely on military forces to provide effective security for any area of the theater that may require joint tactical action to address security challenges. Military force commanders should have greater authority to establish theaterwide directives on tactical brigade and battalion support by national contingents to civil authorities.

*   *   *

Finally, managing security sector challenges can only be successful when integrated within the wider context of a multisectoral peacebuilding process. Three aspects are worth stressing. First, effective judicial reform, with functional legal and penal systems in place, must support the police side of the law and order equation. Second, civil institution building must complement security sector reform by establishing democratic civilian control over paramilitary and police forces. Ultimately, security can only be ensured through institutions that are accepted by the public as legitimate expressions of sovereign authority, and this requires an effective political settlement of the status of the territory in question. Third, it is imperative to build reforms in both security and political sectors with the input of local political and civil representatives. Peacebuilding should be approached as a process that fosters self-sustaining institutions, and this requires the active engagement of the local population. Kosovo's slow but steady progress toward a stable peace suggests that joint action between the UN, NATO, and the OSCE has been applied in some key areas, arising from their Balkans experience to date. Effective interorganizational coordination of joint action on security, in particular, can play a central role in fostering a stable basis for the peacebuilding process, and should become the new standard for civil-military interaction in such complex peace operations.

Notes

A shorter version of this chapter appears in *Global Governance: A Review of Multilateralism and International Organisations* 8, no. 4 (Winter 2002). Copyright © 2002 by Lynne Rienner Publishers, Inc. Used with permission of the publisher.

1. See also John G. Cockell, "Conceptualising Peacebuilding: Human Security and Sustainable Peace," in Michael Pugh, ed., *Regeneration of War-Torn Societies* (London: Macmillan, 2000), pp. 15–34.

2. UNTAES benefited from IFOR/SFOR assistance in the form of "over the horizon" air and ground support. See United Nations, DPKO Lessons Learned Unit, *The United Nations Transitional Administration Mission in Eastern Slavonia, Baranja, and Western Sirmium (UNTAES), January 1996–January 1998: Lessons Learned* (New York: United Nations, July 1998), pp. 46–47.

3. Kofi Annan, "UN Peacekeeping Operations and Cooperation with NATO," *NATO Review* 41, no. 5 (October 1993): 3–7.

4. See George A. Joulwan and Christopher C. Shoemaker, *Civilian-Military*

Cooperation in the Prevention of Deadly Conflict (Washington, DC: Carnegie Commission on Preventing Deadly Conflict, December 1998), pp. 15–16.

5. These reforms have been made as part of the implementation of recommendations made in the final report of the Brahimi panel on UN peace operations. See United Nations, *Report of the Panel on United Nations Peace Operations,* UN Doc. A/55/305-S/2000/809, August 21, 2000, paras. 58, 64 at pp. 10–11.

6. A similar recommendation is made in ibid., para. 64 at pp. 11–12.

7. Joulwan and Shoemaker, *Civilian-Military Cooperation,* pp. 20–22.

8. See United Nations, *Report of the Panel on United Nations Peace Operations,* paras. 198–217 at pp. 34–37.

9. As noted by Derek G. Boothby, *Cooperation Between the UN and NATO: Quo Vadis?* International Peace Academy (IPA) Seminar Report (New York: IPA, June 1999), pp. 7, 10.

10. On the role of the international security presence for Kosovo, see UN Security Council Resolution 1244 (1999), para. 9. The resolution directs the international security presence (KFOR) to coordinate closely with the work of the international civil presence (UNMIK). In the text of the NATO North Atlantic Council's June 10, 1999, authorization for Operation Joint Guardian (establishing KFOR), specific reference is also made to the requirement for KFOR to "help achieve a self-sustaining secure environment which will allow public security responsibilities to be transferred to appropriate civil organisations."

11. KFOR, speech by General Michael Jackson at Transfer of Authority Ceremony, Pristina, October 8, 1999.

12. The JSEC is the highest joint body for security coordination in Kosovo. Its members include the KFOR chief of staff, the UNMIK police commissioner, the Principal Deputy SRSG, and the chair of the Joint Implementation Commission. Interview with deputy political adviser to COMKFOR, Pristina, May 2001.

13. Michael Pugh, "Civil-Military Relations in the Kosovo Crisis: An Emerging Hegemony?" *Security Dialogue* 31, no. 2 (June 2000): 238.

14. By January 2001, UNMIK police personnel had reached a total of approximately 4,500 international police officers (of their authorized maximum strength of 4,718 officers), a level that has been maintained since. UNMIK police do have "police primacy" (i.e., authority for criminal investigations and arrests) in the Mitrovica region, but not "tactical primacy" (i.e., executive authority for the enforcement of law and order). See UNMIK Police, *Annual Report 2000* (Pristina: UNMIK Police, 2001), p. 16.

15. Klaus Reinhardt, "Commanding KFOR," *NATO Review* 48, no. 2 (Summer–Autumn 2000): 16–19.

16. Interview with senior officer, UNMIK Police Operations Department, May 2001.

17. Interviews with UNMIK O/SRSG and KFOR Main J3 Operations senior officers, Pristina, May 2001.

18. Michael C. Williams, *Civil-Military Relations and Peacekeeping,* Adelphi Paper no. 321 (London: International Institute for Strategic Studies, 1998), p. 48.

19. Interview with senior officer in KFOR Main J3 Operations, Pristina, May 2001.

20. International Crisis Group (ICG), *Kosovo: Let's Learn from Bosnia—Models and Methods of International Administration,* ICG Balkans Report no. 66 (Sarajevo: ICG, May 17, 1999), sec. 3.

21. On this point in general, see Annika S. Hansen, "International Security Assistance to War-Torn Societies," in Pugh, *Regeneration of War-Torn Societies,* pp. 41–42.

22. UNMIK, Pillar I press briefing, Pristina, May 21, 2001.

23. A similar recommendation is also made in United Nations, *Report of the Panel on United Nations Peace Operations,* para. 101 at p. 17.

24. This is not to say that there have not been interpillar disagreements at the senior management level of UNMIK (including problems arising from diverging reporting lines to three or four separate organizational headquarters), or that staff in the field have not been able to achieve good examples of ad hoc coordination. The multipillar mission structure is a new experience for all concerned, and in spite of its evident difficulties it has been a significant improvement over previous models.

25. While space limitations preclude a discussion of the role of judicial and penal reform, and rule of law capacity-building programs, these are crucial aspects of the broader management of the security sector and have been the focus of considerable efforts by UN and OSCE staff within UNMIK.

26. David Lightburn, "Seeking Security Solutions," *NATO Review* 48, no. 3 (Winter 2000): 12–15.

27. In its "Undertaking of Demilitarisation and Transformation" of June 21, 1999, the KLA pledged complete demilitarization by September 19, 1999. As part of this process, within these ninety days the KLA turned over to KFOR some 10,000 weapons and over 5 million rounds of ammunition.

28. See UNMIK Regulation 1999/8, "On the Establishment of the Kosovo Protection Corps," September 20, 1999. The regulation limits the total number of KPC personnel to 3,000 active members and 2,000 reservists. The preferred Albanian reading is "Kosova Defense Forces," instead of the official English name used by UNMIK and KFOR.

29. Together with the KPC and the KPS, IOM's (ICRS) program serves to actively assist the transformation and reintegration of former KLA combatants into productive civilian life. Over 10,000 former combatants are registered with the ICRS program.

30. UNMIK, Administrative Department for Civil Security and Emergency Preparedness, "Coordinating KPC Issues," March 16, 2001, p. 4.

31. Agim Çeku, "The Kosova Protection Corps," *RUSI (Royal United Services Institute) Journal* 146, no. 2 (April 2001): 27. The UNMIK mission budget, as approved by the Security Council, does not include funding for the KPC, which leaves the corps dependent on voluntary contributions from the EU and other donors.

32. UNMIK, O/SRSG Human Rights Unit, "Issue Analysis: A Current Assessment of the Kosovo Protection Corps," February 29, 2000.

33. Interview with KPC program managers, UNMIK Administrative Department for Civil Security and Emergency Preparedness, May 2001.

34. The UCPMB later agreed, as a result of sustained mediation efforts by NATO, to demilitarize and demobilize by the end of May 2001. Similar mediation by EU and U.S. envoys in Macedonia led to a political agreement in August 2001 under which the NLA agreed to demilitarize.

35. Agim Çeku, cited in Beth Potter, "Kosovo Corps Chief Fights Image Problem," Reuters, May 3, 2001.

36. See *General Framework Agreement for Peace in Bosnia and Herzegovina,* December 14, 1995, annex 11. This includes background checks and certification for police officers in the Federation and Republika Srpska, but the IPTF is unable to enforce cases of decertification.

37. Greg Schulte, "SFOR Continued," *NATO Review* 46, no. 2 (Summer 1998): 27–30. In Multinational Division Southwest (UK-Canada-Netherlands), SFOR troops have also intervened to ensure that decertified police officers do not continue, in defiance of UNMIBH, to carry out police duties.

38. The KPS is often held up as the only truly multiethnic institution in Kosovo today. It has some eighty Serb officers (roughly 7 percent of the total), as well as Roma, Turk, and Bosniak members in smaller numbers.

39. Espen Barth Eide, "The Internal Security Challenge in Kosovo," paper presented at the UNAUSA/IAI conference "Kosovo's Final Status," Rome, December 12–14, 1999, pp. 5–6.

40. Interview with senior officer in UNMIK Police Operations Department, Pristina, May 2001.

8

Military Forces and Public Security Challenges

Peter Viggo Jakobsen

William Flavin, of the former U.S. Army Peacekeeping Institute, asked the question that is at the heart of this chapter:

> The key is how do you fill the gap which occurs when the CIVPOL [UN Civilian Police] does not engage in a timely manner leaving the military to conduct law and order operations—a mission for which they are not trained and which is not in their mandate? . . . We [the U.S. Army] have engaged in these activities in the past, but does this mean the military must consider judicial systems and bring experts in prisons when they are deployed to peace operations in which these core institutions have failed?[1]

Military forces have been forced to come up with an answer to this question time and again since the 1990s, as this gap has been one of the few constants characterizing the multifunctional peace operations conducted since the end of the Cold War. Prior to the Kosovo Force (KFOR), a North Atlantic Treaty Organization (NATO) operation, the answer to this question was generally no. The military involvement in public security tasks should be as limited as possible, and it did not extend into judging and jailing. After KFOR and the Australian-led International Force for East Timor (INTERFET), this is no longer the case. In both operations military forces ended up acting as police, judges, and jailers, and as a result a growing number of prominent military commanders and UN officials have begun to paraphrase Dag Hammarskjöld, arguing that although peacekeeping is not a job for soldiers, they may sometimes be the only ones who can do it.[2] In the ensuing debate two schools of thought have locked horns: the minimalists and the vacuum-fillers. The minimalists maintain that the answer to Flavin's question is no. The military can provide security but should not act as judge and jailer as well. From

their point of view, the military involvement has gone too far. In the words of
U.S. Brigadier-General John Castellaw:

> [T]hese [rule of law functions] are not our roles. . . . I was pushed by some
> within our military organization in Timor to provide lawyers for investigat-
> ing atrocities and other civil legal issues. I opposed that. . . . That is an area
> that I clearly see as not a military role . . . it's easy to default to the military.
> I think that that's the unfortunate reality and in my view, it's absolutely the
> wrong thing to do.[3]

The vacuum-fillers beg to differ. In their view military involvement in
public security activities will remain part and parcel of future multifunctional
peace operations, and the military must be prepared to arrest, judge, and jail
criminals and armed elements in the initial stage of a peace operation if no one
else can. The appropriate role for the military is "vacuum filling." It must take
decisive action to close any public security vacuum as soon as it arrives in the
mission area. The reasoning behind this position is simple: such vacuum filling is key to mission success and only military forces will have the capacity
to accomplish this task in the initial phase in the foreseeable future.[4] General
Michael Jackson, the first KFOR commander, puts it this way:

> For those who say this is not for the military, my next question to them
> would be, for whom is it when there is nobody else there? . . . Or do you just
> let it go? Do you allow anarchy? What do you do when a foot patrol of sol-
> diers in Pristina comes across a Serb about to murder an Albanian? . . . You
> don't have a secure environment with murderers running around.[5]

The claim made in this chapter is that neither position is viable in practice,
and that no effective solution is visible on the horizon. The vacuum-fillers are
right in theory. The logical solution is to let the military fill the public security
gap in the initial phase if no one else can. The problem is that reluctance and
reactive minimalism will prevent this from happening in practice in the near
future. This is what happened in Kosovo, and although this operation served as
an eye-opener for many, the political will to draw the logical consequences
simply does not exist. Western conflict management has been characterized by
reactive damage limitation rather than proactive policymaking throughout the
1990s, and nothing suggests that this is about to change.[6] The challenge for
practitioners in the near term is therefore to come up with realistic and second-
best solutions rather than pin their hopes on the ideal ones—that is, military or
UN "law and order packages" that are unlikely to materialize.

This chapter is divided into four parts. The first part introduces the problem presented by the public security gap and the solution that everybody can
agree on in theory. In the second part a case study of the military involvement
in public security tasks in Kosovo reveals the abyss currently separating the-

ory from practice. The third part spells out why the lessons learned in Kosovo will not result in robust vacuum filling in the near future, even though this would be the logical thing to do. Policy prescriptions are outlined in the chapter conclusion.

The Problem and Its (Theoretical) Solution

Surprising as it may seem in light of the above, there is consensus at the theoretical or doctrinal level about the nature of the problem and how it should be solved. There is general agreement that the public security gap should be closed as quickly as possible because failure to do so may compromise the long-term success of a peace operation. It has also become generally accepted that the entire security triad, consisting of the police, judiciary, and penal system, must be rebuilt, and that the neglect of the judiciary and the penal system, which has characterized many recent peace operations, is a recipe for failure. Efforts aimed at strengthening the police will not have the desired effect unless the criminals can be judged and jailed.[7]

Second, it is generally understood that the "one size fits all" approach must be avoided. Each security gap is different, and it is important to identify the precise nature of the gap at hand before taking steps to fill it in order to avoid wasting resources or making the situation worse.[8] Without going into details, the different nature of the gaps that peace/intervention forces have encountered can be illustrated schematically by a comparison of recent peace enforcement operations, shown in Table 8.1.

Third, there is agreement that military forces have a role to play in filling the public security gap. To this one may add that military forces have done so more often, and to a far greater extent, than many minimalists realize. Both public security operations and nation building have been part and parcel of the counterinsurgency operations, colonial interventions, and occupations that military forces have conducted in the past.[9] This has also consistently been the case in peace operations with enforcement (Chapter VII) authority authorized or commanded by the UN. Although it is beyond the scope of this chapter to provide a detailed analysis of the latter, Table 8.2, which illustrates the role played by military forces in peace operations, underlines that military involvement in public security tasks has become the rule rather than the exception during the 1990s.

Finally, there is also agreement about a three-phase solution that gradually scales back the military involvement in public security tasks in peace operations. In the emergency phase, the intervening military forces are responsible for restoring stability to the point where international or local police forces can function effectively. The stabilization phase is entered when this objective is achieved and primary responsibility for law and order can be

Table 8.1   Different Types of Public Security Gaps

	Police	Judiciary	Penal System
Operation Just Cause (Panama)	Collapsed	Nonfunctional	Collapsed
UNITAF (Somalia)	Collapsed	Collapsed	Collapsed
MNF (Haiti)	Corrupt, abusive, politicized	Politicized, dysfunctional	Dysfunctional, abusive
I/SFOR (Bosnia)	Corrupt, divided along ethnic lines	Corrupt, divided along ethnic lines	Dysfunctional, abusive
KFOR (Kosovo)	Collapsed	Collapsed	Collapsed
INTERFET (East Timor)	Collapsed	Collapsed	Collapsed
ISAF (Afghanistan)	Nonfunctional	Nonfunctional	Nonfunctional

Sources: Michael Bailey, Robert Maguire, and J. O'Neil G. Pouliot, "Haiti: Military-Police Partnership for Public Security," in Robert B. Oakley, Michael J. Dziedzic, and Eliot M. Goldberg, eds., *Policing the New World Disorder: Peace Operations and Public Security* (Washington, DC: NDU Press, 1998), pp. 215–252; "Filling the Vacuum—Prerequisites to Security in Afghanistan," report of the Consortium for Response to the Afghanistan Transition, March 2002, http://www.ifes.org/news/craft.pdf; Michael J. Dziedzic and Andy Bair, "The International Police Task Force," in Larry Wentz, ed., *Lessons from Bosnia: The IFOR Experience* (Washington, DC: NDU Press, 1998); Anthony Gray and Maxwell Manwaring, "Panama: Operation Just Cause," in Oakley, Dziedzic, and Goldberg, eds., *Policing the New World Disorder;* Michael J. Kelly, Timothy L. H. McCormack, Paul Muggleton, and Bruce M. Oswald, "Legal Aspects of Australia's Involvement in the International Force for East Timor," *International Review of the Red Cross* no. 841 (March 31, 2001): 101–139.

transferred to the UN or local authorities. In the stabilization phase military or constabulary forces may still be called upon to act in support of the civilian authorities and the civilian police forces, but their involvement in public security activities is now secondary. This phase ends when the local authorities assume full responsibility for public security.[10]

The consensus does not extend beyond the general shape of this model, however. Although it is generally agreed that military involvement is all but inevitable in the emergency phase of a peace operation, there is little agreement about the precise nature and extent of this involvement. The ambivalent position of the United States is telling in this respect. In the latest draft of its forthcoming doctrine for peace operations, the U.S. Army acknowledges that it may have to restore law and order, establish and run temporary confinement facilities, and assist in the establishment of a workable judicial system in a failed state situation—the Kosovo experience has in other words found its way into doctrine.[11] This stands in direct contrast to the public position that President George W. Bush and the Pentagon have taken on this issue. This position was succinctly summed up in a comment by General Henry H. Shelton of the U.S. Army, then chairman of the Joint Chiefs of Staff, in November 2000: "We can provide a safe and secure environment, but we don't do the

Table 8.2   Military Involvement in Filling the Public Security Gap

System	Local Police	Local Judiciary	Local Penal
Operation Just Cause (Panama)	Emergency law enforcement Training of police Joint patrols On-call backup Riot control	Legal advice and assistance in reconstruction	Construction and operation of detention centers
UNITAF (Somalia)	Emergency law enforcement Training of police Joint patrols On-call backup Riot control	Material support and protection	Construction and operation of detention centers
MNF (Haiti)	Emergency law enforcement Training of police	Legal advice on reconstruction	Construction and operation of detention centers Training of prison guards
I/SFOR (Bosnia)	Joint patrols On-call backup Riot control Logistical and planning support Support for war crimes tribunal	Support for institution building	—
KFOR (Kosovo)	Emergency law enforcement Joint patrols On-call backup Riot control Support for war crimes tribunal	Emergency judiciary Protection of courts and personnel	Construction and operation of detention centers
INTERFET (East Timor)	Emergency law enforcement	Emergency judiciary	Detention management
ISAF (Afghanistan)	Joint patrols Training Material support	—	—

Sources: Same as Table 8.1 plus "Operation Just Cause: Lessons Learned," *CALL Bulletin* no. 90-9 (Fort Leavenworth, KS: Center for Army Lessons Learned, 1990); *Law and Military Operations in Haiti 1994–95: Lessons Learned for Judge Advocates* (Charlottesville, VA: Center for Law and Military Operations, 1995), pp. 64–65; Mark Warner et al., *SFOR Lessons Learned in the Establishment of Peace with Respect for Law* (Carlisle, PA: U.S. Army Peacekeeping Institute, 2000), pp. 37, 40.

law enforcement, we don't do the court systems."[12] It is the nature and the extent of the military involvement that is the bone of contention in the debate between the minimalists and the vacuum-fillers. The negative implications this lack of agreement can have on the ground were highlighted by the KFOR operation.

KFOR: A Case of Reluctant Vacuum Filling

The Kosovo operation was chosen as a case study because it represents a worst-case scenario.[13] An analysis of the future military involvement in public security tasks must be based on a worst-case scenario to ensure that the full range of potential military tasks are taken into account.

The Nature of the Security Gap in Kosovo

When KFOR began to enter Kosovo on June 12, 1999, there were no police forces and no functioning courts, and the penal system had also collapsed. The Serbs, who had fulfilled most of these functions during the old regime, had fled, and by October the seven Serb judges and prosecutors serving in the emergency judicial system set up by the UN in July had resigned, complaining of a lack of security, the application of the wrong law by their Kosovar Albanian counterparts, discrimination against Serbs in the administration of justice, and lack of sufficient payment. Most of the Kosovar Albanian judges and prosecutors appointed to the emergency system had not served for ten years prior,[14] and they were biased against the Serbs.[15] With respect to the penal system the situation looked equally bleak. The Serb correctional staff had left and their Kosovar Albanian colleagues had not worked for the previous ten years, the prisons were empty or destroyed, and many detainees had been murdered or taken to Serbia (see Chapter 9).

Finally, there was confusion concerning the applicable law. The UN Mission in Kosovo (UNMIK) first decided to apply Serbian and Yugoslavian law because of UN Resolution 1244's commitment to respect Yugoslav sovereignty. This proved impossible because the Kosovar Albanian judges and prosecutors applied the Kosovo criminal code, which had been annulled by the Serbs in 1989–1990, instead of the Serbian code. Therefore, UNMIK repealed its initial decision on December 12, 1999, enabling the application of the Kosovo criminal code and other Kosovo regional laws.[16]

With the Serb forces gone, the Kosovo Albanian majority unleashed a wave of revenge attacks on the remaining Serb, Roma, and other minority groups. In most municipalities, the Kosovo Liberation Army (KLA) moved quickly to assume control, appointing "mayors" and other administrators, but its leadership did little to curb revenge killings, the looting and torching of houses, and the intimidation of the minorities, particularly Serbs and Roma, for which former KLA members were chiefly responsible.[17] Members of the KLA and its successor, the Kosovo Protection Corps (KPC), were also deeply involved in the rise of organized crime that characterized the months following the Serbian withdrawal.[18]

KFOR and UNMIK thus faced the challenge of rebuilding the entire public security triad from scratch in an environment characterized by ethnic violence and rampant crime, and by active opposition from the Albanians and the remaining Serbs at all levels of society to any initiative that they deemed contrary to their ethnic group interests. As a U.S. military police officer in KFOR remarked: "There was no such thing as an Albanian witness to a crime against a Serb."[19]

KFOR Is Drawn into the Public Security Vacuum

UN Resolution 1244 made KFOR responsible for ensuring public security in the emergency phase until UNMIK was capable of taking over, and NATO planners originally envisioned that KFOR would perform policing duties for three months before turning those duties over to UN police.[20] The UN was not able to meet this deadline due to funding problems, cumbersome procedures, and huge problems with respect to finding qualified police officers and other civilian staff in adequate numbers. A year into the operation, UNMIK police had only 3,626 civilian police of its authorized strength of 4,718, and the international civil administration had only 292 professional personnel out of its authorized total of 435.[21] In the first half of 2000 KFOR was still substituting rather than supporting UNMIK police. It was only in the second half of 2000 that the emphasis shifted from substitution to support,[22] and the operation in doctrinal terms can be said to have moved from the emergency phase to the stabilization phase. UNMIK police did not begin to conduct patrols until early August, and it took another month before the process of transferring primary responsibility for policing from KFOR to UNMIK was initiated with the latter assuming primary responsibility for law enforcement in Pristina on September 13.[23] By early June 2000 UNMIK police had only assumed full responsibility for policing in two out of Kosovo's five police regions (Pristina and Prizren),[24] and the handover was still not completed in January 2002, when KFOR still had responsibility for daily police operations in the Mitrovica region.[25] The handover of detention management was also protracted. The process began on August 23, 1999, when UNMIK police took over the Pristina detention center from KFOR; another two facilities were handed over to UNMIK by KFOR before the end of the year, but KFOR still ran two detention facilities by mid-2001.[26]

Although a NATO spokesman in late May 1999 indicated that NATO knew that it would be facing a "law and order vacuum" and that "a heavy force would be required to deter any further breakdown in law and order,"[27] it is clear that NATO had taken a too narrow view of its own role in ensuring public security and order and misjudged the capacity of the UN. NATO came much better prepared for policing than had been the case in Bosnia. A multi-national specialized unit (MSU)—a police force with military status—composed primarily of Italian Carabinieri, was included in the force package from the beginning, and the lead nations commanding the five multinational brigades that make up KFOR also deployed with more military police, criminal investigators, and MSUs than usual. Thus the British contingent deployed 140 Royal Military Police, including 13 detectives from the Special Investigation Branch, and the French arrived with 150 gendarmes.[28] Within the first two months, NATO planned to have a total of 900 military police and gendarmes deployed in Kosovo.[29]

This capacity proved insufficient with respect to preventing a further breakdown in law and order in the first months of the operation. With only 35,000 troops on the ground in early August, KFOR could not be everywhere and was forced to concentrate on the most serious offenses, such as murder, rape, and serious assault, and to ignore the majority of crimes, such as forced evictions, robbery, extortion, and other property crimes.[30] That the limited number of specialized KFOR personnel trained to conduct criminal investigations was completely overwhelmed is self-evident. This problem was compounded by NATO's failure to prepare adequately for the problems created by the collapse of the judiciary and the penal system. Believing that the UN would take over quickly, the U.S. contingent, leading one of KFOR's five multinational brigades, initially had its engineers build a small temporary detainment facility with a capacity to hold 48 detainees. When the mistake was realized, a larger facility for 130 detainees was built and a legal procedure put in place to ensure that each arrest was reviewed by a military lawyer within forty-eight hours.[31] The situation was the same in KFOR's other four sectors, as each lead nation ended up establishing a detention facility and similar procedures.[32] In spite of this improvisation, the combined capacity of the detention facilities operated by KFOR (space for some 250 detainees) only amounted to a drop in the ocean. Lack of detention space thus forced KFOR to refrain from arresting offenders, even those caught in the act of committing crimes, and to let many go shortly after their arrest. Further adding to the problem was the unusually high number of people released by the newly appointed Kosovar Albanian judges.[33]

Judging KFOR: Reluctant Vacuum Filling

That KFOR failed to stem the violence was partly due to its lack of resources and skills. Although soldiers can patrol the streets and arrest people breaking the law, and can conduct weapons searches, disarmament, and riot control, they are not trained to conduct criminal investigations and fight organized crime.[34] It is also clear that KFOR's involvement, not just in public security activities but also in other "nonmilitary" tasks, went much further than had been the case in the early phase of the Implementation Force (IFOR) operation in Bosnia, when such involvement was regarded as "mission creep." Yet in spite of this vast improvement, KFOR remained a reluctant and reactive vacuum-filler. The failure to establish a secure environment must also be explained by a lack of will to take the steps necessary to bring the situation under control.

The reaction from the Pentagon, when it realized that KFOR would have to do much more to fill the public security gap than initially anticipated, was revealing: harsh criticism of the UN for failing to do its job instead of taking the lead in finding an effective solution to the problems at hand. U.S. secretary of defense William Cohen flatly ruled out greater military involvement on the grounds that "the more we do, the less incentive there is for the U.N. to come in and assume that burden."[35] He was not alone. The first two KFOR commanders, and several national commanders, took turns complaining about their troops having to engage too much and for too long in "police-type actions."[36]

KFOR's reluctance manifested itself in three ways that reduced operational effectiveness in the emergency phase. First, it resulted in inadequate planning and preparation. There appears to have been no overall plans for the protection of minorities even though revenge attacks were to be expected.[37] An overall plan for reviewing arrests and running detention centers was also lacking, although the failure of the UN to arrive in time and assume this task was anything but surprising. After all, deployment delays have characterized virtually all UN peace operations since the 1990s, including the one in Bosnia that NATO is part of.[38] Moreover, the lessons learned from the U.S. intervention in Panama and the peace enforcement operations in Haiti and Somalia also suggested a need for a KFOR role in this area.[39] This lack of realism in the planning process complicated the process of handing over responsibility to the UN, which became a principal source of frustration and friction between KFOR and UNMIK in the first year of the operation.

Second, force protection was clearly accorded a higher priority than the rule of law. When the two clashed, force protection invariably came out on top. Several KFOR contingents were criticized for their unwillingness to intervene to stop crimes committed under their noses.[40] KFOR refrained from taking determined action against the KLA despite clear evidence that it was deeply involved in orchestrating the attacks on the Serbs and the Roma, was linked to organized crime, and was acting as an unofficial police force handing out rough justice and detaining people illegally.[41] For the first two months of the operation, KFOR did little to put effective pressure on the KLA leadership. It was not until mid-August 1999, when KFOR came under sustained media pressure for its failure to establish law and order, that it began to take a tougher line with the KLA.[42] Decisive action was never taken, however, out of concern that it would turn the former guerrilla army into an enemy of KFOR.

Another example is provided by the letter sent by the chairman of the Joint Chiefs of Staff, General Henry H. Shelton, to NATO's supreme commander, General Wesley K. Clark, telling him not to use U.S. troops outside their designated sector after an incident on February 20, 2000, in which U.S. soldiers had been forced to retreat from Mitrovica by a bottle-throwing mob.[43]

Finally, KFOR's reluctance also manifested itself in the unwillingness to impose martial law in order to stop a further breakdown in law and order. This step was discussed with UNMIK's leadership on a number of occasions but was eventually dropped since neither leadership liked it. For UNMIK it represented an admission of failure and KFOR was not willing to assume the responsibilities it would entail.[44] KFOR and UNMIK consequently settled for a less drastic step, a widening of the power to detain for up to twelve hours people deemed a threat to public order.[45] Unfortunately, this regulation, which made it possible to remove such people from their hometowns or even to deport them temporarily from Kosovo, did not have the desired effect.

Robust and Proactive Vacuum Filling

As Lieutenant-General Robert H. Fogelsong of the U.S. Air Force explains: "[T]he first thing you have to do when you go in there is to muscle—to stop, to threaten, to no-kidding demonstrate you are not going to put up with hostile action, and if it does take place you are going to respond in such a forceful way as to deter anyone else from doing it. If you do that early, then you can bring in the civil police on early."[46] This is the lesson to draw from the KFOR operation when military forces are deployed in a public security vacuum, and it is the lesson several former KFOR commanders and senior UN officials involved in the operation have drawn. They also agree that war criminals need to be identified and arrested by special forces as soon as possible, because a failure to do so will be seen as weakness.[47]

The conclusion is neither surprising nor new. The same lesson was drawn from the Unified Task Force (UNITAF) operation in Somalia, where this approach was employed by the Australian contingent with spectacular success. When the Australian contingent arrived in Somalia in January 1993 as part of UNITAF, the situation resembled the one in Kosovo, since there was no effective UN presence and the entire public security triad had collapsed. Unlike KFOR, however, the Australian contingent took a proactive and robust public security approach from day one. Since no effective civil authority existed, this approach was based on the laws of occupation, which is the equivalent of imposing martial law. Priority was given to disarmament, removal of the main bandit and warlord elements, reconstruction of the public security triad, and close contact and cooperation with legitimate representatives of the community, the local elders.

Disarmament was undertaken systematically and the Australian contingent confiscated almost 50 percent of the 2,250 small arms seized by UNITAF in the first ninety days of the operation. The Australians intervened whenever they came across fighting or armed criminals, and early shows of strength resulted in eleven armed contacts with Somali gunmen, which left five Somalis dead and at least six wounded.[48] Two key war criminals were identified, arrested, and removed as soon as the Australians had sufficient evidence to build a legal case against them. The result was a drastic improvement in law and order in the Australian sector. Steps were quickly taken to reestablish the local security triad, which was fully operational when the Australians left in May 1993. The triad continued for another two years until it was dismantled by Aideed's forces who took control of Baidoa in September 1995.[49]

Taken to its logical conclusion, robust vacuum filling may leave the military no choice but to run the judiciary and the jails until the UN or the local authorities can take over. It may thus require a willingness from the military to deploy with a complete law and order package.[50] This would certainly have been necessary in Kosovo, where such an approach would have required a detention capacity at least ten times greater than the one established, as well as the use of military judges to run the judiciary for a considerable period of time. Compared to Kosovo, the Australian sector in Somalia presented an easy case, because the warlords had no popular support and local police officers, judges, and jailers were eager to cooperate.

Conclusion: Muddling Through as the Way of the Future

Although robust vacuum filling by the military is the logical solution to the problem presented by the public security gap in the emergency phase, the willingness to engage in it simply does not exist. "Minimalist" resistance to judging, jailing, and even apprehending war criminals remains strong within the Western armed forces,[51] and nothing suggests that their political masters will coerce them into robust vacuum filling in the immediate future. Reactive minimalism has been the standard operation procedure chosen by Western governments on each occasion where they have been presented with an opportunity to engage in robust vacuum filling since the Kosovo operation. Western efforts to prevent and subsequently manage the civil war in Macedonia in 2001 were reactive, reluctant, and minimalist, and the same has been true with respect to the public security gap currently existing in Afghanistan. Repeated calls from the Karzai government for a deployment of a 20,000-strong peacekeeping force to help it extend its authority beyond Kabul have fallen on deaf ears. Although the need for such a force is obvious and generally acknowledged by Western diplomats involved in Afghanistan and the International Security Assistance Force (ISAF) commander,[52] all the West has been willing to deploy is a token force of 4,500 troops.[53] In Iraq it was also déjà-vu as the U.S.-led force was clearly unprepared and unwilling to respond to the chaos and looting that erupted in major Iraqi cities after the fall of Saddam Hussein in April 2003. Pleas from the Red Cross, aid organizations, and Iraqi citizens that the U.S. forces restore law and order got a telling response from a senior U.S. commander: "At no time do we really see becoming a police force."[54] If the West cannot mobilize the will to take robust action to close the public security gap in operations linked to the war against terrorism, it is difficult to see where it can do so.

The public security gap will therefore remain a problem in peace operations for the foreseeable future. Robust action and deployment of military law and order packets will be the exception and not the rule. Military involvement in public security will continue to be reactive and reluctant, as was the case in Kosovo. The prospects for the creation of rapid reaction law and order teams consisting of judges and jailers and other legal experts, along the lines advocated in the Brahimi Report, are not bright either.[55] The efforts undertaken by the European Union (EU), the Organization for Security and Cooperation in Europe (OSCE), the UN, and individual countries to boost the international capacity to deploy civilian police, judges, and jailers at short notice will not make much difference in the short term. While they represent a step in the right direction, they do little to solve the underlying problem: the desperate shortage of qualified personnel, which stems from the fact that, unlike the military, police forces are created with the sole purpose of dealing with internal tasks. The principal effect is to create databases of personnel already deployed in the field. It may sound impressive that the EU made available 5,000 police officers and 200 rule of law experts for deployment on peace operations in 2003. But the EU already had more than 3,300 police officers deployed in the field in 2000, and in 2001 the number of rule of law experts deployed was 150.[56] Moreover, the mere existence of standby arrangements does not mean that personnel will be available for action when required. The UN's standby system is a case in point—standby forces, as John MacKinlay reminds us, "tend to be exactly what the name implies: forces standing by."[57]

Finally, we have the MSUs hailed by NATO, the United States, and several Western countries, who incidentally do not happen to have such forces themselves, as the solution to the problem.[58] They have been oversold. They are short in supply—NATO has been unable to find the number required for Bosnia, their effectiveness has been hampered by doctrinal problems, varying national operational styles, and lack of coordination with both military forces and the police, and they cannot fill the security gap on their own. They only act in support of the military or the police.[59]

The lack of military will and civilian capacity means that the international community for the foreseeable future will be unable to deploy the right number of law and order experts with the right qualifications in the right place at the right time. As a result, military personnel, CIVPOL, MSUs, and rule of law experts all have their role to play in the efforts to close the public security gap that the international community will continue to encounter on future operations. The challenge will be to construct the optimal force mix from the personnel available, when the need arises. Muddling through will remain the way to proceed for the time being, while the international community continues to increase the pool of qualified personnel and improve training, selection methods, and coordination at all levels. Closing the public security gap will be a marathon rather than a sprint.

Notes

1. William Flavin, "Doctrinal Review: American View," in U.S. Army, *Challenges of Peacekeeping and Peace Support into the Twenty-First Century: The Doctrinal Dimension* (Carlisle, PA: U.S. Army Peacekeeping Institute, Center for Strategic Leadership, 2000), p. 80.

2. Dag Hammarskjöld was UN Secretary-General from 1953 to 1961.

3. John Castellaw, quoted in Edith B. Wilkie and Beth C. DeGrasse, *A Force for Peace and Security: U.S. and Allied Commanders' Views of the Military's Role in Peace Operations and the Impact on Terrorism of States in Conflict* (Washington, DC: Peace Through Law Education Fund, 2002), p. 54.

4. Conrad C. Crane, *Landpower and Crises: Army Roles and Missions in Smaller-Scale Contingencies During the 1990s* (Carlisle, PA: U.S. Army War College, Strategic Studies Institute, 2001); Sheila Coutts and Kelvin Ong, *Managing Security Challenges in Post-Conflict Peacebuilding* (New York: International Peace Academy, 2001); Peter D. Menk, *Post-Conflict Strategic Requirements Workshop,* Issues Paper no. 1-01 (Carlisle, PA: U.S. Army War College, Center for Strategic Leadership, 2001).

5. Michael Jackson, quoted in Wilkie and DeGrasse, *A Force for Peace and Security,* p. 38.

6. Peter Viggo Jakobsen, *Western Use of Coercive Diplomacy After the Cold War: A Challenge for Theory and Practice* (Basingstoke: Macmillan, 1998).

7. Gareth J. Evans, *Cooperating for Peace: The Global Agenda for the 1990s and Beyond* (St. Leonards, New South Wales: Allen & Unwin, 1993), p. 56; Michael J. Kelly, *Restoring and Maintaining Order in Complex Peace Operations: The Search for a Legal Framework* (The Hague: Kluwer Law International, 1999); Mark Plunkett, "Reestablishing Law and Order in Peace-Maintenance," *Global Governance* 4, no. 1 (January–March 1998): 61–80; Hansjorg Strohmeyer, "Collapse and Reconstruction of a Judicial System: The United Nations Missions in Kosovo and East Timor," *American Journal of International Law* 95, no. 1 (January 2001): 46–63; UN Doc. A/55/305-

S/2000/809, August 21, 2000 (Brahimi Report); Wilkie and DeGrasse, *A Force for Peace and Security.*

8. Michael J. Kelly, "Legitimacy and the Public Security Function," in Robert B. Oakley, Michael J. Dziedzic, and Eliot M. Goldberg, eds., *Policing the New World Disorder: Peace Operations and Public Security* (Washington, DC: NDU Press, 1998), pp. 399–431; Rama Mani, "The Rule of Law or the Rule of Might? Restoring Legal Justice in the Aftermath of Conflict," in Michael Pugh, ed., *Regeneration of War-Torn Societies* (London: Macmillan, 2000), pp. 94–95; J. W. Rollins, "Civil-Military Cooperation (CIMIC) in Crisis Response Operations: The Implications for NATO," *International Peacekeeping* 8, no. 1 (Spring 2001): 122–129.

9. William Rosenau, "Facing the Unpalatable: The U.S. Military and Law Enforcement in Operations Other Than War," *Low Intensity Conflict and Law Enforcement* 4, no. 2 (Autumn 1995): 187–202; Erwin A. Schmidl, "Police Functions in Peace Operations: An Historical Overview," in Oakley, Dziedzic, and Goldberg, *Policing the New World Disorder.*

10. Variations of this three-phase logic can be found in U.S. Army, *FM 3-07 (100-20) Stability Operations and Support Operations* (Washington, DC: Headquarters Department of the Army, DRAG, February 1, 2002), pp. 4–10; UK Ministry of Defense, *Joint Warfare Publication 3-50: Peace Support Operations* (Northwood, UK: Ministry of Defense, 1998), para. 505; "Nice European Council: Presidency Conclusions," Council of the European Union Press Release no. 400/1/00, Brussels, December 8, 2000; Rollins, "Civil-Military Cooperation," pp. 124–125; Strohmeyer, "Collapse and Reconstruction."

11. U.S. Army, *FM 3-07 (100-20) Stability Operations and Support Operations,* pp. 4-10, 4-26, 4-27.

12. Henry H. Shelton, quoted in "Shelton: Peacekeeping Missions Unavoidable," *Washington Post,* November 17, 2000, p. A02.

13. Although INTERFET in East Timor was also faced with a collapsed security triad, it did not have to contend with ethnic hatred and lack of cooperation and outright opposition from the parties.

14. Only 30 of the 756 judges and prosecutors serving in Kosovo when the war began were Kosovar Albanians. See United Nations, *Report of the Secretary-General on UNMIK,* UN Doc. S/1999/779, July 12, 1999, para. 66.

15. OSCE Mission in Kosovo, Department of Human Rights and Rule of Law Division, *The Development of the Kosovo Judicial System (10 June through 15 December 1999),* Pristina, December 17, 1999.

16. Ibid.

17. Lawyers Committee for Human Rights, *A Fragile Peace: Laying the Foundations for Justice in Kosovo* (New York: Lawyers Committee for Human Rights, October 1999).

18. R. Jeffrey Smith, "Rule of Law Is Elusive in Kosovo," *Washington Post,* July 29, 2001, p. A1; John Sweeney and Jens Holsoe, "Revealed: UN Corps' Reign of Terror in Kosovo," *The Observer,* March 12, 2000.

19. Richard W. Swengros, "Military Police Functions in Kosovo," *Military Police,* May 2000.

20. Gregory Piatt, "Law-and-Order Duties Shifting Away from U.S. Troops in Kosovo," *Stars and Stripes* (European edition), November 27, 2000, http://call.army.mil/products/nftf/julaug00/swengros.htm.

21. UN Doc. S/2000/538, June 6, 2000, paras. 28, 31.

22. Piatt, "Law-and-Order Duties."

23. Lawyers Committee for Human Rights, *A Fragile Peace;* Lawyers Committee for Human Rights, *Kosovo: Protection and Peace-Building* (New York: Lawyers Committee for Human Rights, August 1999).

24. UN Doc. S/2000/538, June 6, 2000, para. 32.

25. UN Doc. S/2002/62, January 15, 2002, para 31. However, UNMIK police had investigative primacy in Mitrovica.

26. Roland Lavoie, "KFOR Press Update," KFOR Press and Information Center, Pristina, November 29, 1999; Chapter 9, this volume; Mannie Mendoza, "Pristina Detention Centre," UNMIK Police Press and Public Information Office, Pristina, August 12, 2000; UN Doc. S/1999/987, September 16, 1999, para. 27; UN Doc. S/2000/177, March 3, 2000, para. 114.

27. Linda D. Kozaryn, "Robust, Ready Peacekeeping Force Needed Soon," *American Forces Press Service,* May 26, 1999.

28. Chris Bird, "Autopsies Delay Burial of Slain Serb Farmers," *The Guardian,* July 27, 1999, p. 12; Isabelle Ligner, "Le 'travail de fourmis' des gendarmes français au Kosovo," Agence France Presse, July 7, 1999. For the U.S. contingent, see Linda D. Kozaryn, "U.S. Forces Help Police Kosovo," *American Forces Press Service,* August 10, 1999.

29. Carlotta Gall, "Twelve War-Crimes Suspects Held By NATO's Police in Kosovo," *New York Times,* July 8, 1999, p. A8.

30. Lawyers Committee for Human Rights, *A Fragile Peace.*

31. Susan Ellis, "Mine Awareness Keeps U.S. Troops Safe in Kosovo," *USIS Washington File,* July 13, 1999; Donald G. McNeil Jr., "G.I.'s in Kosovo Are Judges, Jailers, and Much More," *New York Times,* November 22, 2000; Dana Priest, "Waging Peace in Kosovo," *Washington Post,* November 23, 1999, p. A01; Swengros, "Military Police Functions in Kosovo."

32. Lawyers Committee for Human Rights, *A Fragile Peace;* U.S. Army, *FM 3-07 (100-20) Stability Operations and Support Operations;* Chapter 9, this volume; Friedrich Riechmann, "Military Aspects," in Winrich Kühne and Jochen Prantl, eds., *The Brahimi Report: Overcoming the North-South Divide—Sixth International Workshop, Berlin, June 29–30, 2001* (Berlin: German Institute for International and Security Affairs, 2001), pp. 43–44; G. R. Rubin, "Peace Support Operations and Practical Legal Problems 'on the Ground,'" *RUSI Journal* 144, no. 6 (December 1999): 32–33.

33. Lawyers Committee for Human Rights, *A Fragile Peace.*

34. For a clarification of what "policing" actually entails and what military forces can do, see Alice Hills, "The Inherent Limits of Military Forces in Policing Peace Operations," *International Peacekeeping* 8, no. 3 (Autumn 2001): 79–98.

35. William Cohen, quoted in Eric Schmitt, "U.N. Drags Feet in Kosovo, Pentagon Leaders Declare," *New York Times,* July 21, 1999, p. A10. The blame game continued in the first part of 2000, forcing the UNMIK leadership to point out time and again that it could not police Kosovo without the police officers it had been promised. See Elizabeth Becker, "White House Asks Allies to Bolster the Kosovo Police Force," *New York Times,* February 24, 2000, p. A3; William M. Reilly, "Kosovo Police: Crime Down, Needs Up," *United Press International,* February 2, 2000.

36. Christian Brøndum, "General: Giv os klar besked," *Berlingske Tidende,* February 29, 2000; Carlotta Gall, "General Says Civilians Must Take Control in Kosovo," *New York Times,* September 13, 1999; Carlotta Gall, "Filling a 'Gap,' New NATO Commander Moves to Police Kosovo," *International Herald Tribune,* December 22, 1999, p. 4. Interestingly, the two first KFOR commanders, Generals Michael Jackson and Klaus Reinhardt, have subsequently come to regard vacuum filling as inevitable. See Wilkie and DeGrasse, *A Force for Peace and Security,* pp. 33–38.

37. Alexandros Yannis, "Kosovo Under International Administration," *Survival* 43, no. 2 (Summer 2001): 37.

38. Andrew Bair and Michael J. Dziedzic, "The International Police Task Force," in Larry Wentz, ed., *Lessons from Bosnia: The IFOR Experience* (Washington, DC: NDU Press, 1998), www.dodccrp.org/bostoc.htm; Dziedzic and Bair, "International Police Task Force."

39. *Law and Military Operations in Haiti, 1994–95: Lessons Learned for Judge Advocates* (Charlottesville, VA: Center for Law and Military Operations, 1995), pp. 64–65. Kelly, *Restoring and Maintaining Order;* F. M. Lorenz, "Confronting Thievery in Somalia," *Military Review* 74, no. 8 (August 1995): 46–55.

40. Lawyers Committee for Human Rights, *A Fragile Peace;* ICG, *Kosovo Report Card,* ICG Balkans Report no. 100 (Pristina: ICG, August 28, 2000), pp. 17–20; Steven Erlanger, "Chaos and Intolerance Prevailing in Kosovo Despite U.N.'s Efforts," *New York Times,* November 22, 1999, p. A1. The British contingent was the exception to this rule, as it was generally commended for its robust approach. See, for instance, Dominick Donald, "The Doctrine Gap: The Enduring Problem of Contemporary Peace Support Operations Thinking," *Contemporary Security Policy* 22, no. 3 (December 2001): 127, 138, n. 105, 106.

41. Lawyers Committee for Human Rights, *A Fragile Peace;* Human Rights Watch, "Abuses Against Serbs and Roma in the New Kosovo," *HRW Report* 11, no. 10 (1999). www.hrw.org/reports/1999/kosov2/; Philip Smucker, "U.N. Backs Away from U.S.-Made Deal with KLA," *Washington Times,* August 20, 1999.

42. Carlotta Gall, "NATO-led Forces Begin Crackdown on Kosovar Army," *New York Times,* August 15, 1999; Smith, "Rule of Law Is Elusive in Kosovo"; Sweeney and Holsoe, "Revealed"; "Les Graves errements des Occidentaux au Kosovo," *Le Monde Du Renseignement,* January 11, 2001.

43. Steven Erlanger, "U.N. Official Warns of Losing the Peace in Kosovo," *New York Times,* July 3, 2000; Jane Perlez, "Joint Chiefs Chairman Protests Troops' Mission to Kosovo Town," *New York Times,* March 1, 2000, p. A10.

44. International Crisis Group, *Kosovo Report Card,* p. 15. See also Chapter 9, this volume.

45. See UNMIK Regulation 2, "On the Prevention of Access by Individuals and Their Removal to Secure Public Peace and Order," August 12, 1999.

46. Robert H. Fogelsong, quoted in Wilkie and DeGrasse, *A Force for Peace and Security,* p. 54.

47. Halvor Hartz, "Public Security," in U.S. Army, *Challenges of Peacekeeping,* p. 130; Strohmeyer, "Collapse and Reconstruction"; Wilkie and DeGrasse, *A Force for Peace and Security,* pp. 36–38, 47–51.

48. Robert G. Patman, "Disarming Somalia: The Contrasting Fortunes of United States and Australian Peacekeepers During United Nations Intervention, 1992–1993," *African Affairs* 96, no. 385 (October 1997): 522–528.

49. Kelly, *Restoring and Maintaining Order,* pp. 33–63. The U.S. contingent in contrast employed a minimalist approach to law and order, and this makes one wonder what might have happened if the U.S. contingent had used the Australian approach in Mogadishu. UNITAF's senior legal adviser subsequently concluded that the United States should adopt the Australian approach to law and order in the future. Lorenz, "Confronting Thievery in Somalia." The MNF peace operation in Haiti (1994–1995) also provides evidence in support of a robust approach, as U.S. special forces who adopted a proactive approach during the operation proved far more successful than the soldiers of the Tenth Mountain Division, who employed a minimalist approach. See Walter E. Kretchik, Robert F. Baumann, and John T. Fishel, *Invasion, Intervention,*

"Intervasion": A Concise History of the U. S. Army in Operation Uphold Democracy (Fort Leavenworth, KS: U.S. Army Command and General Staff College Press, 1998), pp. 101–121.

50. For practical suggestions concerning the composition of military law and order packets, see Kelly, *Restoring and Maintaining Order,* pp. 237–279; Michael J. Kelly, Timothy L. H. McCormack, Paul Muggleton, and Bruce M. Oswald, "Legal Aspects of Australia's Involvement in the International Force for East Timor," *International Review of the Red Cross,* No. 841 (March 31, 2001): pp. 101–139.

51. See, for instance, Wilkie and DeGrasse, *A Force for Peace and Security,* pp. 47–51, 54–55.

52. For an assessment of the security situation and a call for greater international support, see UN Doc. S/2002/278, March 18, 2002, paras. 45–54, 123–128. The first ISAF commander, British major-general Sir John McColl, also supported an expansion of the force. See Ahmed Rashid, *Security Concerns in Afghanistan,* March 14, 2002, www.eurasianet.org/departments/insight/articles/eav031402.shtml.

53. This may change since the Western unwillingness to adopt a more proactive approach toward filling the Afghan security vacuum, especially the unwillingness of the Bush administration to support an expansion of the ISAF peacekeeping force, has triggered a barrage of criticism. See "Afghanistan at Risk," *New York Times,* March 27, 2002, p. A22; "A Minimalist Peace," *Washington Post,* March 27, 2002, p. A20; "Security for More Afghans," *Los Angeles Times,* April 11, 2002, p. A14; Flora Lewis, "The Afghanistan War Hasn't Been Won," *International Herald Tribune,* April 10, 2002; Richard Holbrooke, "Rebuilding Nations," *Washington Post,* April 1, 2002, p. A15; Sebastian Mallaby, "And Their Armies," *Washington Post,* April 1, 2002, p. A15.

54. Andrew Buncombe and John Lichfield, "A City in Flames, a Nation in Chaos," *The Independent* (London), April 12, 2003, p. 1.

55. UN Doc. A/55/305-S/2000/809, August 21, 2000.

56. Thomas Papworth and Sharon Wiharta, *Policing Europe: European Policing? The Challenge of Coordination in International Policing* (Stockholm: SIPRI, 2000), p. 3; Michael Matthiessen, "The European Union (EU)," in Kühne and Prantl, *The Brahimi Report,* pp. 115–118.

57. John MacKinlay, quoted in Peter Viggo Jakobsen, *CIMIC: Civil-Military Cooperation—Lessons Learned and Models for the Future,* DUPI Report no. 9 (Copenhagen: Danish Institute of International Affairs, 2000), p. 47.

58. See U.S. Department of State, *Strengthening Criminal Justice Systems in Support of Peace Operations and Other Complex Contingencies,* PDD-71 (Washington, DC: U.S. Department of State, February 24, 2000); Peter Viggo Jakobsen, "The Emerging Consensus on Grey Area Peace Operations Doctrine: Will It Last and Enhance Operational Effectiveness?" *International Peacekeeping* 7, no. 3 (Autumn 2000): 48; Linda D. Kozaryn, "NATO Chief Says More Police Vital in Kosovo," *American Forces Press Service,* February 8, 2000.

59. ICG, *No Early Exit: NATO's Continuing Challenge in Bosnia,* ICG Balkans Report no. 110 (Sarajevo: ICG, May 22, 2001), pp. 5–9; Chapter 7, this volume; Hills, "The Inherent Limits"; Jakobsen, "The Emerging Consensus," pp. 48–49; Gretory Piatt, "Long-Term Policing Options for Bosnia Are High on NATO, U.N. Agendas," *Stars and Stripes* (European edition), November 21, 2001.

9

Reviving the Judicial and Penal System in Kosovo

David Marshall

In 1999 the UN Mission in Kosovo (UNMIK) was faced with the daunting task of reviving a judicial and penal system from the ground up. Since then much has been achieved in that Kosovo now has a functioning judicial and penal system. First, the presence of international judges and prosecutors has to some extent alleviated the concerns of ethnic bias in judicial proceedings. Second, a judicial inspection unit was established to address allegations of judicial and prosecutorial misconduct, something that was initially ignored. More impressive has been UNMIK's success in establishing, within fifteen months, seven fully functioning detention facilities. The mission is currently in the process of developing a framework for the implementation of a probation and parole system. Success in this critical area was due in large part to a coherent strategy that included the early introduction of international experts in penal management.

But the successes have been overshadowed by UNMIK's failure to develop a coherent strategy for dealing with the war crimes trials and its interference with the independence of the judiciary. The introduction of international judicial actors into war crime–related cases was slow and ad hoc. Moreover, these actors had no knowledge of international humanitarian law, had limited experience in trying serious criminal cases, and had not received preentry training on the applicable law. The lack of an experienced human rights lawyer within the Office of the Legal Adviser (OLA) of the UN Special Representative of the Secretary-General (SRSG), the failure to ensure that UNMIK draft regulations were vetted for human rights compliance, and the disenfranchisement of the Organization for Cooperation and Security in Europe (OSCE) also contributed to the crisis in the justice sector. Given the formidable mandate, it is surprising that human rights legal expertise was not made a priority. It seems probable that the presence of such expertise would have prevented the zealous use of executive orders by the SRSG to arbitrarily detain persons in a region where UNMIK had not declared a state of emergency.

Furthermore, UNMIK's failure to consult local legal professionals and adequately inform the public about critical changes in the justice system, as well as the practice of ignoring judicial decisions of UN-appointed judges, generated disillusionment and cynicism about human rights rhetoric within the local population and impeded the development of legal institutions and infrastructure.

The Criminal Justice System

In Resolution 1244 (1999), the UN Security Council authorized the Secretary-General to establish an international civil presence in Kosovo that would provide an interim administration designed to protect and promote human rights.[1] The resolution provides for the establishment of UNMIK, under which the people of Kosovo can enjoy "substantial autonomy and meaningful self-administration" within the Federal Republic of Yugoslavia (FRY).[2] The international civil authorities' responsibilities include the performance of "civil administrative functions where and as long as required."[3] UNMIK initially administered the justice system through the UN Department of Judicial Affairs (DJA), which was responsible for the overall management of the judicial system and correctional service.[4] In 2001, UNMIK Pillar I, for police and justice, was created and brought together law enforcement and judicial affairs. Under UNMIK Regulation 2001/09, "On a Constitutional Framework for Provisional Self-Government in Kosovo," promulgated on May 15, 2001, some of the administrative functions of the judicial system have been handed over to new provisional institutions of self-government, namely to the Ministry of Public Services.

Decades of communist rule and ten years of active repression had an adverse impact on the Kosovo judiciary. At the time when UNMIK was established and deployed, there was no functioning court system because the majority of judges and prosecutors had fled to Serbia. Moreover, prior to UNMIK's arrival, detention facilities were emptied and some destroyed. In the first six months, the international community concentrated on establishing a functioning multiethnic judiciary. However, after the establishment of an emergency judicial system and the process leading up to the appointments to the regular courts, it became increasingly difficult to convince Kosovo Serbs to participate in the justice system. This was primarily due to the new campaign of violence, persecution, and human rights abuses against minorities.[5]

The Emergency Judicial System

On June 28, 1999, the SRSG issued an emergency decree establishing the Joint Advisory Council on Provisional Judicial Appointment. The main mandate of the council consisted of recommending the provisional appointment of judges and public prosecutors in the emergency judicial system for a three-month renewable period. The primary purpose of the emergency system was to conduct pretrial bail hearings of detained defendants following their arrest by the Kosovo Force (KFOR), an operation of the North Atlantic Treaty Organization (NATO). Although some trials were held, the most significant development was that UNMIK allowed the local courts to begin conducting investigations into alleged war crimes.

On July 25, 1999, the SRSG approved UNMIK Regulation 1999/1, which provided that the law applicable in Kosovo should be the law in force before the start of NATO intervention on March 24, 1999. This regulation required that the applicable law be consistent with internationally recognized human rights standards, Resolution 1244, and other UNMIK regulations. Members of the ethnic Albanian legal community resented and resisted the applicable law, namely the "Serbian" laws of the repressive Milošević regime. Judges and public prosecutors willingly disregarded Regulation 1999/1 and conducted criminal proceedings under the Kosovo penal code and FRY criminal code that were in effect before the Belgrade authorities stripped Kosovo of its autonomous province status on March 22, 1989.[6] In response, in December 1999 the SRSG promulgated Regulation 1999/24, which repealed Regulation 1999/1 and reinstated the laws applicable in 1989. The emergency judicial system operated until December 1999.

International Human Rights Standards and the Applicable Law

Though the SRSG clarified the applicable law, he did not provide any guidance for the role international human rights law should play. Was international human rights law part of the applicable law? The regulations stipulated that existing laws must be read in light of the mandate, regulations, and international standards. While public officials were instructed to "observe" international standards, UNMIK failed to clarify whether human rights law was supreme in overriding inconsistent applicable law.[7] Nor did UNMIK clarify whether international standards could be used to fill in gaps, such as creating the right to habeas corpus, a right recognized in international law but that did not form part of the applicable law. Indeed, no attempt was made to clarify which provisions of the applicable law were inconsistent with international standards. Lacking precise instruction on what is or is not an internationally acceptable domestic legal provision, both judges and prosecutors used procedures that were not in compliance with international law. This approach led to much confusion, contradiction, and legal uncertainty within the courts and UNMIK.

Establishment of the Regular Judicial System

UNMIK Regulation 1999/7 established the Advisory Judicial Commission with the mandate of recommending candidates for judicial and prosecutorial appointment on a permanent basis. The commission, which replaced the Joint Advisory Council, was also empowered to recommend disciplinary measures, including the removal of judges and public prosecutors. Significant efforts were made to recruit minorities into the judiciary, but to no avail because the limited number of Kosovo Serb professionals who remained in the province feared for their safety. Of the total of 354 judges and public prosecutors sworn into office between January and March 2000, there were no Kosovo Serb judges or public prosecutors appointed to the district courts.[8]

Other than judicial appointments, the commission was also empowered to investigate judicial misconduct, including bias, and to make recommendations to the SRSG. In its first twelve months it failed to undertake any investigations, notwithstanding allegations of judicial bias against minorities. The SRSG did not renew the commission's mandate and in April 2001 promulgated Regulation 2001/8, establishing the Kosovo Judicial and Prosecutorial Council, composed of nine members, the majority being internationals. Its powers are akin to those held by the Advisory Judicial Commission, with one important addition: it can delegate responsibility for investigating complaints of judicial misconduct to the Judicial Inspection Unit, which forms part of the DJA.

Legal Training

Ten years of repression resulted in a significant number of the current ethnic Albanian judiciary not working since 1989 and, consequently, not having the benefit of using their legal skills or continuing their legal education.[9] Of equal concern was the region's past disregard for international human rights law.[10] Prior to the arrival of UNMIK, the local judiciary had no exposure to these laws or to other modern European laws and procedures.

The political urgency to create the appearance of a legal system within six months of arriving drove UNMIK to give inexperienced or incompetent local judges and prosecutors unfettered authority to carry out their tasks. They received no mentoring or training other than a two-day session for all legal professionals organized by the Kosovo Judicial Institute (KJI) of the OSCE in November 1999. Judges and prosecutors were not selected until December and received no training prior to the courts becoming operational in February

2000. In May 2000, legal professionals received training, in a joint Council of Europe/OSCE seminar, on Articles 5 and 6 of the European Convention for the Protection of Human Rights and Fundamental Freedoms (ECHR). Similar training took place in September 2000 and induction training for newly appointed judges and public prosecutors took place in November 2000. In March 2001, one year after the courts began operating, the KJI provided training on FRY criminal procedure code to all judicial officials, both local and international, though most internationals did not attend.

But training by this method failed to improve the quality of judicial proceedings. First, the training programs focused on European human rights law jurisprudence, an unknown field to local lawyers. Though international human rights law should play a critical role in judicial proceedings, Kosovo legal professionals needed instruction on applying such standards in the courtroom, rather than being informed on the relevant case law. Second, the issues in Kosovo were more basic. Judges, prosecutors, and defense counselors required training on basic legal skills, such as the questioning of witnesses, legal reasoning, the development of evidence, and the role of professional ethics. Third, there was little follow-up to this training, with few visits to courts in order to assess where improvements were needed.

The War Crimes and Genocide Trials

Within six months of UNMIK's arrival, law enforcement had detained forty persons for war crimes–related offenses.[11] During this period there was much discussion among UN policymakers as to whether there should be an international judicial presence in these cases, but no policy was developed.[12] Though no official explanation was provided, UN officials have informally stated that the reasoning behind the decision to permit local courts to investigate such cases was to instill in the Kosovars a sense of local ownership of the justice system.[13]

There was some movement on the issue when in December 1999 the SRSG announced publicly that UNMIK was creating a domestic court to try war criminals and ethnically motivated crime. The Kosovo War and Ethnic Crimes Court (KWECC) was to be established and would comprise a majority of international judges and prosecutors. Both the local and international community, including human rights organizations, welcomed the announcement.[14] KWECC also had the support of the DJA, which according to an UNMIK press release was "in the process" of establishing the court.[15] Pending its establishment in May 2000, the SRSG informed Kosovo Serb detainees that they would receive speedy trials before a mixed trial panel that included internationals and Serbs.[16] Such trial panels never materialized. In September 2000, without public explanation, KWECC was abandoned.

Although the reasoning behind the announcement of KWECC acknowl-edged the potential for judicial bias in war crimes–related cases, in the nine months that preceded the September 2000 decision the UN took no steps to halt the investigations or trials of Kosovo Serbs by ethnic Albanians. On May 15, 2000, the first of many Kosovo Serbs charged with war crimes offenses would stand trial before an ethnic Albanian trial panel.[17]

The War Crimes Investigations

In a civil law system, fact-gathering in a criminal case is done at the inves-tigative stage by the examining judge. In Kosovo, the newly appointed judges had limited experience in conducting criminal investigations and between 1999 and 2001 took few steps to effectively investigate war crimes cases they were assigned. Examination of witnesses was cursory and statements impli-cating a defendant were not adequately explored in order to determine if evi-dence needed to be confirmed, developed, or discarded. The failure to gather facts adequately at the investigative stage led to problems at trial, where wit-nesses would often expand on earlier testimony, leaving the trial panel to determine whether a witness was exaggerating evidence offered earlier. Effec-tive questioning at the investigative stage may have alleviated these problems.

The failure of adequate investigation prior to indictment was exacerbated by chronic delays in the judicial investigations. UNMIK Regulation 1999/26 mandated that in serious cases detainees must be indicted within twelve months of arrest. As the twelve-month deadline approached, Kosovo Serb defendants were suddenly indicted. Delays in their investigations seemed less about problems in collating evidence and more about exacting revenge on an ethnic group or those associated with it. In one case, three brothers were arrested on October 7, 1999, and charged with war crimes.[18] Within a month of arrest, the examining judge ceased the investigation. There were no further developments in the case until October 2000, when, without an explanation, the public prosecutor requested an extension of the investigation and deten-tion, which was granted by a panel of judges, one of whom was an interna-tional. Because the extension would exceed the twelve-month deadline, the order was in violation of Regulation 1999/26. When the error was pointed out to the DJA, the defendants were released without rearrest.[19]

According to the applicable law, a defendant can only be indicted if there is "sufficient evidence to warrant a reasonable suspicion" that the defendant had committed a crime.[20] The FRY criminal procedure code provides various safeguards to ensure that an insufficient investigation will not lead to an indictment but will trigger either a request for further investigation or an aban-donment of the case.[21] Prior to trial, the court also has the power to reject an indictment for insufficiency of evidence.[22] In cases concerning Kosovo Serb defendants, none of these safeguards seemed to apply. With little oversight by the international judges or prosecutors, and notwithstanding the lack of evidence, those Kosovo Serb defendants who had not escaped would stand trial.[23]

Forensic Tools

A significant obstacle to effective prosecution has been the quality of investigations by law enforcement officers. The key to effective policing depends on the investigative skills of police and the existence of reliable forensic analysis of evidence. Law enforcement authorities in Kosovo failed to develop sophisticated and modern forms of investigation and evidence collection, including a surveillance capacity and the utilization of informants and undercover police agents. Two years into the mission, law enforcement officials had not established a crime-scene unit to systematically collect forensic evidence.[24] The lack of forensic capabilities in the war crimes investigations inevitably meant that the fact-finder was denied the full picture.

International Judges and Prosecutors

In February 2000, Mitrovica saw an explosion of violence that resulted in a number of deaths and injuries. Following these incidents and allegations of a judicial failure to investigate them, an international judge and an international prosecutor were appointed to the Mitrovica District Court. UNMIK Regulation 2000/34 extended the power to appoint international judges and prosecutors to all courts in Kosovo. But the introduction of international judges and prosecutors was ad hoc. Although the regulation provided greater discretion for the use of international judges and prosecutors, their presence on war crimes cases was almost nonexistent.

Following criticism from the Kosovo Serb community and a pending hunger strike by Kosovo Serb inmates, in April 2000 UNMIK introduced one international judge into trial panels.[25] But the steps taken proved inadequate because they failed to alleviate the perception or reality of ethnic bias: a trial panel consists of five decisionmakers, all of whom have a vote. The DJA stated that this approach was driven by the lack of international judges, which was somewhat puzzling given the number of European states that were willing to provide significant judicial assistance.[26] Moreover, there was no reason why these trials could not be delayed pending the recruitment of new international judges. There was no urgency emanating from the Kosovo Serb community or from defendants to expedite trials before majority ethnic Albanian trial panels.

Although the limited number of internationals posed a problem for UNMIK, a more serious issue was identifying candidates with relevant expertise for these cases. Of the internationals who were appointed in the period 1999–2001, none had conducted trials involving serious criminal offenses and none had any practical experience in, or knowledge of, international humanitarian law. Indeed, one international judge's experience was exclusively in riparian (water) rights law. Furthermore, no attempts were made to provide preentry training on either humanitarian law or the FRY criminal procedure code. In September 2000 the International Criminal Tribunal for the Former Yugoslavia (ICTY) held a training session in Kosovo on humanitarian law for both judges and prosecutors. The majority of international judges and prosecutors did not attend.

Establishing a working relationship between local and international judges was complicated by the lack of adequate translators and what was considered to be derisory pay for local judges (when compared to the riches bestowed on their international brethren).[27] The UN's behind-the-scenes consultation with international judges and prosecutors on specific cases also engendered a degree of distrust within the local judiciary. This distrust was somewhat alleviated when international judges began ignoring UN directives.

UNMIK Regulation 2000/64

Primarily to address the concerns of judicial bias raised in the war crimes cases, in December 2000 Regulation 2000/64 was promulgated. The regulation authorized parties to apply to the DJA for a criminal case to be allocated to an international prosecutor and a three-judge trial panel comprising a majority of international judges. The final decision on allocation is made by the SRSG, after a recommendation by the DJA, which interprets the regulation to permit a local prosecutor to conduct the case before a majority international trial panel.

Section 1 of the regulation grants to prosecutors, the accused, or defense counsel the right to petition the DJA for the assignment of international judges and prosecutors when "necessary to ensure the independence and impartiality of the judiciary or the proper administration of justice." In the absence of a petition, the DJA may act on its own motion. The regulation appears to contain a significant oversight in that it does not apply to trials or appeals that have already commenced.

Prior to its promulgation, no attempts were made to explain to local legal professionals, politicians, or the general public the rationale behind the regulation. This resulted in widespread resentment throughout the ethnic Albanian community. In court, local judges refused to be recruited for the "64 panels" and the Kosovo Supreme Court sent a letter to the SRSG stating that the regulation was a violation of international law. In the war crimes trial of Sava Matić, which was heard by a 64 panel, the third member of the trial panel, an ethnic Albanian, called a press conference and issued a public dissent to the acquittal of Matić (the local judge had earlier refused to enter court during the pronouncement of the verdict).[28]

The use of Regulation 64 panels also caused much friction within the Kosovo Serb community. This was primarily because of the DJA's failure to ensure that *all* war crimes–related offenses, indeed all serious interethnic crimes, qualified for a majority international trial panel and be prosecuted by an international. Although the regulation was promulgated in December 2000, significant delays in drafting the regulation's procedural rules resulted in war crimes cases proceeding before majority or exclusively ethnic Albanian trial panels. As of mid-2003, UNMIK had not promulgated procedural guidelines setting out the basis on which the regulation would be administered.

The regulation notwithstanding, and with one controversial exception, all Kosovo Serb defendants were convicted of war crimes–related offenses.[29] The appellate court has reversed most of these convictions and ordered retrials.

UNMIK: Criminal Justice and Human Rights Policy

UNMIK's initial approach to the war crimes–related cases was symptomatic of its approach to criminal justice and human rights policy generally. Although the UN Secretary-General in his report to the Security Council stated that "UNMIK will *embed a culture of human rights* in all areas of activity," the implementation of that goal has proven extremely difficult.[30]

Part of the problem stems from an unnecessary perceived tension between ensuring law and order and human rights compliance. In the summer of 1999 there was a general consensus within UNMIK that the breakdown in law and order had reached such a critical stage that there was discussion as to whether a state of emergency should be declared.[31] The UN Civilian Police (UNCIVPOL) force was grossly undermanned, the domestic courts were barely operational, and deadly attacks on minority communities were increasing at an alarming rate. Although such a declaration would have resulted in the derogation of certain human rights for a limited period of time, there was broad agreement among human rights advisers that such a declaration, given the circumstances, was appropriate. In the end no such declaration was made because, one assumes, it was considered politically indigestible. Policy and human rights advisers came to believe that UNMIK had painted a picture of the mission for UN New York that was very different from the emergency developing on the ground.[32] It could not state that the mission was proceeding smoothly and then declare a state of emergency.

Talk of a public emergency arose some twelve months later and coincided with the increasing use of executive powers to detain persons thought to be involved in serious criminal activity. The SRSG justified extrajudicial detentions on the basis of an apparent public emergency, though the precise nature of this emergency was never specified. UNCIVPOL had established primacy throughout Kosovo (and was actually up to its full strength of almost 5,000 officers) and there were seventeen international judicial officials assigned to the courts.

This perceived tension between ensuring law and order and ensuring human rights compliance was primarily fostered through an internal paper generated from the Office of the Principal Deputy to the SRSG and OLA.[33] The paper asserted that UNMIK was faced with stark choices between protecting lives, peace, and stability or enforcing existing law, respecting legal institutions, and observing international human rights norms. Within UNMIK, many critics of international human rights norms argued that strict adherence to legal safeguards frequently impeded the mission's ability to respond to a crisis or to criminal activity. This was particularly the view held by international prosecutors and political advisers to the SRSG. But such a view was both simplistic and unrealistic.

A coherent strategy for justice, even in a de facto state of emergency, can incorporate effective crime detection, prevention, and prosecution and at the same time comply with basic due process rights. A multifaceted approach can address the challenges and problems facing a criminal justice system in transition, engaging law enforcement, legislative, and policy needs. This multifaceted approach would include the creation and development of policing tools such as modern surveillance techniques and the effective use of forensic experts; the introduction of more international judicial actors to alleviate concerns of judicial bias; amending domestic laws that hamper effective policing while at the same time protecting the rights of the defendant (e.g., if the domestic law does not permit the introduction at trial of a defendant's confession to the police, the law can be amended to adduce such evidence as long as it was voluntary); and preentry training on the applicable law, including international standards for law enforcement and judicial officials.

A compulsive reaction to a spate of serious criminal activity severely hampers the effectiveness of initiatives that are taken and often results in ad hoc approaches to criminal justice policy, ensuring a failure to implement meaningful, long-term change in the justice sector. For example, UNMIK promulgated a regulation banning "hate speech," but failed to prosecute persons allegedly guilty of such offenses, fearing it would create a political backlash from the ethnic Albanian community.[34] Equally questionable has been the promulgation of regulations that relate to terrorism and organized crime.[35] In order to combat serious criminal activity, both were drafted and promulgated with great speed, only to lie dormant.[36] Some regulations were drafted with little consultation with local legal professionals and inadequate dissemination to the general public. There continue to be inexplicable delays in the translation of many regulations. As of mid-2003 most regulations and administrative directives had been translated.[37]

Executive Interference

International human rights standards require that persons deprived of their liberty have the right to challenge the lawfulness of their detention before a court.[38] These basic rights have been incorporated into the Constitutional Framework.

Between 2000 and 2001, there was a noticeable increase in the use of executive powers to detain persons, decisions that were initially not thought reviewable by UNMIK courts. According to UNMIK policy, as determined by the OLA in New York, executive detentions were to be in line with a so-called three-prong test. These guidelines recognized the intrusive and extensive nature of the executive power to detain, and as such they required that the SRSG exercise this authority only on an extraordinary basis, when all other legal avenues have been exhausted. The *merits of the case* must be strong enough to warrant executive intervention; it must be established that an unfavorable result, in these cases the release of a person from custody, would pose a *menace* to public security; and there must be a basis for the belief that allowing the case to proceed without executive intervention would result in *manipulation* of the case by judicial or other officials.

As executive orders do not spell out the reasoning behind their issuance, there is no possible way to understand on what basis the test is met. Executive orders to detain merely emphasize the powers provided to the SRSG pursuant to UN Security Council Resolution 1244 and conclude that the person subject to the order poses a threat to "public safety and order." There is no official process or procedure by which a case is considered under this test and, on the instructions of the OLA in Kosovo, detainees were not to be provided a copy of the order.[39] As the mission progressed, so did the frequency of these orders. Executive orders to detain were issued notwithstanding earlier decisions to release made by international judges. In 2001, in a case involving three suspects, executive orders to detain were issued despite the decision of a judicial panel composed of internationals that there was an insufficient basis to detain them.[40]

The rationale behind the appointment of international judges was, among other things, to protect against real or perceived bias in the judiciary. The SRSG's decision to detain, in light of a lawful decision to release taken by international judges, appears to fall foul of the three-prong test, undermine the authority and independence of the courts, and violate the Constitutional Framework.[41]

Possibly in light of the Constitutional Framework, on August 25, 2001, the SRSG promulgated Regulation 2001/18, which established a judicial review commission for detentions based on executive decisions. The regulation is peculiar in that it was to be in force for no more than three months and thus appears to have been promulgated with the intent of dealing with one case only.[42] The regulation fell short of meeting human rights standards because it institutionalized the use of executive-ordered detentions and appears to have been an adjunct of the executive. All members of the commission were selected and appointed under the authority of the SRSG, whose authority the commission was expected to review. It is highly questionable whether the commission was a tribunal under Article 6 of the ECHR.[43] In the case of the three suspects referred to above, the review commission upheld the executive order to detain. Months later, and after fifteen months in detention, the three defendants were released due to the lack of evidence.

Although there has been no public support for the acts allegedly committed by persons detained by the executive, there has been much anger. The reaction within the legal and political community has been one of outrage, comparing such detention decisions to those ordered by the Milošević regime. UNMIK's insistence that executive detention orders are meant to uphold the rule of law is undermined by UNMIK's obstruction of prosecutors' attempts to detain certain political leaders accused of serious criminal activity, including the arrest of a Kosovo Protection Corps commander.[44]

Disenfranchisement of the Human Rights Component

The increasing use of extrajudicial detentions coincided with the disenfranchisement of the human rights component to the mission, the OSCE. The UN Secretary-General's report to the Security Council on July 12, 1999, had assigned the lead role of institution building and human rights monitoring within UNMIK to the OSCE. The Legal Systems Monitoring Section (LSMS) of the OSCE was created to monitor the legal and penal system for human rights compliance and issue public reports to the SRSG.

In 1999, human rights policy in UNMIK was often coordinated between the OSCE, the Office of the High Commissioner for Human Rights (OHCHR), the Human Rights Adviser to the UN Police Commissioner, and the SRSG's Office of Human Rights and Community Affairs (OHRCA).[45] Local actors were also consulted. For example, the Joint Advisory Council on Legislative Matters, which is composed of members of the local legal and political community, was often involved in the review of draft legislation.

Since late 2000 the development of human rights and criminal justice policy has been within the exclusive domain of the OLA and the DJA, with no effective recourse to the OSCE or the Joint Advisory Council. Although the UN would provide advance copies of pending regulations, the time frame permitted for review of a document, usually twenty-four hours, was woeful. Both the Joint Advisory Council and the OSCE may have been considered an impediment to speedy lawmaking. Furthermore, the exclusion of the OSCE appears to be in reaction to its comments on critical criminal justice issues. Rather than seek an accommodation, the OLA and the DJA, departments bereft of any experienced human rights or criminal justice expertise, excluded the OSCE from the relevant working groups, failed to keep them informed of relevant developments, and relied almost exclusively on the advice of an international prosecutor.

The failure of the OLA to consult the relevant human rights experts in the mission and to ensure that draft regulations are vetted for human rights compliance resulted in regulations that violate basic human rights standards. In April 2001 a final draft regulation written by the OLA that related to a detainee's right to counsel included a provision stating that counsel can be present during the interrogation of a detainee but "shall remain silent."[46] It was shown to the DJA and an international prosecutor but no attempt was made to clear the draft with the relevant human rights experts or law enforcement officers. The result was a final draft regulation in a critical field that was in breach of basic international human rights standards.[47]

Regulation 1999/26 amends the domestic law and empowers a court to extend pretrial custody to a maximum of twelve months in serious cases (the domestic law permits pretrial custody of six months). The practice of pretrial detention pursuant to that regulation is in violation of Article 5(3) and (4) of the ECHR and Article 9(3) and (4) of the International Covenant on Civil and Political Rights (ICCPR) in that the regulation fails to make adequate provision for the periodic review of the extension of custody time limits throughout the period of detention covered by the regulation. The regulation also fails to provide the detainee with the right to initiate a review of an order for detention. At no stage is the detainee entitled to challenge the reasons provided by either the investigative judge or the public prosecutor. As of mid-2003, no attempts had been made to amend or repeal it.

Legal System Monitoring

Following the international community's arrival in Bosnia and Herzegovina (BiH), there was an increasing interest by the international community in monitoring transitional legal systems. Competent and, where possible, independent monitoring of legal systems can assist field missions, local governments, and foreign donors in the areas of legal reform, capacity building, and policy development in the justice sector.

The creation of a legal systems monitoring component was a unique addition to the UNMIK structure. The LSMS was not only the largest monitoring unit of any previous OSCE mission, but it was also one of the largest of *any* field mission. Its authority derived from a 1999 report of the UN Secretary-General to the Security Council that instructed UNMIK to develop coordinated mechanisms in order to facilitate monitoring of the respect for human rights and the due functioning of the judicial system. In particular it provided for

> unhindered access to all parts of Kosovo to investigate human rights abuses and to ensure that human rights protection and promotion concerns are addressed through the overall activities of the mission. Human rights monitors will, through the Deputy Special Representative for Institution-building, report their findings to the Special Representative. The findings of the human rights monitors will be made public regularly and will be shared, as appropriate, with United Nations human rights mechanisms, in consultation with the Office of the United Nations High Commissioner for Human Rights. UNMIK will provide co-coordinated reporting and response capacity.[48]

The strategy of the LSMS was to monitor cases that proceeded through the criminal justice system, from the moment of arrest and/or detention until trial and appeal. In order to obtain a comprehensive picture, prior to trial, the LSMS would investigate a case by reviewing documents and conducting interviews with the relevant parties. This investigation formed the basis for the LSMS's analysis of the legal proceedings and subsequent reporting. Systematic violations, observed trends, individual case problems, and issues identified by the LSMS were reported to the DJA and other departments and agencies within UNMIK, as well as the UN Children's Fund (UNICEF) and the OHCHR.

For a significant period, the LSMS was hampered in carrying out its mandate. The courts often denied access to court files and court proceedings on the basis that the LSMS was akin to the public and therefore was restricted in what documents it could access. The DJA, UNCIVPOL, and international judges and prosecutors held a similar view. UNMIK took few steps to address the issue, claiming that to do so would violate the independence of the judiciary. Although agreement was reached in June 2001 that the LSMS would be given access to court proceedings and documents, court monitors continue to report obstruction in carrying out their mandate.[49]

The obstruction notwithstanding, the LSMS's reporting, both internal and external, proved a catalyst for effecting a degree of change in the criminal justice system. The first public report, issued in October 2000, identified the growing problem of ethnic bias in the courts as well as cases of judicial and prosecutorial misconduct that required immediate investigation.[50] These concerns resulted in the promulgation of Regulation 2000/64, which introduced more international judges and prosecutors, and Regulation 2001/8, which established the Kosovo Judicial and Prosecutorial Council, a body that investigates judicial misconduct. The reports also identified concerns about the courts' treatment of juveniles and victims of sexual violence.[51]

The Penal System

When KFOR arrived in June 1999, detention facilities in Kosovo were empty, some destroyed.[52] A large number of detainees had been murdered while others had been transferred to Serbia. Records, files, and all furniture had been removed. With a rising crime rate, KFOR had to amend its peacekeeping strategy to include the management of detention facilities. With much reluctance, KFOR reopened the detention centers that were structurally sound and U.S. KFOR opened its own detention center at its base in Camp Bondsteel. Although no long-term strategy had been developed, one issue was clear: given KFOR's acknowledged lack of expertise in managing detention facilities, its role would be short-term.

In late 1999, UNMIK began developing a strategy to take control of all detention facilities in Kosovo. It would re-create at least five detention facilities over a three-year period with Prizren, in southwestern Kosovo, identified as the first facility to open. This timetable was rejected. UN Penal Management (subsequently the Kosovo Correctional Service) was given only a matter of months to develop a fully functioning prison system throughout the province.

The first difficulty UNMIK faced was finding experienced staff. As with the judges and public prosecutors, most detention staff had not worked for ten years. After identifying fifty-six former detention staff, all ethnic Albanian, a training program was created in order to reintroduce staff into the correctional service and acquaint them with UN and European standards for detention facilities. Prizren opened its doors on November 30, 1999, and within fifteen months a further six detention facilities became operational (two staffed by UNMIK police). The collective planned capacity of the seven facilities is 1,112 (both convicted and pretrial detainees), with a current actual capacity of 1,004.

While the first fifteen months focused on refurbishment, locating and hiring staff, and assuming responsibility for detention facilities, the next eighteen months focused on preparation for all the facilities to be handed over to national staff. Approximately 75 percent of all current national staff have less than one year's experience. With the assistance of the Swiss government, an intensive program was created to assist in the training of senior local staff so that they could assume responsibility for managing the facilities. The next phase also included the development of a probation and parole system as an alternative to custody. UNMIK has also hired social workers and mental health professionals in order to work with detainees.

Given security concerns that prevailed in 1999, Kosovo Serb detainees were removed from regional detention facilities to facilities in Mitrovica and Camp Bondsteel, with most Kosovo Serb detainees located in Mitrovica, which eases the burden for legal and family visits. But this policy has resulted in much anger from the ethnic Albanian community: since April 2000, more than half of Kosovo Serbs accused of war crimes–related offenses have escaped from the Mitrovica detention facility (other than Camp Bondsteel, Kosovo has no high-security detention facility). This embarrassing lapse was partly due to the detention facility being placed in the hands of UNCIVPOL personnel with no experience in penal management or the treatment of high-security prisoners.

Although between 2000 and 2001 most detainees were transferred to UNMIK facilities, Command KFOR continues to operate two detention facilities in the province. U.S. KFOR houses those arrested for illegal boundary crossing from Serbia and those found in possession of weapons (inmates have also escaped from the Camp Bondsteel detention facility). While some were channeled through the district courts, others were detained indefinitely on the basis that KFOR is not subject to the applicable law regarding arrests and detentions. While this may arguably be correct, KFOR is nevertheless subject to international human rights standards, including those that relate to the prohibition on arbitrary detention.

The detention of the mentally ill remains the most critical issue faced by penal management officials. Though the applicable law provides for the "mandatory psychiatric treatment and custody in a medical institution [and] mandatory psychiatric treatment outside of prison," as of mid-2003 there still remained no appropriate facility for the detention and treatment of the mentally ill.[53] Prior to the arrival of UNMIK, persons deemed mentally ill in the context of the criminal justice system were either removed to Skopje, Macedonia, or Niš, Serbia.

In the absence of such a facility, UNMIK has designated a detention center in Lipjan to house the mentally ill and has arranged regular visits by psychiatrists and nurses. Though this initiative is to be welcomed, UN standards mandate that every detention institution requires the presence of at least one medical officer with some knowledge of psychiatry.[54] Moreover, there is no mechanism currently in place for the detention centers to communicate their assessments of detainees' mental health to the court so as to ensure the court is aware of any mental health issues affecting a defendant. In any event, the current applicable law relating to the mentally ill does not conform to international standards because it allows the criminal courts to order the *indefinite* detention of a mentally ill person and makes no provision for review of such detentions. Rather, the applicable law places the emphasis on the medical institution to inform the court when the person has completed treatment. Given that there is currently no medical institution or adequate treatment available for mentally ill criminal defendants, the creation of such a facility must be a priority.

The general success of the UNMIK penal system may be directly attributable to the expertise that was brought in at an early stage of the mission. A strategy was developed by penal management experts from Britain and Canada, persons who had worked in correctional services for more than twenty years. A similar approach was adopted when identifying international personnel most suited to manage the actual detention facilities. As of mid-2003, persons with operational experience managed all detention facilities.

Conclusion

It is acknowledged that establishing a justice system is an enormous and complex task, made all the more difficult when the new regime is confronting societal wounds suffered by various ethnic groups. Transitions from repressive regimes to democracies based on the rule of law and respect for human rights are not achieved in a matter of months. In a very short time and under difficult circumstances, UNMIK accomplished a degree of security, stability, and democracy. The courts have dispensed with a large number of criminal cases in a just manner and the prison system is effectively and professionally managed. It is also recognized that judicial training on new approaches to fact-finding, legal reasoning, and decisionmaking will take years, not months.

But how emerging states respond to past legacies of injustice will determine whether the transition toward a democratic state succeeds. Because it distorts the truth, convicting persons in show trials does not resolve past injustices. Miscarriages of justice risk debilitating any opportunity for national reconciliation between ethnic groups or closure for victims and their families as well as imperil respect for legal institutions that are crucial for political stability. But responsibility for these failings must lie with UNMIK. The failure to provide a clear strategy for the handling of the war crimes trials is incomprehensible.

Future peacebuilding strategies must ensure that a coordinated approach to developing a criminal justice system is adopted. First, a judiciary comprised of internationals must resolve alleged violations of international humanitarian law and serious interethnic crime. Second, peace and order, even in a de facto state of emergency, can be achieved concurrently with respect for the protection of basic human rights. It requires a synergy between all relevant actors in the field, one that engages law enforcement, judicial officials, defenders, legislative and policy experts, and human rights advisers. Failure to ensure the presence of human rights or criminal justice experts in a mission can result in irregular policy decisions and unlawful regulations. But mere presence is insufficient. Human rights advisers need to be consulted during the creation of policy and involved in the drafting process.

Future transitional administrations will need to ensure that less power is vested in the transitional administrator and a more sophisticated system of checks and balances is in place. The continued use of arbitrary detentions by the executive and the rejection of lawful court orders set a precedent that the UN may come to deeply regret, because it undermines the democratic objective of developing an independent and strong judiciary.

Future strategies must also reach out to the local community. Failure to consult relevant local actors in policy and legislative developments can quickly deflect a mission's goals. Effectively transforming society also requires a real engagement with the local populace. Consultation on critical issues and dissemination of information to the public must be substantive and genuine. Justice sector reform requires the international community to take account of local experiences, wishes, and expectations. The success of UNMIK will be determined by whether or not the mission succeeds in nurturing a concept of justice that all Kosovars admire and respect.

Notes

I was head of the Legal Systems Monitoring Section for the Organization for Security and Cooperation in Europe's Mission in Kosovo from 2000 to 2001. The opinions expressed in this chapter are mine alone and do not represent those of any of the institutions that I am or have been associated with.

1. UN Security Council Resolution 1244 (1999), adopted June 10, 1999.

2. Ibid., para. 10.

3. Ibid., para. 11(b).

4. UNMIK Regulation 2000/15. UNMIK regulations can be found at www. unmikonline.org and www.un.org/peace/kosovo/pages/regulations/regs.html.

5. See OSCE, *Kosovo/Kosova: As Seen As Told* (Vienna: OSCE, 1999).

6. See *Observations and Recommendations of the OSCE Legal Systems Monitoring Section—Report 2: The Development of the Kosovo Judicial System,* December 17, 1999, www.osce.org/kosovo/documents/reports/justice/report2.htm.

7. See UNMIK Regulation 1999/24.

8. Information supplied by the DJA. The jurisdiction of the district courts covers offenses that carry a sentence of five years or more. There are a handful of Kosovo Serb lawyers working in the municipal courts.

9. OSCE, *Kosovo/Kosova.*

10. Ibid.

11. OSCE, *Review of the Criminal Justice System,* February 2000–July 2000, p. 74, www.osce.org/kosovo/documents/reports/justice.

12. Information supplied by UNMIK Office of the SRSG.

13. Information supplied by a senior official in the DJA.

14. See Amnesty International, *Federal Republic of Yugoslavia, Kosovo: Recommendations to UNMIK on the Judicial System,* February 2000. See also UN Doc. S/2000/538, para. 60, June 6, 2000.

15. See "Reviving Kosovo's Judicial System," *UNMIK First Anniversary Backgrounder,* June 5, 2000, www.un.org/peace/kosovo/pages/twelvemonths/law.html.

16. "Kosovo Detainees Agree to End Hunger Strike," UNMIK press release, May 22, 2000.

17. Milos Jokić was indicted for genocide. The first day of trial was adjourned due to the failure of the defense counsel to appear. See UNMIK press release, May 15, 2000.

18. OSCE, *Review of the Criminal Justice System,* September 2000–February 2001, p. 79.

19. Ibid. (The DJA offered compensation to the defendants.)

20. Federal Republic of Yugoslavia, *Criminal Procedure Code*, art. 270.

21. Ibid., art. 174(2).

22. Ibid., art. 270(4).

23. By September 2000 more than twenty Kosovo Serb detainees had escaped from UNMIK detention facilities.

24. OSCE, *Review of the Criminal Justice System,* September 2000–February 2001, p. 42. The U.S. Department of Justice is funding the establishment of a crime laboratory.

25. OSCE, *Review of the Criminal Justice System,* February 2000–July 2000, p. 60.

26. See, for example, British foreign secretary Robin Cook's statement that "a dozen judges [had been identified and] the first should arrive before the end of next month." "Foreign Secretary Reports on Talks with Kofi Annan," FCO news release, March 14, 2000, www.fco.gov.uk/news/newstext.asp?3407.

27. The average yearly salary for local judges was approximately U.S.$3,600. The average yearly salary for a UN international judge was approximately U.S.$100,000.

28. "Decision to Acquit Serb Kosovar for War Crimes Absurd," Agence France Presse, January 30, 2001. The Kosovo Supreme Court later reversed the acquittal. On retrial, Matić was acquitted.

29. Following a four-month trial in which the international prosecutor repeatedly questioned the credibility of his own witnesses, Igor Simić was acquitted of genocide. See OSCE, *Review of the Criminal Justice System,* September 2000–February 2001, p. 92.

30. United Nations, *Report of the Secretary-General on UNMIK,* UN Doc. S/1999/779, July 12, 1999, para. 42, emphasis added.

31. Information provided by a senior UNMIK official.

32. Information provided by political affairs and human rights advisers within UNMIK.

33. *A Blueprint for Ensuring Security and Establishing the Rule of Law in Kosovo,* internal document made available to the author.

34. See UNMIK Regulation 2000/04.

35. See UNMIK Regulations 2001/12 and 2001/22.

36. According to UNMIK officials, only one person has been prosecuted under the terrorism regulation, none for organized crime.

37. Of the forty-one regulations promulgated in 2001, only nineteen had been translated into Albanian, thirty-one into Serbian. None of the twenty-five administrative directives accompanying the regulations had been translated. Author visited UNMIK website in spring 2002 and March 2003.

38. See *European Convention for the Protection of Human Rights and Fundamental Freedoms,* art. 5, *International Covenant on Civil and Political Rights,* art. 9.

39. Information provided by a senior official at the DJA.

40. OSCE, *Review of the Criminal Justice System,* September 2000–February, p. 17.

41. The Principal Deputy to the SRSG has also engaged in ordering UN officials to detain persons. See ibid., p. 19.

42. See UNMIK Regulation 2001/18, sec. 10. The only case to be heard was that of the Niš "bus bombers."

43. See *Langborger v. Sweden,* European Court of Human Rights, judgment of June 22, 1989; *Belilos v. Switzerland,* European Court of Human Rights, judgment of April 29, 1988; and *Findlay v. United Kingdom,* European Court of Human Rights, judgment of February 25, 1997, para 73.

44. See OSCE, *Review of the Criminal Justice System,* September 2000–February 2001, p. 87. See also R. Jeffrey Smith, "Rule of Law Is Elusive in Kosovo," *Washington Post,* July 29, 2001, p. A1.

45. In 2001, UNMIK removed human rights from the work of the OHRCA.

46. A copy of the draft regulation was provided to me. The UNMIK Office of the SRSG also confirmed this information.

47. International standards and case law recognize the right to the *assistance* of counsel during detention, interrogation, and preliminary investigations. Silent counsel is, in effect, no counsel. See United Nations, *Basic Principles on the Role of Lawyers,* principles 1, 6, 17, adopted at the Eighth UN Congress on the Prevention of Crime and the Treatment of Offenders (1990). The controversial provision was eventually deleted from the promulgated regulation, although other troubling provisions remain. See UNMIK Regulation 2001/28.

48. United Nations, *Report of the Secretary-General on UNMIK,* para. 87.

49. See OSCE, *Review of the Criminal Justice System,* September 2001–February 2002, p. 10.

50. OSCE, *Review of the Criminal Justice System,* February 2000–July 2000, p. 61.

51. OSCE, *Review of the Criminal Justice System,* September 2000–February 2001, secs. 6, 7. See also OSCE, *Review of the Criminal Justice System,* February 2000–July 2000, p. 77.

52. I am grateful to William Irvine, Kosovo Correctional Services, UNMIK, for providing background on this section.

53. See Federal Republic of Yugoslavia, *Criminal Procedure Code,* arts. 493–498.

54. See United Nations, *Standard Minimum Rules for the Treatment of Prisoners* adopted by the First UN Congress on the Prevention of Crime and Treatment of Offenders (1955).

10

Strengthening Indigenous Police Capacity and the Rule of Law in the Balkans

Annika S. Hansen

The evolution of international interventions in internal security matters has been remarkable, and the civilian police missions in the Balkans reflect this. At the same time, expectations have risen out of step with the international community's ability to conduct police operations effectively. On the surface, enhancing indigenous police capacity may be a matter of selecting and training staff, but it is more fundamentally a process of changing the dynamic of a society. For a long time there has been too much focus on technical and structural aspects of police reform. Gradually it is being realized that consolidating the rule of law means building popular confidence in the police and developing faith in the ability of the population to play an active role in the security sector, for instance in civil society organizations. Enhancing indigenous police capacity also involves bringing about a shift in the self-perception of the police from an instrument of the state to a public service institution, a shift that needs to be supported by a corresponding, propitious political context. In short, police reform is part of a major state-building exercise. The scope and challenges of police reform have two implications for the international approach to police assistance in the Balkans. First, acknowledging the sociopolitical context of police reform means understanding the need to tackle the informal indigenous power structures that obstruct reconciliation and economic reconstruction. Second, recognizing how vast and ambitious police reform is should bring with it more realistic and appropriate standards for the war-torn society in question to better assess the impact of international reform efforts.

Police assistance is nothing new. It has come full circle from the bilateral police assistance of the 1960s. In the meantime, it was subject to restrictions because of taboos associated with supporting potentially oppressive police forces and the more general sacrosanct principle of nonintervention in the internal affairs of other states. It is important to grasp just how momentous the development has been. After all, meddling with the indigenous police goes to the heart of a state's sovereignty and its monopoly of coercive means. What makes the job even more difficult is that other structures have frequently gained access to power and to public trust. In a war-torn society, the state's monopoly is challenged by alternative security arrangements, such as opposing military forces, specialized police forces, or other paramilitary groups. As Brynjar Lia points out, "governments in conflict-ridden societies more often than not have lost control and oversight over the use of coercion and legal violence."[1] It is a fallacy, however, to believe that there is a complete—and certainly not a lasting—security vacuum. Even in Kosovo this was not the case. Although there may not have been an official police force or a formal and generally accepted legal code, there were other corrective social mechanisms to maintain some degree of order. If the state is unable to fill the vacuum, alternative nonstate security providers emerge, such as vigilante groups, or informal rules for social interaction crop up. International assistance to law and order must counter these and essentially resurrect the government's security apparatus. At the same time, international assistance seeks to ensure that government security structures conform to democratic standards.

In the Balkans, strengthening indigenous civil police capacity began with monitoring the performance of local police as a minor element in the UN Protection Force (UNPROFOR). It moved on to training and reform missions in Eastern Slavonia and Bosnia and Herzegovina (BiH) and finally to the executive policing role that international civilian police now fulfill as part of the UN Civil Administration of Kosovo. It is important to remember that efforts are cumulative rather than consecutive. In other words, simply because the UN Mission in Kosovo (UNMIK) has now taken on a police operational authority in the maintenance of law and order does *not* mean that monitoring and training activities have ceased. Monitoring and training or "reform and restructuring" form the essential foundation for any executive policing operation, in that these activities are the ones that ultimately build local law enforcement capacity.

This chapter begins by describing the conditions of police forces and the rule of law in the various Balkan cases. Based on the areas of concern identified here, a presentation of efforts to strengthen local civilian police capacity follows. Throughout the chapter, the political and social contexts resurface as key factors in the potential progress and limitations of police reform. The final discussion on prospects directly addresses these contexts. It offers a brief outline of local and international obstacles and underlines the destructive effect of parallel structures and informal networks. These concluding remarks reiterate the case for realistic expectations.

The State of Law and Order in the Balkans

Clearly, assistance to police reform has to be tailored to local conditions, which means identifying gaps that international organizations might attempt to fill temporarily. Most of the cases in the Balkans contain elements of illegitimacy, corruption, destruction, and dysfunction. The question of legitimacy has to do with the historical legacy. The Balkans, similar to many Eastern European countries, are undergoing a transition from socialist states to democratic market economies.[2] This is a complete reversal of the basic principles of how society is organized and underlines the scope of reform programs.

In prewar Yugoslavia, police forces were well trained and professional, but were underdeveloped as policing systems in that they served the state rather than the public.[3] The situation in Kosovo was aggravated when Kosovar Albanian representation in the police forces was gradually phased out from the late 1980s. The Serb-dominated police force then controlled rather than served the Kosovar population. To serve the needs of Kosovar Albanians, a parallel system of law enforcement, based on traditional clan structures, developed.[4] Throughout the Balkans, a popular perception has emerged that police forces are somewhat sinister instruments of the state and are usually partial to the interests of a particular ethnic group. Clearly the police, and slightly less so courts and prisons, have been severely discredited. Strengthening the rule of law in the Balkans now entails bringing about a fundamental shift in popular attitude toward the authorities and building confidence in their law enforcement mechanisms.[5]

Police behavior and perceptions of threats to personal security or to the security of individuals are inextricably tied to the prior conflict. The operations in BiH are a case in point. The dividing line between armed groups, such as home defense forces and police, was blurred during the war, and all security forces, including the police, were involved in the hostilities and were clearly partisan. At the end of the war, the police force that the UN Mission in Bosnia and Herzegovina (UNMIBH) was then charged with reforming in December 1995 was militarized in equipment and outlook, bloated, and ethnically divided.[6]

In Eastern Slavonia police were also involved in the war. When the UN Transitional Administration for Eastern Slavonia, Baranja, and Western Sirmium (UNTAES) was put into place in January 1996, the local police forces consisted of a core of professionally trained police officers and a group without prior police experience who had signed up during the war. Both were sent to the front line at regular intervals.[7] In Kosovo, the police force, as well as the special police and intelligence counterparts, were closely associated with the oppression of ethnic Albanians by the Yugoslav state.[8] When the security forces withdrew in the wake of the NATO bombing campaign, they left a formal or institutional vacuum. Practitioners and researchers alike expected the UNMIK police to step in to fill that vacuum. Instead, international staff sometimes learned the hard way that they had to take informal indigenous networks, first and foremost the power structures of the Kosovo Liberation Army (KLA), into account in all reform efforts.[9] In Albania, clan structures provided an alternative "rule of law" and represented a combination of political, judicial, and social authority.[10] In the wake of the 1997 collapse and the anarchical conditions that followed, the state was no longer considered a credible or reliable security provider by the Albanian population. Assistance to police reform in Albania is therefore also part of a state-building process, in that a recognized Albanian government requested external assistance to resurrect a defunct security sector in order to consolidate power in an unstable political system.[11]

In all cases, military forces were formed or grew in size during the civil war and were due to be demobilized, be they the military forces of the three parties in BiH or the KLA. International peacekeepers and civilian staff who are overseeing the demobilization and reintegration need to be aware of the pitfalls of allowing demobilized soldiers to join newly established or reformed police forces. First, demilitarizing police forces is a central aim—that is, refocusing them on public rather than national security, stripping them of military doctrines, organizational structures, and equipment. This is more difficult to accomplish and is possibly undermined by the presence of soldiers in the police force. In Kosovo, the alternative was to collect former KLA members in a new body called the Kosovo Protection Corps (KPC), which was designed to be distinct from military and police structures and be responsible for reconstruction and in future crises stemming from natural disasters, such as floods. Although setting up the KPC went smoothly, problems persisted with regard to gathering sufficient funds and the definition of the KPC's role.[12] Also, efforts were made to gradually reduce the share of former KLA personnel—which had been 40 percent in April 2001—in the fledgling Kosovo Police Service (KPS).[13] Second, the problem of reintegration is solved only superficially, as postwar authorities are saddled with an excessively large and financially unsupportable police force. In time, the reduction of police forces may become an unavoidable, highly sensitive, and destabilizing political issue. The protests and accusations triggered by the announcement of the Croatian government in the summer of 2001 to cut police forces are a case in point.[14]

A particularly tricky question in the wake of the conflicts in the Balkans was whether a legal code existed, and how useful—how tainted or how practicable—it was. The relevance of a legal code is discussed in-depth in Chapter 9. In the context of police reform, the existence of an applicable legal code is critical in that it guides the international police officers in those cases where they have to enforce law and order, such as in Kosovo and in East Timor. It is also a necessary precondition for training or reforming indigenous police forces. To the population in a war-torn society, the absence of a generally accepted and applied legal code indicates instability and inconsistency and does little to encourage faith in the rule of law.

Efforts to Strengthen Indigenous Police Capacity

Reform efforts fall into two general categories. First, police reform involves a structural component. This refers to questions of basic restructuring, such as the multiethnicity of indigenous police forces in the Balkans, sustainable force levels, and salary structures. In order to be sustainable in the long run, structural reform must also build an institutional framework, including administrative structures, as well as links to governing institutions and to the other elements of the public security field. Second, structural reform is an empty shell unless police behavior also changes and police abide by democratic standards. The training component of reform is carried out through the establishment of police academies and curricula development, through police field training, and through monitoring the performance of local police forces. Police reform has increasingly been tied more explicitly to the concept of democratic policing and respect for human rights.[15]

Although there is no general agreement on a common approach to providing police assistance, one can nonetheless identify a few key concepts, such as democratic policing, community policing, and perhaps the more value-neutral concept of professionalization. Democratic policing involves two key features: responsiveness and accountability. As David Bayley writes, "A police force is democratic when it responds to the needs of individuals and private groups as well as the needs of the government . . . and [is] accountable to multiple external audiences."[16] The concept of community policing underlines the need for responsiveness and—as the name suggests—close ties to the community. When international assistance emphasizes professionalization of the police force as a key aim, it clothes normative concerns in terms of effectiveness and social value and perhaps renders them less politically sensitive and therefore more acceptable to the indigenous police force.[17] Otwin Marenin points out how the police are a source of change that has gone largely untapped. Rather than promoting one model as the ultimate choice, Marenin suggests four basic, nonnegotiable principles that draw on different models and that a police organization should fulfill: representativeness, semiautonomy, integrity, and transparency.[18]

In this steadily expanding field, the context of the rule of law has been recognized as a critical factor in enhancing indigenous capacity. Therefore, the promotion of civil society and civilian oversight mechanisms has increasingly been linked to questions of public security and security sector reform.

Although the civil society dimension will not be explored in this chapter, it is nonetheless of critical importance. Recognizing the significance of the socioeconomic backdrop again underlines the role of police reform in the wider context of state building and its ties to issues of governance. Linking police reform to long-term democratization brings out the difficult transition from immediate crisis management, that is, providing a secure environment and policing, to long-term development, that is, state building, democratization, and economic development.

Structural Reform: Restructuring
Police Forces in the Balkans

As described above, the police forces in BiH were bloated in the aftermath of the war and had acted as a continuation of military instruments in the conflict.[19] As a result, structural reform meant three things. First, the police forces, which had swelled to 54,000, would have to be reduced to 20,000. This also meant dismantling special police forces and similar armed groups. Reductions were necessary simply to arrive at sustainable force levels and salary structures that the Bosnian governments in the two entities would be able to finance without outside assistance in the long run. The process of reduction, however, was also a convenient filter, where police officers were screened in a systematic vetting process. The process continued for more than five years and developed a corollary, certification. Certification proved a useful enforcement mechanism to back up monitoring activity. Although the vetting and certification process was criticized for taking a long time, the UN's International Police Task Force (IPTF) argued that it would ultimately be all the more stable. Vetting is an example of how a structural technical process becomes an issue of police behavior and a true test of reform.

In both Kosovo and Eastern Slavonia, the new police forces were to be kept separate from the influence and participation of paramilitary forces, such as specialized police forces and other armed groups of different shapes and affiliations. Aside from disarming and removing the influence of the KLA to the greatest extent possible, there was also a need to strengthen the fledgling police force.[20] On the contrary, the challenge, as in Eastern Slavonia, was to train a sufficient number of new police officers as rapidly yet as well as possible. In Kosovo, financing of the police forces remained a problem, as indigenous civil authorities were still in the process of being established and there was little income from taxation to pay for the KPS—and the KPC for that matter. Needless to say, unless addressed, the insecure fiscal basis and low salaries increase the temptations of corruption and black market activity and undermine the efforts to build a democratic, credible, and effective police force.

A second element in the structural reform of police forces in BiH was a reorganization in accordance with the government structures established in the Dayton Agreement. In other words, two entity police organizations were formed, one for the Federation and one for the Republika Srpska. At a lower level, police forces were organized in cantons. Progress was a little slower in the Republika Srpska, in part due to funding difficulties and the internal political split, but cantonal police forces were established throughout BiH. Third, the police force was to be multiethnic, in order to instill greater confidence among the Bosnian population and to reflect the ethnic composition of the state. In practice, multiethnicity proved difficult and informal structures continued to dominate the police organization so that there were not two forces, but in effect three—one for each ethnic group.[21]

In Kosovo too, multiethnicity and minority representation in the police force were considered critical from the outset. In fact, throughout the Balkans, multiethnicity in the police force was a fundamental principle, but in all cases it proved extremely difficult. The Kosovo Police Service School (KPSS) boasted a satisfactory number of minority recruits in 2001 (17 percent, of which 9 percent were Serb), as well as female recruits (20 percent),[22] but the true test would be whether the KPS would be able to retain the desired share of Serb officers over time. Similarly, the International Crisis Group initially saw no evidence of political influence over recruitment and selection of candidates for the KPSS, but suggested there was a danger of this—once control over selection had been handed from the Organization for Security and Cooperation in Europe (OSCE) to local authorities.[23]

Structural reform also entails (re)distributing the responsibility for security and is therefore a highly sensitive issue. Former opponents are likely to be distrustful of each other, but may be forced to share power, territory, and the responsibility for internal security. This was clearly the case in all Balkan theaters. One example is Eastern Slavonia, where the Croatian and the Serb population had to learn to share responsibility for security in a hotly contested area and learn to trust that security would be nonpartisan. A new Transitional Police Force (TPF) was established by the UN for the region, with equal participation of Serbs and Croats to alleviate fears of harassment. From 1996 to 1998, it was under the authority of the UN mission, UNTAES, and was then integrated into the structure of the Croatian police force.

Police reform in BiH was orienting itself toward a tentative end-date, namely December 2002. The Mission Implementation Plan (MIP) for this period outlined several core programs: police reform, police restructuring (reduction), police-criminal justice cooperation, institution building, interpolice cooperation (through such entities as the European Police Organization [Europol]), state border service, organized crime, and regional police cooperation. A possible follow-on mission might consist of about 500–600 civilian police or human rights monitors to replace the IPTF.[24]

Behavioral Reform: Training and
Monitoring Police Conduct

Moving from restructuring to behavioral reform of the police forces, processes become a little fuzzier. When devising grand plans for how external actors can mold an indigenous police force, one has to keep in mind that a police force is a professional organization like any other with a defined occupational culture. This is especially true in the case of BiH, where an existing police force was to be reformed and where the organizational culture of the force was a product of prewar police experience, as well as the experience of the recent conflict.[25] Although it is critical to understand exactly what is to be achieved, in practice the common denominator of efforts to reform and restructure the police in the Balkans appears to have been the absence of a declared aim. Frustrated by the lack of a vision for what the Bosnian police should be like at the end of the reform process—aside from a notion that they should be more "like us," IPTF commissioner Peter Fitzgerald collected his thoughts in a report on guidance for democratic policing in the BiH in May 1996. In that way, the civilian police operation in BiH proved a catalyst for formulating and consolidating what until then had been perceived as a random collection of rules. Still, contrary to common belief, internationally recognized documents on police behavior and legal guidelines did exist, such as the Universal Declaration of Human Rights and the UN Criminal Justice Standards, which were developed in 1994 and merged elements of existing international human rights instruments relating to police work.[26]

Typical activities in behavioral reform include monitoring police performance, conducting police training, setting up police academies, including developing curricula, and establishing procedures for recruitment and selection. In BiH, home to the longest-standing police reform effort, a more sophisticated approach to training evolved. International assistance went to training specialist police forces, such as for border services, crowd control, and criminal intelligence. Human rights monitoring was undertaken in all cases in the Balkans, that is, in BiH, Eastern Slavonia, Kosovo, and Albania. Instilling respect for and protection of human rights in the local police forces was a crucial task for the international community, as the population's confidence in its security depended to a large extent on their day-to-day contact with the police force. The IPTF monitored police conduct from the outset, but lacked clout in its recommendations and reprimands to its counterparts in the indigenous police forces. Closer contact developed and monitoring became more effective when IPTF officers were co-located with their Bosnian colleagues and when the Stabilization Force (SFOR) and IPTF conducted joint patrols.[27] The operation in Kosovo benefited from the experiences in BiH, in that the Kosovo Force (KFOR) developed a better understanding of the needs of the civilian police, and military-police relations fell into place more quickly, despite another disjointed start. As the mission in

Eastern Slavonia was entirely under UN auspices, cooperation was somewhat easier, but the general reluctance of military officers to join in activities that are reminiscent of policing still hampered police operations.[28]

Of all the tasks in behavioral reform, monitoring continues for the longest period of time, as it carries on after initial restructuring and training have been completed. Monitoring began instantly, and training and restructuring were almost concurrent in Eastern Slavonia and in BiH. In Kosovo the emphasis would gradually shift to monitoring, as the KPS emerged and deployed to the streets.[29] When UNTAES was drawn down after two years and the political authority was returned to the Croatian government, the more extensive training role of the civilian police component also ceased. The UNCIVPOL component was replaced by the UN Police Support Group (UNPSG), which had a pure monitoring mandate. Nine months later, in October 1998, the mandate was passed on to a monitoring group under the OSCE.

Efforts to strengthen indigenous police capacity in Kosovo developed out of the operation in BiH in another respect. Whereas assistance to police academies was somewhat neglected and funds were difficult to raise in BiH, the Kosovo Police Service School became one of the centerpieces of the rule of law agenda. Of course, a major difference was that public security issues generally enjoyed a higher profile in Kosovo, not the least because the UN suddenly found itself with the responsibility for maintaining law and order as a necessary element in its civilian administration of the province.[30]

Structural and behavioral reform processes were relatively successful in BiH, Eastern Slavonia, and Kosovo. The major difficulty encountered to a greater or lesser extent in all cases was the political influence on the police forces. Despite their multiethnic composition, ethnic tensions still existed within the forces and were even fostered by the political leadership. Experience from Albania illustrates a key challenge in police training. The Western European Union's Multinational Advisory Police Element (MAPE) in Albania claimed relative success in establishing a police force. Challenges, here as elsewhere in the Balkans, tended to arise when the police were released onto the streets, and problems of corruption, the spread of illegal weapons, and organized crime surfaced.[31] Clearly, reform projects are comprehensive and ambitious undertakings and it will take a long time for the revamped police to come into its own. The reformed or newly established police force has to develop its own culture and internal dynamic and control mechanisms, which are then maintained over time. Each society will also arrive at a level of order that it considers tolerable in the long run.

Developing Regional Cooperation

In the late 1990s, an emphasis on regional cooperation, such as the Stability Pact initiative on police training, was added to the portfolio of police assistance.[32] The West promoted regional initiatives for several reasons. One goal was certainly to lighten the load of international assistance by developing regional networks that would improve the chances for sustainable police reform. This meant encouraging self-styled patterns of cooperation that reflect the prioritization of challenges among countries in the region and views as to how the challenges ought to be met. In the course of 2000 another motivation came to dominate the rhetoric on regional cooperation: Western European governments in particular cited the need to stem the spread of transnational organized crime emanating from the Balkans. In that way, assistance to police reform and the wider security sector was justified in terms of combating organized crime. The rationale was twofold. On the one hand, reforming the security sector meant enhancing an ineffective or a corrupt system of law and order and changing the climate in which organized crime thrives. On the other hand, police reform aimed at making indigenous instruments for fighting crime more efficient.[33] It was generally recognized that the local crime picture had clear regional dimensions.[34] As a result, the governments of Croatia, the two entities of BiH, and the Federal Republic of Yugoslavia (FRY) established in June 2001 a regional working group to fight organized crime, providing some hope that the dynamic might be shifting from externally imposed solutions to local initiatives.[35]

In addition to police cooperation within the Balkans, regional cooperation also refers to those states working with European bodies on fighting crime. EU membership has been a particularly attractive carrot that European governments have dangled in front of various authorities in the region as an incentive for reform and compliance with, for example, the provisions of the Dayton Agreement. It is in the interest of Western European governments to build as many ties as possible at lower levels. By bringing the states into the fold in cooperation agreements just short of membership, European governments hope to soften the blow, when it eventually becomes undeniably clear that BiH, Croatia, the FRY, and Albania are *not* on the short list for EU membership.

All the cases point to the intimate link between police reform, or the wider security sector reform, and processes of state building. In the same way, building regional cooperation was intended "to help the emerging national authorities to communicate, share information, and co-operate in prosecution of international crime."[36] The balance between strengthening the state and strengthening regional, decentralized initiatives is a precarious one. Although regional approaches have much to recommend themselves and are ultimately in the interest of Western Europe, they may threaten the fragile states in the Balkans. Regional initiatives may further deflate an already weak basis of power and arouse resentment, but may also be threatening because they counter the criminal activities that large parts of the political leadership are involved in.

Related Areas of Reform

Strengthening the indigenous police capacity is only meaningful if matched by parallel reform processes of the judicial and the penal system. Challenges of judicial and penal reform are discussed at length in other chapters in this volume. I will therefore limit myself to underlining the link between police reform and judicial reform processes. For police reform, defunct judicial and penal systems mean that the efforts of the police force are discredited. In BiH—as in Kosovo—there was no functioning legal system. Yet crime was rampant and a backlog of cases had accumulated during the war. This increased the pressure on the indigenous police to make a visible difference quickly. There was also a danger that the police force would become demoralized and public trust in the rule of law undermined when arrested criminals were released (because the courts and the legal system were unable to try them). Often the courts were unwilling to try or convict criminals. This typifies a situation where judicial reform is taking place in the absence of democratic traditions and under considerable political pressure. In a review of judicial reform efforts in BiH up until mid-1999, the International Crisis Group commented that "law enforcement institutions protect local power structures rather than the rule of law."[37] Unfortunately, the third-party efforts to reform the judicial system in BiH were dwarfed in comparison to the influence of the political framework, which to a large extent determined day-to-day judicial activity. Although a "court police" was established to provide protection for judges and prosecutors and the IPTF monitored court activity, it proved particularly difficult to combat the intimidation of staff and plaintiffs.[38] In Kosovo, the UN felt the pressure even more keenly, since the international civilian administration itself was responsible for investigation, arrest, detention, trial, and other aspects of criminal justice, rather than monitoring the local, if flawed, system of law and order. A final case in point was the effort to enhance the judicial system in Albania, which rested on the realization that police reform in the absence of judicial and penal reform was futile.[39]

Prospects for the Rule of Law in the Balkans

International contributors are spurred on by the fact that there are very real opportunities to lay a foundation for stability and public security by strengthening the indigenous civilian police capacity. At the same time, there are problems that hem reform efforts both locally and internationally and that should not be taken lightly.

At the international level, the practical problems of UNCIVPOL and calls for clearer mandates and more extensive means, usually requiring more personnel with heavier equipment, are in many ways merely the symptoms of far-reaching problems in the international community's approach to public security assistance. Although coordination at an operational level has improved,[40] at a strategic level there is a pressing need to develop a cohesive vision of the comprehensive reform projects that are being launched and conducted in various war-torn societies. A joint strategic vision is especially important when it comes to the cooperation between the military and the police. When there is a joint understanding of priorities and aims, practical cooperation falls into place. It is important to keep in mind that resolute backup from SFOR and KFOR—to the IPTF and the UNMIK police, respectively—is the product of a conscious political decision by the major contributors to the military force, rather than the result of mere practical arrangements. This also points to the need for sustained engagement as a major challenge for international efforts in the public security field. Although the link between security and development has been generally recognized, the practical consequences, namely that strengthening the rule of law is a long-term prospect, are sinking in only gradually. The recognition that police reform is a long-term proposition has been particularly difficult to translate into practice because it requires unorthodox networks of cooperation, for example between domestic police authorities in contributing countries and the development assistance community.

The influence of external factors pales in comparison to local circumstances in which the international mission is deployed. The political context is salient because security sector reform goes to the heart of the relationship between the citizen and the state, whereby the police are the most visible and most immediate representatives of the state in the citizen's daily life. First and foremost, the effectiveness of international civilian police depends on how they deal with recalcitrant political leaders. The Balkans are infamous for a range of so-called spoilers who are present in political, military, economic, and criminal spheres and who obstruct the reform processes. A related factor for the political context is the outcome of the prior conflict and competing visions for an "end-state." This is particularly true because the police and the other elements of the public security sector are so intimately linked to the state-building project that is under way. Managing the expectations of the local population is an important task for international actors, but is often neglected. A final aspect of the political context is the balance between outside pressure and control and local empowerment. For police reform, finding the balance between local involvement and external pressure means finding a model of policing that is sustainable and that will be sustained by the local police forces and authorities.

High levels of crime and violence are also a major obstacle. Crime and instability form the backdrop for reform efforts and are the challenges that the indigenous civil police capacity will face in the future. If authorities cannot counter persistently high crime rates, they will be tempted to use repressive measures, undermining reform and democratization efforts. The surge in crime in the Balkans was a response to the collapse of a socialist state and the resulting void left by an ineffective security apparatus or a corrupt police. This left an opening for opportunists and entrepreneurs in the criminal realm, who built strong informal networks both throughout and outside the region.

A major shortcoming of international assistance to security sector reform more generally has been the reluctance to deal with informal networks of power—criminal or otherwise. These networks are difficult to identify and usually retreat into the shadows when the sometimes boisterous international community arrives on the scene, as they did in Kosovo. Although they become less visible, these networks continue to control and manipulate and are no less influential. In the present context of police reform, removing informal parallel lines of authority, such as among the three ethnic groups in the Bosnian police forces and their respective irregular paramilitary backups, is critical.[41] In the Balkans, few efforts have been made to address this and draw informal networks into the state-building project to enhance popular support and create a more viable system. Obviously, there is a fine balance between building informal actors into reform projects and marginalizing unacceptable counterparts. Allowing groups to operate that benefit from the instability and tension because it detracts attention from their criminal activity, frankly means selling out the peace process.[42] Although individual measures, such as anticorruption programs, have been initiated in both BiH and Kosovo, there is no cohesive political approach to the issue of informal networks. A first step might simply be to take more consolidated action against politically motivated violence, which still accounts for instability and for lack of progress in minority returns, as well as ongoing displacement.[43] Consistency is lacking when it comes to a coordinated approach among both military and civilian actors, including the police, and individual contributing nations, such as between Europe and the United States.[44] There is undoubtedly a vast amount of intelligence on informal networks, but—to be fair—they are also extremely difficult to deal with. For one, essential political support from local authorities is usually absent for fear of losing their own grip on power. More important, the international community is at a loss as to how to curb the influence of informal actors.

Conclusion

Failure is often easier to identify than success. A recurring and exceedingly difficult question is how to know if success has been achieved and, if so, to what extent. General criteria for measuring success have been and will remain elusive. Goals have tended to be exaggerated, and there is a good argument for being modest. After all, establishing crime-free societies in the Balkans is not the goal, but rather identifying and realizing tolerable levels of crime and instability. Derek Chappell, police spokesman for UNMIK, commented in December 2000 that "the real fight against fear, violence and intimidation must be fought in the hearts and minds of the people of Kosovo, who must confront this casual acceptance of violence."[45] While that is true, the tolerance that the population in the Balkans displays for everyday violence might well be unacceptable to an outside observer, but is ultimately subject to an internal assessment within each society. The real goal is to create relatively stable societies in which respect for human rights is self-sustaining. Police reform is certainly a vital element in a sweeping state-building and transformation exercise. As reform projects steadily grow in size and scope, a more poignant question is how to prioritize and how to sequence different aspects of the reform agenda. After all, the attention span of the international community and the funds that they provide are limited. And in the end, the need is to create something that is tolerable to the locals, sustainable by the locals, and based on respect for human rights.

Notes

1. Brynjar Lia, "Policing Without a State? Palestinian Policing from the British Mandate to the Oslo Accords," University of Oslo, 2003, p. 29.

2. See, for example, Graham Day, "The Training Dimension of the UN Mission in Bosnia and Herzegovina (UNMIBH)," *International Peacekeeping* 7, no. 2 (Summer 2000): 155; Gerald Knaus and Marcus Cox, "Whither Bosnia?" *NATO Review* 48 (Winter 2000–2001): 7.

3. Chris Donnelly, "Rethinking Security," *NATO Review* 48 (Winter 2000–2001): 33.

4. Tor Tanke Holm, "CPN/SWP Balkan Stability Project: Crime and Corruption," paper prepared for the CPN/SWP Western Balkans Stability project, 3rd draft, October 25, 1999, p. 5; International Crisis Group (ICG), *The Policing Gap: Law and Order in the New Kosovo* (Pristina: ICG, August 6, 1999), pp. 3–4, 8.

5. It also means a concomitant change in police culture, which as Graham Day points out was "dominated by the pre-war authoritarian ethos." Day, "Training Dimension," pp. 157, 167.

6. Annika S. Hansen, "International Security Assistance to Peace Implementation Processes: The Cases of Bosnia-Herzegovina and Angola," University of Oslo, 2000, pp. 65–67.

7. Tor Tanke Holm, "CIVPOL Operations in Eastern Slavonia, 1992–98," in Tor Tanke Holm and Espen Barth Eide, eds., *Peacebuilding and Police Reform* (Frank Cass: London, 2000), pp. 139–140.

8. Espen Barth Eide, "CPN/SWP Balkan Stability Project: The Internal Security Challenge—Reforming Police, Judiciaries, and Penal Systems in the Western Balkans," paper prepared for the CPN/SWP Western Balkans Stability project, 2nd draft, November 11, 1999, p. 7.

9. ICG, *Kosovo Report Card,* ICG Balkans Report no. 100 (Pristina: ICG, August 28, 2000), pp. 3–4.

10. Holm, "CPN/SWP Balkan Stability Project: Crime and Corruption," p. 5.

11. See "Albania: Law Ensuring Independence of Judiciary Adopted," ATA news agency, Tirana, in English, May 17, 2001; "Albania, Council of Europe Sign Second Action-Plan for Reform of Judiciary," ATA news agency, Tirana, in English, May 23, 2001.

12. ICG, *Kosovo Report Card,* p. 12; "Kosovo Protection Corps Chief Meets NATO Military Council, Seeks Aid," Kosovapress news agency website, Pristina, in Albanian, July 20, 2001, www.kosovapress.com

13. Steve Bennett, "Briefing on the Kosovo Police School," paper presented at the IISS/DCAF workshop "Managing the Context of Police Reform: Implications for International Assistance," Geneva, April 24–25, 2001.

14. See, for example, "Croatian Police Force to Cut 4,000 Posts by End of 2001," HINA news agency, Zagreb, in English, April 28, 2001; "Police Redundancies in Eastern Croatia Blamed on Serbs Taking Up Posts," Croatian Radio, Zagreb, in Serbo-Croat, August 7, 2001.

15. Francesca Marotta, "The Blue Flame and the Gold Shield: Methodology, Challenges, and Lessons Learned on Human Rights Training for Police," in Holm and Eide, *Peacebuilding and Police Reform,* pp. 69–92.

16. David Bayley, "The Contemporary Practices of Policing: A Comparative View," in *Multinational Peacekeeping: A Workshop Series—A Role for Democratic Policing* (Washington, DC: National Institute of Justice, October 6, 1997), pp. 3–4.

17. Another word of warning is in order: while these concepts are generally accepted, they are still interpreted in the way that advisers are familiar with in their home countries, which can still lead to substantial discrepancies in the field. See Bayley, "Contemporary Practices," p. 5.

18. Otwin Marenin, "Approaches to Police Reform," paper presented at the IISS/DCAF workshop "Managing the Context of Police Reform: Implications for International Assistance," Geneva, April 24–25, 2001. Graham Day points to transparency and accountability as two major goals in the reform of police forces in Bosnia-Herzegovina. Day, "Training Dimension," p. 158.

19. For a detailed description of police reform efforts in Bosnia-Herzegovina, see Hansen, "International Security Assistance," pp. 139–149.

20. For more on the disarmament of the KLA, see, for example, ICG, *Kosovo Report Card,* pp. 10–14.

21. Day, "Training Dimension," pp. 158–159; U.S. General Accounting Office (GAO), *Bosnia Crime and Corruption Threaten Successful Implementation of the Dayton Agreement,* Testimony Before the Committee on International Relations, House of Representatives, GAO/T-NSIAD-00-219, Washington, DC, July 19, 2000, pp. 3–4.

22. Bennett, "Briefing."

23. ICG, *Kosovo Report Card.*

24. UN Mission in Bosnia and Herzegovina, *Mandate Implementation Plan 2000–2002,* www.unmibh.org/unmibh/mip.htm; conversations with mission staff, Stockholm, May 2001.

25. ICG, *Policing Gap,* p. 8. This begs the question of whether it is easier to reform an existing police force or to start from scratch. Case study evidence shows that there can be no simple answer. Whereas Kosovo is a strong argument in favor of starting afresh, the Haitian case illustrates all the difficulties of building a police force in a void of policing traditions, established doctrine and culture, and experienced senior officers. Clearly, progress depends more on the political and socioeconomic context of reform than on the prior existence of an indigenous police force.

26. Espen Barth Eide, Annika S. Hansen, and Brynjar Lia, *Security Sector Reform as a Development Issue,* Room Document no. 7 (Paris: OECD/Development Assis-

tance Committee, Task Force for International Peace and Development, June 2–3, 1999), pp. 15–16. See also Marotta, "Blue Flame," p. 74.

27. Hansen, "International Security Assistance," p. 141.

28. ICG, *Kosovo Report Card,* p. 15; Holm, "CIVPOL Operations in Eastern Slavonia," pp. 144–145.

29. The organizational division of labor is as follows: academy training of KPS candidates is conducted by the OSCE; field training and continuous supervision are conducted by the UNMIK police.

30. On the coordination and division of labor among different international organizations, see Chapter 7.

31. Conversations with MAPE officers, Paris, March 2001, and Stockholm, May 2001. See also "Council of Europe Praises Positive Progress of Police Reform in Albania," ATA news agency, Tirana, in English, July 27, 2001.

32. For an outstanding overview of regional efforts, see Tor Tanke Holm and Kari Margarethe Osland, *Regional Civilian Police Training in Southeast Europe* (Oslo: Norwegian Institute of International Affairs [NUPI], December 12, 2000); Special Coordinator of the Stability Pact for South Eastern Europe, "Chairman's Conclusions," Third Meeting of the Working Table on Security Issues, Sofia, October 4–5, 2000, www.stabilitypact.org/w.../sofia%20conclusions,%october%204-5,%202000.htm.

33. Eide, "CPN/SWP Balkan Stability Project: The Internal Security Challenge," p. 4.

34. Holm, "CPN/SWP Balkan Stability Project: Crime and Corruption," p. 5.

35. "Bosnian, Croatian Police Agree on Closer, More Efficient Cooperation," BH Press news agency, Sarajevo, in Serbo-Croat, May 14, 2001; "Yugoslav, Croatian, Bosnian Police Ministers Set Up Crime-Busting Body," Radio B92, Belgrade, in Serbo-Croat, June 12, 2001. Interestingly, the growth of organized crime triggers similar initiatives in other parts of the world as well. Some East African states have joined police forces to combat transnational organized crime.

36. Eide, "CPN/SWP Balkan Stability Project: The Internal Security Challenge," p. 13.

37. ICG, *Rule over Law: Obstacles to the Development of an Independent Judiciary in Bosnia-Herzegovina,* July 5, 1999, www.int...org/projects/bosnia/reports/bh49rep.htm, p. I.14. The quoted report by the ICG is an in-depth assessment of conditions for and international efforts in judicial reform in Bosnia-Herzegovina until mid-1999.

38. Ibid., pp. II.6–11.7. The international pressure that was exercised on courts in Mostar following the inadequate trial of a number of Croat suspects and that led to the case being reopened is only one example of the effort to bring the entire law enforcement triad into line with international standards.

39. See, for example, "Albania, Council of Europe Sign Second Action-Plan for Reform of Judiciary," ATA news agency, May 23, 2001.

40. For an overview over the most important international organizations that provide assistance to security sector reform in the Balkans and their patterns of coordination, see Chapter 7.

41. Day, "Training Dimension," pp. 158–159.

42. "Doppelspiel," *Der Spiegel,* July 30, 2001, p. 102.

43. Human Rights Watch, *World Report 2001: Federal Republic of Yugoslavia,* www.hrw.org/wr2k1/europe/yugoslavia-kosovo.html; ICG, *Kosovo Report Card,* pp. 2–3.

44. See, for example, Office of the High Representative (OHR), *Report by the High Representative for Implementation of the Peace Agreement to the Secretary-General of the United Nations* (Sarajevo: OHR, May 3, 2000), paras. 43 ff.; GAO, *Bosnia Crime,* p. 4.

45. UN Mission in Kosovo, *News Reports,* December 11, 2000, www.un.org/peace/kosovo/news/kosovo2.htm.

PART 4

Comparative
Regional Perspectives

11

The Regionalization of Peace in Asia

Mely Caballero-Anthony

The structural changes brought about by the end of the Cold War have renewed interest in regionalism and a reconsideration of the security role of regional security organizations in promoting international peace and security. Several factors account for this new enthusiasm. Among them is the fact that in the post–Cold War era, regional relations have expanded and regional areas have become "substantially more important venue(s) of conflict and cooperation than in the past."[1] Juxtaposed with this is the increasing security role of the UN after being involved in major conflicts such as in the Gulf War, Cambodia, Mozambique, and others. This has severely stretched the resources of the UN and has been made even more acute with the expansion of peacekeeping operations it has undertaken in recent years. The UN's capacity to undertake additional responsibilities has become more complex while the will of its dominant members has often been weak.[2] It is hardly surprising, then, that some countries have called for the UN to scale down its involvement in conflict situations and rely instead on so-called coalitions of the willing.

Apart from these factors, the desire for regional autonomy was a characteristic feature of several regional organizations in Asia and Africa, mirrored in such slogans as "Asian solutions to Asian problems." Adopting regional solutions to regional problems was predicated on the fact that regional actors felt they were best suited to mediate in local conflicts, as they understood the dynamics of strife and cultures more intimately than outsiders. Moreover, issues that were related to local conflicts would most likely be given more attention in regional fora than in the global one, since the latter had a much broader agenda.[3] Finally, the effects of economic regionalism reflected in the emergence of regional economic groupings like those based around the North American Free Trade Agreement (NAFTA) and the Association of Southeast

Asian Nations (ASEAN) Free Trade Agreement (AFTA), among others, have had the effect of enhancing self-confidence among regional states and encouraging them to emphasize more self-reliance in security matters.

Thus, in spite of the ambiguous experiences of regional organizations in the past, there is not only the growing realization but also the appreciation that they can play a significant role in managing regional conflicts. More important, experiences have also shown that some regional organizations have in fact demonstrated reasonable success in preventing and managing conflict in their specific regions. In Asia, the experiences of ASEAN and to some extent the ASEAN Regional Forum (ARF) have been instructive in efforts at regionalizing peace. This chapter looks at the mechanisms of conflict management in both ASEAN and the ARF, although the former takes up a larger part of the analysis by virtue of its greater longevity.

The main objectives of this chapter are twofold. First, it will analyze the nature of peace operations in Asia, which are significantly different from the types of peace operations of other regional organizations. Second, it will examine the possibility of closer cooperation and partnership between the United Nations and regional arrangements in the resolution and management of regional conflicts. The chief argument is that peace operations in Asia— which are mostly in the area of conflict prevention as exemplified by the types of mechanisms found in ASEAN and the ARF—have made valuable contributions toward regional peace. In spite of this considerable success, I also argue that the changing strategic environment requires a more proactive engagement of regional organizations, which involves reviewing and changing existing mechanisms to be more responsive to current challenges.

The chapter is divided into three sections. The first section looks at the types of regional security arrangements in Asia—ASEAN and the ARF—and examines their institutional capacities, types of norms and informal processes, and availability of resources in the management of conflicts. The second section analyzes how these two organizations have fared in addressing security challenges in Asia, including a case study of the responses of ASEAN and the ARF on the East Timor crisis. The third section considers the possibilities of an ASEAN-ARF partnership with the UN in its peace operations.

The Experience of ASEAN and the ARF

ASEAN and the Security of Southeast Asia:
Regional Reconciliation and Norm Building

At least until the Asian financial crisis struck in 1997, ASEAN was cited as one of the most successful regional organizations by many observers, scholars, and even its major critics.[4] Its success lies in the very fact that ASEAN has so far prevented its members from going to war with one another, given that ASEAN was considered as the Balkans of the East in the early 1960s.

If one goes back to Joseph Nye's notion of "islands of peace," it could be argued that ASEAN's raison d'être has been mainly about regional reconciliation. As a building block to peace in what was once a trouble-ridden region, the formation of ASEAN in 1967 laid the foundations for bridging the differences between the noncommunist states of Indonesia; Malaysia and Singapore (both then referred to as Malaya); the Philippines and Thailand; and the communist states of Vietnam, Laos, and Cambodia; as well as the isolated state of Myanmar. ASEAN expanded from the original five noncommunist states with the inclusion of Brunei in 1984 (after its independence from Great Britain) and Vietnam in 1995. In 1997, Laos and Myanmar became members and in 1999 Cambodia was admitted as the tenth member. Bringing together all the states in Southeast Asia had always been the original vision of ASEAN's founding fathers.

More important, ASEAN was essentially a response by states within a "subregion" that was bedeviled by intramural disputes between Malaysia and Indonesia over the formation of the Federation of Malaya in 1963. This led to the period of *konfrontasi* and the conflict between Malaysia and the Philippines over the territory of Sabah. These major conflicts were in fact the stumbling blocks to earlier efforts by these states to form a regional association and became the major reasons why earlier attempts to establish ASEAN failed.[5] With the formation of ASEAN, the subregional states provided a stable structure of relations for managing and containing tensions among governments of corresponding political disposition. Thus ASEAN's formation had become, for all intents and purposes, a diplomatic device for regional reconciliation,[6] which in turn underpins regional peace and security.

The processes and mechanisms of conflict management. If ASEAN has been essentially about regional reconciliation, its success has been based in management of conflict. Unlike other regional organizations that have developed more structured and formal conflict resolving mechanisms, ASEAN's processes and approaches are quite different. To understand the particularity of these mechanisms, a distinction is drawn here between the processes of conflict resolution and conflict management. According to C. R. Mitchell, conflict resolution is the elimination and termination of conflict, involving the fundamental differences and grievances underlying the conflict. Conflict management, on the other hand, involves the elimination of violence or a deescalation of hostilities without really eliminating the root causes of conflict.[7]

There are several mechanisms that regional institutions can employ to manage conflicts, and Muthiah Alagappa provides an analytical framework for the strategies of conflict management available to them. These strategies usually depend on the nature of the conflict—whether domestic, interstate, or intrastate; and the stage of conflict management—prevention, containment, or termination. Moreover, the choice of mechanisms, either formal (such as third-party mediation, arbitration, internationalization, peacekeeping, and peacebuilding) or informal (such as assurance building and norm setting), is largely dependent on the capabilities and resources available to these regional institutions.[8] In the case of ASEAN, and to a large extent the case of the ARF, the mechanisms used to manage conflict are mostly informal and characteristically limited to norm building.

ASEAN's mechanisms of conflict management—the ASEAN way? Much has already been written about ASEAN's informal conflict management processes and mechanisms.[9] This does not mean, however, that ASEAN has no formal mechanisms. In this latter category, the institutionalized meetings, such as the ASEAN summits, the annual and ad hoc meetings of ASEAN foreign ministers, meetings among economic ministers, and meetings of other ministers and senior officials, which fall within the ambit of ASEAN's political, economic, and security cooperation, provide the venues and opportunities where bilateral and regional issues are addressed. However, bilateral disputes are handled through joint commissions and committees.

The Treaty of Amity of Cooperation (TAC), which came into force in 1976, has been the only attempt by ASEAN to provide a formal conflict management and conflict resolution mechanism in the region. A salient feature of the TAC was its establishment of a code of conduct among regional states according to explicitly prescribed, universally accepted principles, and its provision for the peaceful settlement of disputes. These basic principles are: (1) mutual respect for the independence, sovereignty, equality, territorial integrity, and national identity of all nations; (2) the right of every state to lead its national existence free from external interference, subversion, and coercion; (3) noninterference in the internal affairs of one another; (4) settlement of differences or disputes by peaceful means; (5) renunciation of threat or use of force; and (6) effective cooperation among members.

The other important feature of the TAC was its provision for a High Council, found in Articles 14 and 15. The High Council is empowered to "recommend to the parties in dispute appropriate means of settlement such as good offices, mediation, inquiry or conciliation. If the disputing parties so agree, it may constitute into a committee of mediation, inquiry or conciliation." However, since 1976 this council has not been constituted at all and to date no member state has sought recourse to any of the given provisions. The only progress as far as the constitution of the High Council is concerned is that ASEAN is now in the final stages of drafting the Rules of Procedures for the High Council—after more than twenty-five years.

In 1999 ASEAN established the Troika, an ad hoc body comprising the ASEAN foreign ministers who represent the present, past, and future chairs of the ASEAN Standing Committee (ASC). The post of the ASC chair is rotated annually in alphabetical order of member countries. The Troika's main purpose was to enable ASEAN to address urgent and important political and security issues in a timely manner. However, the work of the Troika as stipulated must be compatible with the principles enshrined in the TAC, particularly the core principles of consensus and noninterference in domestic affairs of states. Since its inception nothing much has been said or reported about its progress.

Thus when one speaks of ASEAN's mechanisms, it is mainly in reference to its informal mechanisms—the "ASEAN way," translated as the observance and practice of a set of principles and norms of interstate conduct and modes of cooperation and decisionmaking that have evolved and been widely practiced among ASEAN states. The norms and principles include: the process of dialogue, consultation *(musyawarah)*, and consensus *(muafakat)* in decisionmaking as opposed to majority rule; the principle of nonconfrontation (also related to the principle/practice of agreeing to disagree); and the principle of noninterference in the domestic affairs of other states.

While there have been other ways of describing the types of ASEAN norms, one scholar has succinctly encapsulated the "ASEAN way" as a feature secured to "the belief in the wisdom of minimal institutionalization and . . . on the belief that parties in a dispute are less likely to go to war as long as dialogue continues, as well as promoting reassurance that states would not be coerced into supporting a decision to which they have not consented"[10]

A closer look at ASEAN's mechanisms of conflict management. ASEAN's mechanisms and approaches to conflict management may seem incongruous in the types of conflicts prevalent today, particularly in complex intrastate conflicts. But before assessing ASEAN's progress in applying its norms and mechanisms to regional conflicts, certain regional characteristics need to be carefully examined. These few but highly important features are critical in understanding ASEAN's processes and approaches to security.

First, in ASEAN's history as a corporate, interstate organization, it has not resolved any regional conflict. All ASEAN has done so far is to prevent conflict. Second, no dispute has been brought for resolution to ASEAN as a corporate entity. Bilateral disputes are left to the parties concerned to resolve or manage bilaterally through their respective joint commissions and committees. Examples include the General Border Committees between Malaysia-Thailand and Malaysia-Indonesia. These committees are tasked with resolving problems such as border issues and immigration. Third, ASEAN has no established institution within itself to handle bilateral disputes, and so far it does not want such an institution. As mentioned above, the High Council has never been invoked. Finally, it follows that since ASEAN as a body does not involve itself in bilateral disputes among its members, it therefore does not involve itself in the domestic problems of its member states, and does not attempt to resolve intrastate problems.

Against all the self-inhibiting criteria, the question then is: How does ASEAN really manage conflicts? Perhaps from a constructivist perspective of international relations, one could argue that managing conflict in ASEAN is, to paraphrase Alexander Wendt, "what members make of it and how they do it."[11] It follows too that its mechanisms of managing conflict are what "ASEAN make of them." Observance of these mechanisms has prevented interstate conflicts from escalating.

The ARF and Security of the Asia Pacific

The ARF can be regarded as one of the proverbial building blocks of regional peace. Formed in 1994 under ASEAN's initiative, the ARF now has twenty-three states: the ASEAN 10 (Brunei Darussalam, Cambodia, Indonesia, Laos, Malaysia, Myanmar, Philippines, Singapore, Thailand, and Vietnam), ASEAN's dialogue partners (Australia, Canada, China, the European Union, India, Japan, South Korea, New Zealand, Russia, and the United States), plus Papua New Guinea, Mongolia, and since July 2000, North Korea.

The ARF's conflict management role has been guided by its objectives to: (1) foster constructive dialogue and consultation on political and security issues of common interest and concern; (2) make significant contribution to efforts toward confidence building and preventive diplomacy in the region; and (3) work toward the strengthening and enhancement of political security cooperation within the region as a means of ensuring peace and stability.

How these objectives are to be realized has been outlined within the context of a three-staged approach in conflict management as stated in the 1995 ARF Concept Paper.[12] It steps from promotion of confidence-building measures, to development of preventive diplomacy mechanisms, to development of conflict resolution mechanisms. Since its formation, the ARF has maintained its focus on dialogue and confidence building. It disclaims notions that it is aimed at being a military alliance, a deterrent, and an alternative to a balance of power arrangement. Instead, the ARF is more about attempts at cooperative security, fostering habits of dialogue in an inclusive forum of both like-minded and unlike-minded states in the Asia Pacific region.

In its first-stage work, the promotion of confidence-building measures, the ARF has established and broadened the regionwide security dialogue.[13] Through its principle of inclusivity, the ARF has managed to bring together diverse actors with different political orientations. This motley gathering has managed so far to sustain the multilateral security dialogue in spite of the checkered history of bilateral relations among certain members, particularly the major powers.

Since 1994 and at each subsequent meeting, the ARF has broadened and enhanced political and security dialogue, as reflected in the wide array of topics and issues discussed concerning Asia Pacific security. It has, for example, facilitated discussion of sensitive issues and problems on Myanmar, on the Korean peninsula and in the South China Sea. It has also included matters related to the proliferation of weapons of mass destruction and the implications of ballistic missile defense systems, and called for ratification of the Comprehensive Test Ban Treaty and support for the Nuclear Nonproliferation Treaty. Furthermore, the ARF has addressed, and continues to address, transnational issues—especially issues of piracy, illegal migration including trafficking in people, particularly women and children, and illicit trafficking in drugs and small arms.

To push its confidence-building agenda forward, the ARF has held a crowded program of intersessional meetings on search and rescue coordination and cooperation, peacekeeping operations, and disaster relief. These developed into practical and cooperative measures including the publication of annual defense policy statements and increased publication of defense White Papers, which serve to reinforce openness in a region where transparency is not the traditional culture of state policy; military exchanges, including staff college training; and growing participation of defense and military officials in the work and activities of the ARF.

Through its annual ministerial meetings, the senior official meetings, the intersessional activities, and the numerous track-one and track-two meetings, the ARF has created a series of networks. These form a "social capital," a stock of trust, familiarity, ease, and comfort, which could be a crucial asset at critical moments.

In its second-stage work, preventive diplomacy, the ARF has made some progress in developing specific concepts and principles, although discussions on the divergent issues regarding preventive diplomacy issues are still continuing.[14] At its eighth meeting in Hanoi, the ARF also established a register of experts and eminent persons to be used by ARF members on a voluntary basis in conflict situations.[15] It also explored the principles and procedures of enhancing the role of the ARF chairman in providing good offices and coordination in the periods between ARF meetings.[16] Moreover, the ARF has begun producing its Annual Security Outlook.

The four areas mentioned above were the proposals agreed upon earlier at the sixth ARF meeting in July 1999 as a means to move the ARF agenda beyond confidence-building measures to preventive diplomacy and to address the issue of overlap between the two stages.[17] As a compromise, the final agreement was for the ARF to work on the two stages in tandem as long as the focus remained on the first stage.[18] Thus the progress in these four areas sets the stage for pushing the preventive diplomacy agenda forward.

The ARF has been described as a sui generis organization with no established precedent to follow. Its emphases on process-oriented approaches to security have more or less defined its raison d'être. Thus, eight years since its establishment, the ARF has preferred to move incrementally, on the shared understanding by members that it "should not move too fast for those who want to go slow or not too slow for those who want to go fast."[19] As with the case of ASEAN, understanding the security culture of the ARF is essential before one can proceed to assess its prospects. As one scholar notes:

> Structural factors play only a limited role in determining the extent and nature of both multilateral activity and multilateralism in a given regional security complex. It is the cognitive features of the environment—the attitudes of the players toward each other, the rules and norms governing international interaction, the scope and nature of the security dilemmas that the actors perpetuate among themselves—that effectively determine the particular form of regional order that results.[20]

ASEAN and the ARF's Conflict Management Scorecard

It can be argued that ASEAN has so far been successful in preventing bilateral conflicts and avoiding the escalation of bilateral disputes so as not to destabilize the region. These processes can be seen in certain case studies of bilateral disputes that have been successfully managed since ASEAN's formation in 1967 and have lent credence to such claims. One can look back, for example, at the formative stages of ASEAN—the 1963 *konfrontasi* period, during the height of the conflict between Malaysia and Indonesia; the territorial dispute between Malaysia and the Philippines over the territory of Sabah (which at one point threatened the viability of ASEAN); the Indonesia-Singapore crisis in 1968, which was sparked by the execution of Indonesian marines; and in the similar Philippines-Singapore crisis in 1997 over the hanging of a Filipina maid—to the recent episodic crises between Singapore and Indonesia and, of late, heightened bilateral tension between Malaysia and Singapore. ASEAN's "soft" approach in managing bilateral conflicts has so far helped to defuse these crises and prevent them from escalating.

This is not to say, however, that there are no more conflicts or tensions within ASEAN. It would require a more comprehensive study to address the dynamics of the many conflicts and issues faced by ASEAN today. Suffice it to say, however, that it has been the view of most ASEAN political leaders, bureaucrats, observers, and even academics in and outside the region that as a conflict management approach, the ASEAN way has served the grouping well in the past and will hopefully continue to do so in the future. These soft approaches have been largely predicated on the self-restraining principles of interstate relations, particularly the principle of noninterference in the domestic affairs of other states.

However, some critics of ASEAN take the extreme view that the ASEAN way is nothing but rhetoric—an oxymoron, an excuse for really doing nothing. For example, at the height of the Asian financial crisis, ASEAN was dismissed as being irrelevant and incapable of responding to urgent economic and political crises that confronted the region at that time.[21] ASEAN could not do much to mitigate the effects of the air pollution (haze) that originated from Indonesia due to its careless "slash and burn" practices, which consequently ballooned into an environmental hazard enveloping many countries in the region. Moreover, ASEAN's response to the financial crisis was widely perceived as generally inadequate in spite of the various initiatives and concrete measures it had undertaken.[22] Finally, ASEAN was deemed to have been totally ineffective in responding to a major security challenge in the region—the East Timor crisis (discussed below).

ASEAN Regional Forum

As far as the ARF is concerned, its achievements can be assessed by plotting the development of its three-stage activities. The previous section has already detailed its progress on confidence building and preventive diplomacy. But in spite of what may be a long list of achievements, the ARF in fact has major shortcomings. One of these is the diversity of its membership. Given the sheer expanse of the ARF's geographic footprint, not to mention the political, economic, and cultural diversity that come with it, the ARF has been hampered in its attempts to move at a more desired pace to push its three-stage agenda. With the diversity of interests among member states, the task of finding convergence of interests and cohesiveness as a multilateral forum has become in itself monumental.

The multifaceted nature of the ARF's diversity explains the characteristically cautious attitude of members toward any political/security initiative beyond what was earlier agreed upon, consequently impeding the pace of progress. As a result, the ARF has often been dismissed by critics as nothing more than a talking-shop, since so far the ARF has not been able to resolve, let alone act or play any significant role in, any of the current conflicts in the region. In the case of the East Timor crisis, for instance, ASEAN (as a core member of the ARF) was already considered a major disappointment because of its delayed response. But while ASEAN did something, its limited resources notwithstanding, the ARF did not.

The question of approach and decisionmaking by consensus has also been problematic. While ASEAN's experience was relatively successful, this may not necessarily be the "Asia Pacific way" of doing things. Specifically, the soft mechanisms developed by ASEAN are deemed insufficient to address real security problems in the Asia Pacific, like the tensions in the Korean peninsula, the conflicting claims on the South China Sea, and the Taiwan issue.

Closely related to the above limitations is obviously the lack of support institutions within the ARF that could set pragmatic and perhaps short-term solutions to difficult problems. Other than the annual meetings held on the sidelines of the annual ASEAN ministerial meetings and the intersessional groups and meetings, there are no other institutions that provide support for ARF activities nor are there mechanisms that could drive the ARF agenda forward. Note that the ARF does not even have a secretariat.

Another significant shortcoming is the preference of most ARF member states for bilateralism rather than multilateralism. The attitude toward bilateralism and the prevailing cautious mind-set of actors hamper efforts toward and support for the ARF as a fledgling multilateral endeavor.

Finally, there is the contentious issue of leadership in the ARF. ASEAN's continued stewardship of the ARF has also been noted by observers as a disadvantage to its progress. The concerns lie mostly in ASEAN's limited potential and capabilities to set the agenda for addressing issues such as nuclear proliferation in the Korean peninsula and the competing claims in the South China Sea. Furthermore, ASEAN has been regarded as peripheral to some of these emerging security issues. Therefore, its advantage in being a "safe" and "acceptable" power broker among the major players in the region may not be sustained in the medium to long term, particularly when pitched against the desire of some members who have been pushing for shared leadership of the ARF.

ASEAN, the ARF, and the Crisis in East Timor: A Test Case of Regional Mechanisms

Even before the events in East Timor in 1999 reached crisis proportions, the existing regional mechanisms to deal with regional political and security matters found in both ASEAN and the ARF were much criticized for their ineffectiveness in light of the crises faced by ASEAN. But while ASEAN did something, the ARF was absent from the picture.

Within and outside ASEAN circles, critics had argued that the ASEAN way, which had served the grouping well in the past, was no longer adequate and was in fact becoming a serious obstacle to responding to certain conflicts. The principle of noninterference in particular had been singled out as needing readjustments under a much changed external environment. The call to rethink this principle within ASEAN became more pronounced when former Malaysian deputy and finance minister Anwar Ibrahim mooted the idea of "constructive involvement" in 1997 in reaction to the events in Cambodia that year.[23] During that period, Cambodia's formal entry into ASEAN was delayed due to the domestic conflict brought about by the ousting of Prince Ranar-riddh, the first prime minister of Cambodia, by Hun Sen. The events threw the country once again into turmoil and undermined the Paris Peace Agreement, which defined the framework for peace and stability in Cambodia.

This idea was followed in 1998 by the broad proposal from Thai foreign minister Surin Pitsuwan to consider some flexibility in the practice of nonin-tervention, thus the emergence of the term "flexible engagement."[24] However, the formal debate on the notion of flexible engagement stopped at the ASEAN ministerial meeting in July 1998 when ASEAN announced that it would instead practice "enhanced interaction." This new lexicon apparently meant that ASEAN could have a more open exchange of issues with cross-border effects, like the haze problem that was plaguing ASEAN at that time, but while still respecting the principle of noninterference.[25] In spite of the regional consensus to practice enhanced interaction, the tragic events in East Timor in 1999 found ASEAN—and even the ARF—severely criticized for their inability to stem the violence and the gross violations of human rights that followed.

With Indonesia's decision to allow East Timor a referendum on August 30, 1999, on its future status as either an autonomous province or an inde-pendent state, violence erupted throughout large parts of the country and grew steadily worse. During this period, the UN Mission in East Timor (UNAMET) was established to help prepare the region for the referendum. UNAMET comprised 241 international staff, 420 UN volunteers, up to 280 civilian police, and some 4,000 local staff. Within ASEAN, the Philippines con-tributed to UNAMET by sending civilian police, staff members, and electoral volunteers.[26]

In spite of the presence of UNAMET, violence escalated and spread throughout East Timor, leading to the declaration of martial law on Septem-ber 7. By then, East Timor had suffered massive human casualties and prop-erty destruction. Thousands of terrified people were also forcibly displaced to West Timor. A report by the International Commission of Inquiry on East Timor, released by the UN Office of the High Commissioner for Human Rights, and the Indonesian government's report on human rights abuses, drew similar conclusions: that the atrocities were committed by the local militia with the complicity of the Indonesian Armed Forces (TNI).[27]

Many governments, either individually or collectively through the UN, urged Indonesia to enforce law and order in East Timor. While there were indeed expressions of concern coming from ASEAN countries, it took an Aus-tralian initiative to offer a large contingent of troops for a UN peacekeeping force before any international action could begin to stop the violence in East Timor. Even then, it was not until Indonesia consented to an international peacekeeping force in East Timor that ASEAN officials began to discuss their countries' possible participation in it. Discussions took place on the sidelines of the APEC summit in Auckland. Prior to that, no ad hoc ASEAN meeting was convened to address what was at that time a humanitarian crisis in the region.

On September 15, 1999, the UN Security Council adopted Resolution 1264, creating the International Force for East Timor (INTERFET) under Chapter VII of the UN Charter. Australia headed the multinational force, and within ASEAN the Philippines, Singapore, Malaysia, and Thailand contributed forces. Most of the ASEAN volunteers were composed of support, medical, engineering, and security task forces. The intervention of INTERFET allowed the United Nations to begin large-scale humanitarian relief operations in the country. Apart from providing basic relief, INTERFET repaired damaged infrastructure, ran medical clinics, and most important, established security in a war-torn territory.

By October 25 the Security Council passed Resolution 1272 to authorize Secretary-General Kofi Annan to establish the UN Transitional Authority in East Timor (UNTAET) in order to "exercise all legislative and executive authority including the administration of justice" until the state's formal independence. UNTAET's mandate was to provide security and maintain law and order throughout the territory of East Timor; to establish an effect administration; to assist in the development of civil and social services; to ensure the coordination and delivery of humanitarian assistance, rehabilitation, and development assistance; to support capacity building for self-government; and to assist in the establishment of conditions for sustainable development.[28] UNTAET formally replaced INTERFET in February 2000 and a Filipino officer, Lieutenant-General Jaime de los Santos, became the head of the UN peacekeeping force, replacing Major-General Peter Cosgrove from Australia.

The East Timor crisis offers salient insights into the existing regional mechanisms of conflict management in Asia. The crisis showed that ASEAN's and the ARF's mechanisms were grossly inadequate to respond to an unfolding humanitarian disaster in their midst. To be sure, ASEAN failed to respond to the crisis as a group, and individual responses that did come were muted and sensitive to the issue of national sovereignty. It is noteworthy that at the height of the violence in East Timor, members of ASEAN were reported to have hedged on the issue of discussing the possibility of international action before securing Indonesia's consent.

ASEAN's lack of leadership in East Timor contrasted sharply with the proactive role it had assumed in the search for a comprehensive political settlement of the Cambodian conflict from 1979 to 1991. From the start of the Cambodian problem, ASEAN was at the forefront of efforts to resolve the conflict. Throughout the crisis, whatever ASEAN lacked in terms of political authority to influence the behavior of the warring factions and major power dynamics was made up for through its intense lobbying in the United Nations and dialogue facilitation between the warring Cambodian parties, which culminated in two informal meetings in Jakarta. While it could be argued that ASEAN's swift reaction was predicated on its protest against Vietnam's occupation of Cambodia, which violated the international norms of respect for a country's sovereignty and the right of self-determination (principles also found in ASEAN's Treaty of Amity of Cooperation), as against the internal dimension of the East Timor conflict, the latter also presented a strong case of gross violation of international norms.

ASEAN officials have responded to the criticisms by declaring that only the UN had the legitimacy and the capabilities to undertake any peacekeeping operation and mobilize the massive resources necessary to respond to the East Timor crisis. What ASEAN did instead was to "undertake consultations, arrived at consensus and let the individual members decide on what specific contributions to make to the UN effort."[29] Although these were consistent with its processes and mechanisms of conflict management, ASEAN's actions, set against expectations, reflected the stark reality that the nature of regional mechanisms was largely indicative of the availability of resources, or lack of, within regional organizations. It should be noted too that the East Timor crisis happened at the time when most ASEAN states were still recovering from the devastating effects of the Asian financial crisis. Thus most countries were preoccupied with national concerns and could offer no more than limited contributions.

The East Timor crisis also highlighted ASEAN's sensitivity to the issue of national sovereignty when it came to initiating an international inquiry into the atrocities in East Timor. ASEAN member states demonstrated their strict adherence to the principle of noninterference by opposing such a European Union–sponsored resolution. This reservation indicates the fear of some ASEAN countries that a similar kind of international response could be directed against them if and when the international community considered it justifiable to undertake humanitarian intervention.[30]

Finally, an important repercussion of the lack of action in East Timor was the further weakening of ASEAN's value as a regional actor in the promotion of regional political and security cooperation. This was in stark contrast to ASEAN's proactive role during the Cambodian crisis.

ASEAN, the ARF, and the UN:
Task-Sharing Prospects for Peace

The preceding discussion provides a mixed picture of the effectiveness and limitations of regional mechanisms of conflict management found in ASEAN and the ARF. Although at the outset attempts were made to clarify the position of both regional bodies regarding intrastate conflicts and to describe at length the self-inhibiting features of the regional mechanisms, especially in the case of ASEAN, it was argued that in spite of such limitations ASEAN and the ARF have achieved limited success in managing interstate conflicts.

Defining the nature of these achievements may be contentious and largely depends on the kinds of benchmark used to assess success. The argument here is that while the soft and informal nature of regional mechanisms may be ineffective and irrelevant to conflicts like the East Timor crisis (conflicts requiring decisive action and intervention), those mechanisms have proven their usefulness in managing interstate relations, specifically in conflict prevention between states. It is these achievements that can provide a foundation in exploring possibilities for cooperation between the UN and both ASEAN and the ARF.

For a start, the regional mechanisms have built up a solid capital of good and peaceful interstate relations in the region at the bilateral as well as the multilateral level. As far as existing institutions are concerned, both ASEAN and the ARF have also generated a number of these institutions—loose and unstructured though they might be. This reservoir of extensive networks, at track-one, track-two, and even track-three levels, is reinforced by the institutionalized habits of dialogue. A panoply of meetings and intensive socialization takes place in the region. Extensive political, economic, and security cooperation occurs among ASEAN and ARF members. These all amount to a valuable asset that a universal institution like the UN can tap into in the efforts toward world peace.

Thus, one of the first measures to promote closer cooperation should be strengthening the existing dialogue mechanisms between ASEAN/ARF and the UN, and creating new ones. Ironically, given the numerous dialogue mechanisms that have been created, ASEAN is the only major regional organization without observer status at the UN. At the ASEAN-UN summit in Bangkok in February 2000, UN Secretary-General Kofi Annan lamented the fact that both institutions "have found little to say to each other on peace and security at the time when new forms of security challenges are presenting themselves."[31] Much can be gained by exchanging information and sharing experiences between the UN and ASEAN.

As far as the ARF is concerned, it has already initiated contacts with the Organization of American States and the Organization for Security and Cooperation in Europe. But more can be done by both ASEAN and the ARF. They could institutionalize regular meetings with or courtesy calls on the UN Secretary-General. In turn, the Secretary-General and members of his staff could be invited to participate in annual ARF ministerial meetings and, to the extent practicable, in important intersessional meetings and other track-one and track-two Council for Security Cooperation in Asia Pacific activities, especially when the issues are of great importance to UN's work on peacebuilding.

With regard to peacekeeping and peacebuilding, experience has shown that ASEAN and ARF countries have the potential to contribute more to UN operations, regardless of some obvious limitations. Although ASEAN and the ARF have far to go before adopting mechanisms similar to those of NATO, ASEAN could offer to undertake some preventive tasks such as early warning, fact finding, and identifying root causes of conflict. This task also suits the ARF, which has just established its register of experts and eminent persons and is currently discussing the enhanced role of its chairman. The Brahimi Report has emphasized the contribution of regional expertise. Thus the ARF's register and even registers from track-two and nongovernmental organizations should be made available to the UN. ASEAN and the ARF already have a pool of experts who can offer a valuable contribution to regional peace. Their work on confidence building and preventive diplomacy can strengthen the UN's early warning and conflict prevention capacities.

Conclusion

The UN Secretary-General in his Millennium Report has placed much emphasis on the key concept of prevention in the maintenance of international peace and security.[32] This is the type of conflict management work that ASEAN and the ARF can complement best. The types of conflict mechanisms and processes that ASEAN and the ARF have generated over the years in avoiding conflicts and, more importantly, in norm building, would be most useful in assisting this objective.

ASEAN and the ARF have realistically carved out their roles in a regional environment where the dynamics of conflicts are complex. Therefore, the preparedness and willingness of ASEAN and the ARF to work with the UN offer prospects for cooperative, task-sharing arrangements between these two international institutions. As each institution sets about its respective tasks of securing and maintaining stability, the major challenge will be to bridge the efforts by the UN, ASEAN, and the ARF and link these "islands of peace" to create collaborative work toward world peace and security.

Notes

1. For a more detailed discussion, see David A. Lake and Patrick M. Morgan, "The New Regionalism in Security Affairs," in David A. Lake and Patrick M. Morgan, eds., *Regional Order: Building Security in a New World* (Philadelphia: Pennsylvania State University Press, 1997), chap. 1, pp. 6–7.

2. S. Neil MacFarlane and Thomas G. Weiss, "Regional Organizations and Regional Security," *Security Studies* 2 (Autumn 1992): 6–37.

3. Ibid., p. 11. See also Muthiah Alagappa, "Regionalism and Conflict Management: A Framework of Analysis," *Review of International Studies* 21, no. 4 (October 1995): 359–397.

4. See, for example, Michael Leifer, *ASEAN and the Security of Southeast Asia* (London: Routledge, 1989); Tim Huxley, "ASEAN's Role in the Emerging East Asian Regional Security Architecture," in Ian G. Cook, Marcus A. Doel, and Rex Li, eds., *Fragmented Asia: Regional Integration and National Disintegration in Pacific Asia* (Aldershot: Avebury, 1996), pp. 29–52.

5. There are many works that discuss the earlier attempts to form a subregional organization in Southeast Asia within the context of ASEAN. See, for example, Estrella Solidum, *Towards a Southeast Asian Community* (Quezon City: University of the Philippines Press, 1974); Arfinn Jorgensen-Dahl, *Regional Organization and Order in Southeast Asia* (New York: St. Martin's Press, 1982); Leifer, *ASEAN and the Security of Southeast Asia;* and Michael Antolik, *ASEAN and the Diplomacy of Accommodation* (Armonk, NY: M. E. Sharpe, 1990).

6. Leifer, *ASEAN and the Security of Southeast Asia,* p. 150.

7. C. R. Mitchell, *The Structure of International Conflict* (New York: St. Martin's Press, 1981), chaps. 1, 4.

8. For a more detailed discussion on the various types of conflict management mechanisms, see Muthiah Alagappa, "Regional Institutions, the UN, and International Security," *Third World Quarterly* 18, no. 3 (1997): 421–441.

9. For a more detailed discussion on these informal mechanisms, see Mely C. Anthony, "Mechanisms of Dispute Settlement: The ASEAN Experience," *Contemporary Southeast Asia* 20, no. 1 (April 1999): 38–66.

10. Carolina G. Hernandez, "ASEAN 10: Meeting the Challenges," in Mely Anthony and Mohamed Jawhar Hassan, eds., *Beyond the Crisis: Challenges and Opportunities,* vol. 1 (Kuala Lumpur: Institute of Strategic and International Studies, 2000), p. 241.

11. Alexander Wendt, "Anarchy Is What States Make of It," *International Organisation* 46, no. 2 (Spring 1992): 396–421.

12. "The ASEAN Regional Forum: A Concept Paper" *Handbook on Selected ASEAN Political Documents* (Jakarta: ASEAN Secretariat, 1998).

13. For an excellent summary on confidence-building measures that have already been implemented by the ARF, see Alan Dupont, "The Future of the ARF: An Australian Perspective," in Khoo How San, ed., *Future of the ARF* (Singapore: Institute of Defense and Strategic Studies, 1999), pp. 31–48.

14. Chairman's Statement, Eighth Meeting of the ASEAN Regional Forum, Hanoi, July 25, 2001.

15. Chairman's Statement, Eighth Meeting of the ASEAN Regional Forum, Bangkok, July 24, 2000.

16. Ibid.

17. Ibid.

18. Chairman's Statement, Fourth Meeting of the ASEAN Regional Forum, Kuala Lumpur, July 27, 1997.

19. Ibid.

20. Brian Job, "Matters of Multilateralism: Implications for Regional Conflict Management," in Lake and Morgan, *Regional Orders,* p. 176.

21. See, for example, Jeannie Henderson, *Reassessing ASEAN,* Adelphi Paper no. 323 (London: Oxford University Press for International Institute for Security Studies, 1999).

22. There have been numerous accounts of ASEAN's response to the currency crisis. See, for example, Hadi Soesastro, "ASEAN During the Crisis," *ASEAN Eco-*

nomic Bulletin 15, no. 3 (December 1998); John Funston, "ASEAN: Out of Its Depths," *Contemporary Southeast Asia* 20, no. 3 (April 1998): 22–37; and Michael Wesley, "The Asian Crisis and the Adequacy of Regional Institutions," *Contemporary Southeast Asia* 21, no. 1 (April 1999): 53–73.

23. Anwar Ibrahim, interview with *Time* magazine, July 1997.

24. "Thailand to Pursue Constructive Intervention Policy," *New Straits Times,* June 3, 1998.

25. Mely C. Anthony, "ASEAN: How to Engage or Cooperate," paper presented at the ASEAN-ISIS conference "ASEAN 2020: Vision, Crises, and Change," Singapore, July 21–22, 1999.

26. Cited in Carolina G. Hernandez, "The East Timor Crisis: Regional Mechanisms on Trial and Implications for Regional Political and Security Cooperation," paper presented at the ARF Profession Development Program, Bandar Seri Begawan, April 23–28, 2000.

27. For a detailed discussion on the violence in East Timor, see Leonard C. Sebastian and Anthony L. Smith, "The East Timor Crisis: A Test Case for Humanitarian Intervention," in *Southeast Asian Affairs 2000* (Singapore: Institute of Southeast Asian Studies, 2000).

28. *The United Nations and East Timor,* www.un.org/peace/etimor/untaetb.htm.

29. "Sovereignty, Intervention, and the ASEAN Way," address by Secretary-General Rodolfo Severino at the ASEAN Scholars Roundtable, Singapore, July 3, 2000.

30. Hernandez, "The East Timor Crisis."

31. Kofi Annan, "Strengthening ASEAN–United Nations Partnership," remarks at the ASEAN-UN summit, Bangkok, February 12, 2000.

32. United Nations, *The Role of the United Nations in the Twenty-First Century: The Millennium Report,* UN Doc. A/54/2000 (New York: UN Department of Information, 2000), pp. 44–46.

12

Managing Security in the Western Hemisphere: The OAS's New Activism

Monica Herz

This chapter analyzes the role that the Organization of American States (OAS) can be expected to play in the context of the regionalization of security at present and in the future, a theme prominent since the end of the Cold War and widely debated by the academic community since Boutros Boutros-Ghali's *An Agenda for Peace* (1992). The chapter examines the tasks the organization assumed in the 1990s, the organizational, cultural, and political variables that prevent greater participation in the administration of regional security, and its potential for further involvement in this area.

The OAS has become a relevant actor in the security sphere as a result of a new framework generated in the 1990s for the protection of democracy. The association between democratic stability and regional security produced the incentive and the road map for the launching of effective projects and new ideas about reform of the OAS. At the same time, taking part in the new generation of peace operations, which seek to foster democratic regimes, became a reality for the OAS. However, the noninterventionist tradition in Latin America, the unilateral policies of the United States, and the organizational fragility of the OAS form limits to the OAS's new activism.

Direct cooperation between the OAS and the UN is one avenue for enhancing the OAS's participation in the administration of peace and security on a regional level. The institutional framework and practical experiences in this sphere will also be considered. The OAS is among a group of regional organizations that have shown a potential for cooperation with the UN, and its transformation in the last fifteen years allows for a wider debate on future prospects for joint action. In fact, since the 1990s a new pattern of relationship between the OAS and the UN has been developing. This process has been a direct consequence of the debate on the reform of the UN in the context of the organization's new activism, of the debate on the reform of the OAS, of the peace process in Central America, and of attempts by the leadership of both organizations to build a new framework for their relationship.

The OAS in the 1990s

The OAS is among a group of regional organizations that single out security as one of their primary objectives; the OAS Charter allows us to define it as a collective security organization, such as the Organization of African Unity (now African Union) and the Arab League. The Inter-American Treaty of Reciprocal Assistance and Pact of Bogota (Treaty on Pacific Settlement of Disputes) were supposed to be the other pillars of the hemispheric security system. The pact has never been applied. The Inter-American Defense Board (IADB), created in 1942, is an advisory organ to the OAS and is funded by the organization, but it is not accountable to the OAS. It is today engaged in demining projects, cataloging confidence-building measures, disaster mitigation and prevention, and the training activities specific to the Inter-American Defense College in the region. The administration of peace and security in the region has been tackled by ad hoc groupings and by the Summit of the Americas process and the Meeting of Defense Ministers.

The OAS security structure was originally designed for collective security operations and diplomatic consultation. Regarding conflict between states in the hemisphere, the emphasis lies on peaceful means for the settlement of disputes. Nevertheless, in recent years the range of activities in which the organization is involved has grown considerably and new capabilities have been generated.

The organization has had some success in dealing with threats to peace. It has functioned as a forum for discussion of interstate as well as intrastate conflict since its creation, and as the organ of consultation of the Inter-American Treaty of Reciprocal Assistance (the Rio Treaty) on several occasions.[1] Investigative commissions were created in a number of cases to offer assessments and sometimes indicate solutions to situations of conflict or controversy. The organization also had some success in reducing regional tensions and preventing conflicts from escalating through mediation efforts, as was the case in the conflict between Costa Rica and Nicaragua between 1948 and 1979 and the "Soccer War" between Honduras and El Salvador in 1969. Since 2000 the OAS has facilitated the negotiations between Honduras and Nicaragua over their maritime boundary and between Belize and Guatemala.

Nevertheless, the lack of actual consensus in the organization, in the context of a normative tradition of consensual decisionmaking, has not allowed it to play a more active role. The search for consensus is, of course, a mechanism for guaranteeing the protection of state sovereignty. The concept of sovereignty itself acquires a particular significance in the Latin American context, given the history of state formation among different nations, the struggle for independence during the first decades of the nineteenth century, and the difficulty in realizing the Westphalian model in the face of great power influence and lack of central government authority over parts of territory in several cases.

The noninterventionist tradition, based on principles deeply rooted in Latin American political culture, enshrined in several legal documents and embedded in a wider support for a legalist international order that would protect the region from great power interventionism, has hindered the development of a stronger collective security system. The legalist tradition is also associated with the norm of peaceful conflict resolution. Most Latin American governments firmly adhere to the principle of nonintervention, fearing a wider control by the United States of different aspects of domestic and international politics in the region. Furthermore, the OAS is perceived as a tool of U.S. interests. Legal instruments are regarded as a protection against the overwhelming power disparity in the region. There is widespread fear that interventionism could also spread into other spheres such as human rights and the environment, in a context of constant redefinition of "threats to peace and security." On the other hand, the systematic affirmation by successive U.S. governments that the United States reserves the right of unilateral action also hinders the move toward stronger multilateral institutions.

The internal governance structure of the OAS has not been reformed to meet the requirements of a regional organization actively engaged in security management. Moreover, the scarcity of resources impedes rapid response to crises and the generation of preventive mechanisms that would allow for OAS involvement before violence or institutional breakdown occurs.[2]

In addition, the organization's inaction during the 1980s in Central America, the marginal role it played in the Falklands/Malvinas War, and the unilateral decisions by the United States to intervene both in Grenada in 1983 and in Panama in 1989 led to greater emphasis placed on ad hoc regional arrangements.

Moreover, the OAS's impartiality can be easily questioned, not only because vested interests could influence its position, as is the case regarding other organizations, but also because of the enormous power asymmetry in the region.[3] In fact, the intervention of an ad hoc group was crucial to resolving the Central American conflicts. The use of the OAS by the United States in order to accomplish its own foreign policy objectives left significant scars on the attitude of Latin Americans toward the organization. The regionalization of security in Latin America can easily be understood by Latin American governments in terms of the reaffirmation of U.S. control over this part of the world.

Nevertheless, since the end of the Cold War an attempt to redefine the role played by the OAS has been made, prompted by a wide sense of failure, the new consensus on democracy in the region, the admission of Canada in

1990, different interests of regional actors, and the wider debate on the redefinition of the concept of security. The effort to reshape the organization should also be understood within a political environment in which the idea that peace is a regional asset has become prevalent. In the context of globalization and fierce competition for international investment flows, the vision of a peaceful and stable region, in contrast to other parts of the world, is perceived as an advantage that could be explored. Thus the organization became more active in several cases of political crises in which democratic regimes were in danger. At the same time, policymakers and academics engaged in debate on the new role of the OAS.[4] Moreover, the Summit of the Americas process, which began in Miami in 1994, led largely by the United States, has provided the OAS with a renewed agenda.

Subsequent to the Cold War, a collective desire to redefine the role of the OAS in the sphere of security in particular can be observed. Several resolutions on cooperation in this sphere were passed, two important conventions were signed,[5] and a debate on the redefinition of the concept of hemispheric security was launched. The OAS has become active in fostering confidence-building measures,[6] land mine clearing, and the dialogue on border disputes. The Education for Peace Program was also created.[7]

The Hemispheric Security Commission was created in 1991, the Committee on Hemispheric Security having been made a permanent body in 1995. The committee has a mandate to review the hemispheric security system. Among several issues under scrutiny, one can highlight the juridical and institutional link between the OAS and the Inter-American Defense Junta,[8] the drive toward greater transparency in managing military capabilities,[9] the special needs of small states, and the debate on the concept of security itself. The redefinition of security has expanded the concept and involved a shift from collective to cooperative security.[10] Stress on the deterrence generated by the principle that aggressors would face the combined force of a coalition is thus substituted by an emphasis on confidence-building measures, which guarantee transparency of military procedures, and the availability of information. The expanded concept of security involves a perception of the interdependence between economic, social, political, and environmental issues and threats and use of violence.

The OAS Secretary-General acquired new responsibilities in line with Article 99 of the UN Charter. The Protocol of Cartagena of the Indies, an amendment to the OAS Charter, which was adopted in 1985 and came into force in 1988, authorizes the OAS Secretary-General to bring to the attention of the General Assembly or the Permanent Council matters that might threaten the peace, security, or development of member states.

Regarding one of the most pressing security threats in the region—narcotrafficking—a drive toward greater activism can also be observed. The Inter-American Drug Abuse Control Commission (CICAD) was created in

1986 and implemented its first projects in 1988. CICAD has dealt with legislative and preventive measures. Its activities include the dissemination of information, research on drug problems, and forging links with other international organizations such as the UN. In 1992, the OAS General Assembly approved regulations on money laundering and asset forfeiture. In 1993, CICAD launched a project aimed at strengthening the ability of governments to stop the international trade in firearms meant for narcotics traffickers, and in 1996 it was the forum for the negotiation of the Hemisphere Anti-Drug Strategy. The Multilateral Evaluation Mechanism generated its first round of evaluation for the 1999–2000 period, publicizing information about the state of the drug problem and efforts to overcome it in each country and making specific recommendations. More cooperation between the hemispheric countries in the antidrug struggle should be expected in the longer term as a result of this process. Nevertheless, enforcement cooperation has been meager and U.S. bilateral supply-side strategies have dominated measures against drug-related crime and the connection between terrorism and drugs in the region.

One of the hallmarks of the 1990s in the Americas was the new emphasis given by the OAS to the defense of democracy. The 1985 Cartagena Protocol already stated the commitment to the promotion and strengthening of representative democracy. Nevertheless when the Panamanian institutional crisis erupted in 1989, the OAS did not go beyond its declaratory tradition. The 1991 Declaration on the Collective Defense of Democracy, often referred to as the Santiago Commitment, called for prompt reaction of the region's democracies in the event of a threat to democracy in a member state. Resolution 1080, which accompanied the declaration, determined that the OAS Permanent Council should be summoned in case of the suspension of the democratic process in any member state, and thereafter a meeting of ministers of foreign affairs or a special session of the General Assembly could be summoned, all within a ten-day period following the crisis.

Resolution 1080 was applied when a condemnation of the 1991 coup in Haiti led to sanctions, and again over Peru (1992), Guatemala (1993), and Paraguay (1996). In the first three cases, an ad hoc meeting of ministers of foreign affairs followed the meeting of the OAS Permanent Council. The interruption of constitutional rule was condemned in all four cases and some kind of mediation took place in order to deal with the crisis. In Peru a compromise was reached and the limited OAS role is indicated by its inability to guarantee the full respect for the principle of separation of powers or the proper participation of all political forces in the negotiations leading to the end of the crisis. In Paraguay the main pressure was exerted by individual countries, and in Haiti, as we shall see, the need for enforcement prompted the involvement of the UN and the United States.

The 1994 Summit of the Americas in Miami set the tone for a growing responsibility regarding the maintenance of democratic regimes in the Americas. Its plan of action identified the OAS as the main organization for the defense and consolidation of democracy in the Americas. In 1997 a reform of the OAS Charter took place through the ratification of the 1992 Washington Protocols. The agreement strengthens representative democracy by giving the OAS the right to suspend a member state whose democratically elected government is overthrown by force. Finally, in 2001 the Inter-American Democratic Charter was adopted, further institutionalizing the democratic paradigm.

In 1991 the Unity for the Promotion of Democracy (UPD) began working to provide assistance for the development of democratic institutions and for conflict resolution. The UPD, in contrast to the crisis-oriented approach of the actions taken by the Permanent Council, offers an embedded institutional perspective. The UPD took part in several electoral observation missions on the national and municipal levels, supporting training, education, research, and information programs.[11] Since 1990 the OAS has generated more than fifty electoral observation missions in eighteen countries. In spite of wide resistance to interference in the domestic politics of Peru by many Latin American countries, the OAS electoral observation mission openly condemned electoral procedures there in the May 2000 presidential election. The UPD showed in this instance its capacity to assume autonomous positions.[12]

The human rights regime in the region has become more robust, the Human Rights Inter-American Commission having led missions to observe human rights conditions in several countries. Issues such as social, sexual, ethnic, and racial discrimination have been added to the organization's agenda.

A new collective identity was fostered, led by the United States and made possible by the transition of most Latin America countries to democracy in the 1980s. The perception that there is a clear association between democracy and security, in line with a wider concept of security, and the adoption of democratic maintenance as an organizational goal, indicate how the OAS can make a difference in managing security in the Americas. Cohesion is fostered by the perception of a common threat, facilitating the development of more robust institutions. The association between democracy and peace allows for greater concern with peace missions and postconflict reconstruction activities such as demining, demobilization of armed groups, verification of the application of peace accords, and rebuilding institutions. In this context the rule of nonintervention is seen in a more flexible manner and the OAS has effectively intruded into the domestic affairs of several countries. This phenomenon is similar to the view of the Organization for Security and Cooperation in Europe (OSCE) that rule of law at home is related to rule of law abroad and that democracy is essential for the generation of a stable and peaceful regional security order.[13]

This transformation encounters resistance in the nonintervention principle, which Brazil and Mexico adhere to most closely. Brazil's noninterventionist position is, however, modified by its active role in strengthening the region's democratic solidarity doctrine. Mexico is more firmly opposed to collective action for the restoration of democracy. Other important actors such as Argentina and Chile have not played a more creative role for different reasons. Having tilted toward a pro-U.S. alignment, Argentina has undermined its position in Latin America, and Chile has adopted a low-key diplomacy under the governments of Patricio Aywin and Eduardo Frei. Thus in the case of the Peruvian *autogolpe,* a more assertive action through the OAS was not possible, given the opposition of the major regional actors.[14] In the context of the Haitian crisis, Brazil abstained from the UN Security Council vote on Resolution 940 (July 1994), which permitted the creation of the multinational force with Chapter VII powers. Chile, Colombia, Ecuador, Peru, and Mexico refused to take part in the multinational force assembled in order to restore deposed president Jean-Bertrand Aristide to power.[15] Among the major Latin American states, only Argentina supported the idea of using military force to remove the de facto government in Haiti.

The unwillingness of governments to relinquish sovereignty is not peculiar to Latin America, but in this case we observe the odd cohabitation between the acceptance of the hegemonic political model of liberal democracy and resistance to the creation of multilateral institutions that would sustain this same model on a regional basis. Nevertheless, although the tension will remain between noninterventionism and the defense of democracy, the battleground has definitely been redrawn.

Cooperation Between the OAS and the UN

The OAS and the UN have cooperated in specific fields since the 1940s and the OAS Charter establishes its subordination to the provisions of the UN Charter. Nevertheless, a new drive toward greater cooperation between the two organizations can be observed since the 1990s, in line with a wider review of methods of cooperation with regional organizations. In accordance with this perspective, general meetings between representatives of the two systems have taken place, resolutions have been passed, and agreements have been signed. The environment, drug control, concerns regarding gender and children, disaster relief, rural development and agriculture, and indigenous populations were among the subjects addressed.[16] Cooperation between the two organizations effectively takes place in several spheres, such as humanitarian affairs, demining, human rights programs, development of human resources, and economic and social activities.

On April 17, 1995, the Secretaries-General of the OAS and the UN signed a cooperation accord after a series of resolutions of the General Assemblies of both organizations called for intensified cooperation between the two.[17] The accord established that regular consultations between the Secretariat of the United Nations and the General Secretariat of the OAS should take place, that arrangements for the purpose of cooperation and coordination between the two could be added, and that the attendance by observers of one organization in meetings of the other and exchange of information and documentation may occur.

The executive office of the Assistant Secretary-General of the OAS and the office of the UN Secretary-General for Political Affairs (Department for the Americas and Europe) are the focus of the connection between the two organizations. "The mechanism provides for focal points within the departments, offices, programs and agencies of the United Nations System, allowing for direct contacts between the OAS General Secretariat and substantive offices in the United Nations System."[18] The cooperation mechanism works in the field in different countries and a technical working group on coordination deals with the specialized agencies of the OAS. Collaborative activities have also been conducted between specialized agencies and departments of the two organizations.

Since the OAS is the regional organization with the widest experience in electoral observation, this is one of the areas where cooperation has taken place and can be expected in the future. Experience in verification activities and technical assistance to the state where elections are being held have led to the accumulation of knowledge. In some cases, such as the elections held in the Dominican Republic, Paraguay, Peru, and Surinam, the OAS has been the sole observer; in other cases the OAS and the UN have worked together. The first instances of such collaboration were the election in Nicaragua in 1989, the 1990 elections in Haiti, and the 1993 regional elections in Nicaragua. This collaboration takes place at the local, national, and international levels. The OAS Unit for Promotion of Democracy and the UN Electoral Assistance Division are key organs in allowing for exchange of information and a suitable division of labor in each case.

The peace process that occurred in Central America during the 1990s was not only the first instance of UN involvement in peace operations in Latin America but also initiated collaboration between the OAS and the United Nations in peace operations. The OAS was involved in the peace negotiations in Central America and in postconflict reconstruction in Nicaragua.

The peace process in Central America was effectively launched by the Esquipulas II peace plan, proposed by President Oscar Arias of Costa Rica, which drew on the other peace plans but placed more emphasis on the process of democratization.[19] The ingenuity of Arias's plan lay in tying the trend to establishing liberal democracy as a norm for the region to the resolution of civil wars and international disputes in the region. Signed at a meeting of Central American presidents in August 1987, the plan had repercussions in Nicaragua, El Salvador, and Guatemala, opening the path to dialogue. Among several provisions designed to forge national reconciliation and generate democratic regimes in the region, the accord supported the establishment of an international verification commission. Two months after the signing of the Esquipulas II Accords, the OAS General Assembly passed a resolution supporting the peace process. A joint UN-OAS team was sent to Central America but concluded that verification of the vague accords was not feasible amid the continuing conflict.[20] This first instance of collaboration was unsuccessful, and the activities of the mission were terminated in January 1988. This failure prompted the Central American presidents to ask the UN to become involved in the verification of the Esquipulas Accords in 1989. After an accord had been reached in Nicaragua during that same year, the UN Security Council issued a resolution supporting the role of the good offices of the UN Secretary-General and establishing the UN Observer Group for Central America (ONUCA) to verify compliance with the security aspects of Esquipulas II.

The ONUCA operation began as a military observer force and expanded to monitor the ceasefire between the contras and the Sandinista government and to oversee the demobilization and disarmament of the contra forces.[21] It did not enter territory controlled by the Farabundo Martí National Liberation Front (FMLN) in El Salvador but supported the creation of the UN mission in that country. The operation established verification centers in Costa Rica, El Salvador, Guatemala, Nicaragua, and Honduras. The initial mandate specified that ONUCA would monitor the five Central American governments' commitments to cease military assistance to irregular forces, prevent acts of aggression from their territories, and prevent the use of their territories for support of irregular forces.

The expansion of the operation's mandate should be understood in the context of peacebuilding in Nicaragua coordinated by the OAS and UN.[22] ONUCA concentrated on stopping border-crossing violations and demobilizing the troops that remained in Honduras. The expansion of its mandate allowed the UN to play a key role in the demobilization process. First, the Security Council authorized the deployment of an infantry battalion, and a further expansion of the mandate established that the operation would monitor withdrawal, provide security within assembly areas using ground and air patrols, and receive and destroy personal weaponry. At a meeting in February 1989 the five Central American states recommended the creation of an International Commission for Support and Verification (Comisíon International de Apoio y Verificación [CIAV]) to oversee the demobilization of the Nicaraguan resistance and supervise the reintegration of former contras back into Nicaraguan society. In August, the Tela Accord, signed by the Central American presidents, confirmed these tasks and the collection and disposal of weapons. The two Secretaries-General were to determine the appropriate strategies to be employed. Initially the UN was responsible for the repatriation of combatants and their families from Honduras and Costa Rica, where the UN High Commissioner for

Refugees had been responsible for the care of Nicaraguan refugees. The OAS would receive returning combatants and their families inside Nicaragua. The commission aided in the reintegration of approximately 120,000 combatants and their families into postwar Nicaraguan society, was able to include non-combatants in the program, and mediated local conflicts. The OAS also monitored the 1996 elections, which saw a successful transition from one elected president to the next before the CIAV mission ended in July 1997.

The initial operational planning failed to assume that the resistance would not disarm before entering Nicaragua. The tension generated by the presence of a Sandinista movement, which had lost the 1990 election, and by armed combatants reentering Nicaragua led to a redefinition of CIAV's role. Demobilization and negotiations between the new government and the resistance were overseen by CIAV/OAS. On June 9, 1993, the General Assembly extended the mandate of the mission: the rights and guarantees of all groups in the population would be verified; participation in programs was specifically designed to strengthen institutions; social development projects were continued; and the mission was extended for another two years.[23] The operation was involved in the mediation of various local agrarian conflicts and in the process of institutional transition in Nicaragua, with verification officials having participated in meetings with staff from several state institutions. Aid was given in training, transport, and communication. The organization of peace and human rights committees in areas where the state's presence was weak helped to strengthen civil society and played a crucial role in the preparation for the closure of the operation.

The OAS was also involved in assistance to mine clearing in Nicaragua, with OAS Secretary-General João Clemente Baena Soares having requested the Inter-American Defense Board to plan the operations. Subsequently a wider project to remove mines from Central America was implemented. The mine-clearing program in Central America was created in 1991 and conducted under the general coordination of the UPD with the technical support of the IADB.

The OAS faced several difficulties in this operation. It was criticized for lack of impartiality, lack of clear guidance and proper coordination from OAS headquarters, and its incapacity to aid in building institutions that could constrain existing conflicts.[24] This first experience showed that the organization would have to make a significant investment in building up both capabilities and a normative framework for engagement in peace operations.

In El Salvador and later in Guatemala, the UN would play the leading role in mediating the peace accords, verifying their implementation, and institution building. The coordinated approach that shaped the Nicaraguan experience was abandoned, only to be attempted once again in Haiti.[25]

When a coup d'état took place in Haiti in September 1991 the OAS was the first international organization to react, issuing a Permanent Council resolution condemning the coup and demanding respect for the democratically elected government.[26] An ad hoc meeting of ministers of foreign affairs was called, pursuant to the mechanism established under Resolution 1080. The meeting called for full restoration of the rule of law and the reinstatement of President Aristide; suspension of economic, financial, and commercial ties with Haiti was recommended. In October the creation of a civilian mission to reestablish and strengthen constitutional democracy was authorized by the meeting of consultation. OAS human rights observers were sent to Port-au-Prince by Secretary-General Baena Soares. After this initial OAS experience the UN General Assembly approved a plan for joint a OAS-UN mission and a Memorandum of Understanding between the two organizations was signed on May 6, 1993.

The UN General Assembly, following the steps of the OAS, also adopted a resolution (A/RES/46/7, October 11, 1991) condemning the coup and calling for the restoration of the legitimate government. After failure to implement the Washington Protocols,[27] further resolutions by the OAS Permanent Council and Meeting of Ministers of Foreign Affairs strengthened the embargo and added additional sanctions. But only in September 1992 was it possible to negotiate with the de facto authorities for the establishment of the OAS mission.

As a consequence of the mission's ineffectiveness during 1992, the OAS adopted two resolutions (CP/RES/594, November 10, 1992, and MRE/RES, December 4, 1992) calling on the UN to take part. This was justified by the need to make the embargo global and to bolster the regional effort to deal with the crisis. Dante Caputo became a special envoy both to the UN Secretary-General and the OAS Secretary-General. The imposition of a mandatory embargo by the Security Council and the strengthening of the civilian mission in the context of UN-OAS cooperation was followed by the negotiation of the Governor's Island Agreement (July 3, 1993), which established terms similar to the Washington Protocols for the return of President Aristide. A temporary international police force was to be created in Haiti, and the agreement called for a political dialogue between the parties under the auspices of the UN and the OAS in order to generate a peaceful transition to democratic government. With Aristide apparently having guaranteed his return to office and Robert Maval having been nominated prime minister, both the OAS and the UN suspended the embargo.

The peacekeeping mission—the UN Mission in Haiti (UNMIH)—was authorized by the Security Council in September (S/RES/862), but the situation in the country deteriorated rapidly. The return of President Aristide to Haiti was postponed, the UN embargo was imposed again, and the OAS/UN International Civilian Mission in Haiti (MICIVIH) was evacuated. Finally, on September 18, 1994, the Multinational Force entered Haiti under the command of the United States, as authorized by the Security Council (S/RES/940). President Aristide returned to Haiti in October, and the embargoes were lifted. Only on October 26, 1994, did UNMIH return to Haiti and to the task of securing a stable environment in the country.

The MICIVIH was the most advanced experience in cooperation between the two organizations. In the context of the mission, collaboration took place in the areas of electoral observation, humanitarian aid, human rights monitoring, political negotiations, refugees, fuel supply, and the economic recovery program. This was also an interesting experiment in human rights, and electoral monitoring activities being undertaken in an integrated manner, the OAS having been responsible for human rights observation and protection and election monitoring.[28] All military aspects of the mission were the UN's responsibility. The MICIVIH and the OAS Electoral Observation Mission (1995) also enjoyed significant levels of cooperation. In fact, during the presidential elections, one person was appointed to lead both missions. The mission was an important step on the road toward greater interinstitutional cooperation, the UN Department of Political Affairs and the OAS Unit for Promotion of Democracy having maintained constant coordination.

The experience highlights the advantages of cooperation between the two organizations, the OAS having shown a capacity to move rapidly into a crisis scenario both on the political level and regarding assistance on the ground in the context of a mission geared toward the creation of democratic institutions and the respect for human rights. UN participation was fundamental regarding the preparation of complex planning, guaranteeing the necessary funding and ultimately authorizing the use of force. The institution building that took place was made possible by cooperation between the two organizations.

Conclusion

The process of transformation of the OAS, which has been taking place since the 1990s, involving the definition of democracy as a prime organizational objective and the generation of new capabilities, opens possibilities for the organization to take part in peace management on a regional basis, particularly in view of the recognition that internal rather than interstate conflict is becoming more relevant to a new emerging peace system. Nevertheless, the OAS still has a long path ahead in order to fulfill its potential.

In this context, cooperation between the UN and the OAS should be broadened and institutionalized. The initial framework for cooperation between the two organizations has been established and more joint ventures between the specialized agencies and special commissions of the two systems have been generated, but much more needs to be done in terms of coordination and creation of permanent channels of communication and exchange. Cooperation between the OAS and the UN, considering the very specific tasks the OAS is prepared to tackle, was shown to be an efficient strategy. However, cooperation between the two organizations can only rise to a higher level when the OAS acquires capabilities for peace enforcement, complex planning, and a more efficient decisionmaking process. Only then will the subcontracting model based on Article 53 of the UN Charter become a real possibility. The expectation of autonomy that leads the North Atlantic Treaty Organization (NATO) to avoid subordination to the Security Council is not present here. On the contrary, Latin American countries will tend to perceive the wider environment of the UN as a protection against further U.S. determination of policy choices.

NATO could also offer assistance in terms of the constitution of peace operations capabilities, and the creation of a liaison office could be an initial proposition. The Mediterranean Initiative could offer a model for cooperation between the two organizations. Although Argentina's designation as a non-NATO ally in 1998 greatly displeased its neighbors, contact on a multilateral basis would be received more positively.

The role played by the OAS in the Central American peace process, in Haiti, and in reacting to several institutional crises since the 1990s supports the view that regional organizations must play a major role in administering security, given their proximity to problems in question, their contact with the local culture, and their capacity to react rapidly in view of the range of issues they must deal with. In fact, the OAS is today prepared to deal with institutional crises that may not come to the attention of the UN, as occurred initially when the president of Haiti was overthrown in 1991.

The OAS can be expected to be active in conflict prevention, both in fostering domestic stability and in dealing with possible interstate tensions in the region. It has been involved in norm setting on both levels, encouraging the maintenance of democratic regimes, and stressing the rejection of the threat or use of force as an instrument of state policy, along with other regional actors. The OAS has also become effective in fostering confidence-building measures, which are fundamental in a region where territorial disputes still exist and deterrence capabilities are often perceived to be shifting against the interest of one party. It is equipped to focus on possible interstate and domestic tensions that might lead to conflict or the overthrow of democratic governments. The powers added to the OAS Secretary-General's office also indicate more room for maneuver on this level.

The organization is also capable of participating in peacebuilding operations. Unlike the ad hoc groupings that do not develop the mechanisms for investigation, verification, monitoring, and institution building, the OAS has made some progress in this area in recent years. In this respect it should be expected to be responsible for the same kind of tasks the OSCE has been involved with in the former Yugoslavia. In Nicaragua the OAS was able to work for the demobilization of the contras and rendered some help to the reform of state institutions. The organization was also involved in institutional building in Haiti after 1994 and in monitoring peace arrangements in Suriname, apart from special projects such as demining in Central America. Nevertheless, the capabilities of the organization in this area are very limited. The investment in the organization's capabilities did not allow for the creation of knowledge or an apparatus that permits assuming responsibility for multidimentional operations. Despite the experience acquired in Nicaragua and Haiti, cooperation with the UN Department of Peacekeeping Operations would still be necessary if an operation should be devised in Latin America once again. Furthermore, the OAS has not acquired the legitimacy necessary for an agency involved in verification, monitoring, and institution building. One exception is the Unit for Promotion of Democracy, in particular its role in monitoring electoral processes.

In peacemaking operations that require negotiation skills, the OAS can play an active role; international negotiations are part of the OAS's experience, and it did play a role in Central America and Haiti in this area. Nevertheless, as Joaquín Tacsan reminds us, the inter-American system does not allow the OAS to call governments ex officio to the negotiating table, hindering the OAS's mediating capacity.[29]

On the other hand, in contexts in which a violent conflict is established, such as today's Colombia, or Central America in the 1980s, the organization does not have the political clout or the necessary resources to have an impact. Particularly when enforcement becomes a requirement for success, the OAS is not prepared to share the cost of multilateral security administration. The OAS is not prepared for enforcement operations and does not even present a formal mechanism for compulsory cost sharing for peace missions. The regional culture does not support this option. The major regional actors perceive the development of a multilateral peace enforcement capability as a transfer of sovereignty to the United States, which would inevitably control this capability.

The prospects for effective responses to crisis, although enhanced by the mechanisms created during the 1990s, are limited both by the negative attitude toward the use of force and by the fact that sanctions are not obligatory under the OAS Charter. Nevertheless, given the framework now established, proper pressure by individual nations under the umbrella of OAS resolutions can be effective, as was the case when Mercosur nations reacted to the institutional crisis in Paraguay.

In situations when the use of force is necessary, given the conditions for UN involvement, coordination between the two organizations is one path to be considered. In Central America, when it became clear that a military dimension would have to be added to the international efforts to end the conflict, ONUCA was created; in Haiti under comparable circumstances UNMIH was authorized.

The redefinition of the relationship between the OAS and the IADB could offer the OAS a military capability under the control of the organization. This would require clear civilian control over, and the subordination of this organ to, the OAS decisionmaking process. Currently delegates to the IADB are appointed directly by governments to whom the IADB independently submits plans relating to common defense. Since enforcement will always be an important instrument for conflict resolution, an organization capable of providing some strategic planning in advance of missions should be generated. Currently in the Americas the deterrent function performed by NATO in Europe can only be fulfilled by the United States. Multilateral control over an existing institution may be a better solution than unilateral intervention, which has so often occurred in the region. In addition, the experience acquired in UN peace operations by the military and other state agencies could be applied in a different context.

Regional disparities and different cultural traditions also need to be attended to in order to generate coordination between different subregional arrangements. These differences are heightened by the different kind of relations established with the regional hegemon. Anglophone Caribbean, Central America, the Andean countries, the Southern Cone, and North America have produced subregional arrangements that express this reality. In the Caribbean, in particular, the notion of "small-state security" requires special treatment. These small nations tend to define security in terms of the threats posed by nonstate actors such as corporations, organized crime groups, and drug-trafficking cartels.[30]

Ultimately the governments of the region will need to take the necessary steps to make resources available for the OAS, to expedite the decisionmaking process, modernize the organization's internal procedures, and generate more robust institutions. Leadership from the regional hegemon and coalitions of significant actors will have to play a role. At present, change should not be expected to come about quickly. Although the United States did offer some leadership, particularly in generating an agenda for the OAS in the context of the summit process, unilateralism and the emphasis on bilateral relations prevail. Major regional actors, such as Brazil and Mexico, will not offer alternative leadership.

The clearest sign today of the fragility of the OAS is the fact that the organization has not played a role in the most pressing security crisis in the Americas, namely the war in Colombia. The OAS Security Commission has not discussed the conflict, and the Permanent Council has not gone beyond declarations in support of the government and the peace negotiations. The unilateral approach adopted by U.S. administrations, issuing plans that have only been negotiated or debated on a bilateral basis with the government of Colombia—focusing primarily on military aid, the posture adopted by

Colombia's neighbors, largely concentrating on protecting their own borders from the conflict (apart from Venezuela, which has direct connections with the insurgent groups in Colombia)—explain the lack of involvement of the OAS in this conflict. The OAS could play a role in mediation, it could be a forum for other countries to take part in the debate on the crisis, and it should establish the necessary links between dealing with the war in Colombia and countering narcotraffic in the region.

Given the social and political exclusion of large sectors of Latin American societies, the fact that the military remains a very powerful and autonomous political actor in several countries, the effect of narcotraffic and widespread corruption on democratic institutions, the possible generation of violence as a result of the migration of economic and political refugees, remaining border disputes,[31] and guerrilla activity, an effective regional organization ready to tackle institutional crisis and interstate conflict is a vital contribution to regional stability.

Notes

1. Examples include the 1948–1949 and the 1955–1956 conflicts between Costa Rica and Nicaragua, the Caribbean crisis of 1950 (Haiti and the Dominican Republic), the border dispute between Honduras and Nicaragua in 1957, the tension between Nicaragua and Cuba in 1959, tensions between Venezuela and the Dominican Republic in 1960, reactions to the Cuban revolution in the 1960s, the 1963–1965 Dominican Republic–Haiti controversy, the dispute between the United States and Panama regarding the Canal Zone, and the Dominican Republican institutional crisis of 1965. See Carlos Stoetzer, *The Organization of American States* (New York: Praeger, 1993).

2. Andrew Cooper and Thomas Legler, "The OAS Democratic Solidarity Paradigm: Questions of Collective and National Leadership," *Latin American Politics and Society* 43, no. 1 (Spring 2001): 7, 103–126.

3. See Muthiah Alagappa "Regional Arrangements, the UN, and International Security: A Framework for Analysis," in Thomas G. Weiss, ed., *Beyond UN Subcontracting: Task-Sharing with Regional Security Arrangements and Service-Providing NGOs* (London: Macmillan, 1998), pp. 3–29.

4. For example, Cesar Gaviria, *A New Vision for the OAS* (Washington, DC: Organization of American States, 1995); Cooper and Legler, "The OAS Democratic Solidarity Paradigm"; Tom Farer, ed., *Beyond Democracy: Collectively Defending Democracy in the Americas* (Baltimore: Johns Hopkins University Press, 1996); V. Vaky and H. Muñoz, *The Future of the Organization of American States* (New York: Twentieth Century Fund Press, 1993); Robin Rosenberg, "The OAS and the Summit of the Americas: Coexistence, or Integration of Forces for Multilateralism?" *Latin American Politics and Society* 43, no. 1 (Spring 2001): 79–101; Inter-American Dialogue Study Group on Western Hemisphere Governance, *The Inter-American Agenda and Multilateral Governance: The Organization of American States* (Washington, DC: Inter-American Dialogue Study Group on Western Hemisphere Governance, April 1997).

5. Inter-American Convention Against the Illicit Manufacturing of and Trafficking in Firearms, Ammunition, Explosives, and Other Related Materials; and the Inter-American Convention on Transparency in Conventional Weapons Acquisitions.

6. In November 1995 the First Regional Conference on Confidence- and Security-Building Measures in Santiago, Chile, led to the Declaration of Santiago, which contains eleven measures agreed by the states to build confidence, conduct dialogue, and exchange views on hemispheric security-related matters. The Second Regional Conference on Confidence- and Security-Building Measures was held in San Salvador, El Salvador, in February 1998. Member states agreed to nine additional measures, which are contained in the Declaration of San Salvador on Confidence- and Security-Building Measures.

7. The program created in 1999 comprises three areas: education for the promotion of peace between states, education for the peaceful settlement of conflicts, and education for the promotion of democratic values and practices.

8. For example, Organization of American States (OAS), Special Committee on Hemispheric Security, *The Institutional Relationship Between the Organization of American States and the Inter-American Defense Board,* OAS/Ser.G CE/SH-3/93, February 2, 1993.

9. General Assembly Resolutions 1238 (XXIII-O/93) and 1284 (XXIV-O/94) encourage member countries to submit reports to the UN on the registration of conventional weapons. The Inter-American Defense Board, in response to a request by the General Assembly, has also prepared an inventory of confidence- and security-building measures of a military nature.

10. See Ashton B. Carter, William J. Perry, and John D. Stenbruner, *A New Concept of Cooperative Security* (Washington, DC: Brookings Institution, 1992). See also Permanent Council of the Organization of American States, Special Committee on Hemisphere Security, *Support for a New Concept of Hemisphere Security: Co-operative Security,* OEA/Ser.G,GE/SH-12/93 rev. 1, May, 17 1993. For the Latin American context, see Jorge I. Dominguez, "Security, Peace, and Democracy in Latin America and the Caribbean Challenges for the Post–Cold War Era," in Jorge I. Dominguez, ed., *International Security and Democracy in Latin America and the Caribbean in the Post–Cold War Era* (Pittsburgh: University of Pittsburgh Press, 1992), pp. 3–28.

11. See Jean-Philippe Thérien and Gui Gosselin, "A democracia e os direitos humanos no hemisfério ocidental: Um novo papel para a OEA," *Contexto Internacional* 19, no. 2 (July–December 1997): 199–220.

12. Cooper and Legler, "The OAS Democratic Solidarity Paradigm," p. 1.

13. Michael Barnett, "The UN, Regional Organizations, and Peacekeeping," *Review of International Studies* 21, no. 4 (October 1995): 422.

14. Other motivations include President Alberto Fujimori's role in the war against drugs and Sendero Luminoso and the interest of Peru's neighbors in the stability of the country.

15. Guy Gosselin, Gordon Mace, and Louis Belanger, "La Securité coopérative regionale dans les Amériques: Le Cas des institutions démocratiques," *Etudes Internationales* 25, no. 4 (December 1995): 810.

16. OAS, *Report of the General Secretariat on Cooperation Between the Organization of American States and the United Nations System,* OEA/Ser.p AG/doc.3184/95, May 26, 1995; United Nations, *Cooperación entre Las Naciones Unidas y La Organización de Los Estados Americanos, United Nations General Assembly,* UN Doc. A/49/450, September 28, 1994. See also, Margarita Diéguez, "Regional Mechanisms for the Maintenance of Peace and Security in the Western Hemisphere," in Olga Pel-

licer, ed., *Regional Mechanisms and International Security in Latin America* (Tokyo: UN University Press, 1998), pp. 93–111.

17. OAS, *Cooperation Agreement Between the Secretariat of the United Nations and the General Secretariat of the Organization of American States,* OEA/Ser.D/V.14/95, April, 17 1995. The first resolution on the subject was adopted by the General Assembly in 1987 (AG/RES.880 [XVII-/87]). Subsequently, the General Assembly of the OAS adopted resolution AG/RES.941 (XVIII-0/88). An initial meeting was held between representatives from the Secretariats of the OAS and the UN in May 1991. A working group on OAS-UN cooperation was formed in 1993, according to a resolution of the General Assembly. OAS, General Assembly, *Report of the Working Group on Cooperation Between the OAS and the United Nations System,* AG/RES.1244 (XXIII-0/93), 1993.

18. United Nations, *Cooperation Between the United Nations and the Organization of American States: Report of the Secretary-General,* UN Doc. A/51/297, August 19, 1996, p. 4.

19. The first meeting of Central American presidents, called Esquipulas I, took place in Guatemala in 1986.

20. Jack Child, *The Central American Peace Process, 1983–1991: Sheathing Swords, Building Confidence* (Boulder: Lynne Rienner, 1992), pp. 68–69.

21. Cynthia Arnson, introduction to Cynthia Arnson, ed., *Comparative Peace Processes in Latin America* (Stanford: Stanford University Press, 1999), p. 26. On ONUCA, see Brian D. Smith and William Durch, "UN Observer Group in Central America," in William J. Durch, ed., *The Evolution of UN Peacekeeping* (New York: St. Martin's Press, 1993), pp. 436–462.

22. Caesar Sereseres, "Case Study: The Regional Peacekeeping Role of the Organization of American States: Nicaragua, 1990–1993," in Chester Crocker, Fen Hampson, and Pamela Aall, eds., *Managing Global Chaos* (Washington, DC: U.S. Institute of Peace Press, 1996), pp. 551–562.

23. On this new phase of the operation, see OAS, General Assembly, *Extension of the CIAV/OAS Mandate,* OEA/Ser.p AG/doc.3319/96, June 3, 1996.

24. For a review of CIAV/OAS activities between 1990 and 1993, see Jennie Lincoln and Caesar Sereseres, "Resettling the Contras: The OAS Verification Commission in Nicaragua," in Tommie Sue Montgomery, ed., *Peacemaking and Democratization* (Miami: North South Center, 2000), pp. 17–36.

25. Stephen Baranyi, "Political Missions," in Montgomery, *Peacemaking and Democratization,* pp. 11–16. See also United Nations, Department of Information, *The United Nations and El Salvador* (New York: UN Department of Public Information, 1997); Ian Johnston, *Rights and Reconciliation: UN Strategies in El Salvador* (Boulder: Lynne Rienner, 1995).

26. See William M. Berenson, "Joint Venture for the Restoration of Democracy in Haiti: The Organization of American States and United Nations Experience, 1991–1995," paper presented at the conference "United Nations Regional Organizations and Military Operations," Center on Law Ethics and National Security, Duke University and Center for National Security Law, University of Virginia, 1996, www.geocities.com/enriquearamburu/con/col3.html.

27. The agreements called for the reinstatement of Aristide, the selection of a prime minister by Aristide in consultation with the president of the senate and of the chamber of deputies, the reestablishment of democratic institutions, a general amnesty, the separation of the armed forces for the police and the lifting of sanctions, assistance from the international community to rebuild the country's economy, and the establish-

ment of the OEA mission. In March 1992 the Haitian court declared the protocols illegal and they were not ratified by parliament.

28. This aspect is analyzed by J. Taylor Wentges, "Electoral Monitoring and the OAS/UN International Civil Mission to Haiti," *Peacekeeping and International Relations* 25, no. 6 (November–December 1996): 3–5.

29. Joaquín Tacsan, "Searching for OAS/UN Task-Sharing Opportunities," in Weiss, *Beyond UN Subcontracting,* p. 108.

30. Rafael Hernández, "Cooperation in the Caribbean: The Cultural Dimension," in Joseph Tulchin and Ralph Espach, eds., *Security in the Caribbean Basin* (Boulder: Lynne Rienner, 2000), p. 85.

31. They include: Colombia-Venezuela, Belize-Guatemala, Bolivia-Chile, Colombia-Nicaragua, El Salvador, Honduras and Nicaragua, Guyana-Venezuela, Guyana-Suriname.

13

Africa and the Regionalization of Peace Operations

'Funmi Olonisakin and Comfort Ero

The regionalization of peace operations has been most eloquently expressed in sub-Saharan Africa through the interventions embarked upon by the Economic Community of West African States (ECOWAS) since it first intervened to end Liberia's civil war on August 25, 1990. Since then ECOWAS has mandated its monitoring group (ECOMOG) to intervene in the other regional troubled spots of Sierra Leone (1997–2000) and Guinea-Bissau (1999). The intervention in Liberia was the first indication that African states were increasingly prepared to find solutions to crises in their region. By the time they intervened in Sierra Leone and Guinea-Bissau, West African states had demonstrated their willingness to originate "indigenous" formulas to impose order in their region. While critics have charged ECOWAS with exacerbating and contributing to conflicts in the region, notably in Liberia and Sierra Leone, most critics and supporters, however, recognize that with the growing reluctance among the major powers of the UN Security Council to intervene in African crises, ECOWAS leaders had no choice but to evolve mechanisms and structures aimed at tackling conflicts in the region.

The regionalization of peace operations has been a welcome initiative in part because it serves as a useful cover for the UN Security Council choosing to prevent the UN from playing a greater role. This is demonstrated on the African continent, where regionalism or, to use the popular euphemism, "African solutions to African problems," became a convenient slogan for limiting the role of the UN on the continent. In a number of conflicts (e.g., Liberia, Sierra Leone), the Security Council often left regional organizations to manage the crisis or intervened too late. Thus there was no sign of burden sharing; rather it looked from the perspective of several West African states that they carried the weight in the region. A number of African states remain critical of the UN's reluctance to become fully engaged in their conflicts.

At the same time, however, several African states remain hesitant about having the UN play a role in their region. African states took the lead in developing and advancing the regionalization of peace operations because they wanted to lead on a number of conflicts and often found ways to limit the role of the UN. But two factors have become glaringly obvious following ECOWAS's decade-long interventions. First, interventions by African states are no less controversial than those conducted by Western powers. In fact, the struggles between local hegemon and middle-ranking powers led to serious divisions and often propelled states to side with various rebel groups in retaliation. Second, there is growing realization, as seen through the attempted intervention by ECOWAS in the West African region, that African states need significant support and assistance from external bodies such as the UN. It became apparent that ECOWAS lacked substantial capacity to sustain many of its peace missions and that logistical support was required. But such external assistance need not come from the UN alone. Other regional bodies or arrangements may be able to render constructive assistance to the process of developing effective regional peace operations in Africa. The issue is how to create a partnership that improves the region's capacity to manage and resolve crises as they unfold.

This chapter looks at the evolving nature of the regionalization of peace operations on the African continent, with specific attention to ECOWAS, but also looks at the role of Africa's principle regional organization, the Organization of African Unity (OAU), in managing regional conflicts.[1] It analyzes the difficulties encountered by ECOWAS in Liberia and Sierra Leone and the lessons learned. It then discusses the steps that can be taken to enhance regional capacity in the area of peace operations and how partnerships with the UN and organizations like NATO might enhance this process.

ECOWAS: Overview of Its Earlier Security Apparatus

The planning and execution of peace operations, or indeed the maintenance of regional peace and security, were not on the agenda of ECOWAS at its inception in 1975. As indicated in the treaty establishing the organization: "It shall be the aim of the community to promote co-operation and development in all fields of economic activity particularly in the fields of industry, transport, telecommunications, energy, agriculture, natural resources, commerce, monetary and financial questions and in social and cultural matters for the purpose of raising the standard of living of its peoples."[2]

But its members were soon confronted with the realization that the objectives of subregional economic cooperation and integration could not occur in an atmosphere of conflict and insecurity. This led to the signing of the Proto-col on Non-Aggression in 1978 and the Protocol on Mutual Assistance in Defence in 1981. Both protocols, however, were conceived on the assumption that the greatest threats to security in the West African subregion came from interstate sources. It was at the time not conceivable that threats to the secu-rity of the subregion could come from sources within a state, let alone that the peace operations would be staged in response to such threats. The policy of noninterference in the internal affairs of member states, which was also com-mon to other organizations like the OAU and the UN, made such operations unthinkable in a Cold War climate.

The Protocol on Non-Aggression stipulated that "Members States shall, in their relations with one another, refrain from the threat or use of force or aggression, or from employing any other means inconsistent with the Charters of the United Nations and the Organization of African Unity against the terri-torial integrity or political independence of other Member-States."[3] Addition-ally, the signing of the Protocol Relating to Mutual Assistance in Defense was motivated by a need to deal with aggression coming from outside the subre-gion. The fundamental objective of the protocol is that "any armed threat or aggression directed against any member state shall constitute a threat or aggression against the Community."[4] However, many of the obstacles to progress in ECOWAS have come from intrastate sources and this was not given significant attention by the organization during the Cold War era. The responsibility for subregional security, including the initiation of peace oper-ations, rapidly fell upon West African states in the immediate aftermath of the Cold War, the end of bipolar rivalry and the redefining of new conditions for superpower engagement of erstwhile African partners.

The ECOMOG Operation in Liberia

The first experience of a subregional peace mission was in Liberia, and it was vastly different from peace operations that had occurred elsewhere, whether conducted by the UN or by the OAU. A peace force, ECOMOG, had been deployed in response to a vicious intrastate war in Liberia, where civilians were the focus of the violence. Warring parties in Liberia (regular army and irregular forces alike) had blatantly ignored long-standing rules of war and international humanitarian law. The state of Liberia, whose institutions of governance were already weak, rapidly collapsed as power devolved down to the hands of various warlords. Whatever limited level of social services existed collapsed with the complete destruction of infrastructure, as the mas-sacre of innocent civilians continued unabated. More than 500,000 civilians fled within three months of the fighting.[5] And it was virtually impossible for humanitarian organizations to operate within Liberia, as much depended on the goodwill of warring factions, which could not be relied upon. Thus, despite concerns that some ECOWAS member states such as Nigeria had hidden agendas, it was difficult to oppose the ECOWAS intervention in Liberia amid the unfolding humanitarian tragedy, particularly in an atmosphere where no external actor in the international community was willing to intervene to end the carnage.

A peace operation that could deal effectively with the Liberian crisis would arguably be a multifunctional one, with the ability to offer a robust military response in addition to the ability to coordinate its activities with other operational and humanitarian agencies. ECOMOG's mandate was to restore order in Liberia, but the capacity of ECOWAS to effectively achieve this was severely curtailed. Despite immense political will to respond to the Liberian problem, it was clear that the institutional capacity to comprehensively execute the peace operation was lacking.

The ECOMOG peace operation in Liberia was radically different from the classical peacekeeping operations that had been the order of the day in the Cold War era. Conditions on the ground in Liberia shaped the operation. The ECOWAS decision to send a peacekeeping force to Liberia in July 1990 was taken with the expectation that it would monitor a negotiated peace, but the main rebel group, and indeed the only rebel faction at the time, the National Patriotic Front of Liberia (NPFL), had reneged on its earlier assurance to abide by the terms of a peace plan, opposing the deployment of a peace force in Liberia. Thus a conventional peacekeeping operation was no longer feasible, particularly in a situation where brutal fighting and atrocities still prevailed. ECOMOG was deployed under these conditions and it was severely punished by NPFL troops, who repeatedly attacked the force, inflicting serious casualties on it within the first few weeks of deployment.

In light of ECOMOG's humiliation and continued human suffering, its mandate was changed to one of enforcement in September 1990. The single most important benefit of ECOMOG's enforcement action was that it halted the killing and created conditions for operational and humanitarian agencies to resume activities and for peace negotiations to be conducted. This led to the first comprehensive ceasefire in November 1990. However, this did not end the Liberia problem.

The need to keep peace after the enforcement action demonstrated the unique character of the ECOMOG operation in Liberia. After the signing of the November 1990 ceasefire, a series of agreements were signed and reneged upon by the warring factions, which rapidly increased in number. ECOMOG was able to keep a fragile peace from 1990 until 1992, when the NPFL attacked ECOMOG and the capital city, Monrovia, in an operation code-named Octopus, thus creating a fresh state of emergency. ECOMOG was once again compelled to switch to enforcement action. Alternating between peacekeeping and peace enforcement had not been a pattern in peace operations since the UN Operation in the Congo (ONUC) between 1960 and 1964.

The ECOMOG enforcement action in response to Octopus ended with the signing of the Cotonou Accord in July 1993, which led to the active involvement of the UN. In the peacekeeping phase that followed, ECOMOG operated alongside the UN Observer Mission in Liberia (UNOMIL).[6]

The UN and ECOMOG: Sharing the Burden of Peacekeeping?

Secretary-General Boutros Boutros-Ghali described the alliance between the UN and ECOMOG as "the first peacekeeping mission undertaken by the United Nations in co-operation with a peacekeeping mission already set up by another organization."[7] However, this cooperation suffered a number of "teething" problems, as would be expected from such novel efforts. Some problems resulted from the weaknesses of the earlier ECOMOG experience. It is this earlier experience that presents valuable lessons for improving future peace operations.

Perhaps the major weakness of the ECOMOG operation, and one area in which the UN might have made a difference had it been engaged in the peace process at an earlier stage, was in the provision of political direction to ECOMOG in the field. For example, prior to 1995, when a Special Representative of the Executive Secretary was dispatched to Liberia, ECOWAS did not have a political office on the ground. This left the burden of tackling political issues that arose in the area of operation to ECOMOG's commanders, who did this in addition to handling day-to-day operational matters. The problem was due in large part to the fact that ECOWAS was not originally a political or security organization like other European bodies such as the NATO, which has military experience. As such it neither possessed a ready-made structure nor a technical know-how for conducting classical peacekeeping operations, let alone the complex one that it was compelled to conduct in Liberia. The organization merely responded to problems in the area of operation as they occurred.

Additionally, ECOMOG encountered command and control problems, which were more pronounced as a result of the type of operation it conducted in Liberia. The strategy required the blending of peacekeeping training with that of combat operations. This required adequate logistics capacity to match the level of activity, which was lacking in ECOWAS. The UN and other actors might have provided the required level of support. Individual countries such as the United States and the Netherlands provided logistical support to ECOMOG several years after the operation began, but their efforts were few and far between as well as uncoordinated. Furthermore, such uncoordinated support was sometimes a source of division in ECOMOG because some contingents were singled out for support to the exclusion of others. Nigeria, in particular, received minimal international support for its efforts because of its military regime under General Sani Abacha.

Nigeria, with 70 percent of the largest contingent, suffered huge problems of logistics, morale, and invariably, command and control, and this greatly impacted the operation. Commenting, for example, on the impact of logistics problems in the Nigerian contingent, General Adetunji Olurin, one of the ECOMOG field commanders in Liberia, remarked on different occasions:

> The lack of centralised logistics has inherent command and control problems for the commander. Besides, it is bad for morale of troops who share the same accommodation or office or check points to have different standards of feeding and welfare amenities.[8]

> It is however disheartening to note that of all the contingents in Operation Liberty the Nigerian contingent is the most badly turned out. Most of the soldiers had only one pair of boots and uniform. Our troops can easily be seen in tattered camouflage uniforms. Of late they have resorted to purchasing uniforms and boots from Ghanbatt and Leobatt contingents.[9]

Additionally, the fact that troops who participated in an enforcement phase also had to keep the peace created immense difficulty because they were often unable to assume a conciliatory mood toward rebel forces whom they had earlier encountered in combat and to whom they had lost fellow soldiers.[10]

Lessons from a Late UN Intervention

The UN and the great powers were largely absent in Liberia between 1990 and 1992. In the case of the United States, there was complicity in the violence through its decision to ignore or abdicate any responsibility in the tragedy unfolding in its de facto colony. Yet it was inconceivable that such large-scale atrocities, including the massacre of innocent people, could have been left to continue without any intervention. However, the peculiar nature of the Liberian problem, where warring factions had numbered four by late 1992, meant that resolution was difficult to achieve. By the time another crisis broke out in October 1992, with the NPFL's Operation Octopus, the UN became politically involved for the first time.

Failure to become involved in the response to this crisis from the outset had other implications for the UN. ECOWAS had shown that it was able to deal with problems in the subregion, albeit with several rough edges. It was clear that the UN could have provided the valuable political authority that was missing in the ECOMOG operation thus far. Yet it would have been difficult for the UN to supplant ECOMOG in 1992 without serious opposition from the ECOWAS member states, in particular Nigeria, that had carried the burden of the ECOMOG operation. In any case, the UN was not necessarily inclined to become too involved, given that the country and indeed the subregion no longer played a significant role in the strategic consideration of the powers that constitute the permanent members of the Security Council.

This experience offered valuable lessons for the UN in terms of future collaboration with regional organizations. First, early engagement is important, even if at a low level. It is the best way to ensure and maintain UN political and moral authority over a regional actor. The late involvement of the UN created some resentment among ECOMOG officers and other ranks, some of whom felt that the UN was arriving to share the glory at a time when they had performed the difficult task and suffered serious casualties, including the killing of many of their comrades.[11]

The vast disparity in welfare standards between ECOMOG soldiers and their UNOMIL counterparts compounded this problem. ECOMOG troops were paid operational allowances of U.S.$5 per day from the meager resources of the contributing states and this allowance was not paid regularly. The significantly higher allowance paid to UN troops alongside much higher standards of health created some dissatisfaction among ECOMOG men, who were largely of the opinion that the UN force had a relatively simple task in Liberia.

Second, even though the UN might lack the political will to conduct the type of operation required in such difficult conflict environments, it may be able to support (logistically and politically) the required robust action by a regional organization or group or coalition of states. The African security environment at the time indicated that more operations like ECOMOG's in Liberia might be required to address some of the looming crises in the region. Somalia was on fire, tragedy was unfolding in Rwanda, and a war of attrition, sparked off by Liberia, had already started in Sierra Leone.

By the time of the ECOMOG-UN cooperation, the OAU was already rethinking its principles, such as that on nonintervention in the internal affairs of member states, and assessing how best to become relevant in internal conflict situations. However, even with the establishment of the Mechanism for Conflict Prevention, Management, and Resolution in 1993, it was clear that the OAU could only respond at lower levels through early response, including mediation supported by small peace forces performing traditional peacekeeping functions such as peace observation and monitoring. Between 1990 and 1992 the OAU effort to mediate in Rwanda was supported by an observer force, the Neutral Military Observer Group in Rwanda (NMOG), which consisted of fifty-five military personnel.[12]

It would be appropriate if the OAU could respond at this level to all African conflicts before they become the basis for larger crises. However, the organization is severely limited in its ability to respond to conflicts that are not amenable to this level of intervention, which therefore escalate to disaster proportions as seen in Rwanda, where NMOG was unable to address the genocide, particularly when the UN was unwilling to make a greater commitment. Like the UN, the fifty-three-member OAU might not always achieve consensus among its members to contribute human and material resources to difficult humanitarian emergencies. Nor does it have the financial resources to execute the needed peace operations to address such problems.

Instead, many OAU members have shown greater dedication to subregional organizations, where their immediate security needs and interests coincide with those of other members. For example, where a conflict has spilled into neighboring states in terms of an influx of refugees and border incursions and flow of arms, the states affected often have a vested interest in seeking a resolution to such a crisis. This was the situation in which countries like Guinea and Sierra Leone found themselves when the Liberian war erupted. But despite their vested interest or good intentions, the required type of response to such operations will occur only if these neighboring states are able to meet the costs.

Herein lies the need for larger and richer states and regional hegemons. They are often closer to the problem and have comparatively greater resources than the smaller states. Thus, those subregional organizations within Africa that have shown the potential to respond to such crises have been ECOWAS and the South African Development Community (SADC). The former has shown a greater political will to conduct difficult peace operations because of its subregional hegemon, Nigeria. Nigeria holds the key to understanding ECOWAS's capacity to go it alone without the assistance or manpower from the UN. Where such organizations are absent or there is no political will to act among the richer states in the neighborhood, the UN is often expected to bear much of the responsibility for political and military action, as appears to be the case in the Great Lakes region of Africa. But even in such situations, the presence of the UN provides no reassurance of a successful outcome.

Some of the lessons of this early experience in Africa were apparent in other operations and conflict environments. In late 1992 the UN attempted under U.S. leadership a robust response to the Somalia conflict, which moved beyond mere humanitarian action. But this operation came to an abrupt end after an incident in 1993 in which eighteen U.S. Rangers, twenty-five Pakistani soldiers, and hundreds of Somalis were killed. The Somalia factor was later responsible for the unwillingness to respond to the crisis in Rwanda.

The importance of UN cooperation with regional actors in the effort to address the difficult peace missions for which UN Security Council authorization may not be granted was demonstrated in Bosnia with NATO's enforcement of the no-fly zone. It has been the pattern for NATO to embark on more robust actions in Europe, while the UN conducts the more traditional operations. The same rationale appeared to lie behind the UN response to the crisis in East Timor, where Australia led a more robust operation, allowing the UN to conduct the more traditional peace(building) operation.

ECOWAS and the UN in Sierra Leone: Correcting Past Mistakes

In West Africa, the Sierra Leone crisis, though unfortunate, offered the opportunity to assess the way in which UN-ECOWAS collaboration had progressed. Sierra Leone, which itself was undergoing an internal sociopolitical crisis, paid the ultimate price for its participation in the Liberia ECOMOG operation. Sierra Leonean dissidents of the Revolutionary United Front (RUF) and NPFL troops invaded the country in March 1991, marking the beginning of a drawn-out war that was officially declared to be over on January 18, 2002. A coup by a group of junior officers within the Sierra Leonean army in April 1992 led to the overthrow of President Joseph Momoh and the creation of a military junta known as the National Provisional Ruling Council (NPRC). Nigerians and Guineans had lent support to Sierra Leone in various capacities from 1991. International efforts to resolve the crisis led to hurriedly organized elections, which brought Ahmed Tejan Kabbah to power in February 1996. However, dissident forces within the NPRC and the rebels rejected the elections and subsequent Abidjan Peace Agreement in November 1996, citing government failure to properly tackle reform of the army as their reasons. On May 25, 1997, Ahmed Tejan Kabbah was ousted in a military coup by a segment of the army calling itself the Armed Force Revolutionary Council (AFRC). The military junta, led by Major Johnny Paul Koroma, later invited the RUF to enter the "government"; both unleashed terror on Sierra Leone. The international community widely condemned this coup.

As in the earlier ECOMOG intervention in Liberia, Sierra Leone's neighbors were the first to respond to the crisis in the country. It was not immediately apparent that the military operation aimed at reversing this coup was taken under the auspices of ECOWAS. It was more of a unilateral intervention by Nigeria (supported by Guinea) in which its ground-based forces attempted to respond to the situation. But the subregional framework for dealing with this crisis quickly emerged. This entailed the pursuit of diplomacy, after which a more robust response would be pursued in the event that diplomacy failed. The military junta agreed to an arrangement in which Kabbah would be reinstated by April 1998.

However, following violations of the terms of the agreement and an incident in the capital, Freetown, in February 1998, the ECOMOG force (which now consisted largely of the troops who served in Liberia) defeated the junta/RUF troops, driving them out of the capital. President Kabbah was reinstated in March 1998, thus creating an environment in which international and local actors could resume previous efforts to engage in rebuilding the nation. The ECOMOG effort resulting in the successful reinstatement of Kabbah was widely welcomed despite the fact that there were international sanctions against the military regime of Sani Abacha in Nigeria, which led this operation.

ECOWAS had by then embarked on new thinking and a new approach to regional security, but this had not fully materialized or trickled down to the level of the force in the field. A new ECOWAS treaty was signed in 1993, which conceived of security in a broader sense and made provision for dealing with intrastate conflict situations. Among other things, the new treaty provided for the establishment of a commission on cooperation in political, judicial, and legal affairs, regional security, and immigration,[13] a parliament, and a clause on the need for democracy and human rights in member states. Although many of the lessons of Liberia had not been grasped at the operational level, in Sierra Leone the decision to immediately impose sanctions on the junta negotiations was a significant step, in marked contrast to Liberia, where similar sanctions were not imposed on the NPFL until 1992, after it had reneged on several peace agreements.

Under the terms of its Status of Forces Agreement with the government of Sierra Leone (under the Kabbah regime), Nigeria was heavily involved in the task of rebuilding the Sierra Leonean army. Nigerian action, however, came under heavy criticism from extraregional powers, particularly the United Kingdom and the United States.

The efforts by a cross section of actors to contribute to the rebuilding process in Sierra Leone was stalled when in January 1999 the junta once again launched an attack on Freetown, killing hundreds of ECOMOG soldiers (mainly Nigerian) and many Sierra Leoneans, maiming and looting in the process. Nigeria would later send reinforcements to Sierra Leone to repel the rebel attack and maintain security. But this incident had revealed the inherent weaknesses in the Nigerian-led effort, discussed below, to restore peace and stability to Sierra Leone.

As in the Liberia case, the UN did not play a prominent role at the initial stages of the Sierra Leone crisis. But it provided political support to ECOWAS through a UN Security Council resolution imposing sanctions on the Koroma-led military regime following the coup in 1997. There was also wide condemnation of the junta attack and the atrocities committed against innocent civilians in Freetown.

On this occasion, however, the UN employed tactics different from the Liberian experience. The successes of ECOMOG in Liberia and Sierra Leone, despite some of the flaws outlined above, sent a number of key messages. First, they reconfirmed the fact that the UN and the international community were not sufficiently committed to Africa and would not commit human resources to dangerous African conflicts that could potentially lead to a loss of lives. Thus Africans needed to bear primary responsibility for their own security problems. Second, the confidence of West Africans, particularly Nigerians, was greatly boosted and it was clear that they no longer felt the need for the UN or outside actors to come to their rescue.

The UN, which had earlier deployed its Observer Mission in Sierra Leone (UNOMSIL), once again operated side-by-side with ECOMOG. However, like the Liberia experience, the UN had to contend with a more influential ECOMOG, which was in charge of security in various parts of Sierra Leone, and UN military observers had to depend on the ECOMOG presence in key areas to guarantee security.

The confidence of the Sierra Leone community in ECOMOG was high in the period following the restoration of President Kabbah in particular, and it was apparent that the force enjoyed greater respect and popularity among the people, despite many problems and the criticism of some ECOMOG military personnel considered to have displayed unprofessional conduct. ECOMOG's task force commander at the time of Kabbah's restoration, late brigadier-general Maxwell Khobe, enjoyed immense popularity among ordinary Sierra Leoneans during this period. Thus it was clear that the UN would need to reestablish itself in Sierra Leone if it was to retain any credibility and confidence among African actors. However, ECOMOG's reputation waned after the force departed in April 2000, especially after British forces intervened in May 2000 to prevent the renewal of conflict following the UN hostage crisis, which saw up to 500 peacekeepers being captured by the RUF and the collapse of the Sierra Leone peace process. The British appeared to do something that ECOMOG had struggled to achieve over its three-year intervention—to shift the balance of military and political power into the hands of the government of President Kabbah.

Nigeria was unhappy with several issues and this determined, to some extent, ECOMOG's sojourn in Sierra Leone. The operation was in place at great financial and human cost to Nigeria, which was reportedly expending about U.S.$1 million daily. Many of the key issues of concern to ECOMOG soldiers in Liberia were emerging in Sierra Leone. For example, the vast discrepancy between the income of ECOMOG soldiers and that of their UN counterparts, with whom they would operate side-by-side, was a source of discontent. Nigeria requested that assistance should be provided to boost the income of these soldiers. It became increasingly difficult for President Olusegun Obasanjo's regime, given the democratic transition in the country, to justify the cost of the operation.

Withdrawal of Nigerian troops was a source of concern to the Sierra Leonean government and people alike, who felt that the UN would not be committed to taking forceful measures against the RUF if ever an attack on the scale of January 1999 occurred again. But withdrawal of ECOMOG troops would also provide an opportunity for the UN to reassert itself in the country and gave Britain, Sierra Leone's former colonial master, great leverage in the management of the peace process. Thus it seemed more rewarding for ECO-MOG to depart, while Nigerian and other West African troops could be absorbed into the UN peacekeeping force—the UN Mission in Sierra Leone (UNAMSIL). However, for the Nigerians this was once again seen as a situation in which ECOMOG had done all the hard work only for another force to take all the glory.

ECOWAS in UN Missions: A New Trend?

The argument for absorbing ECOMOG forces into the UN Sierra Leone mission seemed to be a wise decision when judged on two levels—resources and political differences within ECOWAS. At the resources level, as noted above, Nigeria was incurring significant financial and human costs of ECOMOG, though much more scrutiny is required in judging the "real" cost of Nigeria's mission in Sierra Leone and Liberia. Moreover, clearer analysis is needed of the cost borne by other ECOMOG troops, especially when one considers the complaints of soldiers in both Liberian and Sierra Leonean missions about their history of low or no pay, which was seen to have been accountable in part for looting.

Placing ECOMOG or West African troops under UNAMSIL was a necessary political move following serious differences among member states of ECOWAS, particularly between Nigeria and its Francophone rivals (notably Burkina Faso and Côte d'Ivoire) over the legitimacy of ECOMOG interventions. What seemed apparent from the moment ECOMOG first intervened in Liberia in August 1990 was that interventions by African states in other African conflicts were no less politically sensitive or difficult to manage than Western-led interventions because they were conducted by Africans. On the contrary, the ECOWAS-ECOMOG story in Liberia and later Sierra Leone is one of geopolitical rivalry, Anglophone/Francophone cleavages, regional power dominance, and reliance on one regional power to sustain the operation. In Liberia, for example, the various rifts and political entanglements resulted in several member states colluding and collaborating with various warring factions in Liberia, thus prolonging the civil war. Operating under the UN banner addressed the issue of legitimacy and dominance of local hegemons.

In many ways, having powerful countries like Nigeria operating under the UN flag can act as a controlling mechanism or a check against the interventionist stance of a hegemon. As Adekeye Adebajo and Chris Landsberg note:

The UN peacekeeping mission in Sierra Leone, with its large Pakistani, Bangladeshi and Kenyan contingents . . . could signify a new, innovative approach to UN peacekeeping in Africa based on regional pillars supported by local hegemons whose political dominance is diluted by multinational peacekeepers from outside the region. By placing largely regional forces under the UN flag, the hope is that the peacekeepers will enjoy the legitimacy and impartiality that the UN's universal membership offers, while some of the financial and logistical problems of regional peacekeepers can be resolved through greater burden-sharing. These new missions should also be more accountable, since the peacekeepers will have to report regularly to the UN Security Council.[14]

For the UN also, placing ECOMOG under the UN was politically necessary. Having been slow in responding to conflicts in the region, and virtually abdicating its responsibility to ECOWAS, the UN needed to redeem itself not just in the region, but on the African continent. The UN needs to be actively and intimately engaged in the conflicts emerging in West Africa, but it can only do this with the military and political support of the regional powers.

In many ways, UNAMSIL provided an opening for the UN and ECOWAS to reshape and rebuild their relationship and credibility in the region. A new trend or model may emerge out of the UN-ECOWAS experience of drawing in regional forces under the banner of the UN not only to limit their dominance, but also to ensure that the UN does not abdicate from its responsibility of managing peace and security. It is a partnership that might yield some interesting results in West Africa and has become a useful model for the continent and beyond.

Partnerships with Other Regional Actors

Since the Sierra Leone ECOMOG experience, ECOWAS has made tremendous progress in evolving a regional security framework. The Mechanism for Conflict Prevention, Management, Resolution, Peacekeeping, and Security was signed in December 1999 and the restructuring of the organization has begun in earnest. A clear framework for addressing the subregion's security threats has emerged. The decision to establish a mechanism was a bid to institutionalize conflict management in West Africa. After a decade of ad hoc approaches, the mechanism is an attempt to standardize key operating procedures, doctrines, and missions in future ECOMOG interventions. Its main aim is to tackle a wide range of security issues concerning conflict prevention, management and resolution of conflict situations, peacekeeping, internal security, humanitarian support, peacebuilding, control of cross-border crime, and prevention of small-arms proliferation.

In spite of the progress that has been realized at this subregional level, it is clear that the above plans would be more effective under a cooperative and partnership arrangement with other regional and international actors. There is greater realization, both politically and practically, that ECOWAS alone cannot build or manage security in the region. It needs to have closer collaboration and cooperation with other key institutions within the global security framework. But how relevant or beneficial will such partnership, with NATO for example, be to ECOWAS member states? African states seem reluctant or skeptical of partnership because there is a perceived arrogance on the part of the West that their efforts in peace operations are not taken seriously. In addition, many wonder why they need to be accountable to the UN when the Security Council is unprepared to fund their missions. In the years of intervening in West African conflicts, ECOWAS members often felt reluctant to seek UN legitimacy primarily because they saw no reason to be answerable to an organization that neither mandated nor paid for their activities. Similarly, NATO acted alone when it intervened in Kosovo without a UN mandate.

The process of restoring peace and security to the subregion would entail efforts at several levels. These include: addressing current violent conflict and preventing the recurrence of armed conflict; postwar recovery, in essence, peacebuilding, involving the strengthening of weak institutions; ensuring good governance; and early response to potential threats. These tasks are difficult for well-resourced bodies like the UN and NATO to manage. The benefits of partnership are numerous and range from burden sharing and shared training and doctrine to maximizing resources, especially where poorer states are involved in peace operations, but the concept of "partnership" is overused, given that it is often one-sided. At times partnership is devoid of a clear understanding or knowledge of the recipient's needs. The customer is not asked, primarily because the strategic interest of the bigger power decides what is needed or the limits of its assistance. Often, the bigger partner assumes that is has nothing to learn from the small player, yet there is much that the Western peacekeepers can learn from the ECOWAS experience.

At an operational level, ECOMOG forces appeared more flexible in their military endeavors than their Western counterparts, shifting as they did in Liberia from a peacekeeping to a peace enforcement and back to a peacekeeping role. Moreover, many of those troops who were deployed in Liberia were taken to Sierra Leone without rotation or leave to see their families, thus showing the degree of stamina and preparedness among ECOMOG troops. Moreover, troop-contributing states mandated missions with limited resources, thus countering the argument that more money makes a military force more effective. Finally, ECOMOG troops were less restrained in their movement, showing a willingness to accept a number of casualties, though after a number of heavy attacks on ECOMOG by rebels troops in both Liberia and Sierra Leone, troops became heavily demoralized and citizens at home wondered about the involvement of their countries in these conflicts.

Partnership with various African organizations became a recurring theme among Western states and the UN at the start of the twenty-first century as a means to counter the charge that African conflicts were of less concern to the international community. But will it be partnership at a distance or will there be serious attempts to work directly with and in various subregional organizations? One must wonder what "partnership" means and how intimate it will be after the experience of the OAU in the 1990s, when Western partners made much fanfare about supporting its conflict mechanism but appeared to be very distantly involved. There is a perception among some African leaders that the concept of partnership has no real substance and is used loosely by Western powers. In essence, there is no real partnership.

For partnership to be credible it needs to be based on a proper assessment of needs and the capabilities that donors can deliver. The burden is also on African states to define what their needs are and the nature of their partnership with the West. Certainly there is a sense in which African leaders, through various initiatives such as the creation of the African Union, aim at providing a more robust and dynamic response to conflicts (internal and regional) than the OAU. But what has seemed painstakingly clear for some time is that some African leaders have yet to define their own view of the continent's security needs, thus allowing donors to manipulate the environment and determine these needs. A key problem also is that African leaders do not necessarily have the luxury to conduct a proper security-needs exercise because the pressures and challenges against the leadership are constant diversions from the opportunities of providing a clear strategic outlook for their countries. Moreover, several states are part of the security problem. One has to wonder, for example, how the neighboring states of the Democratic Republic of Congo can be both aggressors and peacemakers. These processes will occur at both national and regional levels.

Partnership is also viewed with skepticism because burden sharing or equality in missions is not often apparent. Take for example Britain's involvement in Sierra Leone. Although Britain is often credited for its intervention in Sierra Leone in May 2000, its actions on the ground did not resemble the language of partnership that became a key cornerstone of the British government's Africa policy. Rather, its actions prior to and after its intervention were reminiscent of the tendency of great powers in the 1990s to mandate UN missions, but not to fully back them up in terms of troops on the ground. The resumption of conflict, which eventually led to the British intervention and the collapse of the Lomé peace process and the UN mission, appeared to have dented the credibility of the UN mission. On the other hand, the UN peace operation would have been better enhanced by participation of the British.

Arguably, Britain should have been part of the UN mission from the moment UN Security Council Resolution 1270 of October 22, 1999, mandated peace-keepers for Sierra Leone. In fact, Britain, together with Nigeria, was instrumental in influencing Security Council members to vote for the peacekeeping mission. Yet Britain refrained from placing troops within the UN structure. Following the May 2000 intervention, Britain's initial decision to pursue a unilateral strategy distinct from the UN did more damage to an already discredited UN peacekeeping mission.[15] The decision to place military personnel in key positions in UNAMSIL headquarters in Freetown from October 2000 appeared to contribute to the tension that existed between Britain and UNAMSIL's other leading power—Nigeria. From the perspective of Nigeria and other troop-contributing countries, the permanent members of the UN Security Council were prepared to pay and dictate the limits of their mission, but they were not prepared to spill their blood.

Finally, partnership is not often taken seriously because much of the external assistance that it is based on has not necessarily been coherent, nor has it been provided within a clear security framework that recognizes partnership between various national, regional, and international institutions. For example, efforts that might have contributed to this process were initiated by the United States in the form of the African Crisis Response Initiative (ACRI). On the other hand, at a regional level, the French initiative Renforcement des Capacités pour le Maintien de la paix en Afrique (RECAMP; Reinforcement of African Peacekeeping Capacity) did provide a useful concept of partnership when it gave logistical and financial support to the ECOMOG forces (Benin, Niger, Mali, and Togo) that intervened in Guinea-Bissau in March 1999. Like the UNAMSIL mission that was to follow, this was an innovative partnership that could be further developed. Despite the fact that the small ECOMOG force that intervened could quell the tide of conflict, closer cooperation and support such as that between French and West African forces could help in the development of ECOMOG's capacity. Even with French support, such lack of capacity was evident, as noted when then–executive secretary of ECOWAS Lansana Kouyate stated in an address to the UN Security Council on April 16, 1999, that "it would be particularly useful to acquire for ECOMOG appropriate logistics for the deployment of a naval unit, made necessary by Guinea-Bissau's geographical make-up. The acquisition of an aeroplane or a helicopter is also essential to enable ECOMOG to make important, urgent trips between Bissau and points outside the country."[16]

At the national level, Britain and the United States have been involved in the transformation of the security sector in Sierra Leone and Nigeria, respectively. The British effort in Sierra Leone has witnessed significant progress, although this has reflected one of the core problems of such assistance, which is the failure to take a partnership approach to the problem. For example, the

British took over the process of retraining and rebuilding a new army in Sierra Leone from the Nigerians. However, a formula that sought to provide reorientation for Nigerian military personnel while involving them in the process of rebuilding the Sierra Leonean army might not have been viable at the time, given the political climate in Nigeria, where public opinion had compelled a newly elected government to divert greater attention to domestic issues rather than external military assistance.

The ACRI effort has largely focused on peacekeeping practices and doctrine and the role of militaries in responding to humanitarian crises. But according to the testimonies of West African troops who have participated in these peace operations, their problem is not lack of training in peacekeeping or in soldiering skills. Their experiences in Sierra Leone and Liberia have shown that the greatest challenge they faced was operating in guerrilla terrain, compounded by the problem of inadequate logistics. Thus, providing training in traditional peacekeeping or standard soldiering skills would have done very little for the force, though this needs to be qualified. With the possible exception of South Africa (and even this is debatable), African states will need additional unit training and better equipment. The recommendations in the Brahimi Report—the UN review of peacekeeping operations published in August 2000—called for interoperability and the deployment of larger units (brigade rather than battalion) in support of peace operations.[17] In fact, the Brahimi Report could have been written solely about the difficult encounters faced by African states in managing their conflicts. The report points to lessons in the areas of greater cohesion and direction and better rules of engagement, resources, command and control, and equipment, all of which are reminiscent of past ECOMOG failures.[18]

The continuing threat or potential for operations in difficult terrain involving irregular forces has shown that a more robust type of peace operation must be prepared, with the appropriate adjustment made to the peacekeeping doctrine. Without a new approach to the problems of the region, it will be difficult to correctly address many of the problems encountered in previous operations. However, parts of the training now offered through the ACRI and other sources such as ECOWAS and Save the Children (Sweden), including training in child and human rights training, are a step in the right direction and have great relevance for the transformation process in the security sector.

All of these external actors, including the United States, the United Kingdom, and France (even though it is not part of NATO military arrangements), that have been involved in the transformation processes in West Africa are part of NATO, and the subregion might benefit more from an arrangement in which they collectively, within a NATO framework, share experiences with ECOWAS. This might include issues such as how to respond effectively to crises, particularly participation in robust peace operations. This might allow for a more constructive and coordinated approach to the capacity-building needs of West Africa, rather than the present situation in which the different NATO members offer different forms of support and strategies that do not necessarily meet the collective vision and security needs of the subregion.

Such ECOWAS-NATO arrangements can only complement UN-NATO efforts in other areas in addition to strengthening regional peace operations in Africa. Such collaboration might promote the use of common training and doctrine in response to similar challenges as well as a more efficient mechanism for logistical support, all of which can only enhance the UN's role and truly lessen its burden.

Conclusion: What Might the Future Offer?

The future might already be here, so to speak. Following the combined efforts of the UN and ECOWAS in Sierra Leone, it appears that a new trend has emerged. Given the obvious limitations of the ECOWAS effort to restore peace to Liberia and Sierra Leone, and the failure (Somalia and Angola) or the unwillingness (Rwanda) of the UN to intervene in African conflicts, the logical next step is to create a solid and firm partnership where both institutions share the burden of managing conflicts in the West African region. There can be no doubt that West Africa has gone further than any other region in creating structures for building peace, security, and stability, but a glaring problem is that not all actors in the region are equal stakeholders, hence closer cooperation with the UN is pertinent. West Africa and the rest of the continent must be first and foremost key participants in setting a framework and an approach for understanding and responding to their security problems. The ongoing efforts between the UN and regional organizations to develop modalities to enhance cooperation offer the prospect, ultimately, for improved collaboration in peacekeeping. The cooperation between ECOWAS and the UN appears to be far more advanced than what exists between the UN and many other organizations.

The creation of a UN West Africa Office in Dakar, Senegal, in January 2002 might be a consolidation of the efforts begun by UNAMSIL.[19] The aim of the UN office is to support the region and harmonize UN activities with those of ECOWAS. It is an office premised on the assumption that partnership must include all stakeholders. But this office is dependent on the willingness of West African states to make it work for the region. ECOWAS member states need to ensure that it is based on a common or shared vision of Africa's future and a division of responsibilities with tangible commitment by various actors to play roles within this framework relevant to the needs of Africans and their common interests.

Notes

The views expressed in this chapter are entirely those of the authors and do not necessarily reflect the views of their employers.

1. The OAU is in a transitional phase to the new African Union.

2. ECOWAS, *Treaty of the Economic Community of West African States,* May 28, 1975, art. 2(1).

3. ECOWAS, *Non-Aggression Treaty,* April 22, 1978, art. 1.

4. ECOWAS, *Protocol Relating to Mutual Defense,* May 29, 1981, chap. 2, art. 2.

5. For a firsthand account of the early years of the Liberian civil war, see M. Huband, *The Liberian Civil War* (London: Frank Cass, 1998).

6. See UN Doc. S/Res/866, September 22, 1993.

7. Ibid.

8. Adetunji I. Olurin, "Peacekeeping in Africa: The Liberian Experience," *The Peacemaker* 2, no. 1 (September 1992–September 1993): 13, 20.

9. Adetunji Olurin, "Lecture on Military Operations in Liberia," delivered to student officers at the National War College, Lagos, October 2–5, 1993, p. 30.

10. Several interviews with ECOMOG soldiers in the field during 1993 and 1994 confirmed this problem.

11. Personal interviews with ECOMOG officers in June and July 1994.

12. For a detailed discussion, see Monde Muyangwa and Margaret A. Vogt, *An Assessment of the OAU Mechanism for Conflict Prevention, Management, and Resolution, 1993–2000* (New York: International Peace Academy, November 2000).

13. See ECOWAS, *Revised Treaty of ECOWAS,* July 24, 1993, chap. 10, arts. 56–59.

14. Adekeye Adebajo and Chris Landsberg, "Back to the Future: UN Peacekeeping in Africa" in Adekeye Adebajo and Chandra Lekha Sriram, eds., *Managing Armed Conflicts in the Twenty-First Century* (London: Frank Cass, 2001), pp. 183–184.

15. Comfort Ero, "A Critical Assessment of Britain's Africa Policy," *Journal of Conflict, Security, and Development* 1, no. 2 (2001): 57.

16. UN Security Council, *Report on the Situation in Guinea-Bissau Prepared by ECOWAS Executive Secretary,* UN Doc. S/1999/432, April 16, 1999.

17. United Nations, *Report of the Panel on United Nations Peace Operations,* UN Doc. A/55/305-S/2000/809, August 21, 2000.

18. See also International Peace Academy (IPA) and ECOWAS, *Towards a West Pax Africana: Building Peace in a Troubled Subregion* (New York: IPA, 2002).

19. The decision to open a UN West Africa Office followed recommendations made in a UN interagency mission led by Ibrahima Fall, Assistant Secretary-General for Africa, from March 6 to March 27, 2001. The mission recommended the appointment of a UN Special Representative of the Secretary-General for West Africa. See United Nations, Inter-Agency Mission to West Africa, *Towards a Comprehensive Approach to Durable and Sustainable Solutions to Priority Needs and Challenges in West Africa,* UN Doc. S/2001/434, May 2, 2001.

PART 5

Conclusion

14

Strengthening Regional Approaches to Peace Operations

Cyrus Samii and Waheguru Pal Singh Sidhu

The development of a post–Cold War global architecture for peace operations has progressed in fits and starts. A global multilateral architecture, embodied by UN-centered decisionmaking and implementation, has been made unsteady by instances of hegemonic reluctance to comply with multilateral commitments. Regional powers have often stood in the way of global multilateral resolution of "their" conflicts—as in the cases of India in its confrontation with Pakistan; Israel in its confrontation with Palestinians over a Palestinian state; and the U.S. unilateral impulse to evict Saddam Hussein in Iraq.[1]

But at the same time, as the chapters in this volume demonstrate, new initiatives for regionalized capacity development have bolstered the global architecture for crisis management, even if such developments create a higher degree of decentralization. Degradation of the UN-centered approach would seem to be an incentive—though a negative incentive—for capacity development among "regional actors," by which we refer to organizations and groups of states that act in the collective interest of a region. One would expect that the less the UN decisionmaking and implementation framework serves interests of regional actors, the more the regional actors will seek to consolidate and strengthen their capacities. This is assuming that the states involved in the process of regionalization perceive that such regional consolidation will serve their national interests better than the UN.

A potential outcome of these circumstances—of a challenged UN-centered approach and enhanced regionalization—is discord between the UN and regional actors as they compete in zero-sum games for resources and authority. Such discord is aggravated where UN decisionmaking does not seem to represent the interests of regional actors. Such a context characterized the relationship, for example, of the UN Security Council and the members of the

Economic Community of West African States (ECOWAS) as it moved under Nigerian leadership to intervene in Liberia in 1990; the intervention, carried out under the aegis of the ECOWAS Ceasefire Monitoring Group (ECO-MOG), has been described in this volume as marking the beginning of "regionalization" of peace operations. Another potential outcome is discord between the regional actors themselves, particularly in areas where interests overlap. Perhaps the most perverse example is the uneasy relationship among the members of the European Union (EU) and the North Atlantic Treaty Organization (NATO) as each institution attempts to embody particular security objectives in the twenty-first century. This centrifugal tendency has been further accentuated by the present Bush administration and its radical doctrine of preventive war. In a way the U.S.-UK led war on Iraq might well mark the end of this phase of regionalization.

Nonetheless, until the passing of UN Security Council Resolution 1483, the UN-centered approach has been, more or less, preserved in peace operations since the end of the Cold War. As discussed in this volume, the 1998 ECOMOG intervention into Sierra Leone has since transformed into the UN Mission in Sierra Leone (UNAMSIL). In the case of the Kosovo operations, practitioners from both the European regional organizations and the UN have appreciated coordination under a Special Representative of the Secretary-General as an effective organizational model.[2] This trend, though significantly weakened, continued even in Afghanistan. Thus, rather than discord, these operations have been characterized by the emergence of eventual complementarity between the UN and the regional actors. However, Iraq and UNSC Resolution 1483, which clearly puts the occupying powers at center stage and offers only a marginal role to the UN, is a disturbing trend even though it might eventually lead to complementarity between the UN and the occupying powers.

Iraq apart, the emergence of such complementarity is certainly promoted by the headquarters-level interest in avoiding zero-sum relationships between institutions. This interest may be an outgrowth of the institutions' own more parochial interests, including institution preservation in a crowded field or the maintenance of safety nets during institutional transformation. But regardless of the headquarters-level interests in cooperation, systemic factors—discussed in the first section of this chapter as the "demand side"—will compel continued interaction between the UN and regional actors in peace operations. Thus the UN and regional actors will continue to face the need for coordination in this area. From a UN-centered strategic perspective, such coordination with regional actors defines this chapter's theme: "regional approaches." The second section of this chapter looks at certain institutions' initiatives in relation to this need—described as the "supply side." Following that, various modes of matching the supply to the demand are discussed. The final section raises questions addressing processes of and potentials for "cooperative adaptation" to the needs of peace operations.[3] The prescriptive stance of this chapter—"strengthening regional approaches"—calls for the strengthening of regional decision-making and implementation capacity and the improvement of interinstitutional coordination ability (including interoperability). The stance derives from the concept of institutional building blocks—rather than stumbling blocks—for flexible *and* effective response to the needs of peace operations.

The Demand Side

Ongoing Conflicts and Failed States

The first element of this demand side is the continuity of regional low-intensity conflicts and civil wars that show no signs of self-resolution. These conflicts—as in West Africa, Central Africa, southeast Europe, the Caucasus, and Central Asia—often emanate from failed states. As such, the conflicts take place in spaces of weak political administration and tend to involve economic interests and international linkages that promote their prolongation.[4] Intervention in such conflicts—to shore up political systems, adjust economic incentive environments, and sever the international links—is thus required to bring about sustainable resolution.

In other ongoing conflicts where regional powers have blocked global multilateral approaches—as with the conflicts over Palestine and in South Asia—one can nonetheless anticipate intensified international involvement in the postconflict peacebuilding phase. Here, again, Iraq (where the United States and the UK as occupying powers are likely to determine the extent of multilateral involvement in postconflict peacebuilding) might well prove to be the exception. Though the conflicts themselves may not be resolved through global multilateral settlement processes, the massive reconstruction and development projects that will follow will likely require the combination of resources and legitimacy that an internationally coordinated approach provides.

Increased Interest in Intervention and Preventive Security Measures

Since the end of the Cold War, states and security institutions have demonstrated increased interest in intervention and preventive security measures. Such increased interest has led to the emergence of doctrines for a set of security measures including structural prevention,[5] preventive diplomacy, military intervention, and preventive military action. Two particular developments can be identified. First, humanitarian norms have been the source of impulsion for intervention to halt or prevent humanitarian catastrophe with increased frequency since the end of the Cold War in comparison to prior periods. In addition to a proclivity to intervene, the international community operating through the UN has demonstrated a proclivity for multinational intervention.[6] Such norms have not been consistent in their effects, as most visibly demonstrated in the feeble international response leading up to the 1994 genocide in Rwanda. Nonetheless, efforts such as the International Commission on Intervention and State Sovereignty's 2001 report, *The Responsibility to Protect,* demonstrate a continued interest to develop a humanitarian intervention doctrine capable of ensuring consistent and effective intervention and prevention.[7]

Second, the concept of failed states, although well recognized soon after the end of the Cold War, has entered the mainstream strategic discourse of powerful states, particularly as a major element in the strategy of the U.S.-led war on terror.[8] As mentioned above, global linkages to international smuggling and illegal financing networks provide for the prolongation of conflicts; but such linkages also work in reverse: the anarchy in zones of low-intensity conflict and weak political administration is perceived as being a fertile "breeding ground" for transnational terrorist groups. This connection adds a degree of urgency to the need for stabilizing efforts such as structural prevention and postconflict peacebuilding. At the same time, such stabilizing efforts must be seen in the context of the perception that targets abound in such zones for preventive military action. This relationship between peace operations and preventive military action presents a particular doctrinal and normative challenge for international and regional organizations. At the unilateral level, however, Washington appears to have resolved this challenge by giving precedence to the latter over the former.

Whether by definition, as with structural prevention and preventive diplomacy, or as either a complement or a consequence, as with military intervention and preventive military action, each mode of preventive or interventionist security activity involves international and interinstitutional coordination in peace operations. In addition, with the United States interested in maintaining its own high-readiness capacity for preventive military action, regional actors are under pressure to ensure that local regional crisis management capacities are sufficient to meet security needs when U.S. participation and leadership cannot be taken for granted. In the post-Iraq scenario, ironically, it is the overwhelming U.S. use of force and Washington's preference for its own brand of unilateral (or a coalition of the chosen few) peacekeeping action that threatens to keep out the regional or global capacities from Iraq as evidenced by the reluctance of NATO and EU allies to offer meaningful troop commitments for policing Iraq. Thus, the newly emerging capacities in Europe are unlikely to be made available in significant terms for U.S.-sponsored peace operations in Iraq.

Legitimacy

The U.S.-led campaign in Afghanistan that began in the fall of 2001 demonstrated that partnership with international actors continues to be necessary in offensive military action and in peace operations. This necessity is in large part based on the need for legitimacy. The satisfaction of this need for legitimacy in the war and reconstruction effort underpinned the interactions between the United States, U.S. allies, the UN, and other international organizations. This group of actors attempted to negotiate a program of action that met the legitimacy demands arising at the international, regional, and local (i.e., within Afghanistan) levels. The organization of one of these ad hoc bodies, the International Security Assistance Force (ISAF), exposed some of the UN's general deficiencies in providing such legitimacy. First, cultural considerations were significant in the decision to have Turkey take the helm of the ISAF after Britain ended its term in June 2002. The situation in Afghanistan revealed conditions under which the cosmopolitanism that the UN embodies was not an advantage. As discussed in the chapters in this volume, such cultural considerations may give a specific advantage to regional actors.[9]

Second, though legitimacy is certainly measured in terms of the quantity and quality of the states involved in an operation, the degree of legitimacy also derives from the perceived effectiveness of the operation. Effectiveness not only serves in the ex post facto calculation of the legitimacy of an operation, but it also conditions perceptions of the legitimacy of cooperative alternatives for future operations. In the case of the ISAF, numerous factors seem to have contributed to the decision not to have the UN command the operations. These include reluctance on the part of UN officials for accepting responsibility for an operation whose mandate and provisions had not been fully worked out, and reluctance on the part of the United States for accepting limitations on its ongoing offensive operations in Afghanistan.

A third factor, as discussed in the introduction to this book, is whether the UN decisionmaking process adequately represents the interests of actors in the region of the conflict. The lack of a prominent regional organization integrating Afghanistan and its neighbors increases the risks associated with inadequate representation. This concern over representation is also tied to the U.S. strategic leadership in the Security Council, which grew ever more coercive in the wake of the Afghanistan operations. The United States proceeded to use the July 2002 extension mandate for the UN Mission in Bosnia and Herzegovina (UNMIBH) as a bargaining chip for a deal on the International Criminal Court, and then pushed its agenda on action vis-à-vis Iraq. Initially, Washington did persevere for as long as six months with the UNSC to get a resolution that would legitimize its impending military action against Iraq. However, when it became clear that the UN Security Council (particularly France) would not oblige, the United States simply walked away, preferring action over debating legitimacy.

Europeans in particular, but other regional actors as well, have demonstrated an increasing reluctance to leave all strategic direction to be determined in Washington. This split, evident since the present Bush administration took office, was particularly apparent in the run up to the war against Iraq.

In his essay *The Postmodern State and the World Order,* and in addresses that have followed, senior EU official Robert Cooper has made clear that an intention of the EU's Common Foreign and Security Policy (CFSP) is to organize a persuasive European voice to use in strategy discussions with Washington.[10] As 'Funmi Olo/nisakin and Comfort Ero discuss in Chapter 13, certain leaders in West Africa have also expressed their feelings that programs such as the U.S.-initiated African Crisis Response Initiative (ACRI) are unequal partnerships. In conveying an increasing interest in making the idea of partnership clearer to the United States, regional actors have accepted the need to enhance their coordination, decisionmaking, and implementation capacity for peace operations. Thus, with cultural considerations and effectiveness as normative criteria, and with the deficiency of the UN's representation of regional interests, the UN's legitimizing currency is depreciating relative to the currency of increasingly capable regional actors.

The Supply Side

European Regional Capacity
and Out-of-Area Orientations

Over the past twelve years, as European regional actors have been increasingly involved even further afield—in Africa, the Caucasus, Central Asia, and the Middle East—discussions emphasizing out-of-area coordination (presently particular only to European regional actors) and relations with non-European regional and global actors have taken on prominence. The discussions of new out-of-area programs draw upon the innovative regionalized initiatives that have already been established, especially in relation to the ongoing multiorganizational interaction in the Balkans operations.

NATO has made definitive moves to establish itself as a regional facilitator and a quasi-collective security instrument. It has facilitated regional capacity development through its Partnership for Peace (PfP) program and other efforts, mainly through the Euro-Atlantic Partnership Council (EAPC). The programs have worked to strengthen polities and military capacities in regions on the European periphery and beyond, and have included subregionalized capacity building in the Balkans, the Baltics, and the Caucasus.[11] NATO members began to extend the scope of the institution's collective security instrumentality in the context of the U.S.-led war against terrorism, leading to their formal involvement in the International Security Assistance Force in Kabul.[12] The decision to develop a NATO Rapid Response Force is further evidence of NATO's complete transformation away from a static deterrent to a potential quasi-collective security instrument.

In working to satisfy the European Security and Defense Policy (ESDP) terms of CFSP, the EU is moving to develop a military deployment capability

to complement its already far-reaching diplomatic and development assistance activity.[13] This is evident in the deployment of a primarily European
force in the Democratic Republic of Congo. The EU is also complementing
the military capability with a civilian crisis management capability to address
the needs of police, rule of law, civilian administration, and civil protection.
In the Balkans, the EU has initiated two new programs: the Regional
Approach Through the Stability Pact for Southeastern Europe, and the Stabilization and Association Process. The Stability Pact has been organized to
facilitate regional cooperation and to coordinate international assistance in the
region. Through the Stabilization and Association Process, the EU has instru-
mentalized the centripetal force of its own consolidation process to influence
peacebuilding in the Balkans. EU aid and deployments through these two programs fill out the first demonstration of engagement in the full range of activities described in CFSP in one region. They have been coordinated with the
UN, NATO, the Organization for Security and Cooperation in Europe
(OSCE), and other regional and nonregional actors.[14]

Enhancing Regional Capacity in
Africa, Asia, and Latin America

As the West African experiences in the development of ECOWAS and the
deployments under ECOMOG have demonstrated, negative and positive
incentives have compelled regional capacity development. ECOWAS's motivation has come from the perception of the lack of attention from the UN, an
inclination to respond locally, and the actions of a dynamic hegemon—Nigeria—which has defined the agenda. The motivation has resulted in the operationalization of what Olonisakin and Ero describe as ECOWAS's regional
"mutual security principle." The basis for the principle was first articulated in
the 1981 Protocol on Mutual Assistance and Defense, which drew on norms of
sovereignty and impartiality.[15] But following ECOMOG's efforts in Liberia,
Sierra Leone, and Côte d'Ivoire, the principle has come to signify robust intervention and coordination among actors from inside and outside the region—
including the UN, the United States, and European states—to provide for the
"cocktail" of needs and resources in peace operations in West Africa.
    In Southeast Asia, as Mely Caballero-Anthony indicates, the Association
of Southeast Asian Nations (ASEAN), as a preventive regime, appears to have
been successful in reducing the probability of interstate war. However, as the
case of East Timor demonstrates, the "ASEAN way" may be inadequate in
affecting the probability of intrastate war. As a security principle, the ASEAN
way maintains its basis on norms of sovereignty and impartiality. As such, the
ASEAN approach may be labeled "exceptionalist" with respect to explicit
efforts to promote convergence on humanitarian and interventionist norms, as
evidenced at the regional level in the OSCE's 1975 Helsinki cooperation
agreement and ECOWAS's mutual security principle, and at the global level

in the inchoate cosmopolitan intervention doctrine summarized in *The Responsibility to Protect*. The hands-off approach of the ASEAN way lays no such groundwork.

The Organization of American States (OAS) labors under equally powerful limitations. Its lack of institutional robustness, reluctance to get involved in "internal affairs," and dominant influence of U.S. interests and goals mean that unilateralism and bilateral relations prevail. There appears to be little prospect of alternative leadership in the region coming from Mexico, Argentina, or Brazil, for example. Moreover, economic crises in Argentina, Brazil, and Venezuela are likely to debilitate these countries and focus their attention on internal stability. Nevertheless, as Monica Herz shows, there remains potential for the OAS and the UN to develop a new framework for their relationship as a consequence of debates on the reform of both organizations. The OAS may be politically, economically, and militarily deficient for providing peace operations and peacebuilding administration, but there is considerable experience of diplomatic "good offices" and conflict prevention, and growing regional cooperation on promoting democracy, tackling organized crime, and addressing human security issues.

At the UN: Strengthening the Ties

These regional efforts have been occurring against the backdrop of the UN's work over the past decade to promote regionalized capacity building. Though the Brahimi Report's rather light treatment of UN cooperation with regional organizations may not "adequately reflect the latter's importance for peace operations,"[16] the UN has pushed forward in rationalizing its cooperation with regional organizations in peace operations, in line with the modes of interaction described in former UN Secretary-General Boutros Boutros-Ghali's 1995 *Supplement to an Agenda for Peace*.[17] These efforts include framework reports and working-level meetings with organizations. Since 1999, working-level meetings between the UN and NATO, for example, have focused on cooperation in the areas of early warning, conflict prevention, and peacebuilding.[18] However, as most of these interactions are held in a nonoperational context, they tend to be rather more academic than practical.

Matching the Supply to the Demand: Models of Engagement

Certain cases exemplify the various challenges for coordinated engagement, particularly multinational engagements that include significant regional-actor inputs. The cases thus offer a host of lessons for coordinated adaptation by regional actors. In Kosovo, the UN Mission in Kosovo (UNMIK) "four-pillar" and Kosovo Force (KFOR) operation represents a highly structured collaborative effort clearly set out by UN Security Council Resolution 1244. The operation represents, on the one hand, the first multidimensional peace operation where non-UN bodies—the EU and the OSCE—had an operational role under a UN umbrella, and on the other hand, a reaffirmation of the need for robust deployment, under KFOR, that allowed for less constrained command and rules of engagement. Ostensibly, UNMIK combines particular strengths of each of the four organizations: the EU's political pull is the driving force for stabilization, NATO provides the credible deterrent, the OSCE provides its experienced involvement in peacebuilding, and the UN gives consistent authority in allowing the international community to speak with a single voice.

The highly structured arrangement in Kosovo can be contrasted with the complex interaction between ECOWAS, UK forces, the EU, and the UN before and during UNAMSIL's operations in Sierra Leone. UNAMSIL, which emerged out of the 1998 Nigeria-led ECOMOG intervention, came to resemble a "classic" peacekeeping deployment in terms of structure. But its efforts and those of the international community would not have succeeded without the UK taking the lead in the UN Security Council, deploying an "over the horizon" capacity and providing integrative support for political and security sector development. All of this occurred in the absence of any formalized arrangement compelling such UK involvement.

A third modality is evident in the ongoing coordination in Afghanistan between the UN Assistance Mission in Afghanistan (UNAMA), the ISAF, NATO allied forces, and the United States. The absence of any regional organization in this territory, of concern to Europe, Russia, the United States, and other key countries, has been coupled with the reluctance in Washington to undertake peacekeeping operations. Consequently, European actors initially were compelled to provide the military heavy-lifting for the peace operation through the instrument of the ISAF for Afghanistan, which has included troops from thirteen of the EU's fifteen members. This action should also be viewed in relation to EU-led humanitarian, peacebuilding, and reconstruction assistance efforts.[19] The UN geared up to handle the political and economic peacebuilding requirements through the medium of UNAMA while the NATO Secretariat has emphasized its role in force generation and planning assistance.

The multidimensional Afghanistan operation, involving in different capacities the United States, European security organizations, other key countries, and the UN, offers both a challenge and an opportunity for the rapidly changing character of peace operations. It also seems to have set a pattern for future operations. One indication of this was the emergence of "the Quartet"—the United States, Russia, the EU, and the UN——to deal with the crisis in the Middle East. As in Afghanistan, the Quartet also reflects the absence of any regional mechanism to deal with the conflicting interests of the different parties in the region satisfactorily. Iraq too appears to be the hapless victim of a region that is also bereft of an adequate regional mechanism to effectively deal with either inter- or intrastate crises. The Iraqi plight has been further compounded by the unilateral U.S. action and Washington's indifference to obtaining even a post-facto justification of its actions. Resolution 1483, passed in May 2003, did not appear to be designed to work toward a truly multilateral coordinated effort. Instead, it appeared to give precedence for peacebuilding and reconstruction to the United States and UK (as occupying powers) and their close friends, rather than the international community in general. There also does not appear to be much concern regarding cultural sensitivities, as was evident in handing the leadership of the ISAF to Turkey in Afghanistan.

Finally, other smaller-scale operations may also provide lessons for creative UN-sponsored multidimensional responses. Peace operations in Bougainville, for example, demonstrate how a cooperative effort among a UN presiding body (the UN Political Office in Bougainville), the regional actors (the Truce Monitoring Group and Peace Monitoring Group, led by the Australian Defense Forces), and domestic actors (allowing for the organization of the Bougainvillian reconciliation government) can be effective. Such cases highlight a special priority for the UN—to ensure comprehensive, efficient, and effective responses to smaller-scale crises that may not draw the immediate attention of the powerful states. Indeed, many powerful states might well ignore these small successes to their own peril.

Extracting the Lessons

The above-mentioned cases indicate that there can be no single model for multinational/multilateral engagement and also present other areas for consideration. These include:

- examining the connections between the intrastate crises within regions of concern and the security concerns of states in other regions;
- studying how best the abilities of the emerging regional force capacity can be coordinated with those of the UN and other regional actors to conduct robust peace operations in these crises areas; and
- exploring ways in which the UN, in cooperation with regional actors, can effectively build and maintain peace in these areas of concern through innovative security structures.[20]

Recent experiences in peace operations have put emphasis on the strategic concepts of *footprint, transitioning,* and *disengagement* (the so-called exit strategy). Study of these concepts, along with the geopolitical and resource-related constraints, in past operations would equip the UN and regional actors to develop compatible frameworks that may include a host of generic models to help guide future interaction. This process raises the following questions:

- What opportunities exist in developing regional capacities—including standby units, logistics, civilian experts, and intelligence—to augment UN capacities, in line with the Brahimi recommendations?
- How can these actors work to ensure that peace enforcement, peacekeeping, and peacebuilding strategies are aligned? What benchmarks for success—whether political, social, or military—should be used in the transitioning to determine disengagement and handover?
- How can the UN and regional actors best develop their capacities to be trusted recipients of missions?

As John Cockell and Peter Viggo Jakobsen note in Chapters 7 and 8, respectively, there is some evidence to suggest that the civil-military relationship in the areas of policing, judicial reconstruction, and security sector reform has moved from coordination to dependence in complex peace operations. This dependence requires a high degree of strategic alignment between the peace agreement and the capabilities deployed. Though agreements that end conflicts often do not have a policing mandate for the intervening military—as was the case with the Dayton Accords and UN Security Council Resolution 1244—the intervening troops are nonetheless left with the burden of undertaking policing. The lack of an adequate policing and legal mandate can be the source of weakness in an implementation program; in Bosnia this issue has been quite significant indeed. Although the EU proposal for the establishment of rapidly deployable intervention forces composed of legal experts and civilian police to enhance civilian crisis management capability is the most advanced concept, its operationalization has been sluggish.

More generally, matching mandates to capability requires effective interorganizational coordination and consultation in early stages in the development of the mandate. The mismatches of the Dayton Accords are partially attributable to the fact that the UN was not an active party in the U.S.-led negotiations despite the fact that the UN was assigned as a key actor in the implementation. The Dayton process can be contrasted to the more recent case of the continued interaction between the UN Security Council and the South Africa–led regional initiative for peace in Burundi. Such interaction, based on the implementation of the August 2000 Arusha Agreement, has provided for due caution, and hesitancy, in considering a mandate for any UN deployments to support the "African mission" (led by the South African National Defense Force) tasked to monitor and stabilize the implementation.[21] This cautious regional approach vis-à-vis Burundi derives, in part, from the perceived inadequacy of the abandoned 1995–1996 Security Council and Secretary-General proposals for UN-led intervention, which seemed dangerously disconnected from the complex political situation on the ground.[22] Another case rich in lessons on effective and early coordination is the EU, NATO, and OSCE response to the flare-ups in southern Serbia and Macedonia in 2001. Strong regional actor coordination allowed for an early response to the emerging crises. This coordination ability had been developed through the continuing interaction between the organizations in the Bosnia and Kosovo operations and had been nurtured at the headquarters level since 1999 through regular meetings organized by UN Secretary-General Special Envoy for the Balkans Carl Bildt.[23]

Examination of interregional and interorganizational program coordination could uncover opportunities to provide stronger support to regional security and development arrangements. The case of European involvement in crisis management in West Africa provides an example. The ideational and commercial remnants of the colonial legacy, which motivated British intervention in Sierra Leone and the French intervention in Côte d'Ivoire, most likely do not provide strong enough incentives to ensure European leadership in organizing forces with staying power in Africa. Such involvement would most likely be domestically unacceptable in the European states but also in the African states in the long run. Nonetheless, overlap exists, for example, in EU support for ECOWAS and the UN's regional operations, which include the establishment of the Office of the Special Representative of the Secretary-General for West Africa (in Dakar). Coordination of such overlapping programs would amplify their effects. In addition, such coordination would counter the existent linkages between regional conflict formations and global flows of arms, drugs, refugees, and other transnational and transregional threats to security. In enhancing the complementary relationships among the actors from the different regions in order to develop capacities for peacebuilding, conflict prevention, and crisis management, however, certain questions arise:

- How can the UN work with regional actors to ensure a smooth transition from peacekeeping to regional peacebuilding? How can the various intra-UN agencies as well as the inter- and intraregional actors (including nongovernmental organizations) improve coordination to facilitate disarmament, demobilization, and reintegration, as well as land mine removal and small-arms collection?
- How can the UN and regional actors work together to promote region-wide security-sector reform and development?
- How might UN and regional actor efforts be linked and harmonized with other regional capacity-building programs, such as the U.S. ACRI, France's RECAMP, or the ECOWAS Security Mechanism?

In a world of increasingly variable decisionmaking and implementation architecture, security organizations are compelled to continually identify the potential for strategic and operational coordination. The trends, processes, and cases listed above are only a sampling, but they nonetheless demonstrate that regional organizations and regionalized approaches, in cooperation with the UN, have come to serve as key elements in peace operations. The challenge, then, is to relate the potential arising from the regional processes to the needs of the operations themselves in order to ensure an effective and efficient response. The war in Iraq notwithstanding, this challenge has to be collectively addressed by the key actors likely to be involved there—the U.S.-UK combination, other key countries, the UN, and other regional actors. In fact, events in postwar Iraq pose not only a new challenge to the role of regional actors but also lend a new urgency to the need to coordinate efforts of the different actors, particularly the unilaterally inclined hyperpower.

Notes

1. The emergence of the so-called Quartet (comprising the UN, the EU, the United States, and Russia) and its joint Road Map to solve the Israeli-Palestinian conflict clearly counters this phenomenon, though the effect of this ad hoc institution on the conflict remains to be seen.

2. See Sheila Coutts and Kelvin Ong, "Managing Security Challenges in Post-Conflict Peacebuilding," report from the International Peace Academy's Second Working Group conference, June 2001, Ottawa, as part of the IPA's 1999–2002 project "The UN, NATO, and Other Regional Actors."

3. An academic term taken from the economics field of industrial organization, "cooperative adaptation" refers to the capacity of parties to respond to disturbances in a cooperative way.

4. For a collection of essays examining these economic interests and linkages, see Mats Berdal and David Malone, eds., *Greed and Grievance: Economic Agendas in Civil Wars* (Boulder: Lynne Rienner, 2000).

5. For a collection of works discussing such modes of conflict prevention, see Chandra Lekha Sriram and Karin Wermester, eds., *From Promise to Practice: Strengthening UN Capacities for the Prevention of Violent Conflict* (Boulder: Lynne Rienner, 2002).

6. For a discussion of this post–Cold War increase in frequency in relation to the relevant normative developments, see Martha Finnemore, "Constructing Norms of Humanitarian Intervention," in Peter J. Katzenstein, ed., *The Culture of National Security: Norms and Identity in World Politics* (New York: Columbia University Press, 1996). Finnemore also makes the point that multilateral intervention has become the norm. However, from John Ruggie's definition of multilateralism, which implies significant mutuality in the formation and execution of the intervention mandate, multinationalism would be a more apt description. See John Gerard Ruggie, ed., *Multilateralism Matters: The Theory and Praxis of an Institutional Form* (New York: Columbia University Press, 1993).

7. The report was published by the International Development Research Center (IDRC) as *The Responsibility to Protect: Report of the International Commission on Intervention and State Sovereignty* (Ottawa: IDRC, 2001).

8. See, for example, Sebastian Mallaby, "The Reluctant Imperialist: Terrorism, Failed States, and the Case for American Empire," *Foreign Affairs* 81, no. 2 (March–April 2002): 2–7; and Kimberly Zisk Marten, "Defending Against Anarchy: From War to Peacekeeping in Afghanistan," *Washington Quarterly* 26, no. 1 (Winter 2002–2003): 35–52.

9. For instance, the Organization of the Islamic Conference (OIC), though not representative of the concerns of a particular region per se, but of a particular culture, interacts with the UN through the UN's framework for regional organizations.

10. See Robert Cooper, *The Postmodern State and the World Order* (London: Foreign Policy Centre, June 2000). Comments concerning the EU's interest in strengthening its voice in strategic matters were at the heart of Cooper's address to the IPA-EUISS conference "The UN, The EU, NATO, and Other Regional Actors: Partners in Peace?" Paris, October 11–12, 2002.

11. See James Appathurai, "Promoting Regional Security," *NATO Review* 49 (Autumn 2001): 13–15.

12. The decision from within NATO to emphasize the organization's outward orientation was formally presented in the final communiqué from the Ministerial Meeting of the North Atlantic Council in Reykjavik on May 14, 2002. The out-of-area orientation was further articulated on June 20, 2002, when NATO Secretary-General George Robertson stated that NATO could make itself available to "support a non-NATO operation," to work toward the "development of global deployment capabilities," and to "be in a position to take on a wide-ranging facilitating role for UN-mandated operations." The final communiqué from Reykjavik is available at www.nato.int/docu/pr/2002/p02–059e.htm. The quote is from a speech by NATO Secretary-General George Robertson, "Tackling Terror: NATO's New Mission," delivered at the American Enterprise Institute, Washington, DC, June 20, 2002.

13. Preliminary announcements set the boundaries for deployment of the EU force as within a radius of 4,000 kilometers from the EU headquarters in Brussels and for humanitarian action as within a radius of 10,000 kilometers from Brussels. Nonetheless, the ESDP/CFSP process does demonstrate a general reluctance to firmly circumscribe scope or purpose of the emerging EU force. See Jolyon Howorth, *European Integration and Defence: The Ultimate Challenge?* Chaillot Paper no. 43 (Paris: EU Institute for Security Studies, November 2000), pp. 76–81.

14. In addition, some hope may be placed in the EU and NATO enlargement processes for redressing what is frequently considered a faulty incrementalism in the Balkans by providing opportunities to rerationalize the development process. See Carl Bildt, "A Second Chance in the Balkans," *Foreign Affairs* 80, no. 1 (January–February 2001): 148–158.

15. See "Appendix 3: Protocol Relating to Mutual Assistance on Defence," in Margaret A. Vogt, ed., *The Liberian Crisis and ECOMOG: A Bold Attempt at Regional Peace Keeping* (Lagos, Nigeria: Gabumo, 1992), pp. 35–46, cited in Rasheed Dramam and David Carment, *Managing Chaos in the West African Sub-Region: Assessing the Role of ECOMOG in Liberia,* Occasional Paper no. 26 (Ottawa: Center for Security and Defense Studies, 2001).

16. Jeremy Greenstock, International Peace Academy (IPA), and Center on International Cooperation, *Refashioning the Dialogue: Regional Perspectives on the Brahimi Report in UN Peace Operations,* report on regional meetings, February–March 2001 (New York: IPA, 2001), www.ipacademy.org/publications.

17. In *Supplement to an Agenda for Peace,* five modes of interaction between the UN and regional organizations are considered: consultation, diplomatic support, operational support, codeployment, and joint operations. UN Doc. A/50/60-S/1995/1, January 3, 1995.

18. See United Nations, *Cooperation Between the United Nations and Regional Organizations/Arrangements in a Peacekeeping Environment: Suggested Principles and Mechanisms,* March 1999, www.un.org/depts/dpko/lessons/regcoop.htm. The "Framework for Cooperation in Peace-Building" is presented in a letter dated February 12, 2001, from the Secretary-General to the President of the Security Council, UN Doc. S/2001/138, February 14, 2001. As part of the April 10–May 2, 2002, UN-Regional Organizations Working-Level Meeting on Conflict Prevention and Peace-Building, the UN and NATO also held bilateral discussions at the working level.

19. See Lorraine Mullally, "Winning the Peace: The EU in Afghanistan," *European Security Review,* no. 10 (January 2002): 4–5.

20. These issues will be the focus of a new IPA project, "Strengthening Regional Approaches to Peace Operations."

21. See United Nations, *Presidential Statement Requests Secretary-General to Study Ways of Responding Positively, Urgently to Accord's Request for African Mission,* UN Doc. SC/7609, December 18, 2002.

22. See Stephen R. Weissman, "Preventing Genocide in Burundi," United States Institute of Peace Peaceworks Report, July 1998. Accessed on May 22, 2003, www.usip.org/pubs/peaceworks/weissm22/weissm22.html.

23. For a brief narrative of the coordinated preventive efforts in southern Serbia and Macedonia in 2001, see Mihai Carp, "Back from the Brink," *NATO Review* (Winter 2002): www.nato.int/docu/review/2000/issue4/english/art2.htm.

Acronyms

ACRI	African Crisis Response Initiative (United States)
AFRC	Armed Force Revolutionary Council (Sierra Leone)
AFTA	ASEAN Free Trade Agreement
APEC	Asia Pacific Economic Cooperation Forum
ARF	ASEAN Regional Forum
ASC	ASEAN Standing Committee
ASEAN	Association of Southeast Asian Nations
BiH	Bosnia and Herzegovina
CARICOM	Caribbean Community
CFSP	Common Foreign and Security Policy (EU)
CIAV	Comisíon International de Apoio y Verificación (International Commission for Support and Verification; OAS)
CICAD	Comisíon Interamericana para el control del abuso de drogas (Inter-American Drug Abuse Control Commission)
CIMIC	civil-military cooperation
CIS	Commonwealth of Independent States
COMKFOR	Commander KFOR
Coreper	Committee of Permanent Representatives (EU)
CSCE	Conference on Security and Cooperation in Europe
DHA	Department of Humanitarian Affairs (UN)
DJA	Department of Judicial Affairs (UN)
DPKO	Department of Peacekeeping Operations (UN)
EAPC	Euro-Atlantic Partnership Council
ECHR	European Convention for the Protection of Human Rights and Fundamental Freedoms

ECOMOG	ECOWAS Ceasefire Monitoring Group
ECOWAS	Economic Community of West African States
EEA	European Economic Agreement
ESDI	European Security and Defense Identity
ESDP	European Security and Defense Policy
EU	European Union
EUMM	European Union Monitoring Mission
Europol	European Police Organization
FMLN	Farabundo Martí National Liberation Front (El Salvador)
FRY	Federal Republic of Yugoslavia
FYROM	former Yugoslav Republic of Macedonia
G7	Group of Seven
G8	Group of Eight
GCC	Gulf Cooperation Council
HCNM	High Commissioner on National Minorities (OSCE)
IADB	Inter-American Defense Board (OAS)
ICCPR	International Covenant on Civil and Political Rights
ICTY	International Criminal Tribunal for the Former Yugoslavia
IFI	international financial institution
IFOR	Implementation Force (UN)
INTERFET	International Force for East Timor
IOM	International Organization for Migration
IPA	International Peace Academy
IPTF	International Police Task Force (UN)
ISAF	International Security Assistance Force (Afghanistan)
JSEC	Joint Security Executive Committee (Kosovo)
KFOR	Kosovo Force (UN)
KJI	Kosovo Judicial Institute
KLA	Kosovo Liberation Army
KPC	Kosovo Protection Corps
KPS	Kosovo Police Service
KPSS	Kosovo Police Service School
KVM	Kosovo Verification Mission
KWECC	Kosovo War and Ethnic Crimes Court
LAS	League of Arab States
LSMS	Legal Systems Monitoring Section (OSCE)
MAPE	Multinational Advisory Police Element (WEU)
MICIVIH	International Civilian Mission in Haiti (OAS/UN)
MIP	Mission Implementation Plan (BiH)
MNB	multinational brigade
MSU	multinational specialized unit
NAFTA	North American Free Trade Agreement
NATO	North Atlantic Treaty Organization

NLA	National Liberation Army (Kosovo)
NMOG	Neutral Military Observer Group in Rwanda
NPFL	National Patriotic Front of Liberia
NPRC	National Provisional Ruling Council (Sierra Leone)
OAS	Organization of American States
OAU	Organization of African Unity
OCHA	Office for the Coordination of Humanitarian Affairs (UN)
ODIHR	Office for Democratic Institutions and Human Rights (OSCE)
OHCHR	Office of the High Commissioner for Human Rights (UN)
OHR	Office of the High Representative
OHRCA	Office of Human Rights and Community Affairs
OIC	Organization of the Islamic Conference
OLA	Office of the Legal Adviser (SRSG)
OMIK	OSCE Mission in Kosovo
ONUC	UN Operation in the Congo
ONUCA	UN Observer Group for Central America
OSCE	Organization for Security and Cooperation in Europe
P-5	Permanent Five (UN Security Council)
PfP	Partnership for Peace (NATO)
PJC	Permanent Joint Council (NATO)
PSC	Political and Security Committee (EU)
REACT	Rapid Expert Assistance and Cooperation Teams (OSCE)
RECAMP	Renforcement des Capacités pour le Maintien de la paix en Afrique (Reinforcement of African Peacekeeping Capacity; France)
RUF	Revolutionary United Front (Sierra Leone)
SADC	South African Development Community
SARC	South Asian Association for Regional Cooperation
SFOR	Stabilization Force (BiH)
SHAPE	Supreme Headquarters Allied Powers Europe
SHIRBRIG	Standby High Readiness Brigade (UN)
SRSG	Special Representative of the Secretary-General (UN)
TAC	Treaty of Amity of Cooperation (ASEAN)
TNI	Indonesian Armed Forces
TPF	Transitional Police Force (UN)
UCPMB	Liberation Army of Presheva, Medvegja, and Bujanoc
UK	United Kingdom
UN	United Nations
UNAMA	UN Assistance Mission in Afghanistan
UNAMET	UN Mission in East Timor
UNAMSIL	UN Mission in Sierra Leone
UNCIVPOL	UN Civilian Police

UNHCR	UN High Commissioner for Refugees
UNICEF	UN Children's Fund
UNIPTF	UN International Police Task Force
UNITAF	Unified Task Force (Somalia)
UNMEE	UN Mission in Ethiopia and Eritrea
UNMIBH	UN Mission in Bosnia and Herzegovina
UNMIH	UN Mission in Haiti
UNMIK	UN Mission in Kosovo
UNOMIL	UN Observer Mission in Liberia
UNOMSIL	UN Observer Mission in Sierra Leone
UNPREDEP	UN Preventive Deployment Force (FYROM)
UNPROFOR	UN Protection Force (former Yugoslavia)
UNPSG	UN Police Support Group
UNTAES	UN Transitional Administration for Eastern Slavonia, Baranja, and Western Sirmium
UNTAET	Transitional Authority in East Timor
UPD	Unity for the Promotion of Democracy (OAS)
WEU	Western European Union

Selected Bibliography

Adebajo, Adekeye, and Chris Landsberg. "Back to the Future: UN Peacekeeping in Africa." In Adekeye Adebajo and Chandra Lekha Sriram, eds., *Managing Armed Conflicts in the Twenty-First Century*. London: Frank Cass, 2001, pp. 161–188.

Adibe, Clement E. "The Liberian Conflict and the ECOWAS-UN Partnership." In Thomas G. Weiss, ed., *Beyond UN Subcontracting: Task-Sharing with Regional Security Arrangements and Service-Providing NGOs*. London: Macmillan, 1998, pp. 67–90.

Adler, Emmanuel. "Seeds of Peaceful Change: The OSCE's Security Community-Building Model." In Emmanuel Adler and Michael Barnett, eds., *Security Communities*. Cambridge: Cambridge University Press, 1998, pp. 119–160.

Alagappa, Muthiah. "Regional Arrangements, the UN, and International Security: A Framework for Analysis." In Thomas G. Weiss, ed., *Beyond UN Subcontracting: Task-Sharing with Regional Security Arrangements and Service-Providing NGOs*. London: Macmillan, 1998, pp. 3–29.

———. "Regional Institutions, the UN, and International Security." *Third World Quarterly* 18, no. 3 (1997): 421–441.

———. "Regionalism and Conflict Management: A Framework of Analysis." *Review of International Studies* 21, no. 4 (October 1995): 359–397.

Amnesty International. *Federal Republic of Yugoslavia, Kosovo: Recommendations to UNMIK on the Judicial System*. February 2000.

Annan, Kofi. "Strengthening ASEAN–United Nations Partnership." Remarks at the ASEAN-UN summit, Bangkok, February 12, 2000.

———. "UN Peacekeeping Operations and Cooperation with NATO." *NATO Review* 41, no. 5 (October 1993): 3–7.

Anthony, Mely C. "ASEAN: How to Engage or Cooperate." Paper presented at the ASEAN-ISIS conference "ASEAN 2020: Vision, Crises, and Change," Singapore, July 21–22, 1999.

———. "Mechanisms of Dispute Settlement: The ASEAN Experience." *Contemporary Southeast Asia* 20, no. 1 (April 1999): 38–66.

Antolik, Michael. *ASEAN and the Diplomacy of Accommodation*. Armonk, NY: M. E. Sharpe, 1990.

Appathurai, James. "Promoting Regional Security." *NATO Review* 49 (Autumn 2001): 13–15.

Archer, Clive. *International Organizations.* London: Routledge, 1992.

Arnson, Cynthia, ed. *Comparative Peace Processes in Latin America.* Stanford: Stanford University Press, 1999.

Barnett, Michael. "The UN, Regional Organizations, and Peacekeeping." *Review of International Studies* 21, no. 4 (October, 1995): 411–433.

Bayley, David. "The Contemporary Practices of Policing: A Comparative View." In *Multinational Peacekeeping: A Workshop Series—A Role for Democratic Policing.* Washington, DC: National Institute of Justice, October 6, 1997.

Bennett, Steve. "Briefing on the Kosovo Police School." Paper presented at the IISS/DCAF workshop "Managing the Context of Police Reform: Implications for International Assistance," Geneva, April 24–25, 2001.

Bennis, Phyllis. *Calling the Shots: How Washington Dominates Today's UN.* New York: Olive Branch Press, 1996.

Berdal, Mats. *Whither UN Peacekeeping?* Adelphi Paper no. 281. London: International Institute for Security Studies, 1993.

Berenson, William M. "Joint Venture for the Restoration of Democracy in Haiti: The Organization of American States and United Nations Experience, 1991–1995." Paper presented at the conference "United Nations Regional Organizations and Military Operations," Center on Law Ethics and National Security, Duke University and Center for National Security Law, University of Virginia, 1996. www.geocities.com/enriquearamburu/con/col3.html.

Berman, Eric G. "The Security Council's Increasing Reliance on Burden-Sharing: Collaboration or Abrogation?" *International Peacekeeping* 5, no. 1 (1998): 1–21.

Berman, Eric G., and Katie E. Sams. "The Peacekeeping Capacities of African Regional Organisations." *Conflict, Security, and Development* 2, no. 1 (2002): 31–55.

———. *Peacekeeping in Africa: Capabilities and Culpabilities.* Geneva: UNIDIR, 2000.

Boothby, Derek G. *Cooperation Between the UN and NATO: Quo Vadis?* International Peace Academy (IPA) Seminar Report. New York: IPA, June 1999.

Boutros-Ghali, Boutros. *An Agenda for Peace.* New York: United Nations, 1992.

Buzan, Barry. *People, States, and Fear.* 2nd ed. Hemel Hempstead: Harvester Wheatsheaf, 1991.

Buzan, Barry, Øle Wæver, and Jaap de Wilde. *Security: A New Framework for Analysis.* Boulder: Lynne Rienner, 1998.

Cantori, Louise J., and Steven L. Speigel. *The International Relations of Regions: A Comparative Approach.* Englewood Cliffs, NJ: Prentice Hall, 1970.

Carter, Ashton B., William J. Perry, and John D. Stenbruner. *A New Concept of Cooperative Security.* Washington, DC: Brookings Institution, 1992.

Çeku, Agim. "The Kosova Protection Corps." *RUSI [Royal United Services Institute] Journal* 146, no. 2 (April 2001): 25–27.

Chamot, Céline. "Vers un partage des responsabilités entre les Nations Unies et les organisations régionales dans le maintien de la paix?" *L'Observateur des Nations Unies* no. 5 (1998): 29–57.

Child, Jack. *The Central American Peace Process, 1983–1991: Sheathing Swords, Building Confidence.* Boulder: Lynne Rienner, 1992.

Chopra, Jarat. "The UN's Kingdom of East Timor." *Survival* 42, no. 3 (Autumn 2000): 27–40.

Claude, Inis L., Jr. *Swords into Plowshares: The Problems and Progress of International Organization.* London: University of London Press, 1965.

Cockell, John G. "Civil-Military Responses to Security Challenges in Peace Operations: Ten Lessons from Kosovo." *Global Governance* 8, no. 4 (Winter 2002): 483–502.

———. "Conceptualising Peacebuilding: Human Security and Sustainable Peace." In Michael Pugh, ed., *Regeneration of War-Torn Societies.* London: Macmillan, 2000, pp. 15–34.

Cooper, Andrew, and Thomas Legler. "The OAS Democratic Solidarity Paradigm: Questions of Collective and National Leadership." *Latin American Politics and Society* 43, no. 1 (Spring 2001): 103–126.

Cooper, Neil. "State Collapse as Business: The Role of Conflict Trade and the Emerging Control Agenda." *Development and Change* 33, no. 5 (November 2002): 935–955.

Cooper, Neil, and Michael Pugh. *Security Sector Transformation in Post-Conflict Societies.* London: Centre for Defence Studies, 2002.

Cooper, Robert. *The Postmodern State and the World Order.* London: Foreign Policy Centre, June 2000.

Cotton, James. "Against the Grain: The East Timor Intervention." *Survival* 43, no. 1 (Spring 2001): 127–142.

Cox, Robert W. "Social Forces, States, and World Orders: Beyond International Relations Theory." *Millennium* 10, no. 2 (1981): 126–155.

Day, Graham. "The Training Dimension of the UN Mission in Bosnia and Herzegovina (UNMIBH)." *International Peacekeeping* 7, no. 2 (Summer 2000): 155–168.

De Waal, Alex. "Wars in Africa." In Mary Kaldor, ed., *Global Insecurity.* London: Pinter, 2000, pp. 49–51.

Dee, Moreen. "Coalitions of the Willing and Humanitarian Intervention: Australia's Involvement with INTERFET." *International Peacekeeping* 8, no. 3 (Autumn 2001): 1–20.

Deutsch, Karl W., ed., *Political Community and the North Atlantic Area.* Princeton: Princeton University Press, 1957.

Diéguez, Margarita. "Regional Mechanisms for the Maintenance of Peace and Security in the Western Hemisphere." In Olga Pellicer, ed., *Regional Mechanisms and International Security in Latin America.* Tokyo: UN University Press, 1998, pp. 93–111.

Diehl, Paul F. *International Peacekeeping.* Baltimore: Johns Hopkins University Press, 1993.

Dominguez, Jorge I., ed. *International Security and Democracy in Latin America and the Caribbean in the Post–Cold War Era.* Pittsburgh: University of Pittsburgh Press, 1992.

Donald, Dominick. "The Doctrine Gap: The Enduring Problem of Contemporary Peace Support Operations Thinking." *Contemporary Security Policy* 22, no. 3 (December 2001): 107–139.

Dorn, Walter. "Regional Peacekeeping Is Not the Way." *Peacekeeping and International Relations* 27, nos. 3–4 (July–October 1998): 2–4.

Dramam, Rasheed, and David Carment. *Managing Chaos in the West African Sub-Region: Assessing the Role of ECOMOG in Liberia.* Occasional Paper no. 26. Ottawa: Center for Security and Defense Studies, 2001.

Duffield, Mark. *Global Governance and the New Wars: The Merging of Development and Security.* London: Zed Books, 2001.

Dufourcq, Jean. "L'Engagement européen dans la gestion des crises: Un point de situation militaire." *Annuaire Français de Relations Internationales* 3 (2002): 480–485.

Dupont, Alan. "The Future of the ARF: An Australian Perspective." In Khoo How San, ed., *Future of the ARF.* Singapore: Institute of Defense and Strategic Studies, 1999, pp. 31–48.

Eide, Espen Barth. "CPN/SWP Balkan Stability Project: The Internal Security Challenge: Reforming Police, Judiciaries, and Penal Systems in the Western Balkans." Paper prepared for the CPN/SWP Western Balkans Stability project, 2nd draft, November 11, 1999.

———. "The Internal Security Challenge in Kosovo." Paper presented at the UNAUSA/IAI conference "Kosovo's Final Status," Rome, December 12–14, 1999.

———. "Regionalising Intervention? The Case of Europe in the Balkans." In Anthony McDermott, ed., *Sovereign Intervention.* Oslo: PRIO, 1999, pp. 61–86.

Eide, Espen Barth, Annika S. Hansen, and Brynjar Lia. *Security Sector Reform as a Development Issue.* Room Document no. 7. Paris: OECD/Development Assistance Committee, Task Force for International Peace and Development, June 2–3, 1999.

Ero, Comfort. "A Critical Assessment of Britain's Africa Policy." *Conflict, Security, and Development* 1, no. 2 (2001): 51–71.

European Union. *Presidency Conclusions.* Göteborg European Council, June 15–16, 2001.

———. *Statements by the Ministerial Council.* MC(9).DEC/2, December 4, 2001.

Evangelista, Matthew. "Historical Legacies and the Politics of Intervention in the Former Soviet Union." In Michael Brown, ed., *The International Dimensions of Internal Conflict.* Cambridge: MIT Press, 1996.

Evans, Gareth J. *Cooperating for Peace: The Global Agenda for the 1990s and Beyond.* St. Leonards, New South Wales: Allen & Unwin, 1993.

Falk, Richard. *Predatory Globalization: A Critique.* London: Polity Press, 1999.

Farer, Tom, ed. *Beyond Democracy: Collectively Defending Democracy in the Americas.* Baltimore: Johns Hopkins University Press, 1996.

Fawcett, Louise, and Andrew Hurrell, eds. *Regionalism in World Politics.* Oxford: Oxford University Press, 1995.

Finnemore, Martha. "Constructing Norms of Humanitarian Intervention." In Peter J. Katzenstein, ed., *The Culture of National Security: Norms and Identity in World Politics.* New York: Columbia University Press, 1996.

Flavin, William. "Doctrinal Review: American View." In *Challenges of Peacekeeping and Peace Support into the Twenty-First Century: The Doctrinal Dimension.* Carlisle, PA: U.S. Army Peacekeeping Institute, Center for Strategic Leadership, 2000.

Funston, John. "ASEAN: Out of Its Depths." *Contemporary Southeast Asia* 20, no. 3 (April 1998): 22–37.

Gaviria, Cesar. *A New Vision for the OAS.* Washington, DC: Organization of American States, 1995.

Ginifer, Jeremy. "How Civil Wars End." In Anthony McDermott, ed., *Sovereign Intervention.* Oslo: PRIO, 1999, pp. 117–133.

Gosselin, Guy, Gordon Mace, and Louis Belanger. "La Securité coopérative regionale dans les Amériques: Le Cas des institutions démocratiques." *Etudes Internationales* 25, no. 4 (December 1995): 799–817.

Goulding, Marrack. *Peacemonger.* London: John Murray, 2002.

Greenstock, Jeremy, International Peace Academy (IPA), and Center on International Cooperation. *Refashioning the Dialogue: Regional Perspectives on the Brahimi Report in UN Peace Operations.* Report on regional meetings, February–March 2001. New York: IPA, 2001. www.ipacademy.org/publications.

Griffin, Michèle. "Blue Helmet Blues." *Security Dialogue* 30, no. 1 (March 1999): 43–61.

Gurr, Ted Robert. "Containing Internal War in the Twenty-First Century." In Fen Osler Hampson and David M. Malone, eds., *From Reaction to Conflict Prevention: Opportunities for the UN System.* Boulder: Lynne Rienner, 2002, pp. 41–62.

Hansen, Annika S. "International Security Assistance to Peace Implementation Processes: The Cases of Bosnia-Herzegovina and Angola." University of Oslo, 2000.

———. "International Security Assistance to War-Torn Societies." In Michael Pugh, ed., *Regeneration of War-Torn Societies.* London: Macmillan, 2000, pp. 35–53.

Hartz, Halvor. "Public Security." In U.S. Army, *Challenges of Peacekeeping and Peace Support into the Twenty-First Century: The Doctrinal Dimension.* Carlisle, PA: U.S. Army Peacekeeping Institute, Center for Strategic Leadership, 2000.

Heisbourg, François. *European Defence: Making It Work.* Chaillot Paper no. 42. Paris: WEU Institute for Security Studies, September 2000.

Henderson, Jeannie. *Reassessing ASEAN.* Adelphi Paper no. 323. London: Oxford University Press for International Institute for Security Studies, 1999.

Hernandez, Carolina G. "ASEAN 10: Meeting the Challenges." In Mely Anthony and Mohamed Jawhar Hassan, eds., *Beyond the Crisis: Challenges and Opportunities,* vol. 1. Kuala Lumpur: Institute of Strategic and International Studies, 2000, pp. 239–253.

———. "The East Timor Crisis: Regional Mechanisms on Trial and Implications for Regional Political and Security Cooperation." Paper presented at the ARF Profession Development Program, Bandar Seri Begawan, April 23–28, 2000.

Hernández, Rafael. "Cooperation in the Caribbean: The Cultural Dimension." In Joseph Tulchin and Ralph Espach, eds., *Security in the Caribbean Basin.* Boulder: Lynne Rienner, 2000, pp. 83–96.

Hettne, Bjørn, ed. *International Political Economy: Understanding Global Disorder.* London: Zed Books, 1995.

Hills, Alice. "The Inherent Limits of Military Forces in Policing Peace Operations." *International Peacekeeping* 8, no. 3 (Autumn 2001): 79–98.

Holm, Tor Tanke. "CIVPOL Operations in Eastern Slavonia, 1992–98." In Tor Tanke Holm and Espen Barth Eide, eds., *Peacebuilding and Police Reform.* Frank Cass: London, 2000, pp. 135–156.

———. "CPN/SWP Balkan Stability Project: Crime and Corruption." Paper prepared for the CPN/SWP Western Balkans Stability project, 3rd draft, October 25, 1999.

Holm, Tor Tanke, and Kari Margarethe Osland. *Regional Civilian Police Training in Southeast Europe.* Oslo: Norwegian Institute of International Affairs (NUPI), December 12, 2000.

Howorth, Jolyon. *European Integration and Defence: The Ultimate Challenge?* Chaillot Paper no. 43. Paris: EU Institute for Security Studies, November 2000, pp. 76–81.

Huband, M. *The Liberian Civil War.* London: Frank Cass, 1998.

Human Rights Watch. "Abuses Against Serbs and Roma in the New Kosovo." *HRW Report* 11, no. 10 (1999). www.hrw.org/reports/1999/kosov2.

———. *World Report 2001: Federal Republic of Yugoslavia.* www.hrw.org/wr2k1/europe/yugoslavia-kosovo.html.

Huxley, Tim. "ASEAN's Role in the Emerging East Asian Regional Security Architecture." In Ian G. Cook, Marcus A. Doel, and Rex Li, eds., *Fragmented Asia: Regional Integration and National Disintegration in Pacific Asia.* Aldershot: Avebury, 1996, pp. 29–52.

Independent Commission on Kosovo. *The Kosovo Report: Conflict, International Response, Lessons Learned.* Oxford: Oxford University Press, 2000.

Inter-American Dialogue Study Group on Western Hemisphere Governance. *The Inter-American Agenda and Multilateral Governance: The Organization of American States.* Washington, DC: Inter-American Dialogue Study Group on Western Hemisphere Governance, April 1997.

International Crisis Group (ICG). *Kosovo: Let's Learn from Bosnia—Models and Methods of International Administration.* ICG Balkans Report no. 66. Sarajevo: ICG, May 17, 1999.

———. *Kosovo Report Card.* ICG Balkans Report no. 100. Pristina: ICG, August 28, 2000.

———. *No Early Exit: NATO's Continuing Challenge in Bosnia.* ICG Balkans Report no. 110. Sarajevo: ICG, May 22, 2001.

———. *The Policing Gap: Law and Order in the New Kosovo.* Pristina: ICG, August 6, 1999.

———. *Rule over Law: Obstacles to the Development of an Independent Judiciary in Bosnia-Herzegovina.* July 5, 1999. www.int…org/projects/bosnia/reports/bh49rep.htm.

International Development Research Center (IDRC). *The Responsibility to Protect: Report of the International Commission on Intervention and State Sovereignty.* Ottawa: IDRC, 2001.

International Peace Academy (IPA) and ECOWAS. *Towards a West Pax Africana: Building Peace in a Troubled Subregion.* New York: IPA, 2002.

Jakobsen, Peter Viggo. *CIMIC: Civil-Military Cooperation—Lessons Learned and Models for the Future.* DUPI Report no. 9. Copenhagen: Danish Institute of International Affairs, 2000.

———. "The Emerging Consensus on Grey Area Peace Operations Doctrine: Will It Last and Enhance Operational Effectiveness?" *International Peacekeeping* 7, no. 3 (Autumn 2000): 36–56.

———. "Overload, Not Marginalization, Threatens UN Peacekeeping." *Security Dialogue* 13, no. 2 (2000): 167–177.

———. *Western Use of Coercive Diplomacy After the Cold War: A Challenge for Theory and Practice.* Basingstoke: Macmillan, 1998.

Jett, Dennis C. *Why Peacekeeping Fails.* London: Palgrave, 1999.

Johnston, Ian. *Rights and Reconciliation: UN Strategies in El Salvador.* Boulder: Lynne Rienner, 1995.

Jones, Bruce. *Peacemaking in Rwanda: The Dynamics of Failure.* Boulder: Lynne Rienner, 2001.

Jorgensen-Dahl, Arfinn. *Regional Organization and Order in Southeast Asia.* New York: St. Martin's Press, 1982.

Joulwan, George A., and Christopher C. Shoemaker. *Civilian-Military Cooperation in the Prevention of Deadly Conflict.* Washington, DC: Carnegie Commission on Preventing Deadly Conflict, December 1998.

Jung, Dietrich, ed. *Shadow Globalization, Ethnic Conflicts, and New Wars: The Political Economy of Intra-State War.* London: Routledge, 2003.

Kazantsev, Boris. "NATO: Obvious Bias to the Use of Force." In *International Affairs.* Moscow: Russian Ministry of Foreign Affairs, 1999.

Keen, David. "Short-Term Interventions and Long-Term Problems: The Case of the Kurds in Iraq." In John Harriss, ed., *The Politics of Humanitarian Intervention.* London: Pinter, 1995, pp. 167–186.

Kelly, Michael J. "Legitimacy and the Public Security Function." In Robert B. Oakley, Michael J. Dziedzic, and Eliot M. Goldberg, eds., *Policing the New World Dis-*

order: Peace Operations and Public Security. Washington, DC: NDU Press, 1998, pp. 399–431.

———. *Restoring and Maintaining Order in Complex Peace Operations: The Search for a Legal Framework.* The Hague: Kluwer Law International, 1999.

Kramer, Mark. "What Is Driving Russia's New Strategic Concept?" Harvard University Center for Strategic and International Studies, Program on New Approaches to Russian Security, Policy Memo no. 103, January 2000.

Kretchik, Walter E., Robert F. Baumann, and John T. Fishel. *Invasion, Intervention, "Intervasion": A Concise History of the U. S. Army in Operation Uphold Democracy.* Fort Leavenworth, KS: U.S. Army Command and General Staff College Press, 1998.

Kühne, Winrich. "The Brahimi Report: Overcoming the North-South Divide." Report of Stiftung Wissenschaft und Politik, Sixth International Workshop, Berlin, June 29–30, 2001.

Kupchan, Charles. "After Pax Americana." *International Security* 23, no. 2 (Fall 1998): 40–79.

Lake, David A., and Patrick M. Morgan, eds. *Regional Orders: Building Security in a New World.* Philadelphia: Pennsylvania State University Press, 1997.

Lawyers Committee for Human Rights. *A Fragile Peace: Laying the Foundations for Justice in Kosovo.* New York: Lawyers Committee for Human Rights, October 1999.

Leifer, Michael. *ASEAN and the Security of Southeast Asia.* London: Routledge, 1989.

Leurdijk, Dick A. *The United Nations and NATO in Former Yugoslavia, 1991–1996: Limits to Diplomacy and Force.* The Hague: Netherlands Atlantic Commission and Netherlands Institute of International Relations (Clingendael), 1996.

———. "The United States and the United Nations: An Uneasy Relationship." In Marianne van Leeuwen and Auke Venema, eds., *Selective Engagement: Foreign Policy at the Turn of the Century.* The Hague: Netherlands Atlantic Commission and Netherlands Institute of International Relations (Clingendael), 1996, pp. 75–94.

Leurdijk, Dick, and Dick Zandee. *Kosovo: From Crisis to Crisis.* Aldershot: Ashgate, 2001.

Lia, Brynjar. "Policing Without a State? Palestinian Policing from the British Mandate to the Oslo Accords." University of Oslo, 2003.

Lightburn, David. "Seeking Security Solutions." *NATO Review* 48, no. 3 (Winter 2000): 12–15.

Lincoln, Jennie, and César Sereseres. "Resettling the Contras: The OAS Verification Commission in Nicaragua." In Tommie Sue Montgomery, ed., *Peacemaking and Democratization.* Miami: North South Center, 2000, pp. 17–36.

Llorens, Jorge Cadona. "La Coopération entre les Nations Unies et les accords et organismes régionaux pour le règlement pacifique des affaires relatives au maintien de la paix et de la sécurité internationales." In Boutros Boutros-Ghali, *Paix, développement, démocratie,* vol. 1. Brussels: Bruylant, 1998, pp. 264–275.

Lorenz, F. M. "Confronting Thievery in Somalia." *Military Review* 74, no. 8 (August 1995): 46–55.

MacFarlane, S. Neil, and Thomas G. Weiss. "Regional Organizations and Regional Security." *Security Studies* 2 (Autumn 1992): 6–37.

MacKenzie, Mary M. "The UN and Regional Organizations." In Edward Newman and Oliver P. Richmond, eds., *The United Nations and Human Security.* Basingstoke: Palgrave, 2001, pp. 151–167.

Malone, David, and Mats Berdal, eds. *Greed and Grievance: Economic Agendas in Civil Wars.* Boulder: Lynne Rienner, 2000.

Mani, Rama. "The Rule of Law or the Rule of Might? Restoring Legal Justice in the Aftermath of Conflict." In Michael Pugh, ed., *Regeneration of War-Torn Societies.* London: Macmillan, 2000, pp. 94–95.

Marenin, Otwin. "Approaches to Police Reform." Paper presented at the IISS/DCAF workshop "Managing the Context of Police Reform: Implications for International Assistance," Geneva, April 24–25, 2001.

Marotta, Francesca. "The Blue Flame and the Gold Shield: Methodology, Challenges, and Lessons Learned on Human Rights Training for Police." In Tor Tanke Holm and Espen Barth Eide, eds., *Peacebuilding and Police Reform.* Frank Cass: London, 2000, pp. 69–92.

Marten, Kimberly Zisk. "Defending Against Anarchy: From War to Peacekeeping in Afghanistan." *Washington Quarterly* 26, no. 2 (Winter 2002–2003): 35–52.

Martin, Ian. *Self-Determination in East Timor: The United Nations, the Ballot and International Intervention.* IPA Occasional Paper. Boulder: Lynne Rienner, 2001.

Matthiessen, Michael. "The European Union (EU)." In Winrich Kühne and Jochen Prantl, eds., *The Brahimi Report: Overcoming the North-South Divide—Sixth International Workshop, Berlin, June 29–30, 2001.* Berlin: German Institute for International and Security Affairs, 2001, pp. 115–118.

May, Roy, and Gerry Cleaver. "African Peacekeeping: Still Dependent?" *International Peacekeeping* 4, no. 2 (1997): 1–21.

Mayall, James, ed. *The New Interventionism.* Cambridge: Cambridge University Press, 1996.

McCarthy, Patrick A. "Reliable Rapid Action for the UN." *International Peacekeeping* 7, no. 2 (Summer 2000): 139–154.

MccGwire, Michael. "The Paradigm That Lost Its Way." *International Affairs* 77, no. 4 (2001): 777–803.

McCoubrey, Hilaire, and Justin Morris. *Regional Peacekeeping in the Post–Cold War Era.* The Hague: Kluwer Law International, 2000.

Mitchell, C. R. *The Structure of International Conflict.* New York: St. Martin's Press, 1981.

Momtaz, Djamchid. "La Délégation par le Conseil de sécurité de l'exécution de ses actions coercitives aux organisations régionales." *Annuaire Français de Droit International* 63 (1997): 107–108.

Morris, Justin, and Hilaire McCoubrey. "Regional Peacekeeping in the Post–Cold War Era." *International Peacekeeping* 6, no. 2 (Summer 1999): 129–151.

Mullally, Lorraine. "Winning the Peace: The EU in Afghanistan." *European Security Review,* no. 10 (January 2002): 4–5.

Muyangwa, Monde, and Margaret A. Vogt. *An Assessment of the OAU Mechanism for Conflict Prevention, Management, and Resolution, 1993–2000.* New York: International Peace Academy, November 2000.

North Atlantic Treaty Organization (NATO). *The Alliance's Strategic Concept.* Washington, DC: NATO, April 23–24, 1999.

Nye, Joseph. *International Regionalism.* Boston: Little, Brown, 1968.

———. *Peace in Parts: Integration and Conflict in Regional Organization.* Boston: Little, Brown, 1971.

O'Brien, David. "The Search for Subsidiarity: the UN, African Regional Organizations and Humanitarian Action." *International Peacekeeping* 7, no. 3 (Autumn 2000): 57–83.

Olurin, Adetunji I. "Peacekeeping in Africa: The Liberian Experience." *The Peacemaker* 2, no. 1 (September 1992–September 1993): 1–20.

Organization of American States (OAS). *Cooperation Agreement Between the Secretariat of the United Nations and the General Secretariat of the Organization of American States.* OEA/Ser.D/V.14/95, April 17, 1995.

———. *Report of the General Secretariat on Cooperation Between the Organization of American States and the United Nations System.* OEA/Ser.p AG/doc.3184/95, May 26, 1995.

———. General Assembly. *Report of the Working Group on Cooperation Between the OAS and the United Nations System.* AG/RES.1244 (XXIII-0/93), 1993.

———. Council Special Committee on Hemisphere Security. *Support for a New Concept of Hemisphere Security: Co-operative Security.* OEA/Ser.G,GE/SH-12/93 rev. 1, May 17, 1993.

———. Special Committee on Hemispheric Security. *The Institutional Relationship Between the Organization of American States and the Inter-American Defense Board.* OAS/Ser.G CE/SH-3/93, February 2, 1993.

Organization for Security and Cooperation in Europe (OSCE). *Observations and Recommendations of the OSCE Legal Systems Monitoring Section: Report 2—The Development of the Kosovo Judicial System.* December 17, 1999. www.osce.org/kosovo/documents/reports/justice/report2.htm.

———. *Review of the Criminal Justice System.* February 2000–July 2000. www.osce.org/kosovo/documents/reports/justice.

———. *Towards a Genuine Partnership in a New Era.* Chapter 7: "A Common and Comprehensive Security Model for Europe for the Twenty-First Century." Budapest, 1994. www.osce.org/docs/english/1990-1999/summits/buda94e/htm.

———. Mission in Kosovo. Department of Human Rights and Rule of Law Division. *The Development of the Kosovo Judicial System (10 June Through 15 December 1999).* Pristina, December 17, 1999.

Ó Tuathail, Gearóid, and Simon Dalby, eds. *Rethinking Geopolitics.* London: Routledge, 1998.

Otunnu, Olara, and Michael Doyle, eds. *Peacemaking and Peacekeeping for the New Century.* Boston: Rowman & Littlefield, 1996.

Papworth, Thomas, and Sharon Wiharta. *Policing Europe: European Policing? The Challenge of Coordination in International Policing.* Stockholm: SIPRI, 2000.

Paris, Roland. "Echoes of the *Mission Civiliatrice:* Peacekeeping in the Post–Cold War Era." In Edward Newman and Oliver P. Richmond, eds., *The United Nations and Human Security.* Basingstoke: Palgrave, 2001, pp. 100–118.

Plunkett, Mark. "Reestablishing Law and Order in Peace-Maintenance." *Global Governance* 4, no. 1 (January–March 1998): 61–80.

Pugh, Michael. "Civil-Military Relations in the Kosovo Crisis: An Emerging Hegemony?" *Security Dialogue* 31, no. 2 (June 2000): 229–242.

———. "Maintaining Peace and Security." In David Held and Anthony McGrew, eds., *Governing Globalization.* Cambridge: Polity Press, 2002, pp. 209–233.

———. "Postwar Political Economy in Bosnia and Herzegovina: The Spoils of Peace." *Global Governance* 8, no. 4 (2002): 86–108.

Pugh, Michael, and Neil Cooper, with Jonathan Goodhand. *War Economies in a Regional Context: The Challenge of Transformation.* Boulder: Lynne Rienner, 2004.

Reinhardt, Klaus. "Commanding KFOR." *NATO Review* 48, no. 2 (Summer–Autumn 2000): 16–19.

Riechmann, Friedrich. "Military Aspects." In Winrich Kühne and Jochen Prantl, eds., *The Brahimi Report: Overcoming the North-South Divide—Sixth International*

Workshop, Berlin, June 29–30, 2001. Berlin: German Institute for International and Security Affairs, 2001.

Rivlin, Benjamin. "Regional Arrangements and the UN System for Collective Security and Conflict Resolution: A New Road Ahead?" *International Relations* 11, no. 2 (1992): 95–110.

Rollins, J. W. "Civil-Military Cooperation (CIMIC) in Crisis Response Operations: The Implications for NATO." *International Peacekeeping* 8, no. 1 (Spring 2001): 122–129.

Rosenau, William. "Facing the Unpalatable: The U.S. Military and Law Enforcement in Operations Other Than War." *Low Intensity Conflict and Law Enforcement* 4, no. 2 (Autumn 1995): 187–202.

Rosenberg, Robin. "The OAS and the Summit of the Americas: Coexistence, or Integration of Forces for Multilateralism?" *Latin American Politics and Society* 43, no. 1 (Spring 2001): 79–101.

Rubin, G. R. "Peace Support Operations and Practical Legal Problems 'on the Ground.'" *RUSI [Royal United Services Institute] Journal* 144, no. 6 (December 1999): 32–33.

Ruggie, John Gerard, ed. *Multilateralism Matters: The Theory and Praxis of an Institutional Form.* New York: Columbia University Press, 1993.

Russian Federation. *Kontseptsiya vneshney politiki Rossiiskoi Federatsii* [Foreign policy conception of the Russian Federation]. May 2000. www.mid.ru.

Sarooshi, Danesh. *The United Nations and the Development of Collective Security: The Delegation by the UN Security Council of Its Chapter VII Powers.* Oxford: Oxford University Press, 1999.

Schimmelfennig, Frank. *NATO's Enlargement to the East: An Analysis of Collective Decisionmaking.* EAPC-NATO Individual Fellowship Report, 1998–2000. www.nato.int.

Schmidl, Erwin A. "Police Functions in Peace Operations: An Historical Overview." In Robert B. Oakley, Michael J. Dziedzic, and Eliot M. Goldberg, eds., *Policing the New World Disorder: Peace Operations and Public Security.* Washington, DC: NDU Press, 1998, pp. 19–40.

Schulz, Michael, Fredrik Soderbaum, and Joakim Ojendal. "Key Issues in the New Regionalism: Comparisons from Asia, Africa, and the Middle East." In Bjørn Hettne, Andreas Inotai, and Osvaldo Sunkel, eds., *Comparing Regionalisms: Implications for Global Development.* London: Palgrave, 2001.

Sebastian, Leonard C., and Anthony L. Smith. "The East Timor Crisis: A Test Case for Humanitarian Intervention." In *Southeast Asian Affairs 2000.* Singapore: Institute of Southeast Asian Studies, 2000, pp. 64–86.

Seresere, Caesar. "Case Study: The Regional Peacekeeping Role of the Organization of American States: Nicaragua, 1990–1993." In Chester Crocker, Fen Hampson, and Pamela Aall, eds., *Managing Global Chaos.* Washington, DC: U.S. Institute of Peace Press, 1996, pp. 551–562.

Smith, Brian D., and William Durch. "UN Observer Group in Central America." In William J. Durch, ed., *The Evolution of UN Peacekeeping.* New York: St. Martin's Press, 1993, pp. 436–462.

Smith, Dan, and Nina Græger, eds. *Environment, Poverty, Conflict.* PRIO Report no. 2/94. Oslo: Peace Research Institute, 1994.

Soesastro, Hadi. "ASEAN During the Crisis." *ASEAN Economic Bulletin* 15, no. 3 (December 1998).

Solidum, Estrella. *Towards a Southeast Asian Community.* Quezon City: University of the Philippines Press, 1974.

Special Coordinator of the Stability Pact for South Eastern Europe. "Chairman's Conclusions." Third Meeting of the Working Table on Security Issues, Sofia, October 4–5, 2000. www.stabilitypact.org/w.../sofia%20conclusions,%october%204-5,%202000.htm.

Stepanova, Ekaterina. "Explaining Russia's Dissension on Kosovo." Harvard University Center for Strategic and International Studies, Program on New Approaches to Russian Security, Policy Memo no. 57, March 1999.

Stoetzer, Carlos. *The Organization of American States.* New York: Praeger, 1993.

Strohmeyer, Hansjorg. "Collapse and Reconstruction of a Judicial System: The United Nations Missions in Kosovo and East Timor." *American Journal of International Law* 95, no. 1 (January 2001): 46–63.

Suhrke, Astri, "Peacekeepers and Nation-Builders: Dilemmas of the UN in East Timor." *International Peacekeeping* 8, no. 4 (Winter 2001): 1–20.

Tacsan, Joaquín. "Searching for OAS/UN Task-Sharing Opportunities." In Thomas G. Weiss, ed., *Beyond UN Subcontracting: Task-Sharing with Regional Security Arrangements and Service-Providing NGOs.* London: Macmillan, 1998, pp. 91–114.

Tardy, Thierry, ed. *Peace Operations in World Politics After 11 September 2001.* London: Frank Cass, 2003.

Taylor, Paul. *International Organization in the Modern World: The Regional and the Global Process.* London: Pinter, 1993.

Tharoor, Shashi. "The Role of the United Nations in European Peacekeeping." In Espen Barth Eide, ed., *Peacekeeping in Europe,* Peacekeeping and Multinational Operations Series no. 5. Oslo: NUPI, 1995.

Thérien, Jean-Philippe, and Gui Gosselin. "A democracia e os direitos humanos no hemisfério ocidental: Um novo papel para a OEA." *Contexto International* 19, no. 2 (July–December 1997): 199–220.

Tow, William. *Subregional Security Cooperation in the Third World.* Boulder: Lynne Rienner, 1990.

United Kingdom. Ministry of Defense. *Joint Warfare Publication 3-50: Peace Support Operations.* Northwood, UK: Ministry of Defense, 1998.

United Nations. *Cooperación entre Las Naciones Unidas y La Organización de Los Estados Americanos, United Nations General Assembly.* UN Doc. A/49/450, September 28, 1994.

———. *Cooperation Between the United Nations and Regional Organizations/ Arrangements in a Peacekeeping Environment: Suggested Principles and Mechanisms.* March 1999. www.un.org/depts/dpko/lessons/regcoop.htm.

———. *Cooperation Between the United Nations and the Organization of American States: Report of the Secretary-General.* UN Doc. A/51/297, August 19, 1996.

———. *Declaration on the Enhancement of Cooperation Between the United Nations and Regional Arrangements or Agencies in the Maintenance of International Peace and Security of the General Assembly.* UN Doc. A/RES/49/57, December 1994.

———. "Framework for Cooperation in Peace-Building." Letter dated February 12, 2001, from the Secretary-General to the President of the Security Council, S/2001/138, February 14, 2001.

———. *Report of the Panel on United Nations Peace Operations.* UN Doc. A/55/305-S/2000/809, August 21, 2000.

———. *Report of the Secretary-General on Cooperation Between the UN and the OSCE.* UN Doc. A/56/125, June 29, 2001

————. *Report of the Secretary-General on UNMIK.* UN Doc. S/1999/779, July 12, 1999.

————. *Report on Third Meeting Between the United Nations and Regional Organizations.* New York: United Nations, July 28–29, 1998.

————. Department of Public Information. *The Role of the United Nations in the Twenty-First Century: The Millennium Report.* UN Doc. A/54/2000. New York: UN Department of Information, 2000.

————. Department of Public Information. *The United Nations and El Salvador.* New York: UN Department of Public Information, 1997.

————. DPKO Lessons Learned Unit. *The United Nations Transitional Administration Mission in Eastern Slavonia, Baranja, and Western Sirmium (UNTAES), January 1996–January 1998: Lessons Learned.* New York: United Nations, July 1998.

————. Inter-Agency Mission to West Africa. *Towards a Comprehensive Approach to Durable and Sustainable Solutions to Priority Needs and Challenges in West Africa.* UN Doc. S/2001/434, May 2, 2001.

————. Mission in Bosnia and Herzegovina (UNMIBH). *Mandate Implementation Plan 2000–2002.* November 2000. www.unmibh.org/unmibh/mip.htm.

————. Security Council. *Report on the Situation in Guinea-Bissau Prepared by ECOWAS Executive Secretary.* UN Doc. S/1999/432, April 16, 1999.

UN Mission in Kosovo (UNMIK). Administrative Department for Civil Security and Emergency Preparedness. "Coordinating KPC Issues." March 16, 2001.

————. O/SRSG Human Rights Unit. "Issue Analysis: A Current Assessment of the Kosovo Protection Corps." February 29, 2000.

————. "Reviving Kosovo's Judicial System." *UNMIK First Anniversary Backgrounder.* June 5, 2000. www.un.org/peace/kosovo/pages/twelvemonths/law.html.

————. UNMIK Police. *Annual Report 2000.* Pristina: UNMIK Police, 2001.

U.S. Army. *FM 3-07 (100-20) Stability Operations and Support Operations.* Washington, DC: Headquarters Department of the Army, DRAG, February 1, 2002.

U.S. General Accounting Office (GAO). *Bosnia Crime and Corruption Threaten Successful Implementation of the Dayton Agreement.* Testimony Before the Committee on International Relations, House of Representatives, GAO/T-NSIAD-00-219, Washington, DC, July 19, 2000.

U.S. Department of State. *Strengthening Criminal Justice Systems in Support of Peace Operations and Other Complex Contingencies.* PDD-71. Washington, DC: U.S. Department of State, February 24, 2000.

Vaky, V., and H. Muñoz. *The Future of the Organization of American States.* New York: Twentieth Century Fund Press, 1993.

Vierucci, Luisa. *WEU: A Regional Partner for the United Nations.* Chaillot Paper no. 12. Paris: WEU Institute for Security Studies, December 1993.

Wallander, Celeste. "Institutional Assets and Adaptability: NATO After the Cold War." *International Organization* 54, no. 4 (Autumn 2000): 705–736.

————. "International Institutions and Russian Security Cooperation." Harvard University Center for Strategic and International Studies, Program on New Approaches to Russian Security, Policy Memo no. 48, November 1998.

Wallensteen, Peter, and Margareta Sollenberg. "Armed Conflict and Regional Conflict Complexes, 1989–97." *Journal of Peace Research* 35, no. 5 (1998): 621–634.

Walter, Barbara F., and Jack Snyder, eds. *Civil Wars, Insecurity, and Intervention.* New York: Columbia University Press, 1999.

Weiss, Thomas G., ed. *Beyond UN Subcontracting: Task-Sharing with Regional Security Arrangements and Service-Providing NGOs.* London: Macmillan, 1998.

Wentges, J. Taylor. "Electoral Monitoring and the OAS/UN International Civil Mission to Haiti." *Peacekeeping and International Relations* 25, no. 6 (November–December 1996): 3–5.

Wesley, Michael. "The Asian Crisis and the Adequacy of Regional Institutions." *Contemporary Southeast Asia* 21, no. 1 (April 1999): 53–73.

Wheeler, Nicholas, and Tim Dunne, "East Timor and the New Humanitarian Intervention." *International Affairs* 77, no. 4 (2001): 805–827.

Wilkie, Edith B., and Beth C. DeGrasse. *A Force for Peace and Security: U.S. and Allied Commanders' Views of the Military's Role in Peace Operations and the Impact on Terrorism of States in Conflict.* Washington, DC: Peace Through Law Education Fund, 2002.

Willett, Susan. "Insecurity, Conflict, and the New Global Disorder." *Institute of Development Studies Bulletin* 32, no. 2 (April 2001): 35–45.

Williams, Michael C. *Civil-Military Relations and Peacekeeping.* Adelphi Paper no. 321. London: International Institute for Strategic Studies, 1998.

Yannis, Alexandros. "Kosovo Under International Administration." *Survival* 43, no. 2 (Summer 2001): 31–48.

Yost, David S. *NATO Transformed: The Alliance's New Roles in International Security.* Washington, DC: U.S. Institute of Peace Press, 1998.

The Contributors

Mely Caballero-Anthony is an assistant professor at the Institute of Defence and Strategic Studies, Singapore. Her research interests include regionalism and regional security in Asia Pacific, multilateral security cooperation, politics and international relations in ASEAN, conflict prevention and management, as well as human security. She has been very involved in Track II work, having run the Secretariat of the Council for Security Cooperation in the Asia Pacific from 1997 to 2001 and as a member of the ASEAN-ISIS network.

John G. Cockell is a senior policy adviser in the Peacebuilding and Human Security Division of the Department of Foreign Affairs and International Trade, Canada. In 2000–2001 he was seconded to serve as a political affairs officer with the UN Interim Administration Mission in Kosovo.

Comfort Ero is the West Africa project director at the International Crisis Group and is based in Freetown, Sierra Leone. From 1998 to 1999 she was a research associate at the International Institute for Strategic Studies and from 1999 to 2001 she was a research fellow with the Conflict, Security and Development Group at the Centre for Defence Studies, King's College, London. She has written extensively on African regional security issues.

Louise Fawcett is a fellow of St. Catherine's College and university lecturer in politics at the University of Oxford. She works on issues of regionalism, identity, and security in world politics, with particular reference to the developing world. Publications include *Regionalism in World Politics* (with Andrew Hurrell) and *The Third World Beyond the Cold War* (with Yezid Sayigh). Two edited volumes, *The International Politics of the Middle East* and *Regional Governance in the Americas* (with Monica Serrano), are forthcoming.

Nina Græger is a research fellow at the Norwegian Institute of International Affairs. Her main research fields include conceptual studies of security and military thinking, as well as more empirical studies of European security, peace operations, and security organizations writ large. She is writing a doctoral dissertation on changes in the use of military power in post–Cold War peace operations and the security and defense discourse in Norway.

Annika S. Hansen is the deputy chief political adviser in the European Union Police Mission in BiH and a senior scientist at the Norwegian Defense Research Establishment, working on peacekeeping issues, including public security and military-police cooperation in peace operations. A former Fulbright scholar, she was a research associate at the International Institute for Strategic Studies and holds an M.A. and Ph.D. in political science from the University of Oslo and a M.A.L.D. from the Fletcher School of Law and Diplomacy, Medford, Mass.

Monica Herz is a lecturer at the Catholic University of Rio de Janeiro and holds a Ph.D. in international relations from the London School of Economics. Her areas of expertise are Latin American security and Brazilian foreign policy. She recently published *Ecuador vs. Peru: Peacemaking Amid Rivalry* (coauthored with João Pontes Nogueira) (Lynne Rienner Publishers, 2002). She has published several articles on Brazilian security policy.

Peter Viggo Jakobsen is an associate professor at the Institute of Political Science, University of Copenhagen, Denmark. He has written extensively on coercive diplomacy, use of military force, and peace operations and is currently working on a book entitled *The Nordic Approaches to Peace Operations After the Cold War: A New Model in the Making?* (forthcoming, 2004).

Dick A. Leurdijk is a senior research fellow at the Netherlands Institute of International Affairs (Clingendael) in The Hague. As a UN expert, he has specialized in issues related to the UN's role in maintaining international peace and security, including UN peacekeeping and peace enforcement, the relationship between the UN and NATO, humanitarian intervention, and international terrorism, and he has written extensively on these issues.

David M. Malone became president of the International Peace Academy in 1998, on leave from the Canadian government. A career Canadian Foreign Service officer and occasional scholar, he was successively, over the period

1994–1998, director general of the Policy, International Organizations, and Global Issues Bureaus of the Canadian Foreign and Trade Ministries. During this period he also acquired a D.Phil. from Oxford University with a thesis on decisionmaking in the UN Security Council.

David Marshall is a member of the London, New York, and U.S. Supreme Court Bar. His areas of expertise are criminal defense, including death penalty law and judicial reform. From 1992 to 1994 he was on the executive committee of the Bar of England and Wales Human Rights Committee. From 1992 to 1998 he was a legal consultant to Amnesty International on U.S. criminal justice issues. He is currently writing his LL.M. on transitional criminal justice at Harvard Law School.

Ian Martin is vice president of the International Center for Transitional Justice. He has worked for the United Nations in various capacities, including as Special Representative of the Secretary-General for the East Timor Popular Consultation, Deputy Special Representative of the Secretary-General in the UN Mission in Ethiopia and Eritrea, Special Adviser to the High Commissioner for Human Rights, and Chief of the UN Human Rights Field Operation in Rwanda. He also served in Bosnia and Herzegovina (as Deputy High Representative for Human Rights) and in Haiti. He was Secretary-General of Amnesty International in 1986–1992. His writings include *Self-Determination in East Timor: The United Nations, the Ballot, and International Intervention* (IPA Occasional Paper, Lynne Rienner, 2001).

Emily Metzgar was program officer at the United States Institute of Peace in Research and Studies. Her work includes focus on U.S.-Russian relations, Northeast Asian issues, and general U.S. foreign policy. Previously, Metzgar was a Foreign Service officer with the United States Department of State where she served at the American Embassy in Beijing. Metzgar graduated from George Washington University's Elliott School of International Affairs and served as editor of *International Affairs Review*. She has also been editor of the *Michigan Journal of Political Science*. Her publications include "The Role of the Ambassador in Promoting U.S. Human Rights Policy Abroad," an Institute Special Report, and "The Growth of Regionalism: Implications for the International System" in the *Journal of Public and International Affairs*.

Alexandra Novosseloff gained her doctorate in political science from the University of Paris II with her dissertation "The Ability and Inability of the UN Security Council to Use Force: Bases, Practice, Prospects." She is currently the UN expert within the Directorate for Strategic Affairs of the French Ministry of Defense.

'Funmi Olonisakin is a visiting senior fellow at the African Security Unit, International Policy Institute, King's College, London. Prior to this, she worked in the Office of the United Nations Special Representative of the Secretary-General for Children and Armed Conflict. She has been a MacArthur Foundation Post-Doctoral Fellow at the Department of War Studies, King's College, London, and a research associate at the Institute for Strategic Studies, University of Pretoria. She has conducted extensive research on regional security in Africa. She is the author of *Reinventing Peacekeeping in Africa* (2000) and coauthor of *Peacekeepers, Politicians, and Warlords* (1999), among other publications.

Michael Pugh is director of the Plymouth International Studies Centre and reader in International Relations, University of Plymouth, UK. He is the editor of the journal *International Peacekeeping* and has written extensively on peacekeeping, humanitarianism, the political economy of transition, and maritime security issues.

Cyrus Samii was a program assistant for the International Peace Academy's project "The UN, NATO, and Other Regional Actors in the Twenty-first Century: Partners in Peace?" He is currently completing his graduate studies in the International Security Policy Program at Columbia University's School of International and Public Affairs.

Waheguru Pal Singh Sidhu is a senior associate at the International Peace Academy and coordinated its project "The UN, NATO, and Other Regional Actors." He was professor of international relations at Delhi University and has written extensively on South Asian security issues.

Andrei V. Zagorski is deputy director of the Institute for Applied International Research, Moscow. Previously he was at the Geneva Center for Security Policy and was senior vice president of the EastWest Institute in Prague. He is on the editorial boards of the *OSCE Yearbook* (Hamburg), *Helsinki Monitor* (the Hague), and *Perspectives* (Prague). He is a member of the International Advisory Board, Geneva Center for Democratic Control of Armed Forces, and was chair of the Association for Nonproliferation (Moscow) and an expert on Soviet delegations to the OSCE. His recent publications include: "The New Framework for Strategic Stability: An Outlook," in *The New Agenda in the U.S.–Russian Relations* (2002); "Russia and the CIS," in *Foreign Policy of the Russian Federation* (2000) [in Russian]; and "America's Choices Seen from a Russian Perspective," in R. B. Zoellick and P. D. Zelikov, eds., *America and Russia: Memos to a President* (2000).

Index

Abacha, Sani, 238
Abidjan Peace Agreement, 241
ACRI. *See* African Crisis Response Initiative
Activation order, 71
Ad hoc regional arrangements, 28(n12), 77–78; Afghanistan, 259; Latin America, 215; peace and security in the Americas, 214. *See also* Coalitions
Afghanistan: filling the public security gap, 153(n53); lack of NATO support for, 37; NATO involvement, 72, 87; need for international partnerships, 258–260; public security gap, 140(table), 141(table), 147–148; UN-centered approach to peace operations, 256, 263
AFRC. *See* Armed Force Revolutionary Council
Africa: advantages of regionalization, 23; ECOMOG's operation in Liberia, 235–237; ECOWAS's original agenda, 234–235; regional partnerships, 245–250; UN–ECOWAS in Sierra Leone, 241–244; UNSC's lack of involvement in, 233–234. *See also individual countries;* Organization of African Unity
African Crisis Response Initiative (ACRI), 248, 249, 260
African Union (formerly OAU), 2
An Agenda for Peace (Boutros-Ghali), 15, 17, 34, 213

Agreement on Cessation of Hostilities, Ethiopia-Eritrea, 50–51
Aid: economic balancing of central and regional organizations, 41–42; EU aid, military, and civilian deployments, 261; EuropeAid organization, 92(n31); humanitarian aid for Kosovo, 68; NATO protection of, 80; Nicaragua's institutional transition, 222
Air strikes, 67, 82, 96–97, 99, 100, 103, 104, 107
Alba, Operation, 79
Albanians, Kosovar, 124–127, 158–159, 177, 178, 183
Albright, Madeleine, 66
Algeria, 50
Allied Force, Operation, 57–58, 64, 65, 67, 71–72
Al-Qaida, 72
Amity of Cooperation, Treaty of (TAC), 198, 207
Amsterdam Treaty, 86
Angola, 16
Annan, Kofi: ASEAN–UN summit, 208; increasing role of regional organizations, 17; intervention in East Timor, 52; need for unity in peace operations, 26; Nobel Prize, 24; on poverty and conflict prevention, 92(n30); UNTAET establishment, 206
Arab League, 13

government, 47–48; uneven spread of regional competence, 38; UN–OAS cooperation, 219–224
Organization of the Islamic Conference (OIC), 2, 19, 268(n9)
Organized crime, 128–129, 164, 173(n36), 184, 190(n35)
OSCE. *See* Organization for Security and Cooperation in Europe

P-5 countries, 34, 38
Pacific Settlement of Disputes, Treaty on, 214
Palestinian conflict, 255
Panama, 140(table), 215, 217
Papua New Guinea, 200
Paraguay, 217, 220, 226
Pardew, John, 81
Paris Peace Agreement, 205
Partnership for Peace (PfP), 62, 260
Partnerships, 40
Peace: settlements, 69; as ultimate goal, 24
Peacebuilding: BiH's postconflict peacebuilding, 62; EU peacebuilding capacity, 84–85; NATO role in, 59–60; non-European examples of, 19–20; OAS–UN collaboration in Nicaragua, 221–222; security sector management, 132; subcontracting model, 69–71
Peacekeeping operations, 19–20, 82; East Timor, 205–206; Georgia and Tajikistan, 79; Haiti, 223–224; hard and soft, 20–21; Liberia, 236–237; NATO's evolving role in, 58–60; OAS role in, 226; reliance on UN forces, 35; role of EU and regional organizations, 76; Russia's role in KFOR, 96–97, 104–106; UN–centered model of collaborative engagement, 262–264
Peacekeeping Operations, Department for (DPKO), 35, 78
Peace Monitoring Group, 264
Penal systems: Balkan judicial and penal reform, 185; Kosovo, 155–172; public security gap, 140(table), 141(table); security sector management, 132
People's Movement of Kosovo, 127
Perez de Cuéllar, Javier, 17
Permanent Joint Council (PJC), 96–97, 104, 107–108
Peru, 217, 219, 220
Petersberg tasks, 85, 92(n32)
PfP. *See* Partnership for Peace

Philippines, 52, 197, 200, 202, 205
Pitsuwan, Surin, 205
PJC. *See* Permanent Joint Council
Police systems, 189(n25), 265; certification of police officers in Kosovo, 134(nn36,37); civil and military organizations in Kosovo, 127–128; creating the Kosovo Police Service, 127–128; demilitarization and demobilization of the KLA in Kosovo, 124–127; establishment of rule of law in the Balkans, 185–187; EU forces in Bosnia and Herzegovina, 85; indigenous police operations, 127–128, 175–191, 233; judicial and penal reform in the Balkans, 185; KFOR's public security responsibilities, 133(n10); by military forces, 137–153; military involvement in filling the public security gap, 141(table); police reform in the Balkans, 178–185; public security gaps, 140(table). *See also* Civil-military cooperation; UN Mission in Kosovo
Political and Security Committee, 84
Political economy, 39–41
Postconflict peacebuilding, 62
Poverty, 41, 46(n50)
Power networks, 31, 187
Presidential directive PDD25, 35
Prevention of Violent Conflicts, Program for, 84
Preventive diplomacy, 19–20, 31–32, 83, 200–202, 258
Preventive security measures, 257–258
Primakov, Evgenii, 98
Privatization of resources, 41
Protocol on Mutual Assistance and Defence (1981), 235, 261
Protocol on Non-Aggression (1978), 235
Public security: gaps in, 140(table), 141(table); in Kosovo, 142–146; military responsibility for, 139–142; in Somalia, 152(n49); vacuum filling, 142–149. *See also* Police systems
Putin, Vladimir, 109

Quartet, the, 263–264, 267(n1)

Raçak massacre, 65
Ranariddh, prince of Cambodia, 205

policy, 163–168; judicial and penal reconstruction, 5, 155–156, 158–159; Kosovo's penal system, 169–170; NATO placement of, 67–68; operational coordination of civil and military organizations, 119–124; personnel level, 133(n14); public security, 142–143, 176, 178, 186; senior management, 134(n24); subcontracting model of peacebuilding, 69–71; UN–NATO–OSCE cooperation, 79; war crimes trials, 158–163

UN Mission in Sierra Leone (UNAMSIL), 244, 245, 248, 256, 263

UN–NATO cooperation, 95–112; BiH after Dayton, 62–64; coordinating civil-military interaction, 116–117; Kosovo model, 67–68; NATO issuing its own mandate, 71–73; New Strategic Concept, 64, 66–67; Russian approach to, 95–111, 102; Russian cooperation and, 95–112; Russian opposition to, 100–102; Russia's UNSC membership, 103; subcontracting, 57–58, 60–62, 68–71

UN–OAS cooperation, 213–214, 219–225

UN Observer Group for Central America (ONUCA), 221, 226

UN Observer Mission in Liberia (UNOMIL), 237, 239

UNOMIL. *See* UN Observer Mission in Liberia

UN–OSCE cooperation, 75, 77–78, 78–79

UN Police International Group, 79

UN Police Support Group (UNPSG), 79, 183

UN Protection Force (UNPROFOR), 60–62, 79, 115, 176

UNPSG. *See* UN Police Support Group

UN–regional cooperation, 255–257; Bosnia and Herzegovina, 48–49; demand side of peace operations, 257–260; five modes of interaction, 269(n17); Haiti, 47–48; Liberia, 238–241; models of engagement, 262–264; Sierra Leone, 241–244, 244–245; supply side of peace operations, 260–262; UNSC's lack of involvement in African missions, 233–234

UN Secretary-General, 67–68

UN Secretary-General for Political Affairs, 220

UN Security Council, 20; "African solutions to African problems," 233–234; authorizing use of force, 87; damaged

credibility of, 36; diplomatic approach to peace and security, 32; East Timor intervention, 52; establishment of UNMIK, 156; intervention in Haiti, 223–224; post–Dayton Bosnia, 62–63; regional organizations defined, 89(n1); Russia's membership, 103; Russia's opposition to diminution of, 99–100; strengthening regional actors, 255–256; as ultimate authority in intervention, 26; U.S. negotiation for Iraq invasion, 259; variety of conflict management situations, 34–35. *See also individual resolutions*

UN Special Representative of the Secretary-General (SRSG), 49, 50, 69–70, 79, 120, 131, 155, 159, 163–165

UNTAES. *See* UN Transitional Administration for Eastern Slavonia, Baranja, and Western Sirmium

UNTAET. *See* UN Transitional Authority in East Timor

UN Transitional Administration for Eastern Slavonia, Baranja, and Western Sirmium (UNTAES), 79, 115, 116, 132(n2), 177, 181, 183

UN Transitional Authority in East Timor (UNTAET), 206

UN West Africa Office, 250, 251(n19)

UPD. *See* Unity for the Promotion of Democracy

Vacuum filling, 138, 142–149, 151(n36)

Védrine, Hubert, 83

Venezuela, 228, 262

Verification, 65, 79, 82, 221, 226

Vietnam, 197, 200

Vigilante groups, 176

Violence, civil, 126–127, 186–188

War crimes trials, 147, 155–156, 157, 159–163

Warsaw Pact, 14

Washington Protocols, 223, 230(n27)

Washington Treaty, 37, 72

Weapons control, 229(n9)

Western European Union (WEU), 18–19, 76; Balkan embargo, 79; Balkan police reform, 183; formal status of, 2; as regional organization, 89(n2)

World Bank, 46(n50)

World Economic Forum, 41

About the Book

Events in Europe over the past decade have created a dynamic requiring significant conceptual and practical adjustments on the part of the UN and a range of regional actors, including the EU, NATO, and the OSCE. This volume explores the resulting collaborative relationships in the context of peace operations in the Balkans, considering past efforts and developing specific suggestions for effective future interactions between the UN and its regional partners. The authors also consider the implications of efforts in Europe for the regionalization of peace and security operations in Asia, Africa, and Latin America.

Michael Pugh is director of the International Studies Centre at the University of Plymouth, UK. His numerous publications include *Regeneration of War-Torn Societies* (editor) and *Europe's Boat People: Maritime Cooperation in the Mediterranean,* and he is editor of the journal *International Peacekeeping.* **Waheguru Pal Singh Sidhu** is senior associate at the International Peace Academy and was formerly professor of international relations at Delhi University.